The Two of Me

How much of what we do is directed by conscious, deliberate decisions and how much originates in unconscious, automatic directives? This is the question explored in *The Two of Me* via an engaging combination of phenomenological subjective investigation and objective considerations of mental processes and specific structures. John Birtchnell puts forward the thesis that many more of our actions than we might imagine are determined unconsciously. Not only are unnoticed automatic actions motivated unconsciously, but also seemingly conscious or "thought out" behaviours are actually determined and reinforced by unconscious exigencies. Even where we produce a reasoned discourse taking responsibility for why we hold certain thoughts, there is always the possibility that these explanations serve and follow from an unconscious driving force. The conscious mind seems to act as spokesperson for both itself and the unconscious mind. Investigating this dual aspect of the person, the book addresses the issue across a range of mental processes including memory, language, problem-solving, dreams, delusions, hallucinations and more complex constructs such as the arts, humour and religion.

John Birtchnell is Honorary Senior Lecturer at the Institute of Psychiatry and author of *Relating in Psychotherapy* and *How Humans Relate*.

The Two of Me

The Rational Outer Me and the Emotional Inner Me

John Birtchnell

Routledge
Taylor & Francis Group

LONDON AND NEW YORK

First published 2003
by Routledge
27 Church Road, Hove, East Sussex BN3 2FA

Simultaneously published in the USA and Canada
by Routledge
29 West 35th Street, New York NY 10001

Routledge is an imprint of the Taylor & Francis Group

Typeset in Garamond by RefineCatch Limited, Bungay, Suffolk
Printed and bound in Great Britain by MPG Books Ltd,
Bodmin, Cornwall
Cover design: Lisa Dynan
Cover illustration: "Portrait of Lydia Delectorskaya" by Henri Matisse, 1947, © Succession
H Matisse/DACS 2003; Cover photograph © The St. Hermitage Museum, St. Petersburg

This publication has been produced with paper manufactured to strict
environmental standards and with pulp derived from sustainable
forests.

British Library Cataloguing in Publication Data
A catalogue record for this book is available from the British Library

Library of Congress Cataloging-in-Publication Data
Birtchnell, John.
    The two of me : the rational outer me and the emotional inner me /
John Birtchnell.
        p.   cm.
Includes bibliographical references and indexes.
    ISBN 1-84169-323-5
    1. Consciousness.   2. Subconsciousness.   3. Interpersonal
relations.   4. Philosophy of mind.   I. Title.
    BF311.B533 2003
    150.19'8—dc21
                                                                  2003007755

ISBN 1-84169-323-5

For Igor

Contents

Foreword by Paul Gilbert

Humans have long understood that their emotions and motivations can direct and overwhelm their conscious wishes. Indeed, over two and a half thousand years ago, the Buddha recommended that the mind needs training to bring it under control. Without this training it is unruly and prone to impulsiveness. Shortly after, the Stoics in the Mediterranean suggested that animals differed from humans in that humans could reason. They believed that humans should use the power of reason to control and regulate their emotions. They considered that it's not things in themselves that disturb us but the view that we take of them. This basic idea became a founding principle for cognitive therapy, which has been far more influenced by philosophy than the psycho-dynamic schools have. In the sixteenth century, for religious reasons, Descartes split mind from body, thus allowing us to have both immaterial souls and physical bodies. This advanced the split between biological psychiatry (that viewed mental phenomena as the product of physiological processes) and psychology. Eisenberg (1986) aptly named this division in psychiatry brainlessness and mindlessness. Only recently, under the spotlight of modern neuroscience, has this split begun to collapse (Damasio, 1994). With the advent of psychoanalysis in the 1890s the division between emotion and reason was replaced with the concepts of the conscious and the unconscious. In both Nietzsche and Freud our minds are driven by unconscious motives that are the produce of our evolutionary past (Ellenberger, 1970). Since the 1930s, the brain sciences have been illuminating those ancient structures in the brain that are responsible for motivation and emotion (Panksepp, 1998). The more recently evolved cortical abilities that make possible symbolic self-awareness and identity are linked and regulate these emotion centres, but our cognitions are as likely to be products of more primitive emotional processing as they are to generate it. Understanding our minds has then been riddled with many dualisms.

John Birtchnell enters this important arena with original ideas about the linkage between a sense of self and our emotional and motivational dispositions. As he says, he became obsessed with the idea that we actually have two different types of self inside us: the two of me. He suggests that our emotional and motivational dispositions evolved long before our more rational self-reflecting minds. In consequence, we now have at least two types of self; one that guides the motivational direction and one that thinks and reflects on that. The competencies for forming a sense of self also reflect different evolutionary stages. In fact, Sedikieds and Skowronski (1997) suggested that we have three types of self-awareness. The first is subjective self-awareness shared by other animals and it is what enables animals to "understand" there is a difference between them and the outside world. Animals with this level of awareness recognise an injury when it happens to them and that hunger requires "them" to seek food. They may not be conscious of this, of course. These animals will also have a whole array of motivational systems that direct their behaviour in a host of ways (e.g., find food, avoid predators, seek out mates). Objective self-awareness is the ability to recognise the self as a self and goes with self-recognition in a mirror or television monitor. Only the higher apes have this ability. Symbolic self-awareness arises from the capacity to symbolise the self, reflect on and think about the self, have plans and ambitions and be consciously aware of states of mind. Only humans have this, and it may well depend on language. There are other elements to this self, such as the ability to have a private self and a public self. The symbolic self gives rise to an awareness of mental states; for example, animals may be defeated but it is doubtful whether they know or reflect on the fact that they are depressed, they probably also don't reflect on their future as a consequence.

However you want to divide up the psyche, John Birtchnell puts his finger on an essential issue that the "more primitive self" carries forward gene-informed guides for living. We can often find ourselves carried away by our feelings or passions and these are as much part of the person we are as our thoughts about them. He calls this part of the self the "inner me" and suggests that the inner me is both the energy source and navigator for much of what goes on in our minds. The symbolic self is close to what he calls the "outer me". Although this outer me is the self that thinks and reflects, it often has to deal with intrusions of thoughts, that can at times be bizarre and just pop into the mind, flashes of emotion, changes of mood and impulsive urges. The outer me sometimes consciously wants and tries to design and control the inner me.

Birtchnell points out that the inner me, as the emotional me, gives rise to the aesthetics of life and can texture our experience with deep and wonderful feelings. He suggests that it is only the inner me that "remembers" and thus the outer/symbolic me is rather dependent upon the emotional textures in recall. The inner me is also capable of forming associations and linkages of ideas, which make possible inspiration for theorisers as well as composers and artists. These creative abilities flow when released from over-controlling efforts of the outer me. The inner me can give rise to empathy and sympathy and a drive for justice, and may even be the source of religious experience. However, it cannot be relied on to make logical and rational choices. As Paul MacLean (1990) has noted, if we overly rely on our emotional selves to structure the world, then they are just as likely to give justifications for vengeance, as they are love, and justifications for greed as for sharing. And so, as Birtchnell shows, the inner me is morally neutral, simply going about its business, responding to signals and influencing desires in its age-old way.

Birtchnell makes the intriguing observation that while the inner me knows nothing of the outer me, the outer me knows of the existence of the inner me (the older emotional brain). However, the outer me often cannot work out how the inner me comes to its decisions and conclusions. Indeed, as noted by others (Gilbert, 1989), our conscious, symbolic selves can simply make up the reasons for behaving as we do. Thus, our passions appear understood and our retaliatory vengeance justified.

The inner me responds to evolutionary meaningful signals/events, such as finding a sexual partner, allies and so forth, by generating positive affect, while if it fails in these endeavours it generates emotions that inform us that we are off-track. The outer me is thus, at times, a passive recipient of the emotions coming from the inner me as it tracks through life on its evolutionary guided path. The inner me is also set up for relatively "fast-track" processing to come to decisions quickly, rather than with slow reflection. Indeed, this is a key problem for humans and there is much evidence that we can find ourselves emotionally aroused about something before we fully understand what we are aroused or emotional about. As I have argued elsewhere (Gilbert, 1989), when people feel safe they are much more able to reflect on inner and outer worlds and form creative associations. When threat arrives, decisions must be taken quickly and then the brain tends to dispense with creative associations and looks for a well tried and rapid response.

The 1990s were regarded as the decade of the brain by President Bush Snr. However, there can be no such decade for our knowledge of the brain is growing exponentially. Understanding the linkage between genes and neuropsychological pathways, and how development and experience shape these pathways, giving rise to the experience of a conscious self that can reflect on itself remains a key challenge for all. It has implications for psychotherapy and even for our understanding of religious feelings, both of which Birtchnell discusses. He touches on something that we all experience, which is something of a split between the different elements of ourselves. Written in a lucid and informative style, his book brings a fresh and innovative approach to the complexities of our experience as human beings.

Damasio, A. (1994) *Descartes' Error: Emotion, Reason and the Human Brain*. New York: Putnam.

Eisenberg, L. (1986) "Mindlessness and brainlessness in psychiatry". *British Journal of Psychiatry*, 148, 497–508.

Ellenberger, H.B. (1970) *Discovery of the Unconscious*. New York: Basic Books.

Gilbert, P. (1989) *Human Nature and Suffering*. Hove, UK: Lawrence Erlbaum Associates.

MacLean, P.D. (1990) *The Triune Brain in Evolution*. New York: Plenum.
Panksepp, J. (1998) *Affective Neuroscience*. New York: Oxford University Press.
Sedikieds, C. and Skowronski, J.J. (1997) "The symbolic self in evolutionary context". *Personality and Social Psychology Review*, 1, 80–102.

Paul Gilbert is Professor of Clinical Psychology at the University of Derby.

Preface

I have always considered the Preface of a book to be a pleasant, though not too serious, opportunity for the author to introduce himself to the reader, but this one should be rather more than that, because already there has been some confusion about what kind of a book this is, and what it is about, and this will be my last chance to explain.

Let me start with the title. It does not mean that I am a schizophrenic or a manic depressive, or that I have a split personality. It means that I think we all have two parts to us, but I could not call the book *The Two of Us*, or even *The Two of You*, because that would mean two separate people in two separate bodies. What I am trying to say is that it feels as though, for all of us, there are two people in the same body. Hence, the title had to be *The Two of Me*. Using "me" rather than "us" or "you" has been no bad thing because, in many places in the book, I have chosen to write about how I experience things.

More than anything else, what the book is about is an idea; an elusive idea, but an important one nonetheless; one that I have tried to get a hold of all my life; and one that, in the writing of the book, I have tried to tighten my grip upon; but even now, I have not entirely got it sorted out. Since it is an idea with which I have grappled for so long, it would be surprising if you too did not have some difficulty with it. Not that it is a complicated idea or that the book is difficult to read; in fact quite the reverse; the idea is simple and the book might even be considered simplistic. The problem lies more in allowing yourself to accept the idea – and its implications.

So what then is the idea? It is that there is this inner part of me, of which I am unconscious, that knows where I need to go, that motivates me, and that encourages or discourages me with emotion when I am on course or off course. Beyond this, there is this outer, conscious part of me, that likes to think that it is the decision-maker, but whose role is really only to think up new ways of getting me to where this inner part is urging me to go.

Whoever may seek to track down the idea has got to be a jack of all trades, though inevitably a master of none; for it cuts across a range of disciplines, and a person from any one discipline can only know part of the picture. Writing the book has led me into areas of knowledge that hitherto were unfamiliar to me; and I have had to read a great deal and summarise what I have read. I must apologise in advance if there are things I have not got right. The book is not intended to be primarily a source of knowledge. Such knowledge as is imparted is simply to support the idea. It is the wood and not the trees with which I am concerned, so I have not dwelt in any great detail on any single topic.

While the book is predominantly psychological, I am, in fact, a psychiatrist. Having spent the greater part of my career working for the Medical Research Council, I have a scientific orientation, but I also have a psychotherapeutic side, which shows through in various places. Lately, my main concern has been defining and measuring relating. I became interested in the origin and monitoring of the relating objectives, and it was out of this that the book developed.

Evolutionary theory, which ran through my previous two books, also features in this one; and there are sound evolutionary reasons for believing that I have two parts. In my previous book, *Relating in Psychotherapy*, they were called the inner brain and the outer brain; but this got me into all sorts of trouble. My friend Ralph Goldstein asked, "If I lower an electrode into the brain how do I know when I get to the inner brain?" Obviously, I could not take a crayon and draw around a part of a diagram of the brain and say that's the inner brain. This led to my calling the two parts the outer me and the inner me; so now I have not a two-brain theory but a two-me theory.

The book is intentionally pitched mid-way between the subjective and the objective, because that's the way it is. Sometimes it makes more sense to describe how I experience things, and other times I need to consider specific mental processes and specific brain structures. Inevitably the question arises, to what extent do my subjective experiences correspond with the objective observations of others? Somehow, somewhere, there has got to be an objective, brain-based explanation for what I experience, but so far I do not have it.

How do I answer those who ask me what is wrong with the old conscious and unconscious? Well, for one thing, there are now two unconsciouses: the cognitive and the psychodynamic. Where the cognitive unconscious gains in scientific precision, it loses in the range of processes it is able to encompass. You might say that I am introducing a third one; but even though the inner me is unconscious, the fact that it is, is not the main point. I am much more interested in what it does, and why and how it does what it does.

Finally, I would like to say that I have tried to build up the book in stages, so the sequence of the chapters is important. To get the most out of the book I advise you to read the chapters in the order in which they are presented.

Acknowledgements

Figure 1 is reproduced by permission of Sage Publications from Birtchnell, J. "The interpersonal octagon: An alternative to the interpersonal circle", which first appeared in *Human Relations*, 47, pages 518 and 524. Copyright © The Tavistock Institute, 1994.

Thanks are due to John Shaw, formerly of the MRC Clinical Psychiatry Unit, for helping me with the neuroscience; Dale Mathers, of the International Association of Analytical Psychology, for helping me to understand Jung; and Cristina Sheppard for suggesting the terms inner me and outer me.

I would also like to thank Michael Forster, Managing Director, and a series of Editors (Academic Psychology) at Psychology Press, for efficiently steering the book through its stages of production.

Part I

The outer me/inner me dichotomy

In this part I have to get across the idea with which the book is concerned. If I fail, the rest of the book will make no sense; for every one of the remaining chapters concerns the application of this idea across a range of mental functions. The idea is that there appear to be two broad categories of mental functioning, which are almost like two people in the same body. The terms outer me and inner me have been chosen to describe them because there is no existing pair of terms that fully covers the attributes that they include.

1 The birth of an idea

The germ of the idea to be developed in this book lies in a paragraph early in my 1993/96 book, *How Humans Relate: A New Interpersonal Theory*. Here, I was trying to make the point that much of our relating behaviour occurs quickly and spontaneously, without conscious deliberation. I drew the distinction between what I then called the cortex, which I considered to be concerned with the conscious and the deliberate, and the subcortex, which I considered to be concerned with the quick and the spontaneous. "The logic of the subcortex" I wrote, "is often so profound that it feels as though it is the prime mover and that the cortex trundles along some distance behind, long after the main action has taken place" (page 6). I now realise that the terms cortex and subcortex were inappropriate, since the greater part of cerebral cortical activity is not conscious or deliberate; but although the terms were wrong, the point I was making was probably right. By my 1999/2002 book, *Relating in Psychotherapy: The Application of a New Theory*, this short paragraph had grown into a complete chapter (Chapter 2) in which I had replaced the cortex and subcortex with the outer brain and the inner brain. I concluded that the distinction between what I considered to be these two major components of the brain is relevant to our understanding of a broad range of mental activities; but I also suspected that we might underestimate the extent of the inner brain's influence. I wrote:

> A point that cannot be emphasised too strongly is that the inner brain must be responsible for far more of our mental activity than we are normally prepared to admit. Since we have no conscious awareness of what goes on within it, this is a sobering thought (page 28).

I assumed that in the evolutionary sequence, the inner brain was all there was until the gradual emergence of the outer brain, which made all the difference to the way that humans function; but, as Pinker (1997) so rightly observed, ". . . the forces of evolution do not just heap layers on an unchanged foundation" (page 371). Just because the outer brain came into place after the inner brain does not mean that the inner brain has remained unchanged. The human inner brain, as I understood it, is a highly sophisticated set of structures, and, while it appears to remain unaware of itself, it has acquired a number of capabilities that the inner brains of other animals do not appear to have. Yet even these capabilities can only be modifications of capabilities that other animals do have. The outer brain and the inner brain of the 1999/2002 book have become the outer me and the inner me of the present one. This is because I now realise that I am primarily concerned with mental phenomena and not brain structures.

So what are the two of me?

At this stage it will be necessary to provide only the bare bones of an answer to this question, for the main object of the book is to clarify the distinction between them – for both you and me. That which I experience as I, which I formerly called the cortex, but which I now call the outer me, is the self-conscious part of me, the part that figures things out and makes rational decisions on the basis of facts and evidence. The existence of this other me can only be inferred by this self-conscious me (which I call I) from the observations it makes upon my behaviour.

The science journalist Holmes (1998), in a review article, coined the term *the Zombie within* to refer to that which I am now calling the inner me. He wrote, "The Zombie within, not the conscious self, is running the show." This is exactly how it has always felt for me. The idea that an unconscious part of me "runs the show" has such implications for how we view ourselves as humans that I decided to devote an entire book to examine how far the idea can be taken. A feature of the book is to examine what the outer me can do that the inner me cannot do, and how its particular capabilities can enhance our mental functioning. I will examine how well these two parts of me are able to get on together and whether they ever get in each other's way.

The title of the book is in keeping with my intention, as far as possible, to write in the first person singular. This is because, in many instances, I will take my experience of my own mental functioning as a starting point. In adopting this policy, I will assume that, in most fundamental respects, my own mental processes are comparable to those of other people. The title also links up with my efforts to explain what it feels like to be two of me. In explaining the title of the book to other people, I have found myself saying, "There is the me that I experience as myself, and then there is this other me that appears to make decisions on its own, and causes me to do things that I had not consciously decided to do."

I need to emphasise that the outer me and the inner me are both, in their separate ways, me. If, at least metaphorically, the inner me is in a place, it is not a place into which I (outer me) can enter. Neither can it enter into that place that I experience as I. I (outer me) have worked out that it exists, but it cannot work out that I exist, because it does not have the capacity for working things out. It does not know it exists in the way that I know that I exist. It cannot look at itself in the way that I can look at myself (or it). I cannot communicate with it in the way that I can communicate with you, because it is not a you; it is a me, and I cannot communicate with me. I am me and it *is* me. We are parallel and inseparable parts of me.

The inner me is the most fundamental me. The conscious, outer me is only what might be called a bolt-on extra, an added refinement, a very valuable refinement, but a refinement nonetheless. The inner me could survive without the outer me, but the outer me could not survive without the inner me. The inner me is the control centre, the part that knows where I am going. It releases emotions into consciousness that convey whether or not I am on-track in the attainment of its objectives. The primary objectives concern survival and reproduction (Chapters 6 and 7), but there are also a set of secondary objectives that have evolved out of these that concern relating (Chapter 8). The inner me would seem to have no direct means of passing the objectives on to the outer me, but one-way or another, the outer me becomes aware of them, for its main function is to bring additional capabilities into play that contribute to their attainment. It could be said that the inner me "trains" the outer me by causing it to feel good when its objectives have been attained and bad when they have not.

The confluence of ideas

It is reassuring to discover that others have thought this way. In 1923, Groddeck expressed the view that we are animated by "some wondrous force" that directs both what we do and what happens to us. He called this force the "Es" or the "It" and he believed that we are lived by the "It." Milner (1987), who will be considered more fully in Chapter 4, wrote of the mind that "It lives you." This is how it has always felt to me. In 1936, Agatha Christie, the crime fiction writer, quoted Mary Drower, a character from her book *The ABC Murders*, as saying: "Your mind gets made up for you sometimes without your knowing how it happened" (page 103).

The lines of thought of a number of writers are beginning to converge upon the same common pathway; namely, that there is the part of us that we normally recognise to be ourselves, and then there is this other part that feels as though it is buried somewhere deep inside us, which appears to exert control over us. The understanding is that the part that we normally recognise to be ourselves is, in evolutionary terms, a relatively recent development, and this other part that exerts so much control over us is what might be called the original part, which exists in continuity with the nervous systems of all other animal forms, and which carries the original "blueprints." The more recent part appears to have concluded, on the basis of its observations and experimentations, that this other part exists, though it seems unlikely that this other part has concluded that this more recent part exists.

What is so encouraging about recent developments is that there is beginning to emerge a confluence of the introspective contributions of the more subjective theorists, and the objective contributions of experimental psychologists and neuroscientists. People who introspect are not normally good at neuroscience and experimental psychology, and neuroscientists and experimental psychologists are not normally good at introspection. Despite LeDoux's (1998) caution that ". . . introspection is often a blurry window into the workings of the mind" (page 52), I believe that the book will be most successful if I can integrate the theoretical conclusions from self-observation and the observation of others with the conclusions of neuroscientists and experimental psychologists. There is some legitimacy to simply stating what something feels like; and LeDoux (1998) wrote, "According to functionalist doctrine, cognitive science stands on its own as a discipline – it does not require that we know anything about the brain" (page 27). When I speculate about how the mind appears to function, while it may not be necessary to refer to brain structures, and the findings of neuroscientists and psychologists, it provides support to my speculations if I do.

Some thoughts related to the outer me and the inner me

The distinction between the head and the heart is often used to distinguish between the sensible, practical and rational and the romantic, passionate and irrational. The heart is popularly used to refer to that which is intuitive or instinctive. People use the term I feel it in my heart (or sometimes in my bones) to mean they know it in some deep, fundamental way, which they cannot deny. Sometimes it is right to be guided by reason and sometimes it is right to go the way of the heart.

Much of what Evans (2001) wrote about intellect versus emotion comes close to the distinction between the outer me and the inner me. He wrote:

> Reason and emotion can thus be seen as two complementary systems in the human brain for making decisions. When it is important to get the answer right, and we have a lot of time and information at our disposal, we can use the slow and clean method of reasoning things through. When we have little time and information or it is not so important to get the right answer, we can switch to the fast and frugal method of following our feelings (page 130).

Generally, it seems to be the case that the outer me is slow and laborious and the inner me is fast and effortless.

Maintaining a balance between the outer me and the inner me

In his 2000 BBC Reith Lecture, Prince Charles said, "We need to restore the balance between the heartfelt reason of instinctive wisdom and the rational insights of scientific analysis. Neither is much use without the other." There are those who scorn the rational and those who scorn the irrational. There are those who are hopeless at being logical and those who shun everything that is not logical. A feature of inner me functioning is spontaneity. It does not prepare in advance. The outer me is more cautious. It thinks before it acts. While this may have advantages, it introduces a degree of contrivance, even artificiality. Some people get stuck at the outer me level, and are unable to trust the inner me sufficiently to give it free rein. Psychotherapy clients who try to maintain the dialogue at an outer me level are described as intellectualising, and this is thought to be a defence against joining up with their emotions.

The blurring of the distinction between the outer me and the inner me

Since some actions originate in the outer me and, through force of habit, become downloaded to the inner me (McCrone, 1999), there must always be some actions that fall mid-way between the consciously and unconsciously executed. When I am driving, I sometimes consciously decide to change gear and sometimes I do it without thinking. Sometimes I decide to blink and sometimes I blink reflexly. This must apply to many areas of mental activity.

Interactions between the outer me and the inner me

Pinker (1997) wrote, "And the human cerebral cortex does not ride piggy-back on an ancient limbic system, or serve as the terminus of a processing stream beginning there. The systems work in tandem, integrated by many two way connections" (page 371). The book aims to explore those actions and processes that the outer me appears to be responsible for and those that the inner me appears to be responsible for. Each has its separate strengths and capabilities and, in many respects, each depends upon the other.

Can the outer me influence the inner me?

Because the inner me works quite automatically it is quite easy to deceive it. When the outer me perceives that the inner me has been deceived, it has the capacity to modify the inner me's responses. When the outer me perceives that flowers are artificial, the inner me's emotional response to them diminishes. The same modification of response occurs with a statue that looks like a naked woman, or when a man realises that a woman's breast size has been augmented with silicone implants, or when a female impersonator is really a man. Such modification forms the basis of cognitive therapy, when say a therapist convinces a person with snake phobia that not all snakes are poisonous. It is interesting to speculate what neural connections might be responsible for this.

The outer me misperceiving what the inner me wants

Because the inner me does not make its intentions clear, sometimes I (outer me) think I intend to behave one-way when, from outward appearances, I clearly intend to behave another way. Hence the expression actions speak louder than words. A woman may insist that she does not love a particular man, and perhaps even believe this, but cannot stop thinking and talking about him and finding excuses to make contact with him. A man's failure to have an erection may be because he is not turned on by a particular woman, even though he (outer me) thinks he is. A man cannot will himself to have an erection. Hence the expression, attributed to Freud, that the penis does not lie. Karen Horney (1945) introduced the expression the tyranny of the shoulds. I may try to behave in a particular way because I (outer me) believe that I should, but I may find that I have little enthusiasm to do so, and have to struggle to make myself do it. As the saying goes, my heart isn't in it. There are also the expressions that the spirit is willing but the flesh is weak, and you can lead a horse to the water but you cannot make it drink. When I am being lazy, the outer me thinks that I should be doing something, but the inner me is not motivated to do it.

These kinds of difficulty sometimes emerge in psychotherapy. The psycho-analyst tries to understand, on the basis of what the client says and does, what the client really wants to do. When s/he believes that s/he has unearthed the reason why the client is acting the way s/he is, s/he may try cautiously to offer what is called an interpretation. Sometimes the client will refuse to accept it. This is called resistance. Here, it may be that the client (outer me) cannot believe that s/he (inner me) should wish to do such a thing, particularly if it is something which is socially unacceptable. Bateson (1973), the family thera-pist, introduced the term the double bind, by which a parent may confuse a child by making an explicit statement that is contradicted by an implicit action. The explicit (outer me) statement is what the parent believes s/he should be making and the implicit (inner me) contradiction is what s/he really means to convey. These terms explicit and implicit are sometimes used by psychologists to refer to what I mean by the outer me and the inner me.

Examples of the outer me not knowing why

Because so much of what I feel, say and do is inner me determined, I (outer me) am sometimes confused about what is going on. I can only observe myself and try to make sense of it after the event.

Do I know why I feel the things I feel?

LeDoux (1998) wrote, "And if there is one thing about emotions that we know well from introspection, it is that we are often in the dark about why we feel the way we do" (page 52). Westen (1998) observed that people can feel things without knowing that they feel them, and they can act upon feelings of which they are unaware. They can act in a hostile manner towards people they are not aware that they dislike. Emotions come straight out of the inner me. Only the inner me decides whether I should experience an emotion, what form it should take and with what intensity I should experience it. Only the inner me knows what it is I am feeling emotional about. Quite often, I (outer me) am not surprised by the emotion, and I can usually connect the emotion with the circumstances, but only after the event. In general terms, when I succeed in attaining what I am striving for I feel happy; when I fail to achieve it or when I lose it I feel sad; when I am in danger of losing what I have attained I feel frightened; and when I am determined to retrieve what I have lost I feel angry. Sometimes I feel an emotion I did not expect to feel; I thought something would please me and I find it has displeased me, or vice versa. Sometimes I am more emotional than I thought I would be and sometimes I am less emotional than I thought I would be. In these circumstances, the outer me has guessed how the inner me was going to react, but has guessed wrong. Sometimes I think I am feeling angry or sad or whatever about one thing when really I am feeling this way about another thing.

There are times when I feel emotion that I cannot explain. I feel happy, or anxious or sad, when I seem to have no reason to feel any of these emotions. At these times, the outer me is simply out of touch with the inner me's conclusions. It does not realise the importance that the inner me has attached to a particular event or situation. Sometimes the unexplained emotion can persist for long periods, weeks, months or even years. Then one day, the emotion may go. It may be that on this day something has changed like, for instance, a certain person I work with has left. Only then can I (outer me) link the emotion to the situation and discover what all this time had been causing the inner me to generate this emotion.

Do I know why I say the things I say?

Mostly, when I talk, apart from on really special occasions, I do not prepare carefully in advance what I am about to say. The words just come out. Such talk is spontaneous and probably comes straight from the inner me. If I (outer me) listen to what I (inner me) have said, I am often surprised.

Do I know why I act the way I do?

Because motivation comes only from the inner me, and because the inner me has no way of conveying its motives to the outer me, I sometimes find myself doing things without knowing why. One day, when one of our sons had misbehaved, my wife shouted at him, "Why did you do that?" I said, not very helpfully, "He doesn't know." Often, when people are asked why they did something they say, "Because I felt like it." This may be exactly right, but what does feeling like it mean? Presumably that the inner me has prompted them to do it.

Obviously, there are times when I know perfectly well why I am doing something, like when I switch on the light when it is getting dark, put up an umbrella when it is starting to rain, or go to the post-box to post a letter; but how often is this not the case? It is difficult to say, because sometimes I think I know why I have done something, when perhaps this is not why I have done it at all. For every action there must be a motive, and since motives come from the inner me, there must always be an inner me input; but since the inner me does not (cannot) keep the outer me informed of its motives, the outer me is forever having to think up justifications for our actions.

I do not like to admit that I do not know why I do things, because I like to believe that I do things for a reason. I usually manage to convince myself that I know why I do what I do, but more often than I care to believe, I have made up a reason, and most of the time I have not been aware that I have done this. When, under hypnosis, a person is told to do something at a particular time, on a particular day, more often than not s/he will do it, and when asked why, s/he will make up a reason and not realise that s/he has done so. S/he will be quite unaware that s/he is simply obeying an instruction given under hypnosis. In an experiment reported by Pittman (1992), a class of students received a subliminal presentation (see Chapter 9) of a photograph, accompanied by the word GOOD, of one of two possible candidates for a job. The only difference between the candidates was that one was good at writing and the other was good at computing. The students were twice as likely to choose as the most suitable for the job the one whose photograph had been presented to them accompanied by the word GOOD, and when asked to justify their selection, they said that writing was more important or computing was more important, depending upon the skill of the candidate whose photograph had been presented to them. Gazzaniga (1985) demonstrated how patients, who have had the connections between the cerebral hemisphere's severed, can carry out instructions presented to the right hemisphere and offer incorrect rationalisations for their behaviour. (See a similar observation by Sperry in Chapter 19.) These are only experimental situations, but they demonstrate that people are capable of unknowingly making up a reason for doing something which is not the real reason.

Not doing what I say I will do

Sometimes I will say that I will do something and not do it. I (outer me) may say that I want to do it, but still I do not do it. I keep promising to do it, but it never gets done. What is happening here? Probably I (inner me) do not really want to do it, but I (outer me) think that I do. I try to do it because I believe I ought to. Sometimes I (outer me) can get myself to do what I know I ought to do, but sometimes I cannot. Here, the spirit is willing but the flesh is weak.

The implications for research

Westen (1998) made the important point that many research studies ask questions of the participants that they are in no position to answer. He wrote,

"The overreliance on self-reports in personality, clinical and attitude research can no longer be maintained in the face of the mounting evidence that much of what we do, feel and think is inaccessible to consciousness" (page 361).

Advertisements

Advertisers are well aware that people commonly do not decide to buy things on the basis of working through the pros and cons of comparative products. Advertisements do not soberly list the benefits of their products. They are designed, at great expense, by skilled professionals, because they have been proved to vastly increase sales. Their aim is to override the rational (outer me) side of people and to appeal to the emotional (inner me) side. They aim to sell not an efficient motor car, but power, status and success; not a soap that gets you clean, but youth, glamour and attractiveness. The people in advertisements are young, confident, happy people, in exciting places, enjoying themselves. They do funny things to make me laugh. Music is played to make me feel good. I (outer me) may be aware that I am being manipulated in this way, but the inner me responds just as always.

CONSIDERATIONS OF TIME

It has been stated that the inner me just is, or the inner me just does. A consequence of this is that it just acts in the present and for the moment. It does not look backwards and it does not look forwards. It does not take a long-term view or consider the consequences of its actions. It does not plan ahead. Because the outer me can take an objective view of ourselves, it can also set ourselves in time. The time perspective of the outer me is a major advantage. Dawkins (2000) wrote that Nature (inner me) is a short-term Darwinian profiteer. He observed that long-term planning is something utterly new on the planet, even alien. (It exists only in the human outer me.) The future, he wrote, is a new invention in evolution. He referred to our (outer me) capacity to fight against the naturally selfish and exploitative (inner me) tendencies of nature. He considered that our (outer me) brains are big enough to see into the future and plot long-term consequences. The bracketed insertions are mine.

There are at least four examples of the inner me appearing to be aware of time: The first is when it generates anxiety when a person encounters a situation where previously a disturbing event occurred; the second is post-hypnotic suggestion, when a person behaves in a particular way, at a particular time, on a particular day, because s/he has previously been instructed to do so while under hypnosis; the third is the anniversary reaction, when a person becomes emotional on each anniversary of a disturbing event; and the fourth is what I have called the age correspondence reaction in which a person becomes emotionally upset when her/his child reaches the age that s/he was when a disturbing event took place (Birtchnell, 1981). All these could be explained by the inner me simply matching the reaction to the date or the circumstances. Matching is something the inner me is good at, which is why it is constantly pushing associated ideas into consciousness.

Do the outer me and the inner me correspond to specific brain structures?

I must stress that, throughout the book, the terms outer me and inner me do not refer to specific brain locations. Outer me refers to functions that are consciously and deliberately executed, and inner me refers to functions that are automatic and not voluntarily instigated. While inner me functions are performed by what are considered to be evolutionarily earlier regions of the brain, and outer me functions are performed by what are considered to be more recently evolved regions, research suggests that both the inner me and the outer me are served by a variety of regions, and where these are known they will be referred to.

It may never be possible to allocate precisely outer me and inner me functions to specific brain structures, and LeDoux warns us that "the identification of brain regions associated with specific functions should not be taken too literally. Functions are mediated by interconnected systems of brain regions working together rather than by individual areas working in isolation" (page 77). The greater part of outer me functioning is probably located in the frontal cortex. Severe damage to this region seriously disturbs what I would consider to be outer me functioning. It is much more difficult to point to specific locations for inner me functioning. Certainly large areas of the cerebral cortex are involved in unconscious and automatic processes, which must therefore be linked to the inner me. Since much inner me functioning is extremely subtle, it must draw heavily upon cortical structures.

The triune brain

It is tempting to draw parallels between the outer me/inner me distinction and MacLean's (1990) concept of the triune brain. MacLean proposed that the brain evolved from within outwards. The first and earliest part he called the reptilian brain. It comprises the basal ganglia and is concerned with the primitive drives towards food and sex and with the fight-or-flight responses. The second part, which he called the palaeomammalian brain or visceral brain, comprises what he called the limbic system. It is organised around the first part and is concerned with the emotions. Wrapped around the limbic system is the third part, which he called the neomammalian brain or word brain. It comprises the neocortex and is concerned with thinking and reasoning. He considered that fish, reptiles, birds and amphibians have only a reptilian brain, that the lower mammals have both a reptilian brain and a palaeomammalian brain, and that only humans and other primates have all three. MacLean's (1949) understanding that the palaeomammalian brain is the seat of the emotions and does not use words would indicate an alignment with the inner me. His description of the neomammalian brain as the word brain indicates an alignment with the outer me, which relies heavily upon words.

The triune brain theory has met with much criticism. LeDoux (1998) considered that the term the limbic system should be discarded. He said it is anatomically inexact, and damage to the structures covered by the term, e.g., the hippocampus, has relatively little consistent effect upon emotional function. He also observed that so-called primitive creatures do have areas that meet the structural and functional criteria of the neocortex and that it is no longer possible to say that some parts of the mammalian cortex are older than other parts.

The downloading of brain activities

McCrone (1999) summarised a number of brain scan studies, which showed that ". . . paying focal, effortful attention to something (outer me) calls large regions of the brain into action" (page 32). These include lower brain areas such as the basal ganglia and the cerebellum. He observed that "Vast swathes of the brain light up as it throws every vaguely relevant circuit at the task" (page 31) and "Regions all over the brain are alight with effort." He concluded that "The brain does not behave like a collection of isolated pathways, each doing their own thing, but as a coherent system." In contrast, once a problem has been solved, or a task has been mastered, there is a rapid shrinkage of brain activity. He wrote, "The general picture of shrinking patterns of activation as the brain learns from its own fumbling explorations seems well established" (page 32).

Raichle (1998), using a brain scanner, observed that certain parts of the brain, such as the insula cortex and the lower face of the frontal lobes, appear to be switched off when the brain is dealing with novelty. These areas might house the mechanism for converting the tedious learned activities into effortless routine ones (outer me to inner me). Graybiel (1998), using electrodes to record the responses of individual neurons in a monkey's brain, concluded that the basal ganglia might be involved in the same process. When the monkey was involved in learning that a clicking noise signalled the availability of a sip of juice, the basal ganglia cells fired in response to all stages of the sequence, such as moving the body and drinking. When the task was learned, they fired only in response to the clicking. Graybiel concluded that, once the task was learned, the basal ganglia cells alone could trigger the appropriate motor response to the stimulus of the clicking. Graybiel concluded that because all cortical activity feeds through the bottleneck of the basal ganglia, they could perform the same function for any form of mental action. McCrone (1999) observed that the basal ganglia are connected to the cortex above by a mysterious set of looping paths, which collect signals from wide areas of the cortex and funnel them back to the frontal planning region.

This makes them well placed to coordinate information from any area of the cortex.

These studies suggest that when the outer me is confronted with a new and unfamiliar situation it draws upon large areas of the brain, but that once the situation becomes familiar and the response to it becomes routine, the inner me takes over and far less of the brain becomes involved.

The separate functions of each cerebral hemisphere

Interestingly, there is evidence to suggest that the two cerebral hemispheres may to some extent contribute differently to outer me and inner me functioning. Eccles (1989) observed that the two hemispheres in humans are not simply replicas of each other. Each appears to have become specialised in different brain functions. This has enabled humans to make the most economical use of brain space. He wrote, ". . . there is now the exciting prospect that the evolution of cerebral asymmetry may provide the essential process in hominid evolution." Much of the information we have about the functioning of each hemisphere is due to the work of Sperry et al. (1969) on people who have had their hemispheres separated by the severance of the corpus callosum in operations to treat severe uncontrollable epilepsy. The hemispheres used to be classified as the dominant (usually the left) hemisphere and the minor (usually the right) hemisphere, though there is no reason to believe that one hemisphere dominates the other. The so-called dominant hemisphere codes sensory input in terms of linguistic descriptions, and the so-called minor hemisphere does so in terms of images (Levy, 1974). The dominant hemisphere is specialised for verbal, arithmetical, analytical and ideational abilities and making conceptual connections. The first of these are outer me functions but, it will be argued later that making conceptual connections can also be an inner me function. The minor hemisphere is specialised for spatial and imagistic abilities, perceiving wholes from a collection of parts, the intuitive perception and apprehension of geometrical principles, and discriminating musical chords. These are primarily inner me functions. Eccles (1989) observed, "We can still doubt whether the right (minor) hemisphere has a full, self-conscious existence. For instance, does it plan and worry about the future . . .?" (page 210). This is further suggestive of the minor hemisphere being more associated with the inner me.

AN ALTERNATIVE TWO-ME THEORY

Schiffer (2000) also proposed that everyone has two selves or two minds, but believed that each is associated with one cerebral hemisphere. He drew parallels between these two selves and those identified in split-brain patients. He described one as being sometimes more troubled, more dominant or more mature than the other. He linked his theory with what is known about the characteristics of the two hemispheres.

2   The outer me

By the outer me I mean that which I call "I," the spokesperson or representative of that which I experience as myself, that addresses other people and that feels itself to be addressed by other people. The I that sits on this chair, writing this, feels like the person that I am, the person that occupies the space that is the inside of me. This feeling of I-ness that I have is my sense of being a self. Blackmore (2001) proposed that "Consideration of the nature of self is deeply bound up with questions about consciousness" (page 525). She cited Parfit (1987) who considered there to be two types of self-theorists: the ego theorists and the bundle theorists. The first believe in a persistent self who is the subject of experiences, whose existence explains the sense of unity and continuity of experience. The second deny there is any such thing, and maintain that the apparent unity is just a collection of ever changing experiences tied together by the presence of a physical body and a memory. It feels as if I have been the same person from when I was an infant to now that I am an old man, because I have all the I's that I have ever been inside my memory store, and I can click into any of them.

The outer me and time

Where the inner me acts only for the moment, the outer me looks backwards and forwards in time. Eccles (1989) wrote, "We live in a time paradigm of past-present-future. When humans are consciously aware of the time NOW, this experience contains not only the memory of past events, but also anticipated future events." Stebbins (1982) called this ability to think in terms of time, time binding. Eccles wrote, "The role of time-binding in our conscious life cannot be overestimated" (page 230). The outer me can figure out how something came to be. It can plan ahead and imagine the consequences of an action. Fuster (1989) considered that it is the frontal-prefrontal cortex that is able to handle serial information, and Ingvar (1985) provided clinical evidence in support of this. Eccles (1989) observed that bilateral lesions of the prefrontal cortex result in the loss of future syndrome, characterised by lack of foresight and lack of ambition.

Deciding and acting deliberately

The act of deciding and deliberately doing something are features of the outer me. In a sense, the inner me also decides things. It "decides" whether I should act in a particular way, or feel a particular emotion, but when the outer me decides to do something, it is conscious and deliberate. One could say that the inner me does not really decide, any more than traffic lights decide to change colour. I might draw a distinction between consciously and objectively deciding (outer me) and unconsciously and subjectively deciding (inner me), but is unconscious deciding really deciding? In objectively and deliberately deciding I am standing outside of myself, assessing what, on rational grounds, would be a useful and constructive thing to do.

What is it that determines what I decide to do, and what does the act of deciding amount to? Why do, or how can, I decide to do something? I can only do so if I am aware of the inner me's objectives, but I can learn these by registering what experiences cause me to feel pleasure. There are some who would argue that all (outer me) deciding is an illusion. Perhaps the inner me decides everything, and it just feels as if I (outer me) am deciding. When I do something, it feels as though it is that which I call "I" that has decided to do it, and "I" take responsibility for having done it. Deciding to do something is a manifestation of that which some people call free will. Many believe that, with their free will, they are able to decide whether or not they do something socially unacceptable, like commit an offence. Wegner and Wheatley (1999) have conducted experiments that demonstrate how free will can be an illusion, but neuroscientists continue to grapple with the idea (Libet et al., 1999). Objectives at the outer me level are called intentions. I say "I intended to do something," or "I did something on purpose." Suppose I am aware that the inner me is urging me to do something – like panic – and I decide to calm down and think of a sensible solution. Is not that the outer me deciding? Eccles (1989) combined the terms free will and intention in the phrase willed intention (page 43).

Trying

Obviously, humans are not the only animals that try. A mouse will try to get out of a trap, in the same way that a person will try to get out of a burning building. Such trying is automatic and not thought out. This might be termed inner me trying; but there is another kind of trying that would seem to be outer me trying. When someone says, "You can do it if you try," it means that, if I marshal some extra resources from somewhere, I could achieve something that normally I could not; but why would I want to? Presumably because, in the light of what I know, I have decided that the extra effort would be worth my while. When someone says, "You are not really trying," they mean that at an outer me level, I have not decided to try. Trying is linked with terms like courage and bravery. In an act of courage I, the outer me, am deciding to overcome an inner me induced inertia, tiredness or fear. The outer me is overriding the inner me's natural response. Daring is a further variant of trying. Claxton (1998) expressed the view that it is possible to try too hard, and that sometimes, if we stop trying, what we are wanting to do will happen. Trying keeps us in the more focused outer me mode, and we may be focusing on the wrong thing. Trying blocks spontaneity. When we stop trying we slip back into the less focused inner me mode (see Ehrenzweig, Chapter 4).

The outer me and adaptability

Humans, more than any other animal, are able to adapt to changing circumstances. Stebbins (1982) observed that the careful analysis of the behaviour of animals reveals that they are automatic, stereotyped and relatively inflexible. They have wired-in responses and patterns of behaviour that are applicable to a wide range of situations and circumstances, but they have limited ability to modify such instinctive responses and behaviour patterns, or devise new ones when faced with novel or unexpected situations. In contrast, humans are born with far fewer wired-in responses and behaviour patterns (though they still retain their built-in objectives, housed in the inner me). Consequently, they are at a disadvantage in their early years. Over time, they use the outer me to learn a wide and ever increasing range of skills and capabilities (which, once learned, get passed down to the inner me for their automatic execution). Throughout their lives, though less so in later life, humans remain open to the possibility of modifying, extending or even replacing their learned skills in the light of changing circumstances.

In the field of adaptability, the outer me and the inner me form the perfect combination. No organism can function without objectives. If it had no objectives its behaviour would be random. The inner me retains a set of innate, basic objectives, which are of a fairly general nature. They are fully discussed in Part III. The objectives dictate the general directions in which we move. The outer me could be said to operate at the coal face of life. Its task is to devise specific ways (skills, tools, machinery) of attaining the inner me's general objectives. Once these ways are perfected they get passed back to the inner me, which takes over their execution. This frees up the outer me to direct its attention to devising new tasks for meeting new problems.

Learning

Many human skills are long and complicated. They are built up gradually, step-by-step, over a period of time. Humans are motivated less by simple punishments and rewards, and more by seeing their goals get closer. Learning a skill is an outer me activity. It is unpleasant because it involves trying to do something I have never done before and, despite the mistakes I make, forcing myself to keep trying. As each new skill is acquired, it stops being unpleasant and becomes a pleasure. At this point it stops being an outer me activity and becomes an inner me one. It becomes effortless and automatic.

Language

The greater part of outer me functioning is language-based. In contrast, the inner me is more concerned with shapes, patterns and associations. Although the outer me is an inveterate user of language, it relies heavily upon the inner me to provide the underpinnings of language. The outer me thinks of the ideas, which the inner me converts into words and sentences. The inner me stores the words, propels the required words into consciousness, in the right sequence, at the right moment. It also controls the neural and motor mechanisms of speech and writing. The outer me could not indulge so freely in language if the inner me did not do all this background work. It is the sheer speed of operation that enables the inner me's linguistic processing to keep up with the outer me's thoughts.

The human capacity for language is linked to the human capacity for adaptability. Eccles (1989) observed that although monkeys and apes have good development of all the necessary structures for cognitive and motor learning, they are greatly handicapped in a novel situation by being unable to think of the problem linguistically. Converting thoughts and ideas into language greatly facilitates problem-solving. Having verbal symbols for things makes it much easier to think about them and to think sequentially, moving from step to step. Language also enables humans to record ideas or sequences of ideas, which they may refer back to and to pass ideas back and forth, in rational discussion or argument. Language also enormously increases the capacity of humans to communicate. The closeness of human relationships and networks is a consequence of this. This function of language will be further examined in Chapter 13.

Rational thought

The outer me is the seat of that which is called rational thought. Rational thought is deliberate. It takes place within the setting of consciousness. I am conscious of myself thinking when I apply rational thought and I make deliberate steps in the thought process. Weiskrantz (1997) wrote that to be conscious is to be able to manipulate items in thought and imagery. Almost always, rational thought takes place through language, though this must also include the special language of mathematics. I think out the steps of my thinking in words. When I hear myself thinking, I faintly hear the words in my head. I may also speak them out loud either to myself or to someone else or I may write them down. Rational thought is a way of figuring things out (see Chapter 14). It is that which, more than anything else, puts humans in a different category from other animals. The enormous superiority that humans have over all other animals is largely a consequence of the human capacity for rational thought. Rational thought is the basis of that which is called intelligence. Intelligent people are good at it.

Claxton (1998) listed a number of characteristics of d-mode thinking. He noted that, because it is tied to language, it must proceed at the same speed as language. That is, it cannot be very fast or very slow, providing either the inspirational flash or the slow gestation, which are characteristics of inner me functioning. D-mode thinking is disciplined, precise and clear-cut. There is no place for vagueness or ambiguity. It seeks and prefers clarity. It is purposeful and effortful. It is not fun. It is concerned with answering a question, solving a problem or finding an explanation. The person who has solved a problem by d-mode thinking has to be able to enumerate the series of logical steps by which the problem was solved, to show how s/he got to the end point. In d-mode thinking the person proceeds with caution and shuns the impulsivity of inner me mental activity.

Consciousness

The outer me is inextricably linked with that which is called consciousness. However, there are instances in which it appears that there is a delay between my voluntarily making a decision and my becoming consciously aware of my making that decision. Therefore, the outer me and consciousness cannot be one and the same thing. Sometimes it is useful to think of consciousness as though it were a place, where thoughts, ideas and feelings can enter or leave. We speak of ideas entering or leaving consciousness. The term mind is sometimes used in the same way. I may say that something has entered my mind or that an idea has come to mind. When I say that I have something in mind or on my mind, I mean that presently it has my conscious attention. When I say I have put an idea out of my mind, I mean that I have removed it from consciousness. Consciousness in this sense is like a stage or an arena where mental activity takes place, or a computer screen on to which files are loaded, worked upon, and then saved (taken out of consciousness and stored somewhere else). Since I can only concentrate on, or work upon, one idea or task at a time, it is necessary to have this means of limiting what is, at any time, in this place called consciousness. Baars (1997) observed that a classical metaphor for consciousness has been that of a bright spot cast by a spotlight on the stage of a dark theatre "that represents the integration of multiple sensory inputs into a single conscious experience" (page 58).

Ideas can pass from the inner me into the outer me, and when they do, they come, or are being put, into consciousness. Pain is sometimes acted upon (I pull my hand away from a hot plate) before it enters consciousness. Sometimes information from the sense organs does not reach consciousness (see Chapter 9). The inner me houses the memory store and the inner me can put words, thoughts, ideas, tunes etc., out of the memory store into consciousness, simply because something has reminded it of them. The outer me can also ask the inner me for items out of the memory store. If it wants to remember a name or a tune or whatever, it submits a request for it, and then, in due course, the word or tune pops into consciousness, like a dish being pushed out of the kitchen through the hatch in a restaurant. The inner me controls the emotions, and projects them into consciousness so that I can feel them. Sometimes it keeps emotions to itself, and LeDoux (1998) wrote of the emotional unconscious. By this, he meant that all the correlates of emotion are present, such as raised muscle tone, rapid heart beat, high blood pressure and increased arousal, without there being the conscious experience of feeling the emotion. For organisms that do not have consciousness, all emotions are unconscious.

Reber (1992) observed that consciousness, at least in its human form, appears to be a relatively recent evolutionary development, superimposed upon an information processing system that worked quite well for millions of years. In this sense, consciousness is a kind of optional extra. Sensations, ideas, even cognitive processes can be present outside of consciousness, and may or may not pass into consciousness. They may even be present on the edge of consciousness, sometimes popping up into it and sometimes slipping down out of it. They may be not quite conscious, just conscious, vaguely conscious or partially conscious. When trying to remember a half-remembered name, idea, tune or movie, I struggle to pull it into consciousness, catching a bit of it, then losing it again.

Since consciousness is a subjective experience, there is no way of knowing whether any animal other than humans has it. It seems likely that only humans have it. If this is true then consciousness is not essential for survival. If animals do not have a consciousness then they are 100 per cent inner me. They have memories, sensations and emotions of which they are not conscious. That is, there is no place called consciousness where they can enter. This is a strange, though inevitable conclusion. Some anglers justify fishing by arguing that fish do not feel pain, that is they have no consciousness for the pain to enter. Certainly, when an animal shrieks and writhes when it is hurt, it looks as though it is feeling pain, but this may not be so. Greenfield (1995) considered there to be degrees of consciousness. She proposed that all animals are conscious to some extent, and that from the simplest organisms to the most complex, there is a gradual intensification of consciousness, culminating in the high level of consciousness of humans; but this can only be conjecture.

Controlling what enters consciousness

It would seem that one of the functions of the outer me is to control what is allowed into consciousness; yet since consciousness is a component of the outer me, how can this be? I need to postulate the existence of a mechanism, which straddles the inner me and the outer me, which is part of the outer me but which functions outside of consciousness. This I have chosen to call the in-between me. It is comparable to, but not identical with either the censor, or the unconscious ego of psychoanalytic theory (Chapter 4). It is a defensive device that protects the conscious part of the outer me from painful emotion. It imposes controls unbeknown to this conscious part, and this conscious part is unaware that they have been imposed.

The in-between me may keep out of consciousness such things as memories of distressing events, like childhood abuse; memories of acts of which I am ashamed, like cheating or stealing; awareness of unacceptable desires that I may harbour, like sexual perversions; acknowledgement of unpalatable truths about myself, like that I am a snob or a sadist; and experiencing the unpleasant emotion that is appropriate to a particular situation, like I am hurt because someone has insulted me. Westen (1998) cited evidence to support the hypothesis "that people can prevent themselves from consciously experiencing affect as a way of trying to manage unpleasant feeling states" (page 341), but he cited further evidence that "inhibiting conscious access to one's emotions places the body, particularly the heart and the immune system, under considerable stress" (page 342). Sometimes they emerge in dreams (Chapter 17), and some have argued that they are a feature of psychosis (Chapter 16).

The in-between me enables me to convince myself that I am a decent, honest citizen, who would never torture, rape or kill anyone, and yet there is evidence that most people are capable of such things. It has been argued that those who most vigorously protest against such acts in others are defending against their own capability of committing them; and why do people read avidly about them in the newspapers, or watch plays and movies about them?

Core consciousness and extended consciousness

Damasio (2000) took a neurological view of consciousness, which is different from the more subjective, psychological view that I am presenting here. He distinguished between a simple kind of consciousness, which he called core consciousness and a complex kind, which he called extended consciousness. In core consciousness the person is conscious and is aware of and attentive to her/his surroundings. The scope of core consciousness is the here and now. The only past it allows is a glimpse at that which occurred in the instant before. Extended consciousness goes beyond the here and now of core consciousness, both backwards and forwards, and therefore comes closer to my concept of the outer me. He made the important point that extended consciousness is built upon the foundation of core consciousness. Where core consciousness has it origins in a restricted number of phylogenetically old me structures, beginning in the brainstem and ending with the somatosensory and cingulate cortices, extended conscious has its origins in a much broader range of phylogenetically more recently formed structures. Impairments at the level of core consciousness cause the destruction of extended consciousness, but impairments at the level of extended consciousness leave core consciousness intact.

He wrote, "Extended consciousness is everything core consciousness is, only bigger and better, and it does nothing but grow across evolution and across a lifetime of experience in each individual" (page 196): and "If core consciousness allows you to know for a transient moment that it is you seeing a bird in flight or that it is you having a sensation of pain, extended consciousness places these same experiences in a broader canvas and over a longer period of time" (page 196). He meant by this that it brings to mind all manner of associated ideas and feelings that these momentary experiences evoke.

Self-consciousness

That which is called self-consciousness or self-awareness is a characteristic of the outer me. Dobzhansky (1967) wrote, "Self-awareness is, then, one of the fundamental, possibly the most fundamental, characteristic of the human species. This characteristic is an evolutionary novelty; the biological species from which mankind descended had only rudiments of self-awareness, or perhaps lacked it altogether" (page 68). Humans are probably the only animals who are aware of what they are doing. Being aware of myself is having the capacity to stand outside myself and observe myself in the way I might observe someone else. I have objectivity. I can watch myself doing something, but beyond this, I can watch myself watching myself doing something. I know that I am doing something in the way that no other animal knows that it is doing something.

One important point about watching myself is that, through this process, the outer me is able to watch the inner me in action. When I (inner me) automatically, and without thinking, pull my hand away from a hot object, I (outer me) can watch myself doing this and I can speculate that there must be an automatic part of me, which I am calling the inner me, that is doing this thing without any instigation from me (outer me). I can also conclude that there must be this so-called conscious part of me, which I am calling the outer me, that is watching the inner me doing this. The outer me can watch my outer me watching my inner me, but that's about as far as I can go. Perhaps that is all consciousness is: watching myself watching myself. That is something no computer can do. I can turn the spotlight of consciousness on to myself. There is nothing so miraculous about this. If I can look at my body, why can I not look at my body looking at my body?

Damasio (2000) wrote, "What could be more dizzying than to realize that it is our having consciousness which makes possible and even inevitable our questions about consciousness?" (page 4). Popper (1977) considered the emergence of full consciousness to be one of the greatest miracles. Many books have been written on the subject of consciousness. Asking what consciousness is strikes me as a pointless exercise. There comes a point in asking questions when you can go no further. It is like asking what is outside the universe. At that point you simply have to accept that that is as far as you can go.

That which I have written about language and rational thought has some relevance for this issue. Being able to turn ideas into words makes it easier to write about them. If I have a word for awareness or consciousness, I can then try applying that word to myself. If I can write the sentence "I am aware of you," I can try writing the sentence "I am aware of me," to see if it makes any sense. If this is the case, then it is questionable whether a baby has self-awareness. Why would a baby wish to consider whether it were aware of itself? Its only concerns are survival. In fact, the concerns of many people are only with survival. A person in famine-stricken Africa is unlikely to be concerned about whether s/he is aware of her/himself. It is only when I have time on my hands that I am inclined to engage in this kind of speculation.

Issues of right and wrong

Self-judgement

If I am aware of myself and I can observe myself, I can make judgements about myself. This I can do in a number of spheres. I can assess my personal attributes, such as my height, weight, physical appearance, strength, intelligence, fitness and how experienced or knowledgeable I am in various directions. I can assess my capabilities, such as how good I am at various skills, both physical and mental, and at performing various tasks. I can assess my various achievements, such as physical, mental, occupational, academic and success in social situations. I can assess my general behaviour, in terms of how clean, tidy, presentable, careful, conscientious, efficient and hard-working I am. In these various respects I can form an opinion about myself and this will contribute to an overall feeling of self-worth or self-esteem.

I can assess my behaviour towards other people, in terms of how fair, honest, generous, tolerant, caring, respectful and sympathetic I am. Would I lie, cheat or steal if I could get away with it? Would I intimidate, bully, harm, torture or murder people? Would I abuse children or commit rape? Would I prostitute myself? I can form an opinion about my behaviour towards others. Do I approve of the way I behave towards other people? Do I approve of the kind of life I lead, or have led? I can be proud of myself or ashamed of myself. As with self-consciousness, some people do not take time out to assess or make judgements about themselves. Such people are probably more inclined to act unscrupulously.

Is there a relationship between self-judgement and the judgement of the self by others? The answer is that there is enormous variation. Some people who have a secure sense of self, of what they believe in, and what they stand for, rely entirely upon their own self-judgement and show no concern for the judgement of others. Others have no internal standards of their own and are entirely dependent upon the judgement of others. What others say about them, they accept.

Understanding what it feels like to be someone else

How is it that the outer me is able to consider what it might be like to be someone else? Language is part of the answer. With language people can tell other people what it feels like to be them. This is part of the quality of closeness that will be discussed in Chapter 8. Humans have a greater capacity for closeness than any other animal. They tell each other about themselves and ask each other questions about themselves. The strange term theory of mind has been coined to describe the human capacity to imagine what it might be like to be someone else. Tests have been devised to examine this capacity. They show that children younger than age two do not have it, and that autistic children do not have it. It is clearly an outer me quality. It is related to such qualities as identification, sympathy, empathy, feeling pleased for someone and feeling sorry for someone. The extent to which a person is able to put her/himself in the place of another, or imagine what it feels like to be another, is bound to affect her/his morality. Tantam (1988) observed that people with a schizotypal personality disorder, an extreme form of distancing, have no qualms about laughing about the misfortunes of others.

Awareness of what may be going on in someone else's mind can modify my response to that person's behaviour. At an outer me level I may be able to conclude that a person's behaviour towards me is not because of what I have done or said but because of how s/he construes me. Consequently I may not necessarily feel insulted or rejected by her/his insulting or rejecting behaviour.

I am constantly aware of the effects that I may have upon others. Consequently, I greatly modify what I do and what I say in order not to upset others or cause them offence. The outer me is responsible for that which is normally described as being civilised. Civilised people restrain themselves and try to act decently. They do things out of consideration for others, because they can identify with them. Without this universal restraint civilised communities and societies would not be possible. Unlike any other animal, humans like helping and pleasing others. They give things to and do things for them. At their best, humans are cooperative and mutually supporting. They draw up rules and regulations that facilitate harmonious interaction.

The internalised judgemental figure

It is not always easy to decide whether certain standards or moral principles are internally or externally determined. Humans are able to train animals by either punishing them if they take a wrong step or rewarding them (usually with food) if they take a right one. Since, in this way, it is possible to train animals to behave correctly, it is also possible to train humans to do so. Humans may have standards or a moral code imposed upon them, by parents, teachers, ministers of religion and the like, either by the exertion of social pressures or by threat of punishment. These may begin as outer me attitudes, but over time, they may become second nature, and therefore inner me responses. Almost all humans have an internalised judgemental figure, sometimes called a conscience, which prompts them into moral action and causes them to feel guilty if they behave immorally. It can only be an outer me phenomenon. Often it is reinforced by religious beliefs. This issue will be considered further in Chapter 20.

THE OUTER ME CONTROLLING OR MODIFYING THE INNER ME

The outer me watches the inner me and appears to have the capacity either to let it have its way or to stop it in its tracks. In view of its broader understanding and its ability to think ahead, it can ask itself, "Would that be wise?" The inner me decides whether or not I should be emotional, but the outer me appears to have some control over whether I give way to that emotion. Only the inner me can fall in love but I, the outer me can, to an extent, stop myself falling in love.

It is sometimes useful to view the relationship between the outer me and the inner me as being like that between a computer programmer and a computer. In many respects, the inner me acts like a computer. The outer me may decide that the inner me's response to a given situation is based upon out-of-date information. The inner me may have registered that because an accident occurred in a particular place, this place could be dangerous. It may thus cause the person to become anxious on approaching it. The inner me may register a fear of all dogs because once the person had been savagely attacked by a dog. The outer me will appreciate that what caused the original accident is no longer present, or it may reason that not all dogs are dangerous. It will try therefore to "rewrite the computer program" so that the inner me no longer provokes an anxious response to the place where the accident occurred or adopts a more discriminating attitude towards dogs.

Since the inner me does not consider the long-term consequences of its actions, it may prompt the person to act impulsively. The outer me may consider that such behaviour may not be in the person's best interest and may impose a restriction upon it. It may introduce a more diplomatic way of saying something, or even choose to lie or deliberately deceive the other person.

The social life of humans

Because of its adaptability and ingenuity, the outer me can bring about major changes very quickly. Compared to natural evolution, social evolution is extremely fast. In many parts of the world, even over a period as short as 100 years, there have been major changes in the way we live.

Humans do not operate in isolation; they do so within the framework of groups and societies. Human relating and interrelating is complex and subtle

(Chapter 8). The communicational skills of humans are far greater than those of any other animal. Humans discuss, argue, bargain, debate and negotiate. They also bribe, threaten, coerce and deceive.

One of the great strengths of humans is that, due primarily to outer me functions, they can create groups, councils, companies, organisations, nations and governments, with complex administrative and managerial structures, capable of working towards common objectives. Such structures function almost like a single organism. Some, like certain multinational corporations, have mainly a self-serving, profit-making objective, while others, like the United Nations Organisation, benefit humanity as a whole.

Some animals also form colonies, some of enormous size – a single ant colony is believed to extend across several Mediterranean countries – but they are instinct-driven and their objectives are limited.

Over the course of generations, humans accumulate, record and pass on, knowledge for solving recurrent problems. A society has vast stores of knowledge that continues to be added to, which enables its members to function with ever increasing efficiency. If there were a major catastrophe and all this knowledge were lost, the human society would have to start afresh.

So where has it all gone wrong?

Despite the mutual respect and understanding that results from close cooperation, identification, sympathy and empathy, humans are also capable of the most appalling acts of cruelty, both as individuals and as nations. Ironically, the capacity for rational thought has caused humans to become the cruellest and most destructive animals ever to have existed. Remember, the outer me evolved as a means of facilitating the inner me's objectives; so if the inner me seeks power and domination, the outer me has the capacity to invent highly efficient ways of attaining this. The gun and the bomb are simply outer me improvements upon the weapons of other animals. Because the inner me cannot envisage the consequences of a plan of action, it cannot be unscrupulous; and although morality was the invention of the outer me, humans are able to suppress moral issues, particularly when acting as members of a group. Humans think in terms of groups and nations, but so far they have not managed to think consistently in terms of the entire human race.

The possible location of the outer me

Crick and Koch (1995) observed that voluntary, planned behaviour requires activity in the frontal lobes. McCrone (1999) quotes Passingham as saying that the involvement of the prefrontal cortex is essential for people to be sharply conscious of a mental event – a fact long suspected by neuroscientists on the basis of animal studies. Passingham was also quoted as saying that there are general purpose planning centres that seem to come into play whenever the brain is dealing with any kind of novel or difficult mental situation.

Pinker (1997) wrote that, for many decades, neurologists have known that exercising the will, forming and carrying out plans, is a job of the frontal lobes. He further observed that the prefrontal lobes, the seat of deliberate thought and planning, have ballooned to twice what a primate of our size should have.

3   The inner me

That which I am calling the inner me is responsible for far more mental activity than that which I am calling the outer me. Consequently, far more of this book is taken up with inner me processes than with outer me ones. Despite the enormous importance of the inner me, until recently, research interest in it has been relatively slight. This is probably because of the reluctance of people to accept that so much mental activity takes place outside of conscious awareness. Drawing attention to the importance of the inner me is a central aim of this book.

The inner me is that which motivates the person and keeps the person on-track. It is the headquarters, the power house. All directives emanate from it. The existence of the inner me can only be inferred. I know the inner me is there because I observe the things it causes me to do. It has nothing to do with that which I experience as "I." I (outer me) do not decide to do the things it causes me to do; I just find myself doing them. Yet, having done them, I accept them as my own. The inner me appears to have a mind of its own. It does not, cannot, convey to the outer me the factors it takes into account before causing me to recognise a cluster of images as a particular object, before propelling me towards or deterring me against a particular course of action, or before experiencing a particular emotion. It performs its functions with no awareness that there is an outer me observing it and sometimes trying to modify its responses.

Throughout the animal kingdom, the inner me is the norm and the outer me is the exception. The way I see it is that the inner me is just like any other organ. It just is. It just functions. Just as the heart and the liver are unaware that they are a heart or a liver and are unaware that they are part of a body, which has other organs in it, so too is the inner me unaware that it is an inner me and is unaware that it is part of a body with other organs in it. The term awareness simply does not apply to the inner me. If the inner me cannot be aware, it cannot even be aware of the existence of the outer me.

The inner me is of the same order of things as all the other parts of the body. The sense organs take in sensations, but they do not perceive; the muscles move, but they do not know what action their movement is bringing about; broken bones mend, but the bones do not know that they are mending themselves; body temperature gets controlled but the parts of the body responsible for this do not feel the temperature they are controlling; germs get trapped and destroyed, but the blood cells do not know that this is what they are doing.

Wants and objectives

Where do our "wants" come from? I am aware of myself wanting things, but what is it that causes me to want them? What determines that I "want" them? I can acknowledge that hunger, thirst and sexual arousal arise from some inner source, but is this the case for all my "wants"? I do not decide to want things. I just find myself wanting them. Wants arise from my innate objectives. The inner me is not just the source of these objectives; it also serves to monitor their attainment. As and when it is appropriate, it generates in me an appetite for a particular objective, which promotes in me a feeling of restlessness and needfulness. This propels me into action in search of the objective. Along the way, it creates in me good feelings or bad feelings according to whether I am getting closer to (warmer) or further from (cooler) the objective.

How does the inner me know when objectives have or have not been attained?

In some instances this is easy: If I am thirsty and I get a drink, it registers relief, if not outright pleasure; but many circumstances or situations are much more subtle than this. Somehow, every experience I have, everything I do or have done to me, gets analysed in terms of is this good or bad for me, will this improve or worsen my prospects of succeeding? It follows long stretches of discourse, picking up whether I am getting closer to or further from a particular goal, whether I am more or less likely to get my way. I know this because I am aware of the changes it is causing me to have in my mood, which are conveying to me how well or badly I am doing.

The emotions

The inner me is the source of the emotions. The emotions serve to keep me aware of my progress or otherwise in attaining the objectives. They will be fully described in Chapter 10. The outer me cannot generate emotion. It simply has to wait and see whether what I am doing or have done is what the inner me intends, or intended. If I am on the right track, the inner me releases the pleasurable emotion of hopeful anticipation. If I attain the objective, it generates pleasure. If I am in danger of losing it, I am warned by the feeling of anxiety. When the objective is lost, I am caused to feel displeasure. If there is hope of regaining it, I am spurred on by angry determination; and if there is none, I am caused to feel hopelessness or despair.

Misguidedly, people seek happiness, but the only source of happiness is the attainment of the objectives. Happiness is not an objective, though it feels as though it is. Because we like to feel happy, we do the things we think will make us happy. Since we do not know what the objectives are we aim for the happiness instead. That's OK, because that's the way we are made, but the only reliable route to happiness is seeking and attaining the objectives. Although we are not born knowing what the objectives are, we can find out what they are by checking what makes us feel happy (see Part III). It is possible to bypass the attainment of objectives by locating and stimulating those brain centres that generate happiness with electrical stimuli or drugs.

Liking and disliking

Only the inner me is capable of liking or disliking. Liking and disliking is the good or the bad feeling I get when I think about something or someone; so it must be something to do with emotion. I (outer me) cannot decide to like or dislike something or someone. I can decide that I ought to, but that does not cause me to. Because the inner me cannot communicate with the outer me, I (outer me) do not really know what, or who, I like or dislike; or if I do know, I do not know why, because the inner me cannot tell me. I may think I like something or someone, but really I do not, and vice versa. I may think I know, but my reason may not be the right one. In Chapter 10, there are examples of people being trained to like or dislike other people without knowing why. It is also only the inner me that can tell whether someone is attractive or sexually arousing, or whether something is or is not aesthetically appealing, or is or is not funny.

Spontaneity

The inner me functions freely and spontaneously. When I blurt something out or speak my mind, or say the first thing that comes into my head, I am acting out of my inner me. That which I blurt out is more likely to be that which I (inner me) really think or really mean. The outer me is able to exercise some control over what I say and how I say it. It is able to anticipate what the inner me is about to cause me to say, and it can modify it to make it more acceptable, or less offensive. When this happens, my speech is more contrived. That which I say without thinking has a directness to it. Inner me speech is simple and to the point, using fewer and shorter words. Strangely, Anglo-Saxon-based words are more linked to inner me speech than Latin-based ones. Inner me speech follows the natural linking of associations (see Chapter 13), so one idea flows into another. Outer me speech is more consciously pieced together; and this breaks up the flow.

Utterances that come out of the inner me are called unselfconscious. They have not been filtered by the outer me. Because of the close link between the inner me and emotion, I am more likely to be spontaneous when I am emotional. Sometimes, when I (outer me) hear what I (inner me) have blurted out (in the heat of the moment), I (outer me) will apologise for it, and claim I didn't mean it. The listener, realising what I am doing, may say I heard you the first time. I (outer me) am reluctant to express my true feelings for fear of how they will be received. A lover may say "I love you," and then say, "There I've said it." Drugs like alcohol (in vino veritas) and sodium amytal (the truth drug) block the controlling influence of the outer me. Spontaneousness applies to actions as well as to words. Spontaneous acts, like jumping for joy, punching or hugging someone, taking evasive action, slamming on breaks, flattening a skirt caught in the wind, grabbing someone who is about to fall, or taking flight are all inner me-generated.

The inner me appears to be more influential in childhood. Children are more naturally spontaneous, speak more openly and express themselves more freely. With age, the outer me tightens its control over the inner me, and adults are more controlled and more inhibited than children. Child art has a more spontaneous quality, and creative artists sometimes try to shed their adult inhibitions in order to allow themselves to work more like children do.

THE SELF-CENTREDNESS OF THE INNER ME

The inner me has qualities that are similar to those of the psychoanalytic id (Chapter 4). It is entirely self-serving, selfish, amoral, ruthless and inconsiderate; shows no consideration for others, no remorse; seeks immediate gratification, takes what it wants; will steal, rape or torture, fight or kill those who stand in its way, retaliate when attacked, seek revenge. Because of the restraints of the outer me, the inner me is not normally free to cause us to act in this way, though we remain capable of doing so, and under certain circumstances, we do. We do when the frontal cortex is damaged, or under the influence of alcohol, or in a crowd. Those described as having an antisocial personality disorder appear to be less controlled by the inner me.

Bandura et al. (1975) wrote, "By displacing responsibility elsewhere, people need not hold themselves accountable for what they do and are thus spared self-prohibiting reactions" (page 255). At times of war and civil war apparently quite normal people kill and massacre, rape and pillage. Quite normal people can easily be persuaded to perform acts of torture (Haritos-Fatouros, 1988). Even in times of peace, people demand viciously punitive retaliation when others have been found guilty of cruelty, particularly towards children.

Special strengths of the inner me

Even though, in evolutionary time, the inner me came first, and might therefore be considered to be the less well developed of the two me's, it should not be considered to be inferior to the outer me in its capabilities. Over thousands of generations, within its own particular neural structures, it has continued to evolve separately from the outer me, so it has become capable of much sophisticated mental activity; in fact, far more than the equivalent structure of any other animal.

One thing the inner me cannot do is think. Thinking, which mostly takes place within the framework of language, is an outer me activity, which proceeds by conscious and deliberate stages. Unlike the outer me, the inner me cannot talk to itself. It cannot say such things as, "that's very strange;" "I wonder how that can be;" or "that's not a sensible thing to do." Because it does not use language, it is sometimes capable of functioning very quickly; but sometimes it can function very slowly, by what Claxton (1998) called incubation. Things come to it, and then these things get passed up into consciousness (the outer me).

Pattern recognition

The inner me is good at recognising patterns, like, for instance, recognising a face, a voice, a view or a tune. It does this in an instant. The outer me would have to resort to the laborious task of analysing the pattern piece by piece. The inner me functions by matching things up. The pattern, face, voice, view, tune or whatever just matches up with one that has been recorded on some previous occasion. It is easy to say the phrase recognising a pattern, but it is hard to imagine what the mental process of recognising a pattern amounts to. How does the inner me bring together a cluster of images that normally occur in a particular arrangement? It must be able to store data both outwardly, over space, and in sequence, over time. We may think this is easy because a camera can store data in space and a compact disc can store data over time, but how can the brain function like a camera or a compact disc? How can memories be stored in such a way that an entire face, building, landscape, piece of music or the lines of a play be remembered as a single entity?

The visualising, or envisaging capacity of the inner me is of great value in human cerebration. The inner me conceptualises in wholes rather than in parts, in the wood rather than in the trees. It does not fragment like the outer brain does. It is sensory: it grasps the overall appearance, the overall sound, the overall feel. It can tell when two experiences match up or when they do not, when something fits or when it does not. It can tell that all these things are or are not so, but it cannot tell why or how they are so; that is an outer me function. It can tell when a motor car is about to turn right, or when a shape in the distance is a woman on horseback, because it knows what motor cars look like when they are about to turn right, or what women on horseback look like, though it could not explain what it is about the car, or what causes it to conclude that it is a woman on horseback and not something else.

The capacity of the inner me to comprehend

Since it is the inner me that determines whether, when and how I become emotional, I can use my experience of emotion to tell how much the inner me has comprehended of what is being said to me. When my boss explains how short of money the department has become, and how he will shortly need to prioritise certain areas of work, I notice myself feeling afraid. Already, the inner me has grasped that I am in danger of being fired. When I am listening to my wife telling me about a man she recently met at a party, and how well she found she had got on with him, I find myself feeling afraid. The inner me has grasped that I may be in danger of losing my wife. These are not simple reflex responses. They involve taking in what is being said and drawing conclusions from it. On what basis does the inner me decide that a picture is aesthetically effective, or that a remark is funny? The French expression *je ne sais quoi* (I know not what) refers to that undefinable something that has been picked up and that has made all the difference.

The inner me's ability to comprehend concepts and metaphors

I can perceive the inner me's capacity to comprehend concepts and metaphors by noticing the ideas, phrases and even tunes that come into my head (out of the memory store) in response to things that are happening to me or being said to me. When my colleagues did not select me to be a member of a committee, I recalled a moment when I was not given a part in a school play. When I am misunderstood I find myself thinking of other occasions when I was misunderstood. When I jump to the wrong conclusion I think of other occasions when I did this. To the inner me, a concept is a kind of shape and it matches one concept against another. It is also good at transforming a life situation into a visual image, like a watershed, a logjam, a bottleneck, a revolving door, keeping afloat, hitting your head against a brick wall or chasing rainbows. This is also a feature of dreams and works of art.

The inner me is also capable of comprehending abstract concepts like ambiguity, animosity, fanaticism, generosity, jealousy, obsessionality, rivalry and revenge. Interestingly, it must also be capable of comprehending concepts of forms of behaviour of which it is not capable, such as deceit, guile and mischievousness! As far as the inner me is concerned a concept is yet another pattern.

PERCEIVING SIMILARITIES

If the inner me can register patterns and comprehend concepts, it must also be capable of recognising similarities and dissimilarities. This is an extremely important aspect of inner me functioning. It can tell when one face looks like another, or one voice sounds like another, or one view looks like another, or one tune sounds like another, or one idea is like another idea. It can tell when two pictures were painted by the same artist or two pieces of music were written by the same composer. Not only can it register these similarities, it can generate the feeling (of familiarity) that there is a similarity, and project into consciousness that image which is similar. These associations contribute to our ability to make conceptual connections.

The inner me's memory store has a record of how things normally are, so it can register when there are deviations from this. Even if something has been only slightly altered, it can recognise that it is not quite as it should be and project into consciousness the feeling of not quite rightness. Because it recognises things as a whole rather than by their separate parts, it can readily recognise when some part of the perception has been removed or changed. What it is perceiving or experiencing does not match up with what is stored in the memory. It can readily perceive that something is not quite right here, though it cannot always say what. The capacity to do this is a characteristic of the good detective. The murderer, in trying to conceal his crime, often overlooks some small detail that gives him away. What the murderer is doing here is trying to recreate by means of his outer me a situation that would normally be perceived in its entirety by the inner me. It is extremely difficult to do this. The art or antiques collector needs a similar capability in order to recognise when a work of art or a piece of furniture is a fake. S/he looks at the item and just has the feeling that it is not the real thing.

Inner me methods of learning and working things out

Since most animals do not have an outer me, learning must be possible at an inner me level. Quite simple animals are capable of learning. They can learn the route to a supply of food or they can learn to avoid a situation in which something unpleasant once happened. Claxton (1998) used the terms implicit learning and learning by osmosis to mean learning without trying to learn. It involves simply exposing yourself to experiences and allowing them to percolate into the memory. Through repeated exposure, people, places and things become familiar. We come to recognise certain people, places and things as sources of good emotion or bad. Through repetition, necessary skills somehow get remembered. I never learned, or taught myself, to type. I type with only two fingers, yet as I type I do not keep stopping to find the appropriate key to tap. My fingers seem to find their way there without assistance. In fact, if I try to assist them by looking for the right keys my level of performance drops. If I were asked to draw a plan of where the keys were on the keyboard I could not do it.

Memorising

Memorising is one of the most important functions of the inner me. Since almost all animal forms have memory, it must represent one of the most basic and fundamental forms of mental activity. To some degree, the inner me remembers things indiscriminately. As I walk along a street, aspects of the street just get remembered. As I talk to a stranger, I am automatically recording what the stranger looks like. If I walk along the street again, it feels familiar. If I meet the stranger again, he looks familiar. I can watch a movie I saw 20 years ago and realise I have seen it before. Some memories fade rapidly, while others persist for years afterwards. Significant events get remembered with greater intensity and for longer periods than insignificant ones. When I write significant, I mean significant to the inner me. An event is significant to the inner me if it has relevance to the attainment of an objective; so the inner me must be constantly aware of the objectives and of whether or not they are being attained. I remember vividly the first girl I kissed. I remember the place and what the girl was wearing. I even remember what the kiss felt like. As far as the inner me was concerned, this was a significant moment. I (outer me) did not decide to remember it. It (inner me) did. The inner me does not just remember successes; it remembers failures too with equal vividness. Emotion, either positive or negative, gets released at significant moments, and the emotion – gets remembered along with the event; so when I remember the event, I re-experience the emotion.

Working things out

Since the inner me does not use language (though it does generate it for the outer me to use), it must solve problems by non-linguistic means. This must mean that it relies upon memory, pattern recognition and the recognition of similarities. Animals can work things out and they appear to do this by perceiving connections. A monkey is capable of slotting one strip of wood into another to make a tool for reaching bananas on a tree. It sees the two strips of wood and visualises the effect of the one strip being somehow attached to the other strip.

Claxton (1998) used the term the undermind to refer to what he called the intelligent unconscious. This would correspond with the inner me's particular mental abilities. He considered there to be two classes of unconscious mental activity: the one very fast, the other very slow – slower even than rational thought. Of the very fast kind he said that fast intuitions, snap judgements and quick reactions are vital responses for human beings, just as they are for animals. To spend time pondering on insignificant details is wasteful, or even dangerous. He wrote, "Fast intuitions depend on the undermind taking a quick look at the situation and finding an analogy which seems to offer understanding and prediction. These unconscious analogies surface as intuitions" (page 53). Claxton argued that what here I am calling the outer me is too precisely focused to solve certain kinds of problem, that the person takes the problem too seriously and tries too hard. Discipline is important for some problem-solving tasks, but is inappropriate for others. He proposed that if you don't even try to solve the problem, it may solve itself.

He advocates adopting a more playful attitude to the problem and maintains that children are better than adults at solving certain kinds of problem. He gave as an example the puzzle, which was popular during the 1980s, called the Rubic cube. It comprises 27 small cubes with a different colour on each face, which could be rotated in any direction. The task was to arrange the small cubes so that the large cube was of one uniform colour. Claxton explained that it was hopeless to solve if you tried to understand how to do it. It was, he wrote, too complicated for that. The best way to solve it was, as one girl explained, by just messing about with it.

Claxton's slower method of solving problems, he called the gentle art of mental gestation. This is a process that cannot be hurried. He wrote:

> the undermind needs to be left to its own devices for a while, and then the need for patience – the ability to tolerate uncertainty, to stay with the feeling of not knowing for a while, to stand aside and let a mental process that can neither be observed nor directed take its course – becomes important (page 75).

Rokeach (1950) persuaded people to slow down when trying to solve certain kinds of problem. He believed that when people are stressed and in a hurry they are inclined to fall back upon ways of thinking that are clear-cut, rigid and conventional. Claxton argued that wanting an answer too much can interfere with the process of gestation. Viesti (1971) observed that offering financial rewards cause students to do worse at solving the task of detecting the odd one out of three complicated patterns.

THE INNER ME AND AUTISM

There appears to be a link between inner me activity and the capabilities of what are called autistic savants. The amazing feats they perform they do extremely quickly. Only one in ten autistic people have such extraordinary capabilities, but their skills are all of a kind. Matching days and dates is one such feat. They can say in a flash the day of the week of any date in either the past or the future. Another is working out the square root of any number. They appear not to calculate this; they just say what it is. This issue will be examined further in Chapter 14.

IRRATIONALITY

Epstein (1994) described irrational thinking as a separate kind of thinking. This is a useful way of putting it because it implies that it belongs to a separate cognitive system (see Chapter 5). That humans continue to hold irrational beliefs, even though they have the advantages of a rational outer me, is because they still have the option of using that older (inner me) system.

Aids to survival

Perhaps because the inner me has a longer evolutionary history than the outer me, it has several functions that contribute to survival.

Filling in the gaps

In a number of situations, the inner me appears to make a guess on the basis of limited information. If there is missing information the inner me fills in gaps to turn it into the thing it resembles most. If a sentence only partly makes sense, it picks out any bit that does make sense and makes up the rest. If I do not quite hear what somebody says, I make a guess at what s/he might have said and respond accordingly. I am able to guess the answer to the clue of a crossword if there are only two letters that are appropriately placed. The inner me tries to visualise a word that has those letters in those positions. When I am trying to remember a person's name, just some slight association, like it is some kind of a flower, or it has three syllables, or it starts with a particular letter, may be enough to catch a hold of the word and pull it into consciousness. These may seem pretty useless capabilities, but they are linked to capabilities that can be life saving.

Filling in the gaps causes me to make mistakes too. When I am looking for something, I may see something that only slightly resembles it, and react to it as though it were the real thing. When I am watching the football scores coming through on the teleprinter, I get excited when a team that starts the same as the team I support begins to be printed. The more emotional I am at the time the less the thing has to resemble that which I am looking for. It works as much for something I am hoping to find as for something I am dreading. Filling in the gaps has obvious survival value, since if there is only a suspicion of what I need, or what I dread, it is better to go for it, or flee from it, rather than wait until the information is more complete and I can be sure.

This process of filling in the gaps is similar to Nunberg's (1931) idea of the synthetic function of the ego. He observed that humans gather facts together in such a way as to make some kind of sense of them, a process he called rationalisation. This may not always be helpful, but sometimes it is. Interestingly, the process of filling in the gaps also emerges in people with dementia. When they cannot remember, they confabulate. This happens automatically, and they do not know they are doing it.

Selective perception

The inner me is selectively primed to pick out objects of importance for survival or reproduction. If there is something that vaguely resembles an object of threat, it responds to it as if it were that object. A shape that vaguely looks like a snake, it responds to with alarm. A sound that could be the roar of an animal, it responds to as if it were one. In the dark, it is particularly sensitised to sounds, since sounds are all the information there is; so any unfamiliar sound evokes alarm. This is similar to Gagg's (1999) report of a psychotic client in which he suggested that hearing voices might be the client's habit of interpreting any sound as being meaningful.

The process also has a reproductive aspect. A man who catches sight of a shape that vaguely looks like a woman's body responds to it as if it is one. I have sometimes misperceived a photograph of something neutral, like a hand, as being that of a woman's body. A shape I have seen behind a curtain, I have assumed to be a woman. A woman I have seen in a lighted window, I have assumed to be young and beautiful. A woman's underwear on a washing line I have assumed to belong to a young and beautiful woman. I have "seen" what I hoped it would be.

Selective perception operates with words and sentences. If a word is misspelt I am inclined to read it as though it were correctly spelt, and if a sentence does not make sense I am inclined to read it as one that does make sense. These tendencies make proofreading difficult. I am more inclined to read a string of letters or a string of words as an important or desirable word or sentence than as a neutral one. I am likely to misread bar as bra or kickers as knickers, or "I shall wait to hear from you" as "I shall want to hear from you."

PICKING UP CUES AND INNUENDOES

The inner me can tell when something is happening or is about to happen by small perceptions. It can tell when it is going to rain without registering how it can tell. Presumably it notices that the sky is becoming overcast, or that a wind is blowing up, or it is getting colder. It can tell when someone is singing out of tune or when someone is not telling the truth. It can tell when a smile is not a real smile. Mistrusting someone is a similar experience. The question "Would you buy a second hand car from this man?" carries the implication that there are aspects of his appearance or behaviour that convey that he is unreliable. The inner me cannot convey to the outer me what it is picking up that is causing it to reach such a conclusion because it only perceives in wholes. It cannot break down a general impression into its component parts. A person makes a remark like "I just knew." There is nothing mystical or mysterious about this. All the person's inner me has done is match up this man against its impression of a fair and honest man and found something wanting. It is something like the murderer trying to cover up his tracks. The man is intent on cheating the client but he is trying to act the part of someone who is being honest. He is leaving out some vital ingredient.

HUNCHES AND INTUITION

Hunches are usually based upon real information, but they are not always right. The inner me may be generalising from a situation that is not generalisable from. A woman was sexually abused as a child by a man who had a gap between his front teeth. For the rest of her life she mistrusted men with gaps between their front teeth. An association may once have been true but things may have changed, so that it is no longer true. Tap water in a certain district may once have been unsafe to drink, but the water supply may have improved and now it is safe to drink. Despite these exceptions, it is wise to take hunches seriously. Women are more inclined to respect hunches than men, and we speak of feminine intuition. It is unlikely that women have an additional capability; it is more probable that they avail themselves more of a capability that both men and women have. This may be because women do not place as much reliance upon rational thought as men do. They are probably more inclined to believe in astrology, visit fortune tellers and attend seances; though obviously, there are intuitive men and rational women.

Morris et al. (1998) observed that the brain processes facial expressions of emotion at both an unconscious and a conscious level. Because of this they suggested that whenever we have a gut reaction to someone we have never met, it is probable that the stranger resembles someone who has done something bad to us in the past, even though we have no conscious recollection of it.

Is there such a thing as the inner me?

The inner me is a term that is used to cover a broad range of mental functions that are characterised by their automatic and nonconscious nature. Those processes that are referred to as innate are invariably inner me processes. Subjectively, the inner me feels like a separate entity, but there is certainly not a single structure, nor even an area of the brain, which can be identified as the inner me. Because it encompasses so many different functions, it must have a number of locations depending upon the function that is being performed, and these will be referred to in the chapters referring to them.

Part II

Other conscious/
unconscious distinctions

In this part I describe, one after the other, two theoretical systems that propose a division of mental functioning that come close, in varying degrees, to the two categories of mental functioning with which the book is concerned. That both systems propose such a division adds further support to the idea that such a division exists. Clearly, what is happening here is that these two systems, plus the present one, are all attempts to define the nature of the division. The cognitive system drew heavily upon the psychodynamic one (see Westen, 1998), and the present system has drawn heavily on both.

4 Psychodynamic distinctions

Psychoanalysis

Psychoanalysis is both a way of exploring the psyche and a form of psycho-therapy, the one always merging with the other. Its strength lies in its acknowledgement of the irrational. More than any other discipline, it accepts that people express themselves in strange and individual ways, sometimes saying one thing while meaning another; denying what is patently true; appearing upset about one thing while really being upset about another; and not knowing why they say what they say. It acknowledges that people can harbour perverse and offensive intents, and be capable of appalling acts of cruelty. It maintains that awareness of such intents and such acts are denied in order to preserve a veneer of respectability.

The psychoanalytic unconscious

Psychoanalysis is sometimes referred to as the science of the unconscious, and Badcock (1986) wrote that, "Nobody would doubt that it was the discovery of the unconscious that was Freud's greatest and central achievement" (page 42); though Webster (1996) maintained that, in this respect, Freud was following a cultural trend rather than starting one. Although Freud did not discover the unconscious, he set it within a coherent theory. He used the term unconscious both as a noun, meaning a place in the mind, and as an adjective, meaning that which is not conscious. In contrast, he did not consider the conscious to be a place in the mind. For him that which is conscious is simply that which is not unconscious. He likened the unconscious to the submerged nine-tenths of an iceberg, and the neuropsychologist, LeDoux (1998), wrote, "Freud was right on the mark when he described consciousness as the tip of the mental iceberg" (page 17).

Instincts and drives

Freud considered the unconscious to be the source of the instincts, just as I consider the inner me to be the source of the objectives. Although Freud

(1911) wrote of the life instincts, which are concerned with physical functions, like hunger, thirst, urination and defaecation, he was less forthcoming about other instincts. Over a 30-year period (from 1890 to 1920) he vacillated between the terms instincts and drives, and about what exactly these were (Bibring, 1941). In his first formulation he considered there to be two drives: one concerned with self-preservation and one concerned with sex; this corresponds closely with the contents of Chapters 6 and 7. Later, he modified these to the aggressive drive and the sexual drive (Freud, 1920). He was never entirely satisfied that the aggressive and the sexual drives were separate, and often he considered the former to be a component of the latter. For example, weapons are often interpreted as symbols of what he considered to be the sometimes powerful and destructive penis. Unlike most other psychoanalysts, he was never convinced that aggression gave rise to pleasure; but how can a drive be a drive if it does not give rise to pleasure?

The development of the psychoanalytic theory of the psyche

Freud's first attempt to construct a theory of the psychic apparatus featured in the last chapter of his (1900) book, *The Interpretation of Dreams*. In his second attempt (Freud, 1913), called the topographical hypothesis, he conceptualised three mental systems called the unconscious, the preconscious and the conscious. The conscious is currently conscious; the preconscious is currently not conscious, but can be brought into consciousness by an effort of attention; and the unconscious is currently not conscious and cannot be brought into consciousness, even by an effort of attention. It is barred from access to consciousness by some force within the psyche itself, which Freud called the censor, which comes close to my idea of the in-between me. Although the inner me is unconscious and the outer me is largely conscious, I would not consider consciousness to be the main criterion by which they are distinguished.

The thoughts and wishes of the unconscious, though barred from consciousness, are revealed through people's actions, their slips of the tongue or the pen, and their dreams. There is a parallel here with the inner me. Freud invented the psychological technique called psychoanalysis specifically for uncovering the contents of the unconscious. It requires the analysand to lie on a couch and report to the analyst, without exception, whatever thoughts come into her/his mind, and to refrain from exercising either conscious direction or censorship over them.

Freud's followers have added their own variations of the topographical hypothesis. Sandler and Sandler (1984) proposed what they called the three-box model of psychic structures. The first "box" is called the child within the adult, and represents the continuation of the past into the present. It comprises unconscious, infantile reactions, wishes or wishful fantasies that were developed early in life. The second "box" is also unconscious, but is oriented to the present rather than to the past. It consists of "here-and-now adapta-tions to the conflicts and anxieties triggered in the first box" (Fonagy and Cooper, 1999). The third "box" is all that is presently conscious.

An important difference between psychoanalysis and my two me theory lies in the reason why parts of the psyche are unconscious. Psychoanalysis would have it that motives and ideas are kept unconscious in order to protect the conscious. The greater part of that which is called the inner me is unconscious simply because it evolved before consciousness evolved, and it has stayed that way. That which the in-between me keeps out of conscious-ness remains in the memory store which, admittedly, comes within the province of the inner me.

The wild unconscious

Freud viewed the unconscious as the wild, untamed part of us. In contrast, he viewed the conscious as the civilised part. He saw the role of the conscious as keeping the wild unconscious in check, even of taming it (Frosh, 1997). Webster (1996) likened Freud's distinction between the unconscious and the conscious to that found within the Judaeo-Christian dualism between the flesh and the spirit, evil and good. The outer me does restrain and control the inner me, but mainly in the direction of being more tactful and diplo-matic, and in being more able to plan ahead. I see the primary function of the outer me more as furthering the aims of the inner me than of controlling it.

The ego and the id

In 1923, Freud proposed a successor of the topographical hypothesis, called the structural hypothesis. In place of the unconscious and the conscious was the id and the ego. He maintained that at birth there is only the id, and that the ego gradually becomes differentiated from it. The id comes closer still to that of the wild animal. It houses the primitive drives. It is unconscious and presses for expression. The ego tries to restrain it. Trivers (1985) considered the id to represent the individual's self-interest, the internal, innate, egoistic impulses, the source of our selfish urges. One of the functions of the ego is to control and modify these urges, and to delay their satisfaction until environmental circumstances are more favourable. The id houses the basic instincts, described by Badcock (1986) as the "so-called ego-instincts directed to self-preservation and sexual or libidinal ones directed ultimately to reproduction" (page 27). This modification comes closer to my two me theory.

Freud (1923) introduced the term the neutralisation of drive energy to mean that, by the delay of the immediate gratification of the drives (aggres-sive and sexual), energy is saved that may be used in the service of the ego (that is the psychic structure of that name). Part of the use to which this energy is put is rational thought. While I consider rational thought to be an essential component of outer me functioning, I do not see why energy needs to be saved for this purpose.

Webster (1996) tried to normalise the Freudian distinction between the id and the ego by pointing to the pragmatic necessity for us to put off the immediate gratification of appetites such as hunger and sex in order to focus upon the acquisition and execution of useful skills. Such self-discipline is part of the work ethic. By being set a whole range of tasks, children are taught the general lesson that developing the attention span and the ability to concentrate is virtuous.

In his earlier formulations, Freud assumed the ego to be the equivalent of the conscious self, but gradually he felt forced to consider that many of the ego's functions occurred outside of consciousness, so he began to think in terms of the unconscious ego. Badcock (recent communication) now considers that almost all ego functions are unconscious; and Fonagy and Cooper (1999) considered the unconscious ego to be the equivalent of Sandler and Sandler's (1984) second box. Freud believed that the (unconscious) ego functions concern the person's relationship to the environment, and include the various modalities of sensory perception, the control over the skeletal musculature, the affects and the acquisition of what Brenner (1957) called "a library of memories" (page 41). To me it makes more sense to consider anything that is unconsciously controlled to be inner me, and anything that is consciously controlled to be outer me. The in-between me's (unconscious) function is largely that of controlling the entry of certain memories and motives into consciousness.

Another function specified for the ego is that of the executant for the drives. That is, the ego seeks to find acceptable ways of attaining the drives. In this respect the relationship of the ego to the id is similar to that of the outer me to the inner me.

PRIMARY PROCESS AND SECONDARY PROCESS

Freud (1911) drew a distinction between what he called primary process thinking (linked with the id) and secondary process thinking (linked with the ego). The former was considered to be preverbal and prelogical and to do with visual imagery and irrationality. The latter was considered to be linguistic, logical and to do with rational thought. Brenner (1957) described it as ordinary, conscious thinking. It is primarily verbal, and follows the laws of syntax and logic. Clearly, primary process is linked with the more visual and intuitive minor hemisphere, inner me; and secondary process with the more verbal and logical dominant hemisphere, outer me.

Primary process thinking is considered to be a characteristic of those years of childhood when the ego is still immature. The maturational transition from primary to secondary process is gradual. Primary process is the dominant mode of thinking for the immature ego, which in some degree persists into adulthood. It is associated with the immediate gratification of an impulse or need (inner me). The capacity to delay gratification is an essential feature of secondary process (outer me). The linking of primary process with immaturity is unfortunate. I do not propose a similar association between inner me functioning and immaturity.

Primary process thinking bears many of the characteristics of the mental activity of dreams, like a tendency to represent ideas as visual or other sensory impressions, representation by allusion or analogy, part of an object, idea or memory being used to stand for the whole, several different thoughts being represented by a single thought or image, opposites appearing in place of one another, the coexistence of mutually contradictory ideas, and past, present and future fusing into one. This is all consistent with the inner me.

Webster (1996) provided a useful historical setting within which to view Freud's distinction between the rational secondary process and the irrational primary process. He observed that, during the eighteenth and nineteenth centuries, enlightenment, rationalism and materialism (secondary process) gradually gained intellectual ascendency. Views of the self emerged which, either implicitly or explicitly, denied the reality of almost all aspects of human nature that could be deemed irrational. A (primary process) reaction to this trend was the rise of Gothic Romanticism that stressed "all those irrational, dark or demonic aspects of human nature which rationalism had implicitly repudiated" (page 244).

Some variants of Freudian theory

Milner (1987), a psychoanalytic writer who died in 1998, and whose ideas sometimes come strikingly close to my own, wrote, "As far as I remember we never used Freud's words 'primary and secondary process' but talked instead in terms of 'directed and undirected thinking' " (page 3), directed coming closer to (intentional) secondary process and undirected to (automatic) primary process. Milner (1987) wrote of a different kind of thinking, or this other half of thinking, a kind that does not work according to the laws of logic which, she wrote, Freud and the psychoanalysts that came after him called unconscious fantasy (inner me). She considered that people who came to see Freud were trying to manage their feelings and desires by means of a one-sided (outer me) kind of thinking that did not work. They were trying to live their lives as though conscious, common-sense, logical thinking was all there was. By attending to what they freely imagined (inner me) rather than to their common-sense reasoning, they were helped to a freeing of their powers.

Milner was greatly influenced by Ehrenzweig's terms the creative accident (1953) and the creative surrender (1957) to refer to giving way to the irrational side of herself. She wrote of how she struggled, both in her patients and in herself, with the problem of "how truly to trust the unconscious, the blankness, trust what seems to be not there" (page 5). She wrote of her "inner fact" and her "automatic self" which, she believed, expressed her real, deep needs (inner me).

Surface mind and depth mind

Ehrenzweig (1953) distinguished between what he called the surface mind and the depth mind. He considered the surface mind to be articulate and the depth mind to be inarticulate. He also called the surface mind our observing mind, which corresponds with the observing function of the outer me. He wrote that the surface (observing) mind finds the ideas of the lower layers of the mind (inner me) chaotic. Ehrenzweig considered that Freud was so pre-occupied with translating the inarticulate thoughts of the depth mind into rational language that he overlooked the importance of the depth mind's inarticulateness. He considered that the depth mind can do things that the surface mind cannot do. It can encompass a complexity of relationships (thinking in terms of the whole) that is quite beyond the capacity of the surface mind. Linked with Milner's undirected thinking, Ehrenzweig believed that you can only get to the depth mind by the diffused wide (non-focused) stare, not by the narrow focus of ordinary (outer me) attention. He maintained that it is this wide focus that makes it possible to get closer to a more primitive vision of the world, which is not chaotic, only more generalised (see Chapter 2 on trying).

An evolutionary view of the unconscious

Trivers (1981) set the unconscious within the context of cheating. He arrived at this via his exploration of reciprocal altruism, that is the arrangement by which one person agrees to do another a favour in the expectation that the other will return that favour. He observed that there is the temptation to try to get away with not returning the favour. He considered that such cheating is easier to perform if the person is able to deny even to her/himself that s/he is doing it. This he believed became the function of the unconscious. The issue of cheating will be considered further in Chapter 15.

Repression

The process of repression lies at the very heart of psychoanalytic theory (Freud, 1915). It is the means by which material that is considered danger-ous or threatening is kept out of consciousness. DelMonte (2000) observed that repressed memories are unconscious in a double way: firstly, the memory trace is removed from consciousness; and secondly, the act of removing the memory trace from consciousness is forgotten. The phenomenon of repression is linked with the idea that the id, among other things, is a place where unacceptable psychic material is stored. Such psychic material is like nuclear waste: it cannot be got rid of, so it has to be buried and rendered safe. However, even though it is buried, it is not entirely safe, for both Freud and most contemporary psychoanalysts believe that repressed psychic material is the cause of many psychiatric disorders. Therefore, the object of psychoanalytic treatment is to uncover such repressed material and render it less damaging.

The unconscious then is primarily a hiding place for material that the individual (the conscious person) might have difficulty dealing with. By calling the unconscious dynamic, Badcock (1986) would be suggesting that it is able to decide to banish material from consciousness. This gives it discriminatory power, that is it has an awareness of the conscious, and what it may or may not be capable of tolerating. This is quite the reverse of how I would view the inner me; for since the inner me has no awareness of the existence of the outer me, it could not perform such a discriminatory function. Therefore, it has to be that part of the outer me that I call the in-between me, which must control what enters consciousness (see Chapters 2 and 15).

The issue of repression is linked with that of morality, and it seems likely that Freud's preoccupation with repression was very much affected by the moral climate of his time. Webster (1996), who described Freud as "a prisoner of the respectability he believed he had transcended" (page 249), pointed to the extent to which individuals differ in the degree to which they have internalised cultural taboos, particularly sexual ones. It seems likely therefore that what is repressed and how powerfully it is repressed is determined by the person's (outer me) view of how acceptable the particular feelings or experiences are.

Much is written in the psychoanalytic literature about the ego's constant attempts to keep in check the instinctual wishes or impulses arising from the id. Much also is written about the psyche being overwhelmed by an influx of stimuli that is too great for it either to master or discharge. Since sexual and aggressive drives are part of the normal repertoire of the psyche, why are they considered to be so dangerous?

Repression and memory

Brenner (1957) wrote, "Indeed, we may remark parenthetically that we don't know for sure whether there is any type of forgetting other than repression" (page 89). I think we do know for sure, and this reveals how far psychoanalysts are prepared to carry the repression argument. The repression of psychic material is considered to be the basis of the eternal conflict between the ego and the id. The repressed material continues to be charged with what is called drive energy or cathexis, which presses for expression and satisfaction. The repression is maintained by means of a portion of the psychic energy that is called countercathexis.

Psychoanalysts sometimes encounter what they call screen memories. They are apparently trivial memories with which the patient becomes preoccupied, and which are linked with an inaccessible, more disturbing memory. Rycroft (1995) observed that the aptness of these memories for symbolising the more disturbing earlier memory is presumably responsible for them being remembered and for their recurrent nature. The screen memory is used by the psychoanalyst to enable the patient to get to the disturbing, earlier memory. Spinelli (1994) provided the example of a woman who was preoccupied with a pattern of black and white squares. After much therapeutic work she realised that this was the pattern of the linoleum in a room where she had been forced to fellate a friend of her brother.

The role of anxiety

Anxiety features prominently in psychoanalytic theory. Freud considered it to be the central problem of mental illness, and his original conception of anxiety was that it results from the damming up and inadequate discharge of sexual energy. Later, he abandoned this idea, but he continued to view anxiety as an area of central concern. He considered that anxiety was generated by the ego in response to danger, from either an internal or an external source. He wrote more of anxiety arising from an internal source, and that source was largely the pressure of the drives from the id. The main object of repression seems to be the avoidance of the emergence of anxiety. When anxiety is experienced in the course of psychoanalysis, it is assumed that impulses from the id are pressing for expression. There is a fundamental difference between Freud's view of the id and my view of the inner me. While there would appear to be a close correspondence between the drives that emanate from the id and the objectives that emanate from the inner me, I do not recognise a pressure or a threat. The objectives are simply guiding forces that provide us with a sense of direction.

The oedipus complex

The oedipus complex is another concept that is central to psychoanalytic theory. Its presumed existence is the most important justification for the emphasis that is placed upon repression. Freud maintained that he frequently observed in the unconscious mental lives of his neurotic patients the fantasy of having sex with the parent of the opposite sex and the expression of murderous rage towards the parent of the same sex. He later concluded that, between the ages of two and six, all children have oedipal feelings. Róheim (1950) provided evidence that children in all cultures have them, and Watson and Getz (1990) obtained objective evidence that three to six year olds do indeed show significantly more affection towards the opposite sex parent and significantly more aggression towards the same sex parent. Segal (1999) considered that there might be "an inborn structure of an Oedipus complex" (page 97), that gains expression in different ways in different cultures. This is similar to the Jungian concept of an archetypal image (see below). The child, it is maintained, fears retaliation by the same sex parent, and the form that such retaliation is expected to take is the removal of the penis in the little boy and some unspecified equivalent in the little girl. The belief is that, once the oedipal phase is past, all oedipal feelings are powerfully repressed and can be uncovered only during the course of psychoanalysis.

Badcock (1986) maintained that it would be in the best interests of the child to remain unconscious of the sexual and murderous elements of oedipal behaviour and simply to experience the whole procedure as a playful attempt to gain the attention of the opposite sex parent. He further maintained that adults might be inclined to adhere to what he called the fiction of infantile innocence and to resist accepting the oedipal theory as a means of suppressing their own oedipal tendencies.

The oedipus complex exists only in psychoanalytic theory. It raises many questions, like how do small children know about the sexual act? Why would they wish to do it? Why would they know it was pleasurable? Why would they think it was wrong? Why would they want to murder the opposite sex parent? Why would they think the opposite sex parent would object? Why cut off the penis? Why do little girls not fear the removal of their clitoris? Why do oedipal feelings stop after the age of six? If they are universal, why should they be a cause for concern? Why do people not openly acknowledge that they have them? If, during analysis, adults claim to have had sexual feelings towards a parent, is it not more likely that this is a retrospective fantasy? How do oedipal feelings fit into evolutionary theory? Obviously, animals do not have them.

The superego

Psychoanalytic theory would have it that the superego is formed during the oedipal phase of development, and that the oedipus complex plays a major role in its development. It is believed to be the result of an internalised parent, particularly the father. Trivers (1985) considered it to represent the internalised demands of the parents and is developed in interactions with them. The primary sin is the child's desire for sexual involvement with the opposite sex parent and the death of the same sex parent, but other sins become tagged on to it. The ego is viewed as occupying a mid-way position, trying to reconcile the demands of the id with the restraints of the superego.

Freud (1923) considered the superego to be a further extension of the ego, and Rycroft (1995) considered it to be the successor to the censor. It has a powerfully judgemental, even punitive function, particularly in relation to sexual urges.

Analytical psychology

Analytical psychology is a term introduced by Jung to draw a distinction between his own account of mental functioning and Freud's. Jung (1939) did not consider the unconscious to be restrained by the conscious. He conceived of the psyche as a self-regulating system that is in constant movement, covering both the conscious and the unconscious, the unconscious aspect being different from, but compensatory to, the conscious. He believed that the conscious grows out of the unconscious, which is older than it is, and which goes on functioning together with it or even in spite of it. This is similar to Freud's view of the ego growing out of the id.

The Jungian unconscious

Fordham (1968) wrote, "Jung's view of the unconscious is more positive than that which merely sees it as the repository of everything objectionable, everything infantile – even animal – in ourselves, all that we want to forget" (page 21). She acknowledged that "I forget, or I repress, what I do not like, or what is socially not acceptable" (page 21), and this is in accord with the Jungian concept of the shadow, which I will discuss shortly. Jung accepted the idea that the unconscious could serve the function of a repository for repressed, infantile personal experiences, but he also considered it to be a locus of psychological activity. In this way it resembles more the cognitive unconscious (see next chapter) and the inner me.

Jung distinguished between what he called the personal unconscious and the collective unconscious. Where the personal unconscious is specific for the individual, and contains her/his personal memories, the collective unconscious is common to everyone. What Jung appeared to be getting at here is that the collective unconscious is part of our common inheritance, which has evolved in us, is stored within the structure of the brain and has been there from birth. He maintained that the contents of the collective unconscious, in contrast to those of the personal unconscious, have never been conscious and never can be. This resembles the cognitive unconscious and the objective monitoring component of the inner me.

Archetypes

Unlike Freud, Jung worked extensively with psychotic patients. In this work he was struck by the frequent occurrence of what he considered to be universal symbols, which he later called archetypes; and it was this that led him to the idea of the collective unconscious. Sometimes he used the term the archetypes of the collective unconscious. Samuels (1997) observed that Jung always distinguished between an archetype and an archetypal image. An archetype is an unknowable nucleus that never was conscious and never will be. It can only be inferred from the archetypal images that point back to the one essential, basic form of the archetype itself. Ellenberger (1970) considered the archetypes to be one of the three main conceptual differences between Jung and Freud in defining the content and behaviour of the unconscious; and Hillman (1975), who founded a school of archetypal psychology, considered them to be the most fundamental concept in Jung's work.

Jung acknowledged in his introduction to Jacobi's 1959 book that the concept of the archetypes has given rise to the greatest misunderstandings, and different authors have varied in their definition of them. One of Jung's later definitions is an innate tendency to form emotionally powerful images that express the relational primacy of human life (Young-Eisendrath and Dawson, 1997). He believed that, like the collective unconscious, of which they form a part, they are present within the psyche from birth, and are universal; that is they form part of the evolved psyche of everyone. Samuels et al. (1986) defined them as simply the inherited part of the psyche, as hypothetical entities irrepresentable in themselves and evident only through their manifestations. Similarly, Young-Eisendrath and Dawson (1997) defined them as hypothetical constructs to explain the manifestation of arche-typal images. There are powerful links here with the inner me, but the archetypes provide a broader elaboration of it.

Archetypal images feature in dreams, fantasies and psychotic delusions and resemble the universal motifs that are present in myths, legends and reli-gions. They can assume the form of almost anything, and are recognisable as such by their emotional loading, their intensity, their compelling quality and their numinosity, that is their mysteriousness, spirituality, awe-inspiringness or religiousness. Some of the most prominent archetypes are the self, the shadow, the anima and the animus, and these will briefly be discussed.

THE SELF

The self, like the psyche, embraces both the conscious and the unconscious. It is a term borrowed from Eastern philosophy in which it has existed from time immemorial. In Hindu thought, it is the supreme oneness of being. Young-Eisendrath and Dawson (1997) defined it firstly as an archetypal image of wholeness, experienced as a transpersonal power, which invests life with meaning, and which is epitomised as Christ, Buddha and mandala-figures; and secondly as the hypothetical centre and totality of the psyche, experi-enced as that which governs the individual, and towards which the individual unconsciously strives. Jung called it a unifying principle within the psyche, which occupies the central position of authority in relation to psychological life and, therefore, the destiny of the individual. It consists in the awareness, on the one hand, of our unique nature, and on the other of our intimate relationship with all life, and even with the cosmos itself.

THE SHADOW

In her explanation of the Jungian concept of the shadow, Fordham (1968) called Mr Hyde the shadow to Dr Jekyll. She considered it to be the primi-tive, uncontrolled and animal part of ourselves, the inferior being in our-selves, the one who wants to do all the things that we do not allow ourselves to do, who is everything that we are not. It is all those uncivilised desires and emotions that are incompatible with our social standards and our ideal per-sonality, all that we are ashamed of, all that we do not want to know about ourselves. She explained that, since it is unconscious, the shadow cannot be touched by ordinary methods of education. The more restrictive the society is the larger will be its shadow. The more we repress the shadow the stronger it grows. It is the shadow that emerges when apparently harmless people behave in the most appallingly savage and destructive ways.

The shadow need not be negative. It is simply the unexpressed part of ourselves. It is an unconscious aspect of the personality, characterised by traits and attitudes that the conscious ego does not recognise in itself. One of the objectives of Jungian therapy is for the patient to recognise and consciously assimilate the shadow, just as one of the objectives of psychoanalysis is for the patient to assimilate the unconscious.

THE PERSONA

The persona is the reverse of the shadow. It is the mask behind which most people live. It is that which makes us acceptable and presentable. Fordham (1968) observed that people who neglect the development of a persona tend to be gauche and to offend others by their outspokenness. The persona is clearly related to the outer me. Too rigid a persona means too complete a denial of the rest of the personality. A person who has too powerful a persona may be said to be putting on an act. The contemporary term being politically correct is a manifestation of the development of a persona.

THE ANIMA AND THE ANIMUS

The anima and the animus seem to form parts of the shadow. The anima is part of the man's shadow. It is the image of a woman or feminine figure in men's dreams, or the unconscious, feminine side of a man's personality; and the animus is part of the woman's shadow. It is the image of a man or masculine figure in women's dreams, or the unconscious masculine side of a woman's personality. Current belief is that everyone has both an anima and an animus.

ARCHETYPAL TYPES

Archetypes also include particular types of people like the old wise man, the great mother, the tyrannical father and the treacherous friend. These archetypes are considered to represent a danger to the personality if the person becomes excessively identified with any one of them. The woman taken over by the great mother archetype believes herself to be endowed with an infinite capacity for loving, understanding, helping and protecting, and will wear herself out in the service of others. She will also coerce others into adopting the reciprocal role of behaving like her children. Fordham (1968) maintained that "This subtle tyranny, if carried to extremes, can demoralize and destroy the personality of others" (page 61). The great mother archetype is the equivalent of Bowlby's (1980) compulsive care-giver, and my own state of negative upper closeness (Chapter 8). If this is so, there seems to be nothing gained by invoking the more complicated and mysterious concept of an archetype.

THE COMPLEX

The concept of a complex sprung from Jung's conviction that a person has many selves. A complex is an autonomous entity within the psyche. Jung wrote of a complex as a splinter psyche, which can behave like an independent being. It can be conscious, partly unconscious or totally unconscious. If unconscious, it can belong to the personal unconscious, the collective unconscious, or both. For example, in the case of a mother complex, it can be personal in so far as it relates to a person's actual mother and collective in so far as it relates to the archetypal mother. Jung considered the complexes of men and women to be different. In women, erotic complexes, and complexes to do with pregnancy, children and the family are more predominant, and in men, complexes of ambition, money and striving to succeed are.

A SYMBOL

Jung's use of the term symbol is quite different from Freud's. What Freud would call a symbol Jung would call a sign. Freud's most common use of the word symbol is in the term phallic symbol, which is an object like a tower, that a person sees as, or uses to represent, a penis, as a way of avoiding a reference to the penis more directly. A sign, according to Jung, is the representation of something specific, like the male and female signs on the doors of public lavatories. A symbol is something far less tangible. According to Samuels (1997), it is "... the best possible formulation of a relatively unknown psychic content that cannot be grasped by consciousness" (page 94). According to Young-Eisendrath and Dawson (1997), it is "... the best possible expression for something inferred but not directly known or which cannot be adequately defined in words" (page 319). More often than not, a symbol is a visual representation of something, but that something is ungraspable or undefinable. In this respect, it is like an archetype. It is recognised as a symbol because, like an archetype, it appears to have meaning beyond that which it simply depicts. I presume this is because it evokes an emotional response. Jung maintained that, because it moves him, he is compelled to conclude that it alludes to something deeper.

THE JUNGIAN CONCEPTION OF CONSCIOUSNESS

Jung used the term ego, though he was at pains to distinguish between his own use of the term and Freud's use of it. However, there do appear to be a number of similarities. Jung conceived of the ego as being the centre of

consciousness. As with the Freudian ego, the Jungian ego serves as an intermediary between the inner and the outer world. Like the Freudian ego, the
Jungian ego is concerned with reality testing. Like the outer me, the ego is
concerned with continuity over time. Also like the outer me, it is concerned
with discretion. In contrast to the self, the ego is ethical. The ego is also
capable of uncertainty, of staying with not knowing. The self cannot tolerate
the anxiety that goes with not knowing. It has to explain everything. It is
inclined towards what Jungians call premature closure, that is for producing
an explanation, any explanation, rather than no explanation. This leads to
irrationality. In contrast to the self, the ego is rational.

5   Cognitive distinctions

While the psychodynamic theorists consider themselves to be primarily psychotherapists, the cognitive theorists consider themselves to be primarily scientists. Where psychodynamic therapists are concerned with how the mind works, cognitive scientists are concerned more with how the brain works. Unlike the psychoanalysts, cognitive scientists use terms that are more aligned with brain functioning, like processes and mechanisms. LeDoux (1998) observed that "The emphasis on unconscious processes as opposed to conscious content underlies much work in cognitive science" (page 29). Because of its diffuse and varied nature, aspects of cognitive science are included in several other chapters in this book. This chapter will try to focus upon some of its central issues. It has a number of growing points, between which theoretical connections can be made.

Lakoff (1997) wrote:

> Perhaps the most striking result obtained across the various branches of cognitive science is that most thought is unconscious – though not in the sense that Freud meant by the term. To Freud, unconscious thought was thought that could, in principle, be brought into consciousness. It was thought that was, to a large extent, repressed – too painful to be brought into consciousness. The cognitive unconscious is not like this at all. The kind of unconscious thinking studied by cognitive science cannot be done consciously. It is thinking that is extremely fast, automatic, effortless – and completely normal (page 89).

He considered that most of the kinds of thought discussed in the cognitive sciences operate below a level that we could possibly have access to or control over. It was his view that the cognitive unconscious and the psychodynamic unconscious both exist, but are different. He did concede however that, in certain places, they overlapped.

Human instincts

Instincts feature much more prominently in cognitive theory than in psychodynamic theory. Pinker (1997) referred to what he believed to be a common misconception that humans have no instincts beyond the vegetative functions. He considered the idea that, in humans, instincts have given way to the more flexible system of making rational decisions on the basis of available information to be quite wrong. Instead, he argued that "Our vaunted flexibility comes from scores of instincts assembled into programs and pitted in competitions" (page 184). It was his conviction that the advantage that humans have over other animals is not that we have fewer instincts than them, but that we have more. Cognitive scientists have introduced the term hard-wired to refer to innate, mental mechanisms that are in place for solving recurrent adaptive problems. Gilbert (1992) wrote of internal processing modules, and Cosmides (1989) wrote of mental algorithms and rules of inference.

The cognitive unconscious

In contrast to psychodynamic theorists, cognitive theorists attempt to be extremely precise. They use a lot of highly technical jargon, which renders what they write almost as impenetrable to the general reader as that which psychodynamic theorists write. In place of the psychodynamic unconscious and conscious, they (e.g., Jacoby et al., 1992) tend to use terms like automatic processes (which come closer to the features of the inner me) and intentional processes (which come closer to the features of the outer me). LeDoux (1989) wrote, "It is now widely accepted that mental information processing takes place largely outside of conscious mental awareness, with only the end products reaching consciousness and being represented as conscious content" (page 271). He observed that cognitive psychologists sometimes speak of consciousness as being the end product of cognitive processing, but they are much more interested in the processing than of the contents of consciousness that emerge during or as a result of such processing.

Cognitive psychologists do not normally use the noun *the* unconscious, because they do not conceive of there being a place, region or even a structure that could be identified as *the* unconscious. Instead, they use the adjectives unconscious or nonconscious to mean that something happens inside the brain but outside of consciousness. Kihlstrom (1987) did introduce the term *the* cognitive unconscious, perhaps as a way of setting up a rivalry with the psychodynamic unconscious. He considered it to encompass a very large proportion of mental life. LeDoux (1998) wrote, ". . . the cognitive unconscious is not the same as the Freudian or dynamic unconscious. The term cognitive unconscious merely implies that a lot of what the mind does goes on outside of conscious, whereas the dynamic unconscious is a darker, more malevolent place . . ." (page 30). He proposed that the cognitive unconscious consists of ". . . processes that take care of the mind's routine business without consciousness having to be bothered" (page 30), and Lewicki et al. (1992) believed that our nonconscious information processing system is faster and smarter overall than our ability to think and identify meanings in a consciously controlled manner.

Repressed memories

It is perhaps because the process of repression has commanded such a central position in the psychoanalytic theory of the unconscious, that, at first, cognitive psychologists had such difficulty accommodating it into their own theoretical system. In 1991, Power and Brewin wrote, "We would question however whether there is room in a model of the unconscious for repressed material that was previously conscious" (page 307). However, in a more recent study, Brewin and Andrews (1997) cited at least 30 cohort studies, which provided robust empirical evidence of people forgetting childhood sexual abuse, with varying degrees of later recall. Another psychologist (Myers 1998), who has collaborated with both Brewin and Power, has now put repression on to a sounder, scientific basis. She observed that some people, with what she called a repressive coping style, have a greater than normal capacity for forgetting negative information, but have a normal capacity for remembering positive information (Myers and Brewin, 1994). Reynolds and Brewin (1999) observed that people with depression or post-traumatic stress disorder spend much time trying to avoid unpleasant intrusive memories. Brewin and Andrews (2000) now conclude that "The systematic forgetting of negative and traumatic material appears to be both possible and reasonably common among people who have been repeatedly victimised, although the mechanisms are not yet understood" (page 617). In place of repression some cognitive psychologists use the more neutral term cognitive avoidance, which can be applied to either deliberate avoidance or that avoidance of which the person is no longer aware.

Kelly's view of the conscious/unconscious distinction

Kelly (1955) was inclined to view consciousness and unconsciousness not as a bipolar construct but as being on a continuum. He wrote of levels of cognitive awareness and referred to psychological manoeuvres that could defensively restrict awareness. Some of these he termed cognitive restriction, suspension of sense making, loosening of construing, and the selective submergence of one pole of a bipolar construct.

Explicit and implicit cognitive systems

Cognitive psychologists use the terms explicit and implicit to refer to two distinct cognitive systems, explicit referring to the slow, deliberate, conscious one and implicit referring to the fast, automatic, unconscious one. Reber (1993) argued that the implicit one is evolutionarily older. Eagle (1987) considered that implicit cognition (like the psychodynamic unconscious) predominates during early years and explicit cognition becomes possible only after a sufficient degree of brain maturation had taken place. The term implicit has been used to refer to motivation, learning, sensory input, perception, recognition, knowledge, memory, judgements and behaviour and these will be considered in their respective chapters.

Epstein's cognitive-experiential self-theory (CEST)

Epstein (1994) considered there to be ample evidence that "people apprehend reality in two fundamentally different ways" (page 710). The first he described as deliberative, verbal and rational; the second he described as intuitive, automatic, natural, nonverbal, narrative and experiential. His theory distinguishes between what he considered to be two interactive modes of information processing, which he called rational and experiential. He linked rational with the term analytic and experiential with the term intuitive. He considered the rational to be primarily verbal and the experiential to be primarily non-verbal. He considered the rational to be intimately associated with the intellect, and to be relatively affect-free, and the experiential to be associated with feelings. He aligned the rational with the head and the experiential with the heart. An interesting point that no one seems to have noted is that cognitive theory is more closely aligned with the rational and psychodynamic theory is more closely aligned with the experiential.

In an earlier work, cited in the 1994 paper, Epstein (1991) listed 11 differences between the rational (R) and the experiential (E) system, which may be briefly summarised as follows:

R analytic	E holistic
R reason oriented	E pleasure–pain oriented
R logical connections	E associationistic connections
R abstract symbols	E images, metaphors, narratives
R slower processing	E rapid processing
R changes easily	E changes with difficulty
R highly differentiated	E broad generalisations
R highly integrated	E more crudely integrated
R active and conscious	E passive and preconscious
R requires evidence	E self-evidently valid
R mediated by appraisal	E mediated by past experiences

The rational has much in common with the outer me, and the experiential has much in common with the inner me, though the equivalence is far from being a complete one. Epstein described the experiential as being "emotionally driven." Although the inner me is considered to be the source of the emotions, there is no direct alignment of the inner me with emotions in the way that there is a direct alignment of the experiential with emotions. The primary function of the inner me (if it is appropriate to consider it as having a function) is to ensure that the objectives are met, which is why the three chapters of Part III will be devoted to the objectives.

It concerns me that neither psychoanalysis nor cognitive psychology lays any great emphasis upon objectives. Epstein did incorporate into CEST what he called the four basic needs, but they do not appear to be central to the theory. They were derived from psychodynamic sources and are: the pleasure principle (Freud, 1911); the need to maintain a relatively stable, coherent conceptual system (Lecky, 1961); the need for relatedness (Bowlby, 1988); and the need to overcome feelings of inferiority and enhance self-esteem (Adler, 1954; Kohut, 1984). These are neither fundamental nor comprehensive.

Another distinction Epstein drew between the rational and the experiential is that the rational is associated with "impersonal information acquired from textbooks and lectures" (page 711) and the experiential is associated with what he called insight. He distinguished between intellectual knowledge, which he called abstract, and insightful knowledge which he believed to be derived from "personally meaningful experience" (page 711). He saw narratives as appealing to the experiential system "because they are emotionally engaging and represent events in a manner similar to how they are experienced in real life, involving location in place and time, goal-directed characters, and sequential unfolding" (page 711). Experientially derived knowledge he considered to be more "appealing," "compelling," "persuasive" and "more likely to influence behavior." This, he said, is why the Bible used stories and parables rather than philosophical discourse, and why advertisers use pictorial representations rather than intellectual arguments.

Epstein linked the experiential with nonrational or irrational thinking, which he considered to be highly prevalent. This, he maintained, accounts for the appeal of superstition and religion. He made the useful point that even when people know that their thinking is irrational they are still not prepared to abandon it. This is why it is not possible to dispel religious belief with rational argument (see Chapter 20). Irrational thinking is connected to Nunberg's (1931) concept of rationalisation (Chapter 14). Epstein observed that people know that some fears that they have, like the fear of flying and the fear of mice, are irrational, yet such knowledge does not stop them from harbouring them.

I agree with Epstein that there are two kinds of thinking: irrational thinking, which I would associate with the inner me; and rational thinking, which I would associate with the outer me. That the two kinds of thinking exist side by side supports the view that the inner me and the outer me operate in parallel. I explained in Chapter 3 that irrational thinking does make some kind of sense, which must have been of benefit to humans before the more objective, rational thinking of the outer me became a possibility. Although inner me thinking is not perfect, it worked in enough instances for it to be useful. I also explained, and I cited Claxton (1998) in support of this that, under certain conditions, inner me thinking continues to have advantages over outer me thinking.

Epstein (1994) reviewed a whole host of theories that support a two-system approach, some of which will be briefly summarised. Schneider and Shiffrin (1977) distinguished between two modes of information processing: a reflective, rational, conscious mode and an automatic mode that does not require consciousness. Tversky and Kahneman (1983) distinguished between two common forms of reasoning: an extensional, logical mode; and a natural, intuitive mode. They considered that the intuitive mode involved what they called heuristic thinking, that is taking logical short cuts. Labouvie-Vief (1989) distinguished between a rational, analytic mode of information processing called logos, and an intuitive, holistic mode called mythos. She believed that an integration of the two is necessary for well-being and creative accomplishment. Epstein also made reference to Brewin's (1989) three-system approach, which is essentially a two-system approach with an additional component. The first included deliberative, intentional, cognitive processing that is under conscious control; the second included subconscious, automatic, rapid, difficult-to-modify, cognitive processing that is responsive to affect-laden experience; and the third is what he called the prewired dispositions. The dispositions may well have something to do with what I have called the objectives (Part III).

Gilbert's slow-track and fast-track systems

Gilbert (1998) drew a distinction between what he called *slow-track* and *fast-track* modes of brain functioning. It appears to be a derivative of Epstein's model. He considered these two modes to be only partially independent. Slow-track is equivalent to the outer me and fast-track is equivalent to the inner me.

He considered slow-track to be a rational system. It "processes information more slowly, needs to integrate information from memory and knowledge stores and is thus less modularized" (page 449). He considered that rationality evolved more recently and includes building complex, multidimensional models of the world. "It uses logical deductive and symbolic forms of reasoning in a more conscious way and is less influenced by past events and affects" (page 449). Fast-track he considered to be reliant on "affect and how something feels" on "more primitive, earlier evolved appraisal-response systems," (page 449) encoded in limbic and sub-limbic areas. He describes it as being preconscious, as using "crudely integrated information," (page 449) heuristics and an experiential system.

Evans (2001) slightly modified this when he referred to two complementary systems in the brain for making decisions, which he called reason and emotion. When it is important to get the answer right, and we have a lot of time and attention at our disposal, we can use the slow and clean method of reasoning things through, but when we are short of time and information, or it is not so important to get the right answer, we switch to what he called the fast and frugal method of following our feelings.

Teasdale's interacting cognitive subsystems' model

Teasdale and Barnard (1993) arrived at a similar dichotomy when researching into depressive cognition. They proposed nine cognitive subsystems, but only two will be described here. One, called the propositional, represents the logical mind, capable of fine discrimination. It takes an objective, dispassionate view of phenomena and its memory store is coded verbally (outer me). The other, called the implicational, deals with perception of the whole and with emotional meaning. Its concern is with self-worth and threats to position or survival and its memory store is coded in several sensory modalities (inner me).

Claxton's undermind

Claxton (1998) perceived the existence of an unconscious that was, as he put it, quite unlike "the dangerous Freudian dungeon of the mind" (page 7). Interestingly, in contrast to Gilbert's (1998) fast-track, he considered that that which he chose to call the *undermind*, or sometimes the *intelligent unconscious*, to be a slower form of mental functioning. His introduction of this term was, in part, a reaction to two current preoccupations, consciousness and the intellect. While he acknowledged the importance of both of these, he argued that they can only be part of the picture. He maintained that consciousness can only be understood in relation to the unconscious. He saw a danger of our coming to see models of mind that are associated with consciousness as being pre-eminent, and of our ignoring, or undervaluing, those that require a different image of mind. He believed that we have become trapped in a single mode of mind that requires us to be explicit, exact, articulate and purposeful. He referred to us operating in a "high-speed mental climate" (page 6) that placed emphasis upon language and other symbol systems. Claxton considered the undermind to be a leisurely way of knowing that has a tolerance of confusion and uncertainty. He described uncertainty as "a seedbed in which ideas germinate and responses form" (page 6).

Claxton (1998) devoted an entire book to explaining the workings of the undermind, and quotations and citations from the book are included in several chapters of this book. He envisaged the conscious self as "the recipient of gifts from a workplace to which consciousness has no access" (page 223). He wrote of the need to wait for inspiration rather than to manufacture it. He urged us to take seriously ideas that come out of the blue, without any ready-made train of rational thought to justify them. He argued that when the mind slows and relaxes, other ways of knowing automatically appear. He used the term incubation to refer to a period of time, sometimes minutes, sometimes months or even years, during which the undermind is working on a problem without the person being aware of it. In due course the answer just emerges. He wrote of the possibility that we may try too hard to solve a problem, and that if we stop trying the answer may just come; almost as though it is the intensity of our trying that is interfering with the solution emerging.

The title of Claxton's book is *Hare Brain, Tortoise Mind.* The hare brain refers to the conscious intellect and the tortoise mind refers to that which he called the undermind. He sometimes called the undermind the slow mind and he wrote about slow thinking. Since I equate the intellect with the outer me and the undermind with the inner me, and since I consider the outer me to be slow and the inner me to be fast, and cognitive psychologists consider the conscious mind to be slow and the unconscious mind to be fast, this is bound to give rise to confusion. There is little doubt that many inner me processes are fast and I suspect that Claxton would not dispute this. He has drawn attention to the slower ones. When we move away from the verbal, the deliberate and the precise, we enter a timeless world where thoughts and ideas drift into each other, and this is partly what Claxton is referring to. Claxton would entreat us to trust the undermind in the way that Milner (1987) would entreat us to trust the unconscious.

Information-processing theories

Information processing is one of the central concerns of cognitive psychologists. They demonstrate the enormous difference between the psychoanalytic and the cognitive distinction between conscious and unconscious processes. Epstein (1994) wrote that ". . . most information processing occurs automatically and effortlessly outside of awareness because that is its natural mode of operation, a mode that is far more efficient than conscious, deliberative thinking" (page 710). There are a number of theories about it. The classic information-processing model proposes that information from the environment is transferred to sensory registers, one for each sense modality, where it is (unconsciously) analysed by processes called feature detection and pattern recognition. Information which, by these processes is identified as meaningful and relevant to current goals, is then transferred to a (conscious) structure known as the primary or short-term memory, where it is subject to further analysis. Within this structure it may become combined with additional information, which is retrieved from what is called the secondary or long-term memory. The primary memory is considered to have an extremely limited capacity for processing information and it is only the staging area for the cognitive system. Information resides in it only so long as it is attended and rehearsed.

Extending beyond the classic model is one which is called adaptive control of thought (ACT*), the asterisk indicating that, currently, this was the final version (Anderson, 1983). In place of the primary memory of the classic model, there is what is called the working memory (Baddeley, 1986). Like the primary memory, the working memory is also a (conscious) temporary storage structure, but it has a much larger capacity. Within it, that which is called the (unconscious) procedural knowledge (i.e. our repertoire of mental skills, rules and strategies), operates upon that which is called the declarative knowledge (i.e. our fund of general and specific factual information), in order to reach conclusions and make decisions. While the conclusions and decisions are available to consciousness, the procedures employed to reach them are not. As with the primary (short-term) memory, material is retained within the working memory only long enough for updating from moment to moment. The working memory has relevance to working things out, which is covered in Chapter 14.

Kihlstrom (1987) proposed that declarative knowledge might be represented by a graphic structure with nodes representing concepts and associative links representing the relations between them. Procedural knowledge is similarly represented, with nodes representing processing goals and the conditions under which some cognitive or behavioural action will meet them. Activation spreads from one cognitive unit to another along the associative links, activating still other nodes in the memory network.

The term working memory is a misnomer, since it is not really a memory. It is the location where information is held in order that it may be worked with. Logie (1999) referred to it as the desktop of the brain. It allows several pieces of information to be held in mind at the same time, so that they can be compared, contrasted and otherwise interrelated. That which is in the working memory is that which I am currently thinking about or paying attention to. Since I am able only to think about or pay attention to a few pieces of information at a time, the capacity of the working memory has to be limited. As with the classic information-processing model, the working memory needs to be able to draw upon material that is in the long-term memory in order that I can set into context that which I am working upon and to perceive connections between what I am working upon and what I already know. This is like what I wrote about consciousness on page 19.

The lateral prefrontal cortex and the working memory

As far back as 1937, Jacobsen and Nissen worked with monkeys to implicate the prefrontal cortex in the functioning of the working memory. They trained a monkey to watch while the experimenter placed a raisin under one of two objects. They then lowered a curtain between the monkey and the objects for varying periods of time, before allowing the monkey to select the object under which the raisin had been placed. After a delay of a few seconds, the monkey could make a correct selection, but after a delay of minutes, it could not. However, if the prefrontal cortex was damaged, it could not remember at all. Thus, the prefrontal cortex was necessary to retain the memory of the spatial location of the raisin.

The working memory has now more precisely been located in the lateral prefrontal cortex. This region exists only in primates and is much larger in humans than in other primates. Fuster (1989) and Goldman-Rakic (1993) showed that cells in this region become active during the delay period when the curtain was up, indicating that it was instrumental in retaining the image of the two objects while they could not be seen. Damage to it in humans seriously interferes with working memory. D'Esposito et al. (1995) showed that when humans were asked to perform a visual and a verbal task at the same time the lateral prefrontal cortex was activated, but when they were asked to perform them separately, it was not.

The lateral prefrontal cortex has connections with the various sensory systems from which information is gathered, the hippocampus, which plays a vital role in long-term memory storage, and the motor system. Thus it can receive information, make decisions about it, pass it on for long-term storage and instigate appropriate motor responses to it.

Parallel information processing

An alternative information-processing theory is called connectionism or parallel distributed processing (PDP). It is fully described by Rumelhart et al. (1986). Whereas in the two previous theories there is a single, central processing unit (the primary memory or the working memory), in PDP there is a large number of processing units, each devoted to a specific but simple task. Each unit, when activated, excites and inhibits others along a rich network of associative links. Also, in contrast to the previous two theories, it is not necessary for an object to be fully represented in consciousness before information about it can influence experience, thought and action. An important feature of the theory is that unconscious processing is fast and parallel, while conscious processing is slow and sequential.

LeDoux (1998) maintained that information can be simultaneously processed separately by systems that do and do not give rise to conscious content, so that there is the conscious representation in some and the unconscious representation in other systems. Thus, although we can introspect and verbally describe the workings of the systems that create and use conscious representations, we cannot do so when the processing occurs purely outside of consciousness.

Cognitive theories of consciousness

LeDoux (1998) observed that "Consciousness seems to do things serially, more or less one at a time, whereas the unconscious mind, being composed of many different systems, seems to work more or less in parallel" (page 280). He argued that the consciousness (serial) processor works at a symbolic level, whereas the unconscious (parallel) processor works at a subsymbolic level. Presumably, he included using words and sentences within the definition of symbolic. He considered that serial processors create representations by manipulating symbols, and we are only conscious of information that is represented symbolically. The subsymbolic parallel processors operate in codes that are not decipherable consciously. Might this be comparable to that which Pinker (1994) (Chapter 13) called mentalese? He observed that some cognitive scientists consider that consciousness sits at the top of the cognitive hierarchy, above a variety of special purpose (unconscious) processors that are organised in parallel. He cited Johnson-Laird (1988) as saying that consciousness can specify a goal in explicitly symbolic terms. The details of how that goal is attained are formulated in progressively finer detail by the unconscious processors. Ultimately that consciousness receives the results of computations of the unconscious processors, once more in the explicit symbolic form that it can understand.

This to me reflects some of the differences between outer and inner me functioning. The outer me (what LeDoux called consciousness) functions essentially at a verbal (symbolic) level and concerns itself with simple, straightforward, concrete and precisely definable objectives. The inner me (what LeDoux called the unconscious mind) functions at a nonverbal, intuitive level and concerns itself with complex objectives that cannot be simply defined, like the recognition of a face.

The major difficulty I have with this comparison is that I do not consider that it is the (conscious) outer me that dictates the objectives and the (unconscious) inner me that sets about the complex task of attaining them. In other words, I do not consider the inner me to be the slave of the outer me. In fact the reverse comes nearer to the truth. In Chapter 8, under the heading *The underpinning of the attainment or relating objectives*, I make reference to the complexity of both physical and psychological mechanisms that contribute to the attainment of relating objectives. This comes close to the processing that is described here.

Is even the outer me sometimes unconscious?

Libet (1993) observed that before anyone makes an apparent voluntary movement, such as flexing the wrists, a voltage called the readiness potential sweeps across the scalp. He asked people to flex their wrists or fingers whenever they felt they wanted to, and to declare that urge as soon as they were aware of it. He found that the awareness lagged behind the readiness potential by a consistent amount of time, around 0.4 seconds. Challoner (2000) concluded from this that consciousness really is a consequence of the unconscious behaviour of our brains, rather than a deciding factor or guiding light in how we should behave. Claxton (1998) reporting upon the same experiment observed, "These results indicate clearly that it is the unconscious brain which decides what to do, and when; and that what we experience as an intention is merely a post hoc confirmation of what has already been set in motion" (page 160).

These would not be the constructions that I would put upon this experiment. I would consider deciding to flex the fingers to be an outer me action. Normally, rationalising after the event is what I would consider to be an outer me response to something that the inner me had caused to happen. Here, what, in effect, Claxton is saying is that the outer me has unconsciously decided to do something and then subsequently, the outer me again, but this time consciously, has made up a reason for its doing it. This does not make any sense. Why should the outer me need to rationalise about something that it itself has instigated? What I think the experiment is showing is that the outer me really did make the decision to perform the act, and really did know why it did so, but the person does not become conscious of the outer me's decision until 0.4 of a second later. That is the time it takes for the outer me's decision to enter consciousness. One can conclude from the experiment the very important point that the outer me and consciousness are not one and the same thing (see also Chapters 1 and 15). Consciousness is a place, an arena, like a computer monitor, where experiences, happenings, thoughts or whatever are brought to the person's attention. The actions of the outer me inevitably do come into consciousness, but there is a delay before they do so. This is not, cannot, be the case for the inner me.

The function of consciousness

An important feature of cognitive science is the idea that the conscious mind often does not know how the unconscious mind reaches its decisions. However, the conscious mind is extremely reluctant to acknowledge this. Nisbett and Wilson (1977) observed that people are often mistaken about the internal causes of their actions and feelings. They demonstrated, with a number of experiments that, when people do not know the cause, they make up reasons that they firmly believe in. Claxton (1998) remarked that people are not comfortable with the idea that the brain, unsupervised by the conscious intellect, does smart things on its own. He went on to propose that "consciousness per se does not carry out any cognitive function" (page 162). This strikes me as carrying the argument a bit too far.

Both Challoner and Claxton consider that what they call consciousness still has a function. By using the word consciousness in this way they are implying that it is not only a state of awareness; it is also a component of the mind that does things. In this sense it is comparable to the outer me. Their explanations of the function of consciousness were not entirely satisfactory. Challoner (2000) considered it to be working out whether what happened really was the best course of action in the circumstances and learning from it. This is very much like one function of the outer me. He observed that some neuropsychologists believe that the brain reacts automatically in any situation, and that the mind works out what went on, making up reasons for the behaviour shortly afterwards. He described consciousness as an afterthought. This view is similar to one I expressed in my 1993/96 book, and that I cited in the first paragraph of this one, that "the logic of the subcortex is often so profound that it feels as though it is the prime mover and that the cortex trundles along some distance behind, long after the main action has taken place" (page 6). Here the terms cortex and subcortex were the forerunners to the present outer me and inner me.

Claxton (1998) considered that consciousness made its evolutionary appearance in states of disruption and emergency. He saw it as a form of highlighting strange and disturbing situations that cause us to sit up and take notice. "Whatever occupies the centre of conscious attention," he maintained, "is there precisely because its meaning, its significance, its interpretation is in doubt" (page 161). He believed that consciousness is for self-protection, that conscious awareness has the function of checking a situation for concealed threats to the self. He saw it as the detection of some irregularity or threat, either real or imagined, and the instigation of some veto that can block the execution of the evolving plan before it is too late. This also is in line with one of the functions of the outer me. Later he denied this by saying, ". . . even this formulation credits consciousness with power that it does not intrinsically possess" (page 162). Here he seems to be viewing consciousness simply as a passive state of being alerted to what is happening, with, as he puts it, no executive responsibility. This now is denying that consciousness is a component of the mind that does things. This kind of confusion can be resolved by having the two separate concepts, the outer me and consciousness, which often, but not necessarily always, coincide.

LeDoux (1998) observed that we can have introspective access to the outcome of cognitive processing, but not all processing gives rise to conscious content. He concluded that one of the main functions of consciousness is keeping our life tied together into a coherent story. "It does this," he wrote, "by generating explanations of behaviour on the basis of our self image, memories of the past, expectations of the future, the present social situation and the physical environment in which the behaviour is produced" (page 33).

Damasio (2000) who wrote an entire book on consciousness was not very forthcoming on what its function is. He wrote that considering that so much adequate regulation of life can be achieved without conscious processing, that skills can be automated and preferences enacted without the influence of a knowing self, what is consciousness really good for? His answer was ". . . consciousness is good for extending the mind's reach and, in so doing, improving the life of the organism whose mind has that higher reach" (page 303). By this he meant that it enables the individual organism to cope with the environmental challenges not predicted in its basic design. That is, it provides a flexibility that goes beyond the organism's rigid responses.

Taken together, these various explanations are not too far removed from the idea that the outer me can stand aside and decide, for each new situation, what might be the best line of action, given the circumstances. It may be slow and it may be cumbersome, but it has an independence of mind, which enables it to see all around a situation, and view it in both a spatial and a temporal context, which sets it apart from the precisely programmed inner me.

Part III

The human objectives

Surprisingly, little attention has been paid to the human objectives; yet all human behaviour is directed towards attaining them. It seems only right, before examining a broad range of mental mechanisms, to set out clearly what these mechanisms have been shaped to achieve. While the objectives are housed within, and monitored by, the inner me, the outer me has somehow come to be aware of them, and equally strives to attain them. An innovation is the introduction of the relating objectives which, while derived from the objectives of survival and reproduction, have greater relevance for the complexities of human behaviour.

6   Survival

Before proceeding with this section, I need to say that organisms do not really have objectives. They are as they are because the way that they are enables them to survive. When I say that plants have flowers in order to attract bees, I am implying that attracting bees is one of their objectives. This is not so. It is simply that plants that happen to have flowers get their pollen transferred. However, it *looks as though* attracting bees is one of their objectives. It is a convenient lie to say that humans have objectives. I know that it is a lie, but I am going to use it all the same.

Survival is the principal objective of all life forms, including humans. A brain is not essential for survival. Plants have evolved without brains. In fact, plants are better at surviving than animals. They survive in locations where animals cannot, tolerating extremes of temperature, extremes of desiccation, even forest fires. Although plants can survive without animals, animals cannot survive without plants. If all plants were killed off, all animals would die too; because only plants can trap the sun's energy. Without the sun, there would be no life on the planet. By photosynthesis, plants create chemical compounds that retain the sun's energy. Animals survive only by eating plants, so the first animals had to be herbivores. Later, carnivores evolved that survived by eating herbivores; and later still, carnivores evolved that ate other carnivores. Plants do not move. Animals need to move to find more plants (or animals) to eat. In order to move, animals had to become vastly more complex than plants. They needed brains to control and coordinate the necessary extra sensory, motor, digestive and excretory systems.

Survival and body structure and function

The greater part of body structure is necessary for survival. The brain exerts control over the body structure via the endocrine system, the autonomic nervous system and the central nervous system. Damasio (2000) introduced the term the proto-self to refer to a collection of neural patterns and interconnected neural pathways that map, moment by moment, the state of the physical structure of the organism in its many dimensions and regulate the state of the organism. The proto-self occurs in many brain locations and at many levels, from the brainstem to the cerebral cortex. All that has been described so far would come within the control of the inner me, but in some regulatory functions, the outer me also plays a part. For example, the body temperature is maintained within narrow limits, quite automatically, by the autonomic nervous system; so when we are too hot we become flushed and perspire, and when we are too cold we become pale, shiver and develop goose pimples. However, this autonomic control of body temperature can be supplemented by the outer me putting on or removing clothing or turning on the central heating or the air conditioning, or in a more general way, by the design and manufacture of clothing, or central heating or air conditioning systems.

The motivation to survive

The motivation to survive comes straight out of the inner me. I (the outer me) do not decide, or strive, to survive. The inner me causes me to. The compulsion to survive is extremely powerful. People who are trapped underground, or lost in wild places, or shipwrecked, manage to stay alive for long periods. Of course, the outer me contributes to their survival by devising methods of protection, or escape, or finding food; so somehow, the outer me becomes tuned in to the inner me's objectives. People who are horribly deformed or disabled, or in constant pain, or who live in circumstances of extreme deprivation, continue to be highly motivated to stay alive, as do people who have severe, or terminal illnesses. The couplet of Dylan Thomas (1951) typifies the determination to survive:

> Do not go gentle into that good night.
> Rage, rage against the dying of the light.

Death and the fear of death

From an evolutionary point of view, death makes a lot of sense. No organism lives for ever, and although some trees live for a 1,000 years or more, few animals, including humans, live longer than a 100 years. In adverse conditions, such as drought, it is advantageous that a plant should die and leave its genes preserved in its resilient seed, in order that they may spring to life when conditions become more favourable. As animals grow old, they become damaged and inefficient; so it is to the advantage of the species that, having produced and reared their young, they should die.

Animals must sometimes encounter the dead of their species, but, because they have no outer me, they cannot conclude from this that they themselves must die, because, without an outer me, that has a conception of time, they cannot reach such a conclusion. Animals sometimes kill other animals, yet they still cannot conclude from this that they themselves can be killed. In fact, without an outer me, animals cannot reach conclusions. Dobzhansky (1967) observed that our early ancestors did not have death awareness either.

Burial customs were first inaugurated by Neanderthal man about 80,000 years ago. Children only gradually become aware that they can die. Anthony (1940) observed that children younger than seven or eight have only a limited conception of death. They ask questions like "What do dead people do?" and "What does it feel like to be dead?" By age nine, they understand that death is irreversible, involves the lack of functioning and is universal (Speece and Brent, 1984). It is only the outer me that understands about the irreversibility of death, because such understanding requires the kind of working things out that only the outer me can do. To the inner me, death is just loss, whether it be reversible or not.

Even though adult humans are capable of comprehending that they die, many find the idea intolerable. They believe in life after death and speak of passing to the other side. In effect, they are creating the delusion that they can survive death (see Chapter 20). In some cultures, food and possessions are placed with the dead for use in an afterlife. Those who do not have the protective delusion of immortality become increasingly anxious as the time for death approaches.

Danger

Preparedness and reaction

Humans are equipped with a range of emotions that reinforce their striving for survival. These could be classified as preparedness and reaction. Terms such as primed, vigilant, alert, aroused and on edge describe the condition of preparedness. Everyone, all of the time, is in some degree of preparedness; so we "jump" when something unexpected happens. While we can talk ourselves into a state of preparedness (outer me), usually, it just happens (inner me). Preparedness may be raised or lowered according to past or recent experiences. Some people are always keyed up, others are not keyed up enough. Some are inclined to see difficulties when there are none; others fail to notice them even when they stare them in the face. Some are paranoid; others are not paranoid enough. Extremes of either can be a disadvantage.

Reaction

Most reaction is inner me-determined. Alarm is aroused at unexpected touch, sound, smell and sight. We have an innate fear of the dark, thunder and heights, all of which are potential dangers. Touching a very hot or very cold object evokes an immediate withdrawal of the limb. The approach of a fast-moving object evokes an instant avoidant action that may involve the entire body. Humans have few predators, so fear of predators is less prominent in humans than in most animals. Fear of a dog's bark and a lion's roar are probably innate, as are fear of snakes, rats, mice and spiders. Pinker (1997) reported that the psychologist D.O. Hebb observed that chimpanzees born in captivity scream in terror when they first see a snake. Parasites, bacteria and viruses are what pose the greatest threat to humans. Perhaps part of the human fear of rats (plague) and barking dogs (rabies) is a protection against these. Strangely, humans do not naturally fear mosquitoes, which cause the spread of malaria; though now we (outer me) know they do, we take precautions against them.

Cleaning

Many animals naturally clean themselves (by washing, dust baths, preening and licking), though, of course, they do not know that this is what they are doing. Perhaps the human obsession with swimming is connected to this. Some have an obsessive fear of dirt and some are compelled to wash almost continuously, particularly if they have been touched, and some have a fear of handling coins, which pass from hand to hand. The important point about compulsive hand-washing is that it is inner me driven. The outer me would like to stop it but it does not know how. It may be connected to an innate need for cleanliness, but strangely, many humans do not regularly wash, and regular washing is a relatively recent development in civilised countries. In fact washing, laundering and sterilisation are largely outer me driven, though are they linked to an innate tendency?

The two responses to threat

LeDoux (1998) wrote of two neural avoidant pathways, one quick and non-discriminating, the other slower and discriminating. Respectively, these are inner me based and outer me based. Gilbert (1998) differentiated between what he called a fast-track and a slow-track system; the former involving automatic responses; the latter, rational thinking. In potentially threatening situations, speed is more adaptive than rationality. The animal takes flight on the simplest of cues, like a movement or a smell. This is the principle that it is better to be safe than sorry. Evans and Zarate (1999) observed that it is better to react quickly and undiscriminatingly to avoid possible danger than to wait to be sure. They wrote:

> The fast and dirty mechanism gets you out of trouble quickly but gives off some false alarms. The slow and clean mechanism tells you when the alarms are false, and so stops you wasting too much energy in reacting to them. Sometimes the slow and clean mechanism doesn't click in, and we continue reacting to false alarms. This may be what happens in some phobias (page 56).

Generalised response reactions

Throughout the animal kingdom, reactions fall into three broad categories called flight, fight and freeze. All three are automatic and instant, though it is difficult to say what determines which is adopted. Some animals are predisposed to one; others adopt a different one at different times.

FIGHT-OR-FLIGHT RESPONSE

The fight-or-flight response is mediated via the sympathetic division of the autonomic nervous system. Its effect is to redistribute the blood away from the visceral organs towards the muscles, where additional energy is needed to meet the emergency. It is accompanied by deep breathing, the rapid and powerful beating of the heart and increased muscle tone. The flight response is more widespread than the fight response, and occurs in reptiles, fish, birds, insects and most animals.

Humans respond sometimes by flight and sometimes by fight. Flight is linked to the emotions of panic and terror, and fight is linked to the emotions of anger, affront, indignation and rage. Within a fraction of a second the inner me has to decide whether to flee or to fight. Presumably it does so on the basis of assessing the chances of overcoming the adversary. In a slower, more considered response to threat, the outer me would play a part, and in a more complex situation, an army or a whole nation may have to decide.

FREEZE

The freeze response derives from the fact that many predators respond to movement; so if the animal stays still it will not be attacked. Not all animals freeze. Laboratory-bred rats who have never seen a cat will freeze at their first encounter with one. As LeDoux (1998) observed, the sight of the predator goes straight to the amygdala and out comes the freeze response. Perhaps there is a vestige of the freeze response when humans become frozen to the spot or paralysed with fear.

MODIFICATION OF RESPONSES BY THE OUTER ME

The outer me is aware of our innate reactions to danger, and sometimes it overrides them. In fact, this is the basis of cognitive behaviour therapy. Panic has its place, but sometimes it does more harm than good. The plea of don't panic can be a useful one. Panic may be a cause of death, because in states of panic people act rashly and do stupid things. The outer me is able to cause us to stand back, assess the situation, to decide what is wrong and work out a considered solution.

Selfishness versus cooperation

All animals are naturally selfish: They compete for territory, shelter, food, the best place in the herd and the best mate. In the survival of the fittest, only the fittest survive, that is the strongest, the most powerful, the fastest, the most capable, the most healthy, the most persistent, the most determined and, in humans, the cleverest. Humans, being animals, are also selfish, as conveyed by the expressions looking after number one, every man for himself and dog eat dog. Selfishness also extends into groups: Families look after their own, races look after their own (racism) and nations look after their own (xenophobia and nationalism).

In civilised societies, selfishness is scorned upon, but it remains prevalent and emerges in many situations. When a crowd is trying to escape from a sinking ship or a burning building, people do not step aside to allow others to go in front. They stampede, and many get trampled under foot. Most forms of crime are manifest forms of selfishness.

Aggression

Aggression is an emotion that serves selfishness. It too extends into groups. Gangs, races and nations fight to destroy or suppress their adversaries.

Revenge, retaliation and retribution

These are powerful responses, which are particularly prominent in humans, but which must surely also occur in the wild. They are the basis of the expression an eye for an eye and a tooth for a tooth. Their aim is to even up the score, redress the balance. Punishment, and many forms of so-called justice, would appear to be modifications of them. When people offend, others argue that they should not be allowed to get away with it. They would appear to be inner me driven, primitive responses, and some would maintain, at an outer me level, that they have no place in a civilised society.

Competition

Competition is a sublimated form of aggression. People compete for mates, social position and recognition. Within a capitalist system, competition is considered to promote efficiency. Aggression can be safely channelled into competition. Teams, towns and nations compete in games and sports. Supporters and spectators identify with competitors or teams and derive vicarious pleasure from the competitor's or the team's success.

Cooperation

Cooperation occurs in many animal species. They cooperate because they have evolved with a cooperative tendency. Species with the cooperative tendency survived where species without it did not. In animal hierarchies the fit and the less fit survive together, for the fit are protected by being surrounded by the less fit, and the less fit benefit from the greater hunting capacity of the fit.

In some animal colonies some animals have innate characteristics that enable them to perform specialist functions.

It may be that humans too have an innate (inner me), cooperative tendency, but beyond this, over time, they have learned, by way of the outer me, the advantages of cooperation. So cooperation has become woven into the human, social fabric. The essence of cooperation is that, if we all work together, we will get the job done more quickly or more efficiently. An extension of cooperation is specialisation. People with different capabilities work collaboratively together. This leads to a division of labour. People train to be good at different skills so that people with different forms of training are able to collaborate efficiently together.

Exchange

Exchange is another outer me development. The principle of exchange is quid pro quo: I will do this for you if you will do that for me. Animals cannot conceive of exchange. An ape can be trained to press a button in order to get food. It might even be trained to give tokens in order to get food, but it would not be prepared to do a service for someone in order to get another service back. Yet even a small child would be willing to exchange one thing for another, and see the point of it. The idea behind exchange is that each of two people have different capabilities so that what one cannot do the other can. Therefore they each are able to benefit from the exchange.

THE INFLUENCE OF THE OUTER ME UPON HUMAN SURVIVAL

The inventiveness of outer me has led to technical developments that have contributed substantially to human survival but, in turn, such developments have brought with them serious threats to the human race. By developing means of protection against extremes of temperature and by the worldwide distribution of food, we have been able to colonise the entire surface of the planet. By the development of weapons we have become the most powerful species ever. By developments in medical research we have created methods of preventing and treating many diseases, such that the expectation of life in modern countries has been greatly extended. These developments have not been without their downside. By the elimination of the rain forests and the pollution of the atmosphere we have brought about a progressive rise in the earth's temperature that could melt the polar ice-caps and extend the deserts. Increasingly, we have turned our weapons upon ourselves, and become the most self-destructive species of all time. The proliferation of nuclear weapons has created the possibility of a nuclear holocaust that could bring about the total extinction of the human race. The overuse of antibiotics has resulted in the evolution of antibiotic-resistant bacteria that is faster than the development of new antibiotics. It seems likely that the AIDS virus, which is now killing millions of people in the African continent, was transferred to humans from chimpanzees during the manufacture and administration of an anti-polio serum to a million people.

Food and drink

Hunger and thirst

Hunger and thirst are hard-wired inner me devices that ensure survival. Hunger is triggered by the emptiness of the stomach and a fall in the concentration of blood sugar. Thirst is triggered by high blood salt and sugar concentrations. Both these sensations become increasingly compelling until the person is totally obsessed by the thought of food or water and cannot concentrate on anything else. Under conditions of extreme food or water deprivation, the need to eat and drink becomes so compelling that the person will eat or drink anything. People have been known to eat their own clothing and to drink their own urine, or the most foul and infected water. In concentration camps, people would fight and even kill each other for scraps of food. Survivors of air crashes have eaten the flesh of dead passengers.

Obesity

The threshold for hunger and thirst were set at a time in our history when food and water were scarce. Today, in the modern world, food and water are readily available. People do not need to travel large distances in search of them, and with modern methods of transport, they take little exercise. Consequently, they eat and drink far more than they need, and obesity is common. In earlier times, because food was scarce, those who had a heightened appetite for foods with high calorific content, like sugars and fats, were the most likely to survive. Humans still retain a selective appetite for these foods, and food manufacturers take advantage of this by extracting and concentrating them and making them readily available. This further leads to high levels of obesity. In Britain, in the year 2000, one in five women and one in six men were obese, twice as many as 10 years previously. In America, one in four adults were obese. The American health care system spends £60 billion per year on the consequences of obesity (Meek, 2000).

The phenomenon of obesity is then largely the result of the failure of evolution to catch up with the greater availability of food in modern societies. Human attitudes to obesity are complex. In some societies it is a sign of power and men strive to, and actually do, become extremely fat. In a number of affluent societies, many successful men are incidentally obese, so obesity has come to be associated with affluence, and women have come to find at least moderately obese men attractive. In other societies, obese women are considered to be the most attractive. As a reaction to the trend for women to become slim, some feminist women consider it demeaning to have to lose weight in order to attract men. Consequently, they take no steps to do so and are proud of their fatness.

Many people, both men and women, at an outer me level, consider being overweight undesirable. They consider it to be incapacitating, unhealthy and physically repellent. Many claim to be helpless to prevent it. They join weight-watchers' associations. Books on dieting abound. Some people, particularly women, smoke because they believe that nicotine suppresses appetite. Others take stimulant drugs for the same purpose. Others pay to have their excess fat surgically removed or to have their stomachs made smaller. Almost half a million Americans per year have fat removed by liposuction.

In earlier times, water was also scarce, but excessive water drinking is not a problem. This is because the thirst-regulating centre is so sensitive to salt and sugar concentrations. Excessive water drinking is not a problem because, unlike excessive food, excessive water is rapidly excreted from the body in the form of urine. Many people do drink large amounts of water but only when it contains drugs such as caffeine and alcohol. Such drugs have a diuretic effect, so the person becomes dehydrated and the thirst returns. It is possible that alcoholism, a common social problem, is contributed to by a level of thirst that is no longer appropriate in modern societies, though the main causative factor is addiction to alcohol. Some alcoholics do become overweight because of the calorific content of alcohol.

Greed

Greed has its origins in hunger. It benefits animals to gorge in times of plenty, so that they may draw upon their reserves in times of scarcity. In humans, greed has become generalised to the accumulation of wealth and possessions. Opulence is the material equivalent of obesity.

THE DISTASTE FOR VARIOUS FOODS

Humans have an innate distaste for foods that are potentially poisonous. They are repelled by the sight of maggots. They avoid food that smells rotten or decayed or has an offensive taste. These foods evoke the experience of nausea and may even induce vomiting. Vomiting is also induced by the smell of vomit or by the sight of others vomiting, presumably because people who see others vomit are likely to have eaten the food that caused the others to vomit. Unlike certain other animals, humans have a marked disinclination to eat vomit. Humans have the capacity to become tolerant of certain kinds of potentially poisonous foods, presumably because they develop antigens to the bacteria in them. Meat and fish decay quickly, particularly in hot countries, and in countries where refrigeration is not readily available; yet many people are able to eat it without becoming ill. Since the introduction of refrigeration people in Britain have become less tolerant of slightly bad meat and fish which, in earlier times, would have been considered to be more flavoursome.

Young children are more cautious than adults about eating certain foods. Commonly, they do not like greens. Such cautiousness may be well founded since their digestive systems may not be as capable of coping with certain foods than those of adults. Pregnant women are also more choosy about what they eat and are also more disposed to vomit. Pinker (1997) has argued that this may be because the woman is protecting the foetus, which may be less tolerant of certain foods.

DISGUST AND NAUSEA

Disgust is a specific emotional response to the prospect of eating that which is considered to be harmful or poisonous. Disgust deters people from eating certain things or, if it is too late, makes them spit or vomit them out. It is accompanied by a characteristic facial expression. Perhaps the most disgusting substances are excrement, vomit and maggots. Disgust is often accompanied by the sensation of nausea or the act of vomiting. The state of disgust can be induced by witnessing another person expressing disgust. There is a precise location in the brain that is responsible for the experience of disgust. The disgust response and the sensation of nausea have spread to other offensive experiences such as mutilation and rape.

Although the disgust response is universal, the substances considered to be disgusting vary from culture to culture. Children younger than age two will eat practically anything, but they harbour the potential for disgust. Rozin (1996) considered disgust to be an adaptation that deterred our ancestors from eating dangerous animal stuff. People are revolted by plastic replicas of faeces and vomit because, to the inner me, they look sufficiently like the real thing to trigger the response, just as people are frightened by imitation snakes. People can overcome their fear of animal products if they see others eating them, just as they can overcome their fear of snakes. People will not drink out of a brand new bed-pan because bed-pans are not normally brand new and have usually contained human excrement. The inner me has learned to associate the appearance of the bed-pan with that which is disgusting.

THE OUTER ME AND FOOD PRODUCTION

The outer me has been instrumental in increasing access to food and water. By sinking wells, constructing dams, reservoirs and irrigation systems, humans have cultivated vast, new areas of land. They have improved food production with efficient agricultural equipment, fertilisers and pesticides; bred more successful varieties of crops, improved methods of hunting and fishing, bred and reared farm animals and fish, and developed ways of preserving food. This has resulted in an enormous expansion of the population, but it has not been without its costs. Short-sighted farming policies have led to the destruction of forests, the erosion of soil and the creation of deserts. By polluting seas and rivers and by overfishing, humans have greatly reduced the fish population.

To maintain profits, food producers have destroyed crops and restricted their distribution. Paradoxically, this has resulted in millions of people dying of starvation.

Apparent contradictions to the survival objective

Suicide

Only humans commit suicide, because only humans are aware that death can happen and know what to do to bring it about. Once suicide becomes a possibility, humans will resort to it. Although only the outer me knows about death and how to bring it about, the suicidal urge has to come from the inner me; so the person often does not know what it is due to. The outer me can restrain the suicidal urge by producing reasons for not acting upon it, a common reason being an awareness of the effect that it will have upon close friends and relatives. The suicidal urge sometimes persists over months or years, and a person may make several attempts before finally succeeding. Often it is an impulsive act, particularly when committed under the influence of alcohol. Some who do not succeed are relieved to find they are still alive; though others are not.

There is no single explanation for suicide. It is easier if the person believes in an afterlife. Sometimes it is a way of becoming united with God. A person in constant physical or mental pain (including depression) may commit suicide to end it. Increasingly, these days, the suicide is simply a byproduct of an act of aggression, as with kamikaze pilots, or terrorists who detonate explosives strapped to their bodies or fly an aircraft into a building. Sometimes an entire religious sect will commit suicide at the command of their leader.

The suicidal motive is commonly an interpersonal one: A person may commit suicide if s/he has lost status, importance or popularity, or to escape the torment and persecution of others, or if s/he feels s/he has become a burden to others, or has let others down, or because s/he has acted in what s/he considers to be a shameful way and cannot face the disapproval of others. S/he may commit suicide at the door of someone who has offended her/him, as an expression of pride. The act of hara-kiri, the ritual falling upon a sword, is committed when a person feels disgraced or under sentence of death. Sometimes suicide is a reaction to losing the friendship of someone important, or a means of becoming reunited with someone close who has died.

Risk-taking

Risk-taking behaviour would appear to run counter to the objective of survival, but Challoner (2000) stressed that, although risk-takers sometimes get killed, most take precautions to avoid doing so. Taking risks, providing adequate precautions are taken is, in fact, advantageous to the individual, because it enables her/him to tackle dangerous tasks and progress beyond her/his present circumstances. What risk-takers seek is the thrill of doing something dangerous but surviving. When people expose themselves to danger they feel frightened, and when they are frightened, they secrete the hormone adrenaline, which makes them feel elated. Being frightened but knowing you have a good chance of survival is not the same as being frightened and knowing you are going to die. The risk-taker is frightened because the inner me responds to what it perceives as a situation of danger, but s/he feels encouraged to continue because the outer me is aware of the precautions s/he has taken. Challoner reported upon the work of Farley, who introduced the term type T personality to describe someone who seeks thrills, risks and arousal. Farley produced evidence that thrill-seeking is a trait which is as much as 69 per cent inherited. Risk-takers are characterised by low blood levels of the enzyme monoamine oxidase, type B (MAO B). In contrast, chronically phobic individuals have high blood levels of MAO B.

Altruism

Altruism is a stage beyond exchange. In altruism, one person does something for another, without necessarily getting anything back in return. Evolutionists have been puzzled by human altruism, because by the principle of the survival of the fittest, it should not happen. Badcock (1986) observed that organisms have evolved to be little more than the elaborate packaging and guardians of their genes, so in answer to the conundrum, which came first, the chicken or the egg, he cited Wilson (1975) as saying that the chicken is the egg's way of making another egg. According to this logic, it matters less that the individual should survive than that the species should. Interestingly, although animals do not exchange things, they do, under certain circumstances, act altruistically. Again, as with cooperation, they do not do this because they decide (at an outer me level) to, but because it is bred into them to do so. Badcock (1986) pointed out that the purely instinctive altruism of say soldiers indicates that altruism must contribute to the survival of the species, otherwise it would have been bred out over the course of evolution.

In animals, altruism occurs most commonly as part of their parenting behaviour. They protect and defend their young and find food and bring it back to them. Sometimes this activity breaks down, and they eat their young. Humans also act altruistically towards their young and this is inner me driven; they do not decide to, they are compelled to. They also act altruistically towards other people's children and to animals, particularly small ones. In fact, recently, an ape in a zoo was observed to act protectively towards a child that was harmed when it had fallen into its enclosure. Humans act altruistically towards other adults, sometimes to complete strangers, even strangers of a different race. Europeans provide aid for famine victims in Africa and Asia. This they do because they feel for them. They empathise or identify with them. It will be explained in Chapter 8 that, in humans, though not in other animals, apart perhaps from domestic pets, it is safe to express needfulness towards others, that humans respond to the needfulness of others and that others reward those who help them with the expression of gratitude.

SELF-SACRIFICE

An obvious and understandable act of self-sacrifice is when a parent sacrifices her/his life to save the life of her/his child. Similarly, an adult will sometimes sacrifice her/his life to save any child. Evolutionists would argue that the child is more important than the adult. Some forms of altruistic behaviour make little sense in terms either of inclusive fitness or of reciprocation. It is possible for a young adult to sacrifice her/his life to save an old person. Commonly, in times of war, a soldier will sacrifice his life to save the other members of his regiment. A driver whose vehicle is out of control may steer it off the road in order to avoid hitting a crowd of pedestrians. Often, acts of self-sacrifice occur quite spontaneously, which indicates that they are occurring at an inner me level. Many people cannot stand by and watch others in pain or distress.

ANOREXIA AND BULIMIA

Because, in most contemporary, Western societies the ideal for female beauty is slenderness, young women experience much difficulty conforming to this ideal. Many are able to exercise restraint over their appetite for fattening foods, but others resort to one of two maladaptive practices: either they suppress their appetite completely and do anything to avoid eating food (anorexia nervosa), or they indulge in bouts of binge eating, mainly of sweet food, followed by self-induced vomiting (bulimia nervosa). In anorexia, the fear of putting on weight is so extreme that the woman defeats her original objective and becomes repellingly thin. She manages to convince herself that this is not the case. It is not uncommon for anorexic women to starve themselves to death.

It is hard to explain how anorexic women are able to overcome so powerful a drive as hunger, to the extent of bringing about their own death. Like compulsive hand-washing, anorexia would appear to be inner me driven, but why would the inner me be so motivated? It could be argued that, in the initial stages of anorexia, the woman is putting the objective of reproduction before the objective of personal survival; yet some have argued that the motivation to lose weight is more to do with the fear of looking like a mature woman.

7   Reproduction

If an organism does not reproduce, it becomes extinct. Therefore, both plants and animals must reproduce (pass on their genes) before they die. This idea has led writers like Dawkins (1976) to suggest that the mortal form of each organism is only a vehicle for its genes, and that the survival of its genes is all that matters, but what is the point of genes if not to produce organisms? Apart from in the very simplest of organisms, the form of reproduction that is most effective is sexual. This involves the fusion of genetic material from two members of the same species, most usually of separate genders. Sexual reproduction evolved quite independently in plants and animals. Its advantage is that it allows for chance variations in structure, some of which may be more suited to survival in new environments. Sexual reproduction is much easier for animals than it is for plants for, because animals can move, those of the opposite gender can move towards each other. Where animals depend upon plants for their survival (because only plants can trap the sun's energy and store it within themselves), most plants depend upon animals for their reproduction. Although some plants rely upon the wind for pollination and the wind and water for the spread of their seed, many need to tempt insects, and some birds, with nectar to spread their pollen, and tempt birds and animals with fruit and nuts to spread their seed.

The male and female members of each species must locate and identify each other. This is easy for gregarious species, but not for solitary ones, since there may be no member of the opposite gender within close proximity; so signals have to be emitted that are detectable over long distances. These may take the form of smell (e.g., with butterflies) or sound (e.g., with birds). Members of these species need to have extremely sensitive sense organs that are capable of detecting these signals. Since humans are gregarious they do not need to rely upon smell or sound to attract members of the opposite gender over long distances. Their main source of sexual attraction is the relatively short distance signal of vision.

Sex and male power

In many gregarious species, the group comprises a single, dominant male who has possession of a number of females. As the male offspring reach maturity, they are expelled from the group but the female offspring are allowed to stay. Any male intruder into the group is expelled by the dominant male. As the dominant male grows older and weaker, he is challenged by the male offspring, and eventually overthrown and expelled by one, who then becomes the new dominant male. He takes possession of, and mates with, the females, and kills their offspring to the former dominant male.

In continuity with this arrangement, throughout history and across cultures, powerful men have claimed the right to possess large numbers of young women. This attitude is so prevalent that it seems likely to have a biological basis. Buss (1994) has argued that it is biologically advantageous for the man to spread his sperm to the maximum number of women. In contrast, the woman needs to retain one man who will protect her throughout pregnancy and protect and support her children. The stronger and the more powerful the man, the more wives he claims the right to own: In a harem, the head man has 10 wives, the chieftain has 100 and the emperor has 1,000. Even in more egalitarian, Western cultures, there are examples of male domination and possessiveness towards young women. Brezhnev in the USSR, Chairman Mao in China and President Ceausescu in Rumania claimed access to large numbers of them. Monarchs, aristocrats and, even recently, American presidents have considered it appropriate to have many sexual partners. The leaders of religious cults such as Bhagwan, and David Koresh, the leader of the Branch Davidians in Waco (Young, 1994), have claimed the right to have sex with all the young women in their cults. In a number of Western cultures, the possession of mistresses by husbands is condoned.

In many cultures, the wife is considered the possession of the husband, and often the man, or his family, has to pay large sums of money or offer gifts to the wife's family. The wife is expected to show total fidelity. Adultery means making impure, i.e. the mixing of the sperms. Sexual infidelity of the wife is frequently considered to be justification for murder of the wife by the husband. For such murder, the husband receives no punishment. In contrast, men have no requirement to be faithful. Wife abuse is condoned in many cultures. Sexual possessiveness by the man is often extreme. In certain Mediterranean cultures, until comparatively recently, women were allowed out of the house only a few times during their entire life; sometimes only once, in order to get married (Morris, 1985). In some cultures, even today, the wife is confined to the house or forbidden to go out alone. If she goes out she must be either totally or largely covered by clothing. Her face may be entirely covered, leaving only gauze patches over her eyes to see where she is going. Wives are sometimes fitted with chastity belts or other forms of restrictive clothing. The practice of female circumcision, which includes the removal of the clitoris, is intended to prevent the woman experiencing sexual pleasure and thus having the incentive to have sex with any other man. In some cultures, if a low ranking man has sex with a high ranking man's woman, both he and the woman are killed, and possibly also the rest of his family.

In many cultures it is essential for the woman to be a virgin at marriage. Virginity is evidence that the woman has not borne children to any other man. If she is discovered not to be a virgin, the marriage may be annulled and she may be returned to her family. So great is the requirement of virginity that women who are no longer virgins seek surgery to repair the ruptured hymen (Lindisfarne, 1998).

Buss (1994) has demonstrated that there is a universal tendency for men and women to have different sexual preferences, and this serves to promote the powerful male/dependent woman relationship. Men are attracted to young, healthy, women and women are attracted to men who are successful, powerful, wealthy and of high status. Men prefer women to be younger and shorter and women prefer men to be older and taller. Men in their thirties prefer women who are roughly five years younger, but men in their fifties prefer women who are 10 to 20 years younger (Kendrick and Keefe, 1992). James (2000) reported that, in a survey of 454 traditional societies, the average age of brides at marriage was between 12 and 15. He observed that many believe that men are responding to neotenous, infantile features when they are attracted to women, and that the more infantile a woman looks the more men she will attract. Interestingly, despite our increasingly egalitarian society, women continue to have sexual fantasies of being a prostitute, treated like a slave, spanked, tied up, lying naked with a team of rugby players, forced to have sex, raped, even by a series of men, one after another. They are also turned on by powerful, muscular men, firemen and men in officers' uniforms (*Female Fantasies*, UK Channel 5 documentary, August, 2000). The relationship between men and prostitutes, strippers and lap-dancers is a reflection of the sex for power transaction: women offer themselves for sex (or sexual arousal) in exchange for money, a symbol of male power. The universality of these sexual practices and attitudes suggests an inner me determined tendency.

The diminution of male power in many western cultures

In many Western cultures, the possession of women by men has greatly diminished. In most Western cultures, men are legally restricted to one wife; and to be concurrently married to more than one woman is a punishable offence. The physical and sexual abuse of wives by their husbands is now a punishable offence in many cultures. Women are frequently not virgins at marriage and most Western men do not object to this. Women are permitted to move freely within society and, far from being totally covered by clothing, women now wear clothing that is ostensibly seductive. This reduction of male power and increase in the freedom of women would seem to be an outer me overriding of an inner me tendency.

Sex versus love

Men are generally considered to have a greater preoccupation with sex and women are generally considered to have a greater preoccupation with love. Men, it is said, tolerate love to get sex and women tolerate sex to get love.

Buss (1994) reported a study in which the greater proportion of men said they would be more distressed if their partners had sex with another man than if they were in love with another man, and the greater proportion of women said the opposite. It is because sex requires no commitment that men tend to be more promiscuous than women. Again, these universal tendencies would appear to be inner me determined.

Homosexuality

Though male homosexuals prefer male partners and female homosexuals prefer female partners, in all other respects, male homosexuals behave like men and female homosexuals behave like women. Homosexuality is of interest because it reveals the true nature of the (hard-wired, inner me determined) attitudes of the two genders towards sex. Although there are male couples who live together and stay loyal to each other over long periods of time, promiscuity is far commoner in male homosexuals than it is in either male heterosexuals or female homosexuals. Symons (1979) argued that every heterosexual relationship is a compromise between the wants of a man and the wants of a woman. He maintained that the promiscuity of men is limited by the disinclination of women to indulge them in their promiscuity.

Attractiveness

Generally speaking, people are most attractive when they are young and healthy. Young people are more attractive than old people, which is why people in the media are predominantly young, and why people try to conceal the signs of aging. People who are deformed, disabled or obviously unwell are less attractive than people who are not. Unhealthy looking skin is particularly unattractive because the condition of the skin is a ready guide to the condition of the body as a whole. People without teeth or with irregular or discoloured teeth are unattractive, again because the condition of the teeth is a ready guide to general health. Symmetry is attractive, because asymmetry is often the result of disease. Averageness is also attractive. People who are very tall or very short, or very fat or very thin are unattractive. People with very large or very small features like hands, feet, breasts, bottom, belly, ears, nose mouth and chin are unattractive. Teeth contribute significantly to attractiveness. Women with moderately prominent teeth are attractive because they look as though they are smiling. People who are happy and successful are more attractive than people who are unhappy and unsuccessful. All these preferences are quite automatic and therefore probably inner me determined.

Sexual attraction

Sexual attraction is a state of pleasurable interest in a person, most usually of the opposite gender. At the stage of attraction the progression to actual sexual intercourse remains only a possibility, but even at this stage, the germ of such an objective is present (to the inner me). Sexual attraction is an evolved (inner me) function for bringing male and female members of a species together. Animals of the same species are programmed to respond to specific smells, sounds and appearances. In humans, as in most animals, the genders are physically distinct and this physical distinction intensifies the attraction between them. Singh (1994) has carried out a number of studies that clearly show that men are attracted most to women whose waist-to-hip ratio is 0.70 or less. However, a recent study showed that hunter-gatherer men in Tanzania prefer women with a higher waist-to-hip ratio (Marlowe and Westman, 2001); and another recent study showed that an attractive face overrides the waist-to-hip ratio (Furnham et al., 2001). It seems likely that other preferred ratios, like large breasts and a narrow torso, could also be demonstrated.

Generally, men find female characteristics appealing, and women find male characteristics appealing. Consequently, at an outer me level, women tend to exaggerate their female characteristics and men tend to exaggerate their male characteristics. I (outer me) do not decide to be sexually attracted to a particular woman. I just find that I am. I can note the characteristics of the woman who has attracted me and conclude that this must be the kind of woman that the inner me prefers. I might even reach a conclusion about why the inner me prefers women of this kind. I might then start to tell people that this is the kind of woman I prefer; but I would only be guessing.

Modifying the appearance so as to be attractive

Throughout history, women, and to a lesser extent, men, have modified their appearance, particularly their facial appearance in order to be what they consider, rightly or wrongly, is more attractive. In effect, their aim, albeit an unconscious one, is to be more sexually arousing. Increasingly, women are resorting to cosmetic surgery in order that their bodies should conform to the condition and shape that they believe men find arousing. By such surgery they can reduce the signs of aging, eliminate deformities, remove fat from places where they think it should not be and introduce simulated fat into places where they think it should be. Even if a man (outer me) is aware that a woman's body has been changed in this way, he (inner me) can still be aroused by it.

Perfume

Human skin, in common with the skin of most other animals, produces natural odours, particularly in those parts of the body where hair grows. In fact, the hair facilitates the spread of the oily substances that smell. The oily substances are produced by glands called apocrine glands, and these are particularly active from adolescence onwards. It seems likely that, until recent times, such odours had the effect of increasing sexual attractiveness. In recent times, in a number of Western countries, humans have become so pre-occupied with cleanliness that these body odours have become interpreted (by the outer me) as indicative of dirtiness and have ceased to be considered attractive; in fact, deodorants are worn to dispel them. These natural odours have been replaced by artificially produced perfumes that mostly incorporate the smells of flowers. They are sufficiently like natural odours to have an arousing effect. Interestingly, perfumes smell differently on different people, so the person's natural odour becomes acceptable and arousing, provided it is combined with, or perhaps masked by, an artificial perfume. Perfumes are equally arousing to men and women.

Clothing and sexual attraction

Clothing plays a major role in the sexual attractiveness of women than it does of men. In marketing terms, clothing is packaging, and one of the objects of packaging is to make what is packaged appear more appealing than it really is. A physically unattractive woman can appear attractive in carefully selected clothing. Through the ages, women have used clothing as a means of positive deception. They have used corsets to make their waists look thinner, padding and reinforcements to make their breasts and bottoms look larger and more shapely. Even though the outer me knows that it is being deceived, the inner me is still responsive to these deceptions. Pinker (1997) observed that we (inner me) are inclined to imagine that the body beneath the clothing is more beautiful than it really is. This is part of the inner me's tendency to fill in the gaps. Whatever clues or hints the inner me receives it elaborates upon. Thus, men may be more aroused by women in clothes than by women who are nude; and apparently, men on a nudist beach sometimes fantasise about what the women might look like in clothes.

Sexual arousal

A fine line divides sexual attraction from sexual arousal. Sexual arousal is a more intense and more emotional response than sexual attraction. In arousal there is the perception that sexual intercourse is likely. People can be aroused by reading about sexual intercourse or watching simulated sex in a movie. To the inner me, this is close enough to the real thing to cause arousal. Arousal is entirely inner me. I simply find myself being aroused. I (outer me) can observe those things that apparently have aroused me and I can conclude from this that the inner me finds them arousing. I (outer me) cannot will myself to be aroused, though I can choose to recall memories or think thoughts that I suspect will arouse me, or I can place myself in situations where I suspect that arousal will happen.

Adolescence

Sexual arousal is most intense at adolescence and during early adult life, when the bodies of males and females become distinctly different, and when they are best equipped for sexual reproduction. The more rapid increase in sexual behaviour in male adolescents has, in part, been attributed to their higher testosterone levels. Women also find that testosterone increases their arousability. Sexual arousal promotes anatomical and physiological changes that both intensify attractiveness and promote sexual intercourse.

Sex and the endocrine system

The importance of the endocrine system is that it produces hormones that enter the bloodstream so they can rapidly effect changes at a number of sites around the body. Hormones play a vital role in the development of sexual differences and in sexual arousability. In a study of 18 male pseudohermaphrodites, who were born looking like girls and reared as girls, 16 (89 per cent) changed at puberty to a male gender role, despite parental consternation and considerable social pressure not to. The study concluded that it was the extent of exposure to hormonal rather than cultural influences that finally determined the sexual identity and behaviour in the sample (Imperato-McGinley et al., 1979).

Eccles (1989, pages 110–111) described how the hypothalamus produces a follicular stimulating hormone releasing factor that causes the pituitary to secrete follicular stimulating hormone (FSH). This activates the oestrogen production of the ovaries. The raised oestrogen evokes female libido by its action upon the hypothalamo-limbic system. The gonadotrophins stimulate the biosynthesis of testosterone by the testes. The gonadal biosynthesis of testosterone is also regulated via the hypothalamo-pituitary-gonadal axis by a negative feedback mechanism. When the concentration of androgens in the circulating blood falls the release of luteinising hormone-releasing hormone (LHRH) by the hypothalamus is increased and, in consequence, there is an increased release of gonadotrophins from the anterior pituitary (Neumann and Kalmus, 1991). Increasing testosterone levels leads to an increase in sexual activity (Knussman et al., 1986).

Denial and arousability

It is a general feature of inner me functioning that the threat of the denial of an objective intensifies the hunger for it. This applies to sexual arousal in both men and women. When one partner appears to be losing interest, or showing interest in another, the other becomes more aroused. When one appears easy to mate with, the other may lose interest. Therefore, sometimes one partner will intentionally play hard to get in order to intensify the other's desire. Uncertainty is provocative and such teasing is an important component of seduction.

Sexual arousal in women

That which arouses women is not the same as that which arouses men, and men are not always aware of this. Women are more likely to find male nudity threatening than arousing and women rarely seek excitement by looking at photographs of naked men (Pinker, 1997). A woman is more affected by romance and to the way she is treated than by provocation. More than a man, a woman will find watching a romantic movie or reading a romantic novel arousing. She will respond to being treated gently and respectfully, being made to feel special, to kindness, politeness, understanding and tenderness; to being paid compliments and given treats, surprises and presents. In effect, she is judging, though perhaps not consciously, the suitability and trustworthiness of the man, the likelihood that he will be protective, supportive and caring. Perversely, the reverse of all these things can also sometimes be arousing.

Women's clothing and sexual arousal in men

In many Western countries, women use clothing to convey ease of access. It is difficult to write this because it is considered unmentionable, and making it explicit, like explaining a joke, detract from its effectiveness; however, it does appear that the inner me responds emotionally to signs of ease of access or the possibility of access. Skirts are interpreted by the inner me as being easy to lift. Low-cut or open necklines appear easy to get into. The resemblance of the cleavage to the genitalia must surely be significant. Garments that are thin or can be seen through create the impression that penetration is a possibility. Women's clothing also represent a challenge. By covering their bodies with clothes, women provoke men into wanting to gain access to them. The principle that denial is provocative applies here too. Any sign of change, like a woman opening a button, pulling down a zip or lifting a hem will arouse the inner me. Even when the exposure is not actively induced by the woman, as when her dress is caught in the wind, the inner me will respond by being aroused. In this respect, the inner me is quite automatic: When the sensory input is adequate it will respond.

Women's clothing is arranged in a series of layers, and the removal of each layer creates a degree of exposure. A woman may sometimes keep on her overcoat not because she is cold but because of what removing it may convey. Women's underwear has particular significance, because it represents the final stage of the exposing process. Underwear is a private and special kind of clothing which, in most areas of social interaction, is kept concealed. A woman does not permit a man to see her in her underwear unless she trusts him. Underwear is frequently thin and flimsy and easy to remove. It conveys to the man that he has almost reached his goal, and because of this, it is especially arousing to him. The word "knickers" is highly emotive because it represents the final barrier to entry. Because of its usual significance, men even find women's underwear arousing, when it is on display in a shop, or hanging on a washing line. Women's soiled underwear may be arousing because it bears evidence of having been worn. Some sex shops actually sell soiled underwear.

Nudity and near nudity when sex is not invited

Despite the general understanding that nudity is an invitation to sex, there are situations in which women are able to be nude or nearly nude without inviting sex. On naturist beaches, and sometimes even in public parks, men and women are allowed to be naked. Somehow here, the outer me has to convince the inner me that sex is not on offer. Beside swimming pools and on bathing beaches, a form of minimal garment called swimwear conveys the same message. For this to be possible, swimwear has to be qualitatively different from underwear. Wearing underwear, which has the same degree of exposure, in these situations *is* sexually arousing; as is wearing swimwear in situations other than beside a swimming pool.

Controlled exposure

In the dance of the seven veils, Salome became progressively more exposed. With the removal of each veil, she generated in the men who watched her a new surge of arousal. When strippers do the same, the inner me responds even though the outer me knows it is being manipulated. In certain carefully controlled establishments men pay to observe and even interact with women who are nude or nearly nude. Though sexually aroused by the women, they are not allowed to act upon their arousal. In recent years, women have paid to have similar experiences with men, but it is unclear whether they are affected in the same way.

The displacement of sexual arousal

The inner me is capable of responding to other bodily gaps or orifices (cleavage, crossed legs, gaps between the toes or fingers, and the umbilicus) as though they were the vagina. The orifices of the face (eyes, nostrils, lips and ears) have erotic significance because they are in full view. Women display or adorn them, and adjust the degree of separation of the legs, fingers, eyelids and lips as a form of provocation. This substitution of a non-desired object for a desired one was called displacement by Freud (1902). It occurs in dreams (Chapter 17) and sometimes in art (Chapter 18).

The inhibition of men's responses to sexual provocation

Many women would object to the suggestion that their choice of clothing is largely directed towards inducing men to have sex with them, and to the extent that it does not normally have this effect, they would be right. However, the pleasurable response that their clothing evokes in men is probably because the inner me interprets their clothing in this way. This being said, it should be acknowledged that, in civilised societies, the understanding is that, however provocative the dress of women may be, men are not entitled to act upon it, unless there is a further, more explicit, invitation from the woman. Such understanding is reinforced by severe legal restraints and heavy punishments imposed upon men who sexually harass, indecently assault or rape women. At an outer me level, men have to learn, though it is never explicitly stated, that they are not expected, or permitted to act upon their arousal, and they need to impose restraints upon what to the inner me is an invitation. Thornhill and Palmer (2000) have proposed that young men should receive instruction so they do not mistake a woman's friendly comment or tight blouse as an invitation to have sex.

Respecting the conventions

The inhibition of men's sexual responsiveness to women's sexual provocations has enabled women to behave openly in a sexually provocative manner as part of their normal social interactions, and this has contributed to a general social cohesiveness; but such an arrangement is not without its dangers. The understanding that sex cannot happen unless women grant men permission affords women considerable power. Men, particularly young men, often find attractive women frightening. This is partly because they need to suppress their arousal and partly their fear of rejection.

Women and rape

The normality and acceptability of sexual provocation by women places them in a position of vulnerability. They are physically weaker than men and are always in danger of men forcing themselves upon them. Rape is an expression of male domination. During periods of war, invading armies freely indulge in raping women. In the Russian invasion of Germany, in 1945, two million women were reported to have been raped, and a substantial minority, if not a majority, appear to have suffered multiple rape (Beevor, 2002). In rape, the convention that the man must wait for permission for sexual intercourse to be granted by the woman is broken. The man is sexually aroused but the woman is not. As the man overcomes the woman's resistance his excitement intensifies and he usually reaches orgasm. The fact that the woman finds the experience of being raped extremely disturbing is so obvious that it may seem offensive to write it, but it is also, from a scientific viewpoint, an important fact. The woman experiences it as a violation of her private self. Her sense of personal pride is shattered and she feels used, insulted, humiliated, soiled and shamed. Following it, she is profoundly shocked and intensely emotional and may vomit. She may suffer an enduring loss of confidence and an inability to trust anyone, but particularly a man to come close to her. Commonly she hates the man who raped her and wants him to be punished. Her disturbance may persist for months or even years afterwards. She may never feel the same about herself again. She may have nightmares and disturbing flashbacks of the event.

Thornhill and Palmer (2000) maintain that rape, although inexcusable, must be viewed as a natural biological phenomenon. They point out that young women at the peak of their childbearing years are over-represented among rape victims, and conclude that this suggests that reproduction is the prime motivation. They also point out that rape occurs in other species.

Prostitution

In prostitution, women permit sex in exchange for money. Although women do not like prostitution, it is important to register that they do not experience the same adverse reaction to it that they do to being raped. Although the woman does not desire the man she offers sex to, she does not feel invaded by him because he has agreed to make the concession of paying her money. This is sufficient to enable her to feel that she is in control.

Sexual excitement

Sexual excitement is a stage beyond sexual arousal. It marks the attainment of the ultimate goal of all that has gone before, and consequently it is highly emotional. It is simply the body's automatic (inner me) preparation for intercourse. For the man, it is induced when the woman's normal restraints are removed and, directly or indirectly, her permission is granted. For the woman, it is provoked largely by actual physical contact, particularly in certain sensitive areas. Although, for both the man and the woman, excitement is enhanced by penetration, orgasm can occur for either without penetration, and can be induced even without the presence of the other, by fantasy and self-stimulation.

Men imprisoned for sexual offences have had erections when shown appropriately provocative photographs, even though they (outer me) knew that this may prolong their period of detention. An intelligent, young woman told me that she was reading a Mills & Boon novel and noticed her vagina becoming wet. She was shocked that what she considered to be such a trashy novel could have had this effect upon her, and she (outer me) shouted at herself (inner me), "What are you doing?" Another woman recalled how she had had a similar experience while being held in terror at knife point by a rapist (Parkyn, 2000). All that concerned the inner me was that sex was a possibility; so it had prepared her for it.

The sex act is almost 100 per cent inner me. In fact, it may become inhibited if the outer me tries to intervene. The autonomic nervous system (the most basic component of the inner me) takes complete control. An emotional state akin to fear is induced, accompanied by increased muscle tone, trembling, quickening of the pulse and breathlessness. The penis becomes erect, the clitoris swells, the breasts enlarge, the nipples become protuberant and the vaginal secretion increases. The excitement is increased by stimulation of the penis, the breast and the clitoris. Excitement culminates in orgasm that is accompanied by spasmodic movements for the woman and ejaculation for the man. At the point of climax, both the man and the woman experience intense euphoria followed by relaxation, inertia and sometimes sadness.

Pregnancy and birth

Women sometimes say that they can tell within a matter of days that they are pregnant, though it is hard for them to say what exactly they feel. On the other hand, some women can reach an advanced state of pregnancy, even to the point of going into labour, without realising that they are pregnant. The process of labour is predominantly controlled by the automatic nervous system. However hard she tries, the woman cannot prevent the process of birth going ahead, though she can augment it by voluntary (outer me) effort.

Child rearing

The rearing of young is a further stage in the reproductive process. Plants, of course, do not rear their young, neither do most fish, insects, reptiles and amphibians. Birds rear their young intensively, but over a brief period. Some mammals rear their young over periods of years, and humans rear their young over the longest period of all. In animals that do rear their young, there are innate responses in both the young and the parents that enable the parents and young to recognise each other and stay in close proximity. Parent birds create nests, protect their young against predators, seek food and return it to their young. The young have innate strategies for eliciting care and parents have innate responses to signs of distress in their young.

Adult humans respond to the smallness and helplessness of their babies. To a lesser extent, they respond to the smallness and helplessness of other people's babies, and also the smallness and helplessness of the young of other animals. The fondness of humans for pets is, to a large extent, an extension of their natural parenting disposition. They often treat and speak to their pets as though they were children and pets have acquired innate behaviours that evoke a parental response in adults. Babies and young children too, of course, have innate ways of behaving towards adults that evoke parental responses.

The sexual arousal of adults by children

The inner me is capable of being sexually aroused by children, sometimes even by infants. Sometimes parents are sexually aroused by their own children, but it is much commoner for step-parents to be aroused by their partner's children. Parents do not consciously suppress their sexual feelings towards their children, so does the parental in-between me do so? Some children who have had sexual experiences with their parents begin to behave in a sexually provocative way towards other adults. Some adults, particularly men, are sexually aroused by other people's children. The appeal of children is that they are less intimidating than adults. Because children are weaker than adults, some adults compel them to submit to sexual behaviour. For these adults, the compulsion to become sexually involved with the child overrides feelings of parental concern or adult responsibility. Often, children who have been so abused remain deeply traumatised for the rest of their lives. This is similar to the woman's response to being raped. Adult women, and sometimes even adult men, adopt child-like behaviour as a way of evoking parental responses in their partners. Such responses become easily transformed into sexual responses. Adult women sometimes try to look like small girls as a form of sexual provocation.

Do children have sexual feelings towards adults?

Although humans are born with the capacity to become sexually aroused, children appear to show little interest in sexual behaviour until adolescence; though Freud (1905a) wrote a great deal about childhood sexuality. My recollection of my own childhood is that sexual feelings towards both girls and women were always around, though they did not have the intensity of adult feelings. Girls sometimes behave seductively towards their fathers and other male adults, and this may cause their fathers and other male adults to become aroused by them. It seems unlikely that these girls are trying to induce these men to have sex with them. It is more probable that they have discovered this as a way of gaining their affection. It is less common for boys to behave seductively towards their mothers or other female adults.

8   Relating

Evolutionists would argue that all the human objectives have been covered in Chapters 6 and 7; so why have I introduced a third chapter? I have done so because I consider there to be an alternative way of viewing objectives, and that is according to the way that people relate. Although it ought to be possible to reduce all human attitudes and behaviour to serve the two basic objectives of survival and reproduction, the lives of humans have become so much more complicated than, and so different from, those of any other animal that it is unhelpful to try to force all forms of human relating into one of these two very broad categories.

Relating is vastly more complex in humans than in any other animal. In fact Humphrey (1983) has argued that one reason why the human brain became so large was in order to make possible the processing of the interactions that took place within emerging social groups. Relating was the subject of my previous two books (Birtchnell, 1993/96, 1999/2002). In these, I concluded that people relate because they have relating objectives. I shall propose that these, like the survival and the reproductive objectives, originate in, and are controlled and monitored by, the inner me. Shortly, I shall consider the relationship between the relating objectives and the survival and reproductive ones but, for now, suffice it to say that they cut across and, to some extent, overlap with, them.

My starting point will be the general principle that the more rigid and instinct-driven behaviour of animals has been replaced in humans by general dispositions towards certain fundamental forms of behaviour, upon which are based learned skills that are more suited to specific environments and are more adaptable to changing life circumstances. Somewhat serendipitously, in a series of articles (Birtchnell, 1987, 1990, 1994), I hit upon the idea that human relating behaviour can usefully be classified within the framework of two intersecting axes; the one, usually considered to be the horizontal one, concerns moving towards or moving away from others; the other, usually considered to be the vertical one, concerns relating to others from a position of relative strength or relating to others from a position of relative weakness. These four ways of relating I have called closeness, distance, upperness and lowerness. They are, I maintain, the four basic dispositions from which all forms of human relating can be derived.

This system of classification can also be applied to non-humans, even though their relating behaviour is much more rigidly set within a range of instinctual actions. That it can indicates that the relating classification is somehow superimposed upon, or interwoven with, the survival and reproductive one; but certainly in humans, it is much more useful in analysing what people do to each other. All animals are, in relation to other animals, sometimes close, sometimes distant, sometimes upper and sometimes lower. It seems likely then that the system had its origins in the relating of animals and became, through the course of evolution, modified and further developed in humans. If this is so, there must be biological advantages to each of the four forms of relating (relating positions), for both animals and humans. Therefore, no one form of relating should be considered preferable to, or more important than, any other; and there must be occasions when any one of the positions is the most appropriate.

Do plants relate?

Relating depends heavily upon mobility, which is why it is not a prominent feature of plant life. However, there are some characteristics of plants that could be viewed as forms of relating. Many plant species grow in masses, a form of closeness, which must be to their advantage. Plants manifest closeness when they attract insects and small birds to themselves for pollination and the broadcasting of their seed. Insectivorous plants manifest closeness by their brightly coloured, but sticky or entrapping leaves, by which they collect insects for their own nourishment. Plants manifest distance when they protect themselves from animals by thorns, stings, or an unpleasant smell or flavour. There are upper plants that block the light from and consequently kill the plants beneath them, and lower plants that are parasitic upon other plants. The point about demonstrating that plants relate, even though they do not have brains and do not move, is that it stresses that relating is simply that which plants, animals and even humans do. We relate in certain ways because we have evolved in order to do so.

The four relating positions in animals

Let us examine then how the four positions can be applied to the relating behaviour of animals. Taking first closeness: Many kinds of fish, birds, insects and animals operate together in shoals, flocks, herds and swarms. In this, they form a more effective force both in defence and attack, and some groups of animals work cooperatively together. Even the most solitary of animals need to come together, at least briefly, for the purpose of sexual reproduction and, in some species, the parents remain together to share in the rearing of the young. For protection, the young need to stay close to the parents and to each other.

Some animal species are naturally solitary (distant) and this in itself carries certain advantages, particularly in environments where food is scarce. Solitary animals are more difficult for predators to find. Distance (taking flight) is a means of escaping from predators. In many species, distance (or, more correctly, keeping other animals at a distance) is a means of defining and defending territories for the purpose of both feeding and breeding. Even in a group, maintaining a degree of distance from the other members of the group reduces infestation and infection. In species that rear their young, when the young have attained an adequate level of maturity, they are expelled from the nest (pushed into distance) and encouraged to fend for themselves. Distance may also take the form of exploring new territories, seeking new sources of food and seeking a mate.

Upperness is a feature of the struggle for survival. It is what evolutionists call fitness. The most upper animals are the fittest, the strongest and the better fighters, the most likely to kill and the least likely to be killed. In animal hierarchies, they get first access to food and get the best mates, and are protected by being surrounded by the least upper ones. By staying in the centre of the shoal, flock, herd or swarm, they are the least likely to get eaten by predators.

It might be considered that lower animals, being the least powerful and the least strong, are always at risk of being trampled upon, killed or ejected from the group. Although this sometimes does happen, the lower animals in a group are mostly tolerated and permitted to survive for without the lower ones, the upper ones would have none to be upper to. They survive by being deferential. They gain protection from remaining in the proximity of the upper ones. When the upper animals have taken their fill of the animals they have caught, and eaten, they allow the lower ones access to the remainder. In most animal species, the females adopt a position of no threat, even helplessness (lowerness), in relation to the males, in order to allow access to themselves. The young adopt a posture of helplessness in relation to their parents in order to induce them to protect and feed them.

The four relating positions in humans

In humans, closeness includes friendship formation, interdependence, sharing, communication, making revelations to and showing an interest in, identifying with, sympathising and empathising; distance includes self-protection and self-preservation, defence against invasion and intrusion, the creation of secure boundaries, privacy, the development of a secure sense of self, communication with the self, individuality and originality; upperness includes judging, managing, leading, guiding, teaching, advising, praising, consoling, helping, protecting and caring for; and lowerness includes obeying, respecting, admiring, looking up to, seeking and accepting judgement, leadership guidance, advice, help, protection and care. Lowerness is much more apparent and beneficial in humans than it is in any other species.

It might be argued that replacing the two objectives of relating and reproducing with the four of relating represents no major advance; but it does make a difference, because it then becomes easier to accommodate those forms of relating (like passing judgement upon and assuming responsibility for) that are exclusively human into an appropriate category. Since each of the four relating positions is generic, it can embrace a broad range of attitudes and forms of behaviour. Taking distance as an example, its various forms, like fleeing from an enemy, exploring, erecting barriers, developing a separate identity, creating a private space, being original, being pleasurably alone, meditating and keeping secrets, are united by the single, abstract and meaningful concept, distance which, and this is very strange, the inner me seems capable of comprehending.

The connection between the four relating positions and the two objectives of survival and reproduction

I refer to the four relating positions as the four relating objectives. As I have stated, I do not consider them to be additional to the objectives of survival and reproduction, merely developments out of them. Many survival mechanisms, like temperature regulation, the avoidance of danger and feeding, would not normally be regarded as forms of relating. However, it is not stretching the definition of distance too far to regard it as a preoccupation with the centrality of the self, relating to the self, looking after the needs of the self, indulging the self, protecting the self, respecting the self and holding the self in high esteem. However, some aspects of closeness also have relevance for survival, such as people join forces in defence or attack, sharing, being mutually supportive. Upperness has obvious relevance for survival, since it is the driving force behind competing, defeating, winning and gaining supremacy. Yet lowerness too contributes to survival. People need to put themselves in the hands of others, seek their advice, help and encouragement; and the young need to have strategies for coercing others to protect, care for, comfort and nourish them.

The processes involved in the attainment of the objectives of reproduction have a more obvious connection to relating. They include the complexities of human courtship and living together as a family. The striving for closeness, in all its forms, is central to this; but distance has its relevance too. Couples need their own personal space and privacy, and need to be able to respect each other's differentness and separateness. The relevance of human upper to lower relating is less obvious. While in many cultures, the man maintains a dominant position in relation to the woman, in certain others the arrangement is one of interdependence in which the man is upper to the woman in some respects and the woman is upper to the man in others.

States of relatedness

The end point of a relating objective I call a state of relatedness. When I am being close, distant, upper or lower I am in a state of relatedness. A state of relatedness must be something that the inner me is capable of recognising. It must be aware of whether or not I am in one. It must be capable of generating a feeling of needing to be in one, of generating encouraging emotion (expectant excitement) when I am getting close to one and generating discouraging emotion (hopelessness, despair) when I am drifting away from one.

It is helpful to view relating in the way that I might view eating. I become hungry for each state of relatedness in the way that I become hungry for food. When I have been deprived of a state of relatedness for any length of time my need for it intensifies, just as when I am hungry, my need for food intensifies. Taking closeness as an example if, say, I have been working in a solitary place, I begin to long for human contact. As the days go by, this longing intensifies, until there comes a point when almost anyone would do, even just to see someone. This is analogous to the man who becomes so hungry that he would eat anything.

In relating, as with food, I can be in either an appetitive or a consummatory state. In an appetitive state, I am needful of relating to someone in a particular way, just as I might be needful of a particular kind of food. I have an obsession with it and I strive to attain it. In a consummatory state, I have it and I am indulging in it.

A state of relatedness can extend over any time period from a minute or two to an entire lifetime. At any moment, I can be in any number of states of relatedness in relation to any number of people. I may be close to my wife, distant from my neighbour, upper to my children and lower to my solicitor. I may be in various degrees of any one of these.

There is much variation in the form that any particular state of relatedness can take. I can be close to one person by exchanging ideas, close to another by being kind and understanding, and close to a third by being in love. I can be upper to one person by giving instructions, upper to another by leading or teaching and upper to a third by being helpful. Because of this variation in the form that a state of relatedness can take, I can relate to any given person in opposite ways at the same time. I can be close by listening sympathetically, but distant by keeping ideas to myself. I can be upper by giving instructions and lower by feeling reassured. The inner me seems capable of keeping track of all this.

Sources of states of relatedness

Continuing the food analogy, I need to have sources of states of relatedness in the way that I have sources of food. When I need closeness, I need to know where to go, or whom to go to, to get it. Some people rely heavily on just a few close friends or relations, while others take small amounts of closeness from a large number of acquaintances. In order to get distance, I need to have ways of shutting others out or keeping others at bay, or I may have my own private places where I can go to be myself. Some people derive upperness from one particular ability, like being an expert craftsperson, while others derive it from a range of abilities. Some people enhance their upperness by surrounding themselves with people of low ability, while others prefer to compete within a broader context. Sources of lowerness are people to go to for help or advice or people to look up to and rely upon.

Being related to

I both relate to others, and am related to by others. On the horizontal axis, the relating of the other tends to be complementary; that is if I am close to someone, that person is close to me; and on the vertical axis it tends to be reciprocal, that is if I am upper to someone, that person is lower to me. Interestingly, my state of relatedness may be as much to do with another person's relating to me as with my relating to her/him. Someone can give me that state of relatedness called closeness by relating closely to me and can give me that state of relatedness called lowerness by relating in an upper way towards me. Mostly, the people I relate to also relate to me, but this is not always so. I may feel close to someone who does not feel close to me, or be admiring of someone who is quite indifferent to me.

Relating fatigue

Gardner (1991) once drew the analogy of satisfying relating needs to filling buckets. When my closeness bucket is empty, I get the urge to fill it, and when it is full I enjoy a sense of well-being. When it starts to overflow, I get the urge to turn off the flow. The more it overflows, the more desperate I become to turn it off. This state of desperation I call relating fatigue.

A consequence of relating objectives being on two axes is that when I have had too much of one end of an axis, I may start longing for the other end. Continuing with the example of the solitary place, it is quite possible that when I first arrived there, I experienced it as blissful: not a soul for as far as the eye could see; just me, alone with myself. Yet after a month or so, I might find myself longing to get away from it, starting to suffer from distance fatigue.

In the reverse direction, I might anticipate with pleasure going on holiday and sharing a house with a group of friends; spending all day together, and talking long into the night, exchanging ideas; but however good the company may be, gradually, the pleasure will pall. I will find myself thinking, what wouldn't I give to have an evening to myself. Eventually, I just cannot bear to spend another day with these people. Closeness fatigue has set in.

On the vertical axis, I may strive for a position of seniority. For a time I enjoy the power, being top dog, being in control, taking charge, being looked up to and respected; but a time will come when upperness fatigue sets in, when I will long for someone else to take over; someone to tell *me* what to do and take responsibility for *me*. After a period of this, lowerness fatigue may set in, and I may begin to long to be back in control again.

The role of the inner me in regulating relating

The inner me seems able to recognise what closeness, distance, upperness and lowerness are. Considering what a diversity of behaviours each must include, this is an astonishing capability. Somehow, it must hold the abstract concept that incorporates the very essence of each, so that it can recognise one in whatever form it may assume; and it can also recognise if one is being feigned, as when I (outer me) am trying to convince myself that someone likes me when really I (inner me) know that s/he does not; or when someone assures me that s/he is trying to help me when something tells me (inner me) that s/he is not.

When the inner me generates the needfulness for a particular state of relatedness, I experience a condition that is akin to hunger. That particular state begins to feel desirable. I feel restless and try to seek ways of attaining it. I think of possible sources of it. As I get closer to it or further from it, the inner me generates encouraging emotions or discouraging emotions that keep me on course. Once the state has been attained, the inner me withdraws the feeling of needfulness for it. I now enter a consummatory phase in which I pleasurably indulge in it.

What provokes the inner me to impel me towards a particular state of relatedness? Obviously, circumstances play a part. If my car breaks down, I need the help of someone to fix it, that is I need a particular form of lowerness. If my neighbour's dog has been barking loudly all day, I need to go and knock on his/her door to complain. That is, I need some distance. Fatigue of one state may propel me towards the opposite state.

Finally, there is reactive relating. That is, if someone relates to me in a particular way, how do I respond? If someone talks to me (seeks closeness), do I talk back? If someone I like walks away (seeks distance), do I chase after them? If someone asks me for advice (seeks lowerness), am I inclined to offer it (assume a position of upperness)? If someone insults me (pushes me into lowerness) do I insult them back?

A possible location for the control of all the objectives, including the relating objectives, is that which Panksepp (1999) has called the seeking system. It connects the midbrain to the limbic system and the frontal lobes. Panksepp maintained that this system instigates goal-seeking behaviours and an organism's appetitive interactions with the world.

The underpinnings of the attainment of objectives

Goal-directed action operates from the objectives outwards, and there can be no attainment of objectives without an organism being geared up to attaining them, and having a coherent collection of neural networks that ensure that all parts of the organism work together in a coordinated fashion. Mobility is an important aid to relating. Mobility enables me to move closer to or further away, to move into a position of power and influence or to move into a position of weakness and needfulness. Thus, when the inner me puts out the directive, get closer, the body is stimulated into acting in a way that enables me to move towards the person I choose to get close to. Obviously, relating is not simply a matter of attaining a position in space. Language is another aid to relating. I relate by speaking; but of course I can relate without moving or speaking, by simply feeling close or distant or whatever.

The role of the outer me in relating

While it is the inner me that generates the need for particular states of relatedness, it is the more flexible, adaptable, ingenious and scheming outer me that devises the interpersonal strategies that enable me to attain them. It makes long-term plans for ensuring relating success. It comprehends the characteristics of the people I relate to. It recognises their strengths and limitations. It learns what works and what does not work with them, and what pleases and what displeases them. It uses tact and discretion, and even deception, and, over time, it learns what is and is not the most likely way of attaining and maintaining each particular state.

Converting dispositions into specific forms of relating

If it is so that we are born simply with general dispositions towards these four forms of relating, we need during our early years to build upon these general dispositions and develop more specific capabilities. This we achieve with varying degrees of success. Essentially, we need to have a pleasurable exposure to each state of relatedness, and we need to feel comfortable in each, and to develop the competence to attain each. All of this depends upon the influential figures in our childhood being good enough at relating themselves so that they are able to provide us with this pleasurable exposure in order to encourage us in developing this competence. This way, we gradually become confident in our ability to relate in any of the four ways as and when we need to. A person who is capable, competent and confident in each of the four relating positions, I describe as being versatile. Such a person should have no difficulty functioning in any interpersonal situation.

Negative relating

Few people attain a level of total versatility and most are deficient in one or more forms of relating. Competent relating in a particular direction is called positive relating, and relating that falls short of complete competence is called negative relating. A person may relate negatively because (1) s/he was born with a diminished capability of relating in a particular way (2) s/he has not had pleasurable exposure to a particular state of relatedness or (3) s/he has never acquired the capability of relating in that particular way.

Some people who are deficient in a particular form of relating simply avoid relating in that way. This is called avoidant relating. When they do this, they tend to cling anxiously to the opposite form of relating for fear that others will try to coax them out of this relating position towards the dreaded, opposite position. Thus a person who is deficient in closeness will try to keep distant from people, and will become anxious, and withdraw even further, when others try to get close; and a person who is deficient in distance will try to stay close to people, and will become anxious and cling, when others try to leave.

Those who are unsure of their capability of relating in a particular way will make an attempt to relate in that way, but will be uncertain of their ability to hold on to that state of relatedness. This is called insecure relating. A person who is unsure of this ability to get close will make an attempt to get close, but will be constantly afraid that the other will go away.

There are those who adopt a particular relating position irrespective of whether this is acceptable to the person with whom they are relating. Either they are insensitive to the feelings of the other or they are not concerned about what the other feels. This is called egocentric or imposed relating. A person who is determined to get closeness will force her/himself upon another with little concern for whether closeness is what the other wants. Being the recipient of this form of relating can be depressing because it is denying the person that form of being related to that s/he may really want.

Finally, there are those who attain and maintain a particular relating position by playing upon the guilt of those to whom they relate. This is called coercive relating. A person will get into a close position, and will make the other feel so bad about breaking up the relationship that s/he cannot bring her/himself to do it, even though s/he may want to. She will make remarks like, "You know I can't live without you," "I could never manage on my own," and "You will never leave me will you?"

People who relate negatively are restricted in the way that they can relate to others. In turn, they restrict the way that others can relate to them. When a versatile person is being related to by a person who relates negatively, s/he is compelled to adopt a style of relating that accommodates the negative relater's negative relating. When parents relate negatively to their children, they prevent their children developing a full range of relating competencies. If a parent cannot get close, the child will not have sufficient exposure to closeness to find it pleasurable or to become competent in close relating. If a parent cannot get lower, the child is constantly forced by the parent into a lower position, so that s/he cannot become competent in upper relating. Hopefully, the child, or even the adult, will interact with others who do not have such relating restrictions and will make good her/his relating deficiencies with them. Relating therapy (Birtchnell, 1999/2002) is a specific method for helping a person to do this.

The intermediate relating positions

The two relating axes seem to function independently. My relating position on the horizontal axis can be quite independent of my relating position on the vertical axis; so my relating to someone, or to some group of people, needs to be defined separately for each axis. In relation to my solicitor, I might be lower and distant, but in relation to a consoling friend, I might be lower and close. Since people are constantly relating on both the horizontal and the vertical axes, there are a number of relating styles that result from various combinations of horizontal and vertical relating. Therefore, in addition to the four main relating positions, there are what are called the four intermediate positions. These are called upper close, upper distant, lower close and lower distant. The four main positions and the four intermediate positions together form what is called the interpersonal octagon. Each of the eight positions of the octagon is given a two-word name, the first word referring to the vertical axis and the second referring to the horizontal axis. In the four main positions, where there is no contribution from the other axis, the word neutral is inserted in the two-word name where the word for the other axis would have been; for example a state of pure upperness, with no close or distant component, would be called upper neutral. The octagon is best viewed as if there were two spectra ranging across its upper half and its lower half. Taking first the upper spectrum, upper relating can range from upper distant, through upper neutral to upper close. Upper distant relating includes the more formal and impersonal ways of being upper, like controlling, judging, imposing restrictions and issuing commands; upper neutral relating covers the more intermediate forms such as leading, teaching and advising; and upper close relating includes the more compassionate and caring ways of being upper, like protecting, encouraging and consoling. For each of the eight positions of the interpersonal octagon there are positive forms and negative forms of relating, and these are summarised in Figure 1.

The interpersonal circle

Some readers may be struck by the resemblance between the interpersonal octagon and that which has come to be called the interpersonal circle (Leary, 1957; Kiesler, 1983). Clearly, the two structures are parallel attempts to define the same basic truth, namely that there are two broad categories of relating that are represented by the two main axes. There are however significant differences between both the descriptive terms and the underlying theory of the two structures, and these have been enumerated elsewhere (Birtchnell, 1994; Birtchnell and Shine, 2000). To avoid confusion, no further reference will be made to the circle, but it is acknowledged that it has a considerable literature that readers may wish to consult.

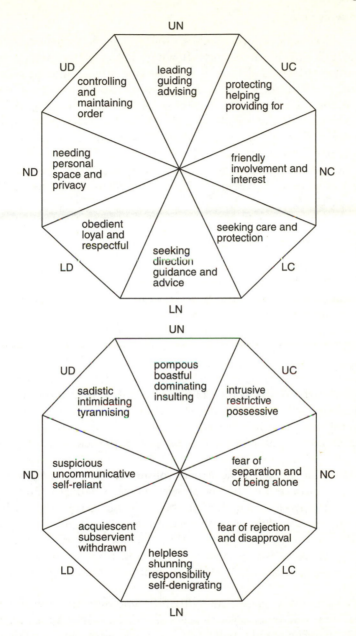

Figure 1 Positive (upper diagram) and negative (lower diagram) forms of relating. The pairs of initial letters are abbreviations for the full names of the octants given in the text.

Source: The diagrams first appeared in Birtchnell, J. The interpersonal octagon: An alternative to the interpersonal circle. *Human Relations*, 47, pages 518 and 524. © The Tavistock Institute, 1994. Reproduced by permission from Sage Publications.

Attachment theory

The reader may wonder how the present theory may relate to the more widely acknowledged attachment theory (Bowlby, 1969). Attachment is clearly a state of relatedness, and there is a secure form that might be considered to be positive relating, and anxious, ambivalent and dismissive forms that might be considered a negative relating. Attachment was originally construed as the relating of a child to a parent, and as such, it would fit into the category of lower closeness. Later, it was expanded to include the relating of one adult to another, and as such, it would fit into the category of neutral closeness. Because it fits into only one quarter of a biaxial system, its scope as a general explanatory theory of relating has to be limited (Birtchnell, 1997).

IS THERE A GENETIC BASIS TO RELATING?

Evidence that people are born with a particular relating deficit is limited, but it seems to be strongest within the horizontal axis. Moir and Jessel (1991) observed that girls have a greater capacity for closeness than boys. They are more sensitive to touch and to sound, even at just a few hours old. They respond better to emotional speech, and they are more easily calmed by a soothing voice. At an early age, girl babies are more interested in communicating with other people than boys, who tend to be more interested in inanimate objects. This early tendency is reflected in the behaviour of adult women and men. When women talk together they tend to be more interested in interpersonal matters, and when men do so they are more interested in technical matters. Challoner (2000) observed that women are generally better than men at identifying the emotion expressed in photographs of faces.

The condition known as autism is considered to be largely genetic in origin. It is characterised by social withdrawal. Challoner (2000) wrote, "While most other schoolchildren are busy playing games with each other, sharing experiences, children with autism are spending most of their time with their own thoughts, investigating not the people but the objects around them" (page 30). As would be expected from what was written in the last paragraph, autism is 10 times more common in boys than it is in girls.

Another condition known as Williams' syndrome (Rosner and Semel, 1998) appears to have an effect that is opposite to that of autism. Children with this condition are unusually disposed to closeness, and are able to perceive when other children are happy or sad. They communicate freely and express both happiness and sadness about other children's feelings.

The brain structures called the amygdalae have long been suspected of being responsible for the recognition of emotion in other people (Calder et al., 1996), though only for fear, anger and disgust. Challoner cited Bauman and

Kemper as showing that the amygdalae of autistic children are smaller than those of normal children, but the amygdalae of Williams' syndrome children are the same size as those of normal children. Challoner cited Baron-Cohen as showing that, according to MRI scans, autistic children, in contrast to normal children, do not use their amygdalae when evaluating facial expression from a photograph.

The possibility exists that genetic factors may also play a part in a person's disposition to relate in a particular way on the vertical axis. Boys tend to be more controlling than girls. Men are more inclined than women to seek positions of high office. Throughout history, and across cultures, there have been far more male leaders than female leaders. In many cultures women are dominated, exploited and abused by men. In relationships between men and women, men are more inclined to adopt the dominant position and, in many relationships, women prefer it that way. The question of whether some people are born leaders and others are born followers has never been thoroughly researched, though some children appear inclined to take the lead from an early age, and since there is a difference between the leadership qualities of men and women, this is always going to be a possibility.

INTERRELATING

The term interrelating is used to describe that which takes place between two people in a relationship. It seems probable that a relationship is most likely to succeed if both people are versatile. That is that either person is able to adopt towards the other whatever form of relating the situation may require. This means that the relationship is flexible and that neither person, due either to her/his own limitations or the limitations of the other, needs to adopt a rigid and permanent role in relation to the other. This way neither runs into, nor is driven into, a state of relating fatigue. Sometimes they can be close and sometimes they can be distant; sometimes one can adopt the upper position and sometimes the other can. Hopefully too, each would be perceptive to the other's relating needs and neither would be inclined to force a particular form of being related to upon the other.

The situation would be quite different if one person or both were limited in their relating capabilities. If one person cannot be close the other needs to stay distant too, and if one person cannot be distant they both have to stay close all of the time. Sometimes one cannot be close and the other cannot be distant. Consequently, each pushes the other towards a more extreme position, so that the distant one becomes increasingly more escaping and the close one becomes increasingly more clinging. On the vertical axis, if one cannot be lower, the other has to agree to be lower all of the time, and if one cannot be upper the other has to be upper all of the time. If both cannot be lower, there is a constant struggle for domination, and if both cannot be upper each tries constantly to lean upon the other.

Limited adjustment is possible when relating deficiencies match. Thus if neither can be distant they stay close all the time and if neither can be close they stay distant all the time. If one cannot be upper and the other cannot be lower the one is always lower and the other is always upper. These rigid relationships survive so long as circumstances do not change.

Part IV

The receptive and responsive me

The three chapters in this part are concerned with taking in, interpreting, responding to, storing and retrieving information. The information cannot be responded to until it has been taken in and interpreted, and it cannot be stored until it has been taken in, interpreted and responded to. All these processes are automatic and unconscious in their execution, and therefore belong to the province of the inner me; but while the processing is inner me, the products of this processing, the sensations, perceptions, emotions and retrieved memories, which are consciously experienced, belong to the province of the outer me.

9   Sensory input

The sensory input of humans is not outstanding compared with that of some other animal species. Compared with many animals, humans have a poor sense of smell. It is significant that the olfactory centre is one of the few brain centres that is smaller in humans than it is in closely related species. Butterflies can pick up the scent of other butterflies over a distance of miles. Whales and dolphins can communicate by sound with members of their own species over a distance of miles. Nocturnal predators are much better at seeing in the dark than humans. On a beach where there are thousands of penguins and their young, the parent penguins can locate their young by recognising the sound that they make. The visual acuity of monkeys that leap from branch to branch at great speed is better than that of humans. Humans have used their ingenuity (outer me) to create devices such as spectacles, microscopes, telescopes, hearing aids, radar, radiography and underwater sonar devices to vastly enhance their sensory input in certain areas.

The sensory system has two parts: the sense organs that register the sensations and convert them into a form that can be transported to the brain, and those areas of the brain that interpret this encoded and transported information. Sensations from the sense organs do not pass straight into consciousness. They pass from the sense organs into information processing centres where they are analysed and made sense of, and only then are they passed on to consciousness. Libet (1981) demonstrated that about half a second of continuous activity in the sensory cortex is needed for a person to become aware of a sensory stimulus. Blackmore (2001) observed that even though consciousness takes half a second to build up, events seem to happen in real time. LeDoux (1998) pointed out that the mental representation of that which we consciously perceive is created by unconscious processes. That is, it gets handed across the border between conscious and unconscious by an unconscious mechanism.

Pinker (1997) observed that information about an object being perceived is scattered across many parts of the cerebral cortex. Therefore, information access requires a mechanism that binds together geographically separated data. Claxton (1998) wrote, "The undermind (inner me) routinely makes all kinds of adjustments to the data it receives before it hands them on to consciousness – because it is usually advantageous to do so" (page 104). He explained that conscious perception is a useful fiction that misrepresents the world around us in our own interests.

In so far as these things happen without my making any conscious decision to cause them to happen, the sensory system is entirely an inner me system. The inner me has the capacity to interpret a complex set of visual stimuli as one complete entity. It does not, as the outer me would, examine what is being experienced piece by piece and, by fitting the pieces together, draw a conclusion about what it is. The process of interpreting what I am experiencing happens in a flash. I have the experience and, immediately, I know what it is that I am experiencing. I see a pineapple and immediately I conclude this is a pineapple. I do not say to myself, as I would if I were functioning at the outer me level, this is a round, hard browny-yellow object with prickles and spiky green leaves shooting out of the top of it. Therefore it must be a pineapple. Normally, I look at a face and know instantly whose face it is. I hear a voice over the telephone and know immediately whose voice it is.

Sensations from within

Sensations from within the body are the means by which the brain gets to know about what is happening in the various parts of the body, in order that it may make responses and adjustments to them. Sensations from within are generally much simpler than sensations from without. Whereas there are many different kinds of smells, tastes, sounds and sights, there are very few kinds of pain. All the brain needs to know is where it is coming from and how intense it is.

Pain

Pain is quite similar to emotion and it is often associated with emotion. Some emotions, like anxiety and depression, are called mental pain. Pain, like anxiety and depression, is a way of registering that all is not well. There are pain receptors in the skin, but also in muscles and internal organs. Strangely, there are none in the brain. Pain receptors somehow respond to tissue fatigue or tissue damage. When certain tissues, like muscle, are overused they begin to hurt. When tissue is damaged chemicals are released that stimulate them. Pain can be registered at various levels of the nervous system. The body can register pain, and respond to it, without the person (outer me) being aware of it. A comatose patient will withdraw a limb that has been pinched. A person can feel pain without it hurting. Damasio (2000) described a patient with a very painful condition of the face called trigeminal neuralgia. After an operation, which produced small lesions in a specific region of the frontal lobe, the patient said the pain was still the same but it did not trouble him any more. Damasio concluded that the actual conscious experience of pain is not necessary, though it does have the important effect of causing the person to rest, immobilise or protect the fatigued or damaged part while the recovery or repair of the damaged part is taking place.

Sensations and physiological functions

Some internal sensations are difficult to define: How could I explain what being "full of gas" feels like? What is it that makes me feel I am about to fart or to vomit; or that I need to pee or to shit? Presumably these are the sensations of the walls of organs being stretched.

Proprioception

By coordinating the information from the proprioceptors around the body I have a perception of where, at any time, the parts of the body, but particularly the head and the limbs, are in space. Because this is an experience I have had from birth, I pay little attention to it, but if through brain or spinal injury I lose this capability, I would experience an unpleasant disconnection from my body.

Intermediate sensations

Some sensations are neither entirely internal nor entirely external. They are part one and part the other, or somewhere in between.

Temperature

There appear to be two ways of registering temperature: there are temperature receptors in the skin that register whether particular areas of the skin are hot or cold, and there is the means by which my brain is made aware of whether my entire body is hot or cold. The temperature receptors in the skin not only register that the area is hot or cold, they also register how hot or how cold I am. If I am too hot or too cold I have an unpleasant subjective experience that urges me (outer me) to move the affected part of the body away. If I am extremely hot or extremely cold, my inner me steps in and the part of the body moves involuntarily. The means by which my brain is aware of the overall temperature of my body can automatically bring into play mechanisms that will increase or lower my body temperature.

Touch

From the touch receptors around the body, I am made aware of my physical contact with someone or something outside of myself. Interestingly, being touched by others is a quite different experience from being touched by myself. When I touch myself, I have two different sensations at the same time: in the place that I am touched, I have the sensation of being touched, and in the place that I do the touching, I have the sensation of touching something. Somehow, if the two sensations coincide, my brain concludes that I have touched myself. When I am touched by something or someone else I only get the single sensation. Somehow, the brain interprets this differently. I cannot tickle myself, even when I do to myself what others do to me when they tickle me.

Touch and sexual excitement

Being touched at all, if it is by a desired person, and if it is intentional, is exciting, but being touched in certain places, which were called by Freud (1905a) the erogenous zones, is particularly exciting. People are able to excite themselves by touching these zones, but are generally more excited when they are touched by someone, or something, else. A woman can be excited by a vibrator or even by sitting on a spin dryer. The genitalia, the breasts and the lips are the most obviously erogenous zones, but different people are sensitive in different places. Being lightly tickled in sensitive places is exciting, but strangely, pain can also be exciting for some people. Being tickled will be further examined in Chapter 19.

Sensing myself

Directing my sense organs on to myself contributes powerfully to my sense of being a person. Not being able to see, hear or smell myself would seriously affect my experience of myself.

Seeing and hearing myself

Because my eyes are in my head, the view of myself I normally have is from above downwards. It is a strange, foreshortened view, but because it is the view I have always had, I do not register its strangeness. There are parts of myself I never see, like my back, the top of my head and the bottom of my feet. Women can only see their breasts from above, and cannot see their genitalia.

The sound of myself that I hear the most is the sound of my voice, but because my larynx is inside my head, and my ears are outside my head, I hear it through the flesh and bones of my face. It is not at all like what other people hear. When I think to myself, I hear, very faintly, the words I am thinking. If this were to stop happening, I would find thinking more difficult.

The simple device of the mirror enables humans to see what they look like from the outside. It also enhances their ability to develop a relationship with themselves. Most animals react to a reflection of themselves as though it were another animal. Some chimpanzees and orang-utans, from adolescence onwards, if they see a mark on their face in a mirror, they will reach up to their face to investigate. It was recently demonstrated (2001) that dolphins also have the ability to recognise themselves in a mirror. Humans can recognise themselves in a mirror from about age 18 months onwards, but how do they know that the face they see is theirs? It continues to feel strange when I look at myself in the mirror, and talking to my reflection feels even stranger.

The tape-recorder enables humans to hear what they sound like from the outside. I was an adult when I first heard myself on a tape-recorder. I knew that it was me because I remembered what I had been saying, but I found it difficult to own the voice I heard. The camcorder enables humans to see and hear themselves from the outside at the same time. This is an experience no human has ever had before. Because of this, there can be no brain mechanism for acknowledging that the person I am seeing and hearing is myself. I was quite old when I first had this experience and I found it disturbing. I responded to it as though it were another person who looked and sounded like myself.

Smelling myself

Most people smell and many people enhance their smell with perfume. Provided my smell stays the same, I do not smell it. Even when I put on perfume, I smell it only for a short time. I smell my own fart, but probably not as strongly as others do, and strangely, because it is my own, I do not find it offensive.

Sensations from without

Sensory input and the environment

Humans map out their environment mainly through sight and sound, and many, totally unconscious and automatic, mental mechanisms are involved in this. These are fully described by Pinker (1997). For both seeing and hearing, the inner me is able to judge how far away an object is by the intensity of the sensory input. If the intensity is high, it assumes that the object is close and if it is low, it assumes it is far away. To make these assumptions, it must know how bright or how loud the object normally is at various distances. I had the experience of thinking that my next door neighbour was speaking outside my living room window. In fact he was speaking through a megaphone at a local fete, some distance away. For seeing, the inner me assumes that objects appear small when they are some distance away and large when they are close up. Again, to make these assumptions, I must know how small or how large particular objects normally look at various distances. The inner me can be fooled if the object is created smaller or larger than it normally is, or if a small object is closer than I think, or a large object is further away than I think. Lying in the garden, I thought I saw a giant fly. In fact it was a normal fly that was much closer to my eye than I realised. For hearing, the inner me assumes that if a sound is louder in the right ear than in the left ear, the source of the sound is somewhere to the left. Again, the inner me can be fooled by artificially altering the intensity of sound in the two ears.

The inner me does not actually know or decide anything; it does not make all these adjustments to perception because it is trying to help me. The information processing capability of the visual and auditory cortex has evolved the way it has because the adjustments that are made to sensory input gives me a clearer perception of what the world looks and sounds like, and this gives me a survival advantage. By means of the outer me, neuropsychologists have been able to work out how the brain does this, and then set up experiments to deceive the inner me, to prove that they are right.

The automatic adjustments the eye makes

When I am looking at a source of bright light, the iris of my eye contracts, and limits the amount of light impinging upon the retina, and when I am looking at a source of dim light, it expands, and allows more light to impinge upon the retina. The consequence of this is that the light impinging upon the retina is kept more or less constant, irrespective of the brightness or the dimness of the light source I am looking at. Beyond this, when I switch off the light, although at first everything around me appears to be uniformly dark, within a few minutes I am able to discern fairly clearly the objects around me in the room. These adjustments are made quite automatically, and I, the outer me, have no part in them, and can neither instigate them nor inhibit them.

Recognition of sensory experience

For each of the senses, there is an area of the brain concerned with recognising the sensory input. This is called the association cortex for each sense. Damage to one of these areas can cause the person to have the sensory experience but not to know what the experience is. This condition is called agnosia for each of the senses. The neural pathways concerned with experiencing and with interpreting what I experience are different. If, as sometimes happens, the pathway concerned with having the experience is intact, but the pathway concerned with interpreting it is broken (due, for example, to a head injury) the person can have the experience but cannot say what the experience is. S/he may then resort to the tedious (outer me) process of trying to fit the parts together and drawing a conclusion.

These interpreting parts of the brain appear to be like a filing system, but different files are in different parts of the brain. We know this because sometimes, following a head injury, a person can recognise some classes of experience and not others. There appear to be files for things, animals, fruit and faces, and probably more. There appear also to be files within files; thus a person can say that s/he can see a fruit, but not know what kind of fruit it is.

S/he could know that s/he is looking at a face, recognise it as a familiar face, but not be able to say whose face it is. The capacity to recognise faces is lost (prosopagnosia) when there is a lesion of the ventromedial occipotemporal cortex. The person who has such a condition may try to use (outer me) tricks like noting that Mary has red hair and Bill has a moustache.

The recognition of objects occurs in an all-or-nothing kind of way. This is an inner me way of functioning. The difference between having the experience and knowing what the experience is applies separately to each of the senses. There is an obvious link here between sensory input and memory. I can only recognise a face if I have seen it before and committed it to memory; so somehow recognition and memory are connected. A further connection is with language for, having recognised the experience, the next step is to give a name to it.

The transition from perception to conception

What is important for humans is not so much the sensory acuity as the brain connections that are made with the sensory input. I can recognise that a sound I am hearing is a tune; I can recognise the tune and I can recognise the person who is singing it; by linking up with my memory, I can remember a particular time when I last heard the tune, whom I was with when I heard it, and what I felt at the time; so instantaneously I can have the experience, plus the associations and the emotion.

In general, the brain is good at linking together associated experiences. It must help that, whenever I experience something, I experience it through all the senses at the same time. There is a region of the brain (the hippocampus) that coordinates the sensory input from the same source via the different senses. This enables me to have an integrated experience of some place, thing or person, so that I can see it, feel it, smell it and hear it all at the same time. When I remember the experience I remember it in this integrated way.

The hippocampus coordinates the sensations from a multiplicity of sources, and the main region that links the hippocampus to the neocortex is called the transition cortex. This region receives inputs from the highest stages of neocortical processing in each of the sensory modalities. LeDoux (1998) observed that once a cortical sensory system has done all it can with a stimulus, it ships the information to the transition cortex where the different sensory modalities can be integrated. This means that we can begin to form representations of the world that are no longer just visual or auditory or olfactory, but that include all of these at once. He wrote, "We begin to leave the purely perceptual and enter the conceptual domain" (page 198). Rudy and Sutherland (1992) have argued that the hippocampus creates representations that involve blends or configurations of sensations that transcend their component parts.

The idea of concepts is crucial to so much that the inner me does. In Chapter 8, it was explained that the inner me needs to hold on to the concept of each of the relating objectives in order to determine whether an objective had been met. Concepts, and establishing connections between similar concepts, contribute to abstract thought (see Chapter 14). Concepts are a manifestation of the inner me's capacity to visualise wholes, but once concepts have been created by the inner me the outer me seems able to make use of them.

First impressions

It is because the inner me visualises in wholes that it can make an immediate judgement about another person that frequently turns out to be sound. Experiments have shown that the judgements that people make about others in the first few minutes of meeting are borne out by later, more detailed assessments. The inner me works both for the judger and for the person being judged. People give themselves away by a stance, a gesture or a tone of voice, and people respond to that stance gesture or tone of voice when making a judgement. I do not know on what basis the inner me makes its first impression; I only get to know what this impression is by the inner me's emotional response: I feel either good or bad about the person without knowing the reason why. I (outer me) can go back over the experience of meeting the person and check her/him out feature by feature until I hit upon what it might have been that caused the inner me to make the judgement it did. Cues that seem to be important are mood and health: When someone looks or sounds depressed or unhealthy, I notice that I am immediately put off that person. Often, there is no time to assess a person in detail, so making a quick decision is advantageous, which is why the capacity to form first impressions has survived.

Familiarity

The question of familiarity will be addressed in Chapter 11 on memory, but it is useful to consider it here as well. What do I feel when I experience something as being familiar? One thing I feel is emotion. If it is someone I know and also someone I like, I feel happy; if it is someone I know and also someone I dislike, I feel unhappy; but I do not go through a complicated sequence of remembering all the good things and the bad things that I and this person have done together, and deciding whether, on balance, I like or dislike her/him; the emotion comes straight out. Familiarity is also something to do with the intensity of the memory. Some memories are strong and some are faint; and the strong ones are often the more familiar ones.

There are a number of variations of the condition first described by Capgras and Carrette (1924) and subsequently called the Capgras syndrome. In this, something that is familiar is experienced as unfamiliar. Ramachandran and Blakeslee (1998) described a young man who believed that his home was not really his home and that his parents were not really his parents. They hypothesised that he could not recognise his home as his home or his parents as his parents because the experience was not associated with the usual strong emotion. Because his inner brain did not produce the usual response to the sight of his parents, the only conclusion his outer me could reach was that his parents were imposters.

In the temporal lobes, just behind the auditory association area, is a region of association cortex involved in visual recognition. The visual association areas are connected to the amygdalae, the brain structures that are involved in generating emotional responses. Ramachandran believed that the Capgras syndrome is the result of the rupture of this connection. He tested this by measuring the galvanic skin response (GSR) of a man while being shown a series of photographs of people's faces. Some of these were of his mother and father and others were of strangers. The GSR is an objective measure of someone feeling emotion. Normal subjects produce a response when looking at their parents but not when looking at strangers. The man produced no response to any of the pictures. When he spoke to his father over the telephone, thus experiencing him through his auditory system and not his visual system, he recognised him as his father. Presumably, the auditory association area, which is further forward in the temporal lobe, remained connected to the amygdalae (Challoner, 2000).

The Capgras syndrome normally applies only to parents or marital partners, but it would seem that a similar condition might also apply to parts of the body. I once met a patient who protested that his hands were not really his hands; they were someone else's hands, and he named the man whose hands they were. There are people, with the rare condition called apotemnophilia, who request the amputation of one or both their legs because they do not experience it or them as their own. After the amputation they feel relieved. I might conclude from this that there is a connection in the brain that confers the feeling of familiarity upon sensory experiences and that sometimes this connection is broken.

Unconscious aspects of sensory input

Conscious and unconscious awareness

Claxton (1998) used the term conscious awareness, which is a characteristic of the outer me, and distinguished it from what he called unconscious awareness, which is a characteristic of the inner me. When I am consciously aware of something, I (outer me) know that I am experiencing it. When I am actively looking at something, I know that I am seeing that which I am looking at, and when I am actively listening to something, I know that I am hearing that which I am listening to; but I can also see things that I do not know that I am seeing, hear things that I do not know that I am hearing, and have sensations from any of my sense organs that I do not know that I am having. In Chapter 2, I wrote of consciousness being like a place where

thoughts, ideas and feelings can enter or leave. Thus, in unconscious awareness, my sensory experiences simply are not entering that place, which is
consciousness. I walk into a friend's sitting room and am convinced that there
is something missing from his mantelpiece. I enquire and he admits that
there is normally a clock there. On previous occasions that I have entered this
room, I (inner me) must have made an unconscious mental note of the appearance of his mantelpiece. A well-known example of unconscious awareness is
the sound of a clock ticking. If it stops ticking, I (outer me) become immediately aware that it has stopped even though, up to that moment, I had not
been aware that it was ticking. This is a process sometimes referred to as
selective inattention. In the interests of efficiency, I cannot be aware of everything that is going on around me. It is better to select out distracting sensory
experiences. Only I (outer me) do not do the selecting out; the in-between me
does. Ross (1989) argued that the ability to attend to information requires the
ability to dissociate irrelevant sensory input from that which is relevant to the
focus of my attention.

Priority sensations

The in-between me screens out many of the sensations I have, since they
would otherwise distract me from what I am doing. Most of the sensations I
feel, the smells I smell, the sounds I hear and the sights I see, I (the outer me)
am unaware of, but the inner me is, and is constantly scanning them for
anything that might be important. I do not feel the pressure of my clothing,
but if my trousers started to slip down, I would notice it and immediately
become alarmed. I do not hear the conversations of the people around me, but
if someone came up behind me and spoke my name, I would hear it and turn
to see who it was.

Nonconscious sensory input

Normally, sensations are passed from the sense organs to those parts of the
brain that coordinate and interpret them, and only then am I (outer me) made
consciously aware of that which has been picked up by the sense organs.
Sometimes, however, that which has been picked up by the sense organs is not
brought into consciousness. Concar (1998), a science journalist, reviewed the
research that has been carried out upon people who are totally blind on one
side of their visual field yet who can respond to images presented to them
within that field. They can see things in this field without being conscious of
the fact that they can see them. They have what is called blind sight, which is
due to damage to the primary visual cortex. Using brain scans, researchers
have shown that such unconscious seeing produces a different pattern of brain
activity than conscious seeing.

Concar reported that the Oxford psychologist Weiskrantz believed that
there are secondary visual pathways that bypass the main reception site for the

affected visual field, and that these pathways serve a different – probably defensive – function. He considered that it would be a waste of effort for the brain to spend time making events conscious that don't really require it. Concar reported upon a study by Marcel in which words shown on the person's blind side can influence her/his response to words shown on the visible side.

Claxton (1998) devoted an entire chapter to what he called perception without consciousness, and provided some striking examples. Damasio (2000) described an experiment in which a person with prosopagnosia, that is who is unable to recognise faces, was shown a random selection of photographs of faces, some of which were of people she had never met and some were of friends or relatives. Although, to her, all of the faces were unrecognisable, when shown the photographs of friends or relatives, a distinct skin conductance response was recorded.

Neglect

Neglect, or anosognosia, is a condition that affects both sensory and motor function. It is due to damage to the right, inferior, parietal cortex. The person simply lacks awareness of one side of both her/himself and the world around her/him; but s/he is unaware that s/he is unaware. If asked to clap hands s/he will clap with one hand believing s/he is clapping with both. If asked to copy a picture s/he will copy only one half of it. When reading a book s/he will begin each line from the middle. If asked to close her/his eyes and imagine walking down a familiar street s/he will describe everything on one side but not on the other. If asked to imagine turning round and walking in the other direction s/he will describe only everything on the other side (Bisiach and Luzzatti, 1978). However, a magnetic resonance imaging (MRI) study has shown that an emotionally stimulating picture presented to the unaware side will activate the emotional centres of the amygdala and the orbitofrontal cortex (Vuilleumier et al., 2002).

Subliminal perception

In each sensory modality there is what is called a limen. This is the weakest detectable stimulus. To identify the limen, the intensity of a weak stimulus is increased until it is reliably detectable, and the intensity of a strong stimulus is decreased until it is no longer detectable. There is now irrefutable evidence that sensory material that is below the limen can be perceived, processed and stored by the brain. A machine called a tachistoscope is capable of flashing images at such a high speed or low intensity that the person is unaware of having been exposed to them. Yet later, when these images are presented to the person, along with other images, the person responds differently to the ones that were flashed. In Chapter 1, a study of Pittman (1992) was reported upon in which a class of students were exposed subliminally to faces accompanied by the word GOOD. When subsequently asked to select people for a job, they were twice as likely to choose the one whose photograph had been presented to them subliminally, accompanied by the word GOOD, and furthermore, they offered spurious reasons for their selection. In fact, a later study by Bornstein (1992) revealed that the accompanying word GOOD was unnecessary. In this, people were subliminally exposed to a series of photographs of faces and then shown a larger series of photographs of faces, some of which had been pre-exposed and some of which had not. When asked to say how much they liked them, the pre-exposed ones received the more positive ratings. This phenomenon, first described by Zajonc (1980), is called the mere exposure effect. It means that the mere subliminal exposure to stimuli is enough to create preference; or perhaps it means that we prefer that which is familiar to that which is unfamiliar.

Evans (2001) maintained that when something has been perceived subliminally, it is stored in a part of the memory that is inaccessible to conscious recall. Things that are registered subliminally when the person is in a state of fear may be stored in the unconscious memory with a negative tag, so that when encountered later, they evoke a curious aversion that cannot be explained (Morris et al., 1998).

Like other forms of nonconscious sensory input, subliminal perception is a means of bypassing the normal conscious pathway. It seems likely that it forms part of a rapid reaction system by which the person perceives and responds to weak sensory inputs that may be signs of potential danger. It may even be a component of that which we would normally call intuition. An important point about subliminal perception is that it provides the means by which one person can introduce information into the memory store of another without the other being aware of it. In acquiring the ability to do this, humans seem to have made use of a system that has existed because of its survival value.

Hypnosis

Hypnosis is another means by which one person can influence another without the other being aware of it, even though the other is a compliant participant. Hypnosis can affect a number of brain functions, but here attention will be restricted to its effect upon sensation. The first stage of the hypnotic process is to persuade the subject to go to sleep. The sleep is the same as normal sleep with the one exception that the subject remains able to hear and respond to the voice of the hypnotist. By this means the hypnotist appears to have gained access to the subject's in-between me. The hypnotist can tell the subject that s/he cannot experience sensation via a particular modality and somehow the subject is able to block out that sensation.

The commonest use of hypnosis is to block out pain for surgical procedures. Sutcliffe (1961) observed that, although the subject does indeed appear not to be concerned during the course of the operation, s/he is still capable of making the kind of physiological responses that normally accompany the experience of pain, for example the galvanic skin response.

Claxton (1998) quoted an experiment performed by Hilgard. The subject was told that he was deaf, and indeed he did not flinch at the sound of loud noises; though paradoxically, he could still hear the hypnotist's voice. Hilgard whispered into the subject's ear that although he was deaf, he could still respond to instructions, and he invited the subject to raise a finger, which he did.

Hysteria

The topic of hysteria will be discussed in Chapter 15, but brief reference will be made to it here. A hysterical subject can maintain that s/he cannot see, cannot feel or cannot hear, just as s/he can maintain that s/he cannot move a limb or open her/his eyes. An important feature of hysteria is that the person genuinely believes that these things are so. It seems that the in-between me is able to block off a particular sensation.

10 Emotion

Fehr and Russell (1984) observed that everyone knows what emotion is until they are asked to define it. While emotion is perhaps the strangest of all subjective experiences, it is not all that difficult to define. Damasio (2000) wrote that ". . . all emotions have some kind of regulatory role to play . . ." (page 51), and this is an opinion with which I would agree. Oatley (1998) drew attention to Turing's (1950) question concerning how we might distinguish between a human and a computer, and suggested that emotion might be the single most distinguishing feature. This may well be true. He considered that emotions are ". . . those processes that relate outer events to the inner states that are called goals" (page 286). This comes close to my own definition, namely that they are messages generated by the inner me to keep us on-track in the attainment of our objectives. Rolls (1997) maintained that pleasure is the subjective state corresponding to reinforcement. From my own theoretical viewpoint, emotion is of immense importance, because it is the surest way of comprehending what, at any given moment, the inner me is doing. By noting what emotion is being felt and when it is felt, I can infer how the inner me is reacting to what is happening and this, in turn, tells me what the inner me's objectives are and whether and when it considers these have been attained.

Emotion and the attainment of objectives

Emotions are the way that the inner me conveys that I am on-track or off-track, getting warmer or getting colder, getting closer to or further away from its objectives. Since it is the inner me that houses the objectives and monitors their attainment, it must be the inner me that generates emotions. It is ironic that the inner me does not itself experience the emotions that it generates. It has no "intention" of communicating emotions to the outer me. It is just something that it does; so emotions are not really "communications." They do not even always get communicated. Damasio (1994) demonstrated that patients with a form of brain damage that left them emotionless had difficulty achieving their goals, and consequently made a mess of their lives. When asked to make a decision they just rambled because they had no sense of where they were trying to get.

From my own theoretical standpoint, four emotions are necessary for monitoring the attainment of objectives: an encouraging or rewarding one (pleasure), conveying that the animal/person has succeeded in attaining its objective; an alerting one (anxiety), warning it that it is in danger of losing it; a determined one (anger) aroused in the defence of an attained objective or in an endeavour to regain a lost objective; and a discouraging or punishing one (displeasure), conveying that the objective has been lost. It is useful to view pleasure as the one positive emotion (communicating that the objective has been attained or is about to be attained) and the other three as negative emotions (representing varying degrees of the objective not having been attained or in danger of being lost).

The intensity of emotion

The intensity of emotion is proportional to the importance (to the inner me) of the circumstances that give rise to it. The inner me "decides" how important the circumstances are and, therefore, how intense the emotion that is released should be. There are times when there is a discrepancy between how important I (the outer me) consider a situation to be and how much emotion the inner me releases. Sometimes I find I am being more emotional than I thought I was going to be and sometimes I find I am being less. Do I take my cue from the emotion I feel or do I hold on to my previous assessment of the situation? Probably the former.

The duration of emotion

Emotion is most intense at moments of change, because at these moments, the inner me is able to inform me whether the change has been advantageous or disadvantageous. When I have a success I experience a surge of pleasure, and when I have a failure I experience a surge of displeasure, but as I get used to the success or the failure the intensity of the emotion diminishes. This is necessary in order that there may be a new emotional release at the moment of the next change. Thus, when playing a game, I experience pleasure at the successful moments and displeasure at the unsuccessful ones. Sometimes a particular emotion can linger on for minutes, hours, days, months or even years. Grief, hate, bitterness and resentment are emotions that tend to linger. One factor in maintaining them is the constant experiencing of circumstances that remind me why I am feeling that way; so in effect, they get constantly retriggered.

Seeking the reward without gaining the objective

Because people feel happy when things are going well, they form the impression that the object of life is to be happy. In fact, as far as they are concerned, the object of life *is* to feel happy, because that is all they have; the happiness that keeps them on-track. Only the inner me has objectives, but it cannot tell people (outer me) what the objectives are; it can only direct them by spurts of emotion. I know that there are objectives because I (outer me) have worked this out. The emotions are the only way of ensuring that the objectives are met. If some authority figure were to announce that these were the objectives (like Moses with the Ten Commandments) people would not have the incentive to attain them. They only respond to emotion. The real object of life must be the attainment of the objectives, and if people attain them they are caused to feel happy.

In a much cited study (Olds and Milner, 1954), rats had electrodes chronically implanted into the septal nuclei of the medial forebrain bundle. By depressing a lever, the rats could stimulate this area, and this gave them a sensation of pleasure. They continued depressing the lever repeatedly and had no interest in doing anything else. If all rats were wired up to such a pleasure centre they would die of starvation, cease to reproduce and rapidly become extinct. The same would happen to humans. An extension of the Olds and Milner study was one in which rats could be navigated by the microstimulation, by remote control, of the pleasure centre and the centre that registered responses from the rat's whiskers (Talwar et al., 2002). Thus when they took the correct turn they were rewarded and, by this means, they were trained to follow particular routes. This is analogous to the way the inner me navigates us in the attainment of our objectives. Drugs exist that create degrees of euphoria. By means of these, people can gain the reward without attaining the objectives. They become addicted to them just as the rats became addicted to the lever. The future of the human race depends upon people continuing to seek their objectives rather than simply seeking the sensation of pleasure.

The specificity of emotions

How many emotions are there?

In common with most other contemporary writers, Damasio (2000) maintained that there are six so-called primary or universal emotions. These are happiness, sadness, fear, anger, surprise and disgust. They were probably selected because they each have a characteristic facial expression. Beyond these, there are a number of what he called secondary or social emotions, such as embarrassment, love, shame and jealousy, which he considered to be adaptations of the primary emotions to specific situations. If the general consensus is that there are six primary emotions, how can I maintain that there are only four? My basis for defining an emotion is that it is an aid to attaining an objective.

Although people are emotional when they are surprised, and although there is a facial expression that is associated with being surprised, I would still not call surprise an emotion. There are pleasant surprises and unpleasant surprises. One might experience joy (a form of happiness) at a pleasant surprise, and dismay (a form of sadness), or terror (a form of fear) at an unpleasant surprise. Surprise then is simply an emotional response to the unexpected.

While I would not deny that disgust is an emotional state, I would not consider it to be a primary emotion. Having originated as a response to food being poisonous (Chapter 6), it has spread to being a rather upper feeling (Chapter 8), drawing away from something that is despicable or contemptible. It bears certain similarities to racism.

More recently (2002) Damasio considered surprise not to be an emotion, and expressed doubt about disgust. On the issue of secondary emotions Damasio (2000) observed that several such emotions are not apparent at birth. This may be because the circumstances that give rise to them are not present until later in life; though he believed it likely that the propensity to experience them may still be innate. Other secondary emotions may, in part, be shaped by social and cultural pressures.

There are many words in the English language that refer to emotional states, but it would be wrong to consider each of them to refer to a separate emotion. In fact, they are mostly variants of the four basic ones, but applied to specific situations. I tried listing these words under the four main headings and stopped when I got to around 30 under each. Here are 12 variants for each:

Happy: amazed, contented, delighted, ecstatic, glad, hopeful, jolly, pleased, proud, overjoyed, relieved and triumphant.

Sad: abandoned, defeated, dejected, depressed, disappointed, disheartened, downcast, forlorn, grief-stricken, hopeless, regretful and sorrowful.

Afraid: anxious, alarmed, apprehensive, jittery, nervous, panic-stricken, petrified, shocked, suspicious, tense, terrified and timid.

Angry: affronted, determined, cross, embittered, enraged, furious, hateful, indignant, offended, resentful, vengeful and wrathful.

Fear

Fear was probably the earliest emotion to evolve. It is the emotion most closely linked with survival. It is clearly observable, and has physiological correlates that are measurable in a wide range of life forms. For this reason, a great deal of research has been carried out on the fear responses of animals. That which I fear is that which stands between me and the attainment of an objective.

LEDOUX'S HIGH ROAD AND LOW ROAD TO THE FEAR RESPONSE

LeDoux (1998) drew the important distinction between what he called the high cortical road and the lowly thalamic road in the processing of fear. There is a neuronal route that passes from the thalamus to the amygdala via the primary auditory cortex, and another that passes directly from the thalamus to the amygdala. Neurons that pass to the primary auditory cortex and then on to the amygdala are narrowly tuned, so that they respond only to a precise stimulus, but those that project directly upon the amygdala are broadly tuned, so that they respond to a broader range of stimuli. The ability of a rabbit to discriminate between two stimuli, the one noxious the other not, is lost if a lesion is made in the auditory cortex. LeDoux concluded that the pathways that bypass the cortex do not involve the subtle discrimination of stimuli. For this, the cerebral cortex is necessary. The thalamic pathway cannot tell the amygdala exactly what is there, but can provide a fast signal that warns that something dangerous may be there.

LeDoux (1998) discovered this distinction by tracing the neural pathway by which an auditory stimulus can evoke fear. He started at the point that a conditioning stimulus entered the brain and tried to trace the pathways forward from this system towards the final destinations that control the conditioned fear responses. He did this by systematically creating lesions in the different stages of the pathway and determining what effect these lesions had upon the final response. He found that damage to the auditory cortex had no effect at all, but that damage to the auditory thalamus and the next auditory station down in the midbrain, the auditory brainstem nuclei, did. He concluded from this that the auditory cortex could be bypassed. By injecting tracers into the auditory thalamus he discovered four routes out of it. He blocked each of these routes in turn, and found that blocking only one route, the one to the amygdala, prevented the conditioning taking place. Further studies (LeDoux, 1995) revealed that it was the central nucleus of the amygdala that was essential for the conditioning.

Anxiety

Where fear is a relatively short-lived experience, anxiety may extend over long periods. It is characterised by high arousal, increased muscle tone, rapid pulse, high blood pressure, restlessness and sleeplessness.

Depression

I would argue that depression is the emotional response to losing an objective, though I would acknowledge that some people have such a high propensity to become depressed that they will do so with only the slightest provocation, and that some may even become depressed in response to biochemical agents, e.g., hypotensive drugs. While it is relatively easy to conclude, from external behaviour and physiological measures, that an animal is afraid, it is much more difficult to conclude that it is depressed.

In both animals and humans the state of depression can be inferred from external behaviour, like slowness of movement, turning away from others and the avoidance of gaze; but it is certainly possible for humans, and therefore probably also for animals, for quite profound states of depression not to be inferable from external behaviour. In a state of extreme depression, a person can lose interest in everything, see no point in anything, derive no pleasure from anything, neglect everything, not speak, not move and even sink into a condition of mute immobility (stupor).

Worry

Worrying is an apparently unproductive mental activity in which the same disturbing thoughts recur over and over. Borkovec and Lyonfields (1993) proposed that it has the effect of blocking access to more specific feared thoughts and images. In this respect it resembles obsessive rumination. It can be resolved by (the outer me) weighing up the pros and cons of the possible options and deciding upon a deliberate line of action. Later in the chapter I will describe how I (in-between me) seem able to exclude worrying thoughts to enable myself to focus upon the matters of the moment. Most worries are dispelled in this way. When they are not the emotional pressure is too great for this to happen.

Mania

The state of mania is the reverse of that of depression. The person is highly aroused, overactive and overtalkative, and is sometimes acutely perceptive. There may be lability of mood, but often elation predominates. Some have argued that it is a defensive protection against depression, what Klein (1934) has called the manic defence, but it is unlikely that this is the most usual cause.

EMOTION VERSUS MOOD

Evans (2001) distinguished between emotions and moods. Emotions are our response to a change in circumstances and are short-lived. Moods, like Damasio's (2000) background emotions, persist over longer periods. Evans explained that a mood state raises or lowers our susceptibility to emotive events. In a chronically anxious state we are more easily frightened and in a chronically depressed state we are more likely to cry at bad news. A mood state also has an effect upon the recall of events. Bower (1981) demonstrated in a series of experiments that when we are in a happy mood we tend to recall pleasant events more easily and more accurately, and when we are in a sad mood we tend to recall unpleasant events more easily and more accurately. This phenomenon is called mood-congruent recall. It is highly relevant to those studies that seek to find explanations for depressed moods by asking depressed people about past events. Because they are depressed, they are more likely to recall unpleasant experiences. Bower asked people to describe a number of events in their childhood. The next day, he found that whether they recalled good or bad events depended upon whether their mood had been artificially raised or lowered by hypnotic suggestion. Evans (2001) proposed that this may be because memories are linked to the emotion experienced at the time of the original event. When we recall events from memory, those that are linked to our current emotional state are given more salience.

Emotion and consciousness

Damasio (2002) concluded that if emotions have a bioregulatory function, then all animals, even unicellular organisms, must have emotions; and he claimed to have some evidence for this. In order to accept this line of reasoning, one needs to be clear about what an emotion is. Put at its most simple, it has to be some kind of electrical discharge that motivates the organism into achieving its ends.

If Damasio is right, since the vast majority of organisms do not have consciousness, emotions need have nothing to do with consciousness. This is a strange idea for us humans to take on board because we cannot conceive of ever having an emotion without being conscious of it; but Damasio (2000) has shown that sometimes we do. He cited the example of a man who had extensive damage to both temporal lobes including the hippocampus and the amygdala. Consequently, if he experienced something, he could not remember it, and if he met someone he could not recognise him again. Despite this, he was capable of being attracted to a person who had pretended to be pleasant and avoiding a person who had pretended to be unpleasant. When shown photographs of the previously pleasant and the previously unpleasant person, and asked, "Who do you think is your friend?" and "Who would you turn to for help?" he consistently chose the person who had pretended to be pleasant. When he was asked why, he could not say.

LeDoux (1998) wrote an entire chapter on the emotional unconscious without specifically defining it. On the penultimate page of this chapter he wrote, "Emotions are notoriously difficult to verbalize. They operate in some psychic and neural space that is not readily accessed from consciousness" (page 71). Operate is all right: I can live with operate, because it simply means that there are unconscious processes that cause emotions to happen. On the same page he wrote, "Animals were unconscious and nonverbal long before they were conscious and verbal." That is undoubtedly true: so if emotions exist in animals that have no consciousness, they must be capable of existing independently of consciousness.

One could argue that an emotion without consciousness is not an emotion at all; it is simply a mechanism for responding to danger. Did LeDoux's rabbits, either by the low thalamic route or the high cortical one, actually experience the fear? But what about Olds' and Milner's rat? If it liked having the pleasure centre stimulated, it must have had the subjective experience of pleasure. When dogs wag their tails, or cats purr, are they not experiencing pleasure? Does the spider experience pleasure when it catches a fly in its web?

The conclusion I seem to be coming to is that there is something akin to emotion that happens at a nonconscious level, which later gets shunted up into consciousness for us to feel it; but perhaps it is not the same for all emotions. The two emotions of fear and anger appear to differ from happiness and sadness in that they are concerned with the recognition of and response to danger. These actions need to be immediate. Therefore, there would be some advantage to their bypassing consciousness. Happiness and sadness do not require immediate action, and it is less easy to imagine them not being conscious. Presumably the eventual shunting of emotion up into consciousness intensifies the experience and drives the message home. Eccles (1989) observed that the pathways between the limbic system and the neocortex provide an essential link in bringing about the conscious experience of emotion.

Some would argue that the experience of emotion is simply the sum total of its anatomical and physiological accompaniments. Lowen (1967) maintained that the muscles are important vehicles for the experience of emotion; that emotion is locked within the muscles, and relaxing the muscles releases the emotion. When people are paralysed, their experience of emotion is diminished. Dolan (2002) found that patients with the rare condition of pure autonomic failure experience a flattening of emotion, but that it does not disappear altogether. He also showed that the autonomic accompaniments of emotion occur slightly before the subjective experience. This is similar to the observation that a hand is withdrawn from a hot object before the subjective experience of pain. The qualitative, subjective difference between the different emotions must be something analogous to different tastes.

Keeping unpleasant emotion out of consciousness

It is inefficient for me to be constantly aware of disturbing thoughts. Hence I have ways of excluding them from consciousness in order that I may devote my attention to the matters of the moment. The terms suppression and repression are too grand to describe what is after all a fairly mundane process. When reminded of these disturbing thoughts I can recall them with little difficulty and experience the accompanying emotion. It seems likely too that they emerge in dreams or as I am emerging from sleep, before I have had a chance to exclude them. This issue is raised again in Chapters 15 and 17, and is linked with the idea that I have a more optimistic attitude than my circumstances would justify. It is another example of the work of the in-between me.

Separating emotion from thoughts

It is possible to hold on to an emotional thought without experiencing the emotion; so although the emotion continues to exist it is no longer experienced. Rachman (1978) made the important point that removing the subjective experience of emotion does not eliminate its psychophysiological component, which can be measured. This is similar to the suppression of pain (Chapter 9). Sometimes it is possible to speak of an emotional experience without feeling the emotion. A child can say, in a cold, matter of fact sort of way, "My mother died last night." The listener may think that the child is being callous, but this is simply a defensive manoeuvre, presumably executed, though not deliberately, by the in-between me. The emotion can be released if the child is caught off guard or if some association is made that bypasses the block. Such dissociation is not only made by children.

Emotion in relation to the outer me and the inner me

Emotion is the most important issue in the book, because it is only through emotion that the inner me makes its presence felt. It provides a continuous flow of encouraging or discouraging promptings to my actions, and responses to what I have done and what has been done to me. Over the years, I (outer me) have worked out the connection between events and what I feel about them; so roughly I know what pleases me and what displeases me, what makes me feel frightened and what makes me feel angry. Perhaps, more often than not, the emotion that I expect to feel is the emotion I do feel, but still there remain the occasions when the match is not as I think it should be. I can anticipate that I may feel a particular emotion in a particular situation; sometimes I feel it and sometimes I do not. I can experience a particular emotion when not expecting to. I can expect to feel one emotion and find I am experiencing a different one. People vary in the way they cope with this. Sometimes they ignore the inappropriate emotion, or try to behave as though they are not experiencing it. Sometimes they try to behave as though they are experiencing the emotion that they think they should be experiencing.

Emotion, more than anything else, reveals the extent of the separation between the inner me and the outer me. People sometimes go to their doctor because they are feeling an emotion that they think they should not be feeling, particularly anxiety or depression. Quite often the emotion is an appropriate one but they are not prepared to acknowledge the appropriateness of it. The inner me is totally logical: It seems unlikely that it ever releases an emotion when it should not have done, or withholds an emotion that it should have released. It also seem unlikely that it ever releases the wrong emotion. That it releases more or less of a particular emotion than it should have does remain a possibility, since some people appear to be genetically disposed to certain kinds of emotion, but mostly it probably gets it right.

However, where emotion is concerned, the inner me is not infallible. It may have insufficient information to make a correct judgement: It may register a fear of all snakes, because it is unaware that only some snakes are dangerous. It may register fear when exposed to a representation or an enactment of a dangerous situation, such as in a movie.

Assuming that the inner me is responding appropriately, how can I tell what is causing me to feel a particular emotion? The best way is to chart accurately the circumstances under which it starts and goes away, or even to experiment by adding and removing the suspected stimulus. One morning I noticed myself feeling unexpectedly happy. I traced my happy state back to a conversation I had had 10 minutes earlier with an attractive young secretary. This forced me to acknowledge that it was important to me that she liked me. Sometimes the cause of an emotional response is complex. It may be due to a connection of a present insignificant event with a more significant one in the past. Sometimes it takes an independent observer to pick up this connection. I find that noting what events and experiences cause me to feel what emotion is a valuable way of discovering those things the inner me considers to be important. These days, I sometimes find myself curious to know how my inner me is going to respond to a particular situation.

Emotion-induced ideas and delusions

Some people who are extremely depressed or manic develop delusions, and sometimes also hallucinations, which are in accord with their mood state. It is as though the person is trying to think of circumstances that would justify the extreme emotional state s/he is experiencing. Depressive delusions include feelings of having done wrong, sinned or let people down; feelings of being the cause of everything that is wrong in the world, of being in the way and a conviction that others would be better off if one were dead; feelings of being dead inside, of rotting away, of having an incurable disease; feeling that the future is bleak and hopeless. Manic delusions include believing oneself to be someone powerful like Jesus Christ; believing oneself to have immense wealth, power or wisdom. People act upon these delusions. People with depressive delusions punish or kill themselves. People with manic delusions give all their possessions and money away.

The facial expression of emotion

Darwin (1872) produced evidence to demonstrate that there are many physical actions that accompany emotion, and that these are largely innate. Emotional expressions are particularly evident in the face, and Argyle (1988) reported that facial expression conveys an individual's emotional state more clearly than words. Darwin observed that the same expression is apparent when a particular emotion is felt in people of all human racial and national groups. They are also apparent in people who have been blind from birth. Darwin further showed that the bodily expression of certain emotions are apparent in many animal species and that these expressions are most similar in species that are closely related. Emotional expression, as with smiling and laughing, is under the control of the inner me, and it is difficult for the outer me to imitate it convincingly. It seems that the purpose of an emotional expression is to convey to another the emotional state that is being experienced; but why is this important? The expression of a particular emotion in one member of a group may induce or reinforce the same emotion in other members of the group. Thus all group members will harbour the same emotion at the same time, and this may promote group cohesiveness. This might be useful for fight-or-flight. I can see that the show of anger may induce an adversary to back off, and this would be an advantage, but the show of fear may induce an adversary to attack, and this would be a disadvantage; so we are more inclined to show anger to an adversary and less inclined to show fear.

The recognition of emotion in others

There are reasons for believing that the amygdalae are necessary for both the expression of fear and the recognition of fear. Damasio (2000) reported the case of a young woman who showed calcification of both her amygdalae. As a result, although she had no difficulty learning new facts, she could not recognise either fear or untrustworthiness in the faces of others and she was incapable of expressing either fear or anger. She had no difficulty recognising other facial expressions. Damasio concluded from this that the amygdalae play no part in the recognition of happiness, surprise or disgust, but damage to the right somatosensory central cortex will lead to the inability to recognise emotion in others. Morris et al. (2001) showed that a patient with blind sight (see previous chapter) was able to discriminate emotional facial expressions when presented in his blind hemifield, indicating that such discrimination is possible without conscious (outer brain) perception of these faces. This ability, called affective blindsight, depends upon a subcortical visual pathway comprising the superior colliculus, posterior (extrageniculate) thalamus and amygdala.

Emotion in crowds

The effects of crowd emotion were described by Le Bon (1895). People in a crowd feel freer to express emotion and express it more intensely. Emotions become intensified and spread rapidly through a crowd. This may be because crowd members lose their individual identity (outer me) and adopt a crowd identity. When crowds become enraged they become a more effective fighting force. People mourn more intensely in a crowd. They laugh more freely at comedy television programmes when these are accompanied by the sound of an audience laughing. Crowds respond emotionally to a leader, whether it be an officer, a politician, an evangelist or a comedian, and Evans (2001) observed that Hitler was aware that collective emotion can drown out the individual voice of reason. This is apparent in warfare, in religious gatherings, at political rallies, at sporting events and in theatre audiences. The effect may have advantages for survival. When crowds panic they flee faster from danger, even though some crowd members get trampled under foot.

The association of emotion with memory

I do not remember everything I experience. Whether I remember something depends upon how emotional I feel at the moment I experience it. The stronger the emotion, the more likely I (inner me) am to commit it to memory. Whenever I remember something, the accompanying emotion, both the type and the intensity, is remembered too, and when I recall the memory I also recall the accompanying emotion, in the same form and intensity. The stronger the accompanying emotion is, the more inclined I will be to recall it. There is, of course, one exception to this: Memories that are accompanied by extremely unpleasant emotion get repressed, and become extremely difficult to recall. When I am reminded of things (people, experiences), it is the memories with the strongest emotional accompaniments that I am most reminded of, so just the slightest link is enough to evoke a highly emotional memory.

Emotion in dreams

Emotions feature prominently in dreams, and there are few dreams that do not have emotion in them. It may be that it is the stored emotion that induces the dream. It seems likely that the in-between me is relaxed in dreams, and that one of the benefits of dreaming may be the controlled release of unexpressed emotion. Highly emotional experiences, such as war experiences, sexual abuse and rape, are repeatedly relived in dreams.

Emotion in psychotherapy

LeDoux (1998) wrote that "Psychotherapy is interpreted as a process through which our neocortex [outer me] learns to exercise control over evolutionarily old emotional systems [inner me]" (page 21) (brackets inserted). In fact, the outer me exercises control over the inner me all the time; but it is quite true that a major concern of certain forms of psychotherapy is enabling the client, by way of the outer me, to correct some of the inner me's inappropriate emotional responses.

Emotional reactions may be excessive either in intensity or duration. Sometimes a reaction appears to be greater than is warranted by the circumstances in which it is generated, or sometimes it appears to persist long after the circumstances that have precipitated it have passed. The therapist needs to be careful about making judgements of this kind, since the inner me may "have its reasons" for determining the intensity or duration of an emotional response. An apparently trivial event may have greater significance than the client may be willing to acknowledge. An emotion may persist for long periods because the circumstances giving rise to it persist.

It is advantageous first to examine what is causing the emotion and whether, in the circumstances, such emotion is reasonable. Being frightened in frightening circumstances, or depressed in depressing ones, or angry when someone is behaving intolerably, is natural and acceptable. Acknowledging the reasonableness of experiencing a particular emotion, and that it is appropriate to the situation, can be therapeutic.

Sometimes there are therapeutic gains in helping the client to establish contact with blocked-off emotion. This is done by watching and listening for small signs of emotion. When the client speaks certain words or phrases, there is a quiver in the voice. The therapist encourages the client to hold on to these and to elaborate upon them. Grunbaum (1993) observed that even Freud had realised quite early in his clinical career that such release had only limited therapeutic value. Getting to the emotion is rather like a miner getting to the coal face. The real therapeutic work takes place when therapist and client explore the original traumatic event and seek ways of living more comfortably with the memory.

Brain locations associated with emotion

The location of the origin of different emotions has become possible from examining patients with disease or damage to specific brain sites and by the neuroimaging of normal individuals. Damasio (2000) observed that the brain induces emotions from a remarkably small number of brain sites, the main ones being in the brainstem region, the hypothalamus and the basal forebrain. This would be in keeping with the idea that the inner me, which must have its roots in the earliest evolved areas of the brain, is responsible for emotional responses. Damasio concluded that there is no single brain centre for processing emotions, though the amygdalae must play a major role in the conditioning and expression of fear. When the amygdalae are lost the person knows what fear is (outer me) but cannot experience it (inner me). The same applies to anger. Damasio (2002) distinguished between induction sites, which have what he called a brokering function, and are located in the amygdalae and the ventral medial frontal cortex, and the effector structures, which are located in the hypothalamus and brainstem, which produce the emotional states.

Different emotions are produced by different brain systems, and there are discrete systems related to separate emotional patterns. Positive emission tomography (PET) has demonstrated that the induction and experience of the four major emotions of happiness, sadness, fear and anger lead to activation in several of the sites listed above, but that the pattern for each emotion is distinctive. For example sadness consistently activates the ventromedial prefrontal cortex, hypothalamus and brainstem, but anger and fear activate neither the prefrontal cortex nor the hypothalamus. Where the fight and flight responses are processed in the ventrolateral column of the periaqueductal grey matter of the brainstem, the freeze response is processed in the lateral column.

11 Memory

Memory is essential for the survival of all animals. They need to remember sources of food and water. In a large forest, a squirrel can remember where it has hidden its nuts. Animals also need to remember how to get to their breeding places. Turtles can remember, over a period of 30 years, the beach on which they were hatched, in order that they may return to the same beach to lay their eggs. Salmon and eels, after crossing the Atlantic, can remember the British rivers where they breed. Swallows, migrating from South Africa, can remember the route to the exact farm in Britain where they built their nest the previous year. The extent of the memory of even quite simple animals is sometimes astonishing. Pinker (1997) cited the example of the Tunisian desert ant, which can travel a distance of 50 metres from its nest, a hole in the sand 1 millimetre across, and find its way back. When moved out of position, it will travel the same distance and in the same direction, though obviously, it will not find the nest. This demonstrates that it has a way of recording the direction and distance it has travelled.

Memory is almost 100 per cent inner me. The outer me has no idea how memories happen and has no idea how to remember. Memories, like emotion, just happen, and simply get projected into consciousness. The outer me can think of things it wants to remember, and can think up tricks, like mnemonics, which make remembering easier, but that is as far as it goes. Of course, it can design research projects to find out how memory works.

Types of memory

The simplest division of memory is between short- and long-term memory. Short-term memory is what is currently in consciousness. It is necessary to permit the constant flow of ideas. The patient H.M. had the surgical removal of large regions of both temporal lobes (Scoville and Milner, 1957), and short-term memory is all that remained. He could remember things for no more than a minute. Long-term memory is memory of any other duration. A special kind of short-term memory, called working memory, was discussed in Chapter 5.

Winograd (1975) drew a distinction between what he called declarative and procedural memory. Declarative memory refers to the remembering of knowledge and procedural memory refers to the remembering of skills; this includes both physical skills and cognitive processing skills. Declarative memory can be further broken down into episodic or autobiographical memory and semantic or general knowledge memory (Sherry and Schachter, 1987). Episodic or autobiographical memory is concerned with those things that have happened in my life and semantic or general knowledge memory is concerned with information that I have acquired. Episodic memory applies to events, like leaving school and getting married, and semantic memory applies to generalities, like birds lay eggs.

Memory and the self

My sense of self depends upon my recollection of all the experiences and feelings I have ever had, and the way that I have behaved in different kinds of situation. Eccles (1989) wrote, "It is a universal human experience that subjectively there is a mental unity, which is recognised as a continuity from one's earliest memories" (page 204). The brain has a way of searching through vast memory stores and selecting out memories that are related. This is particularly true of memories that relate to the self. Eccles continued, "So there would be building of the memory stores in the cerebral cortex, which give an enduring basis for the unity of the self. Without such memory, there could be no experience of the unity" (page 205).

Laying down memories

As I pass from experience to experience, memories just automatically get stored. Remembering is an involuntary act; so it must be a function of the inner me. Cork (1996) has demonstrated that certain kinds of memorising are possible even under general anaesthesia. Each afternoon, I can remember almost everything that happened to me during the morning, even though I have made no effort to do so. A week later, unless something really important had happened on that particular morning, I will have remembered nothing. I (outer me) do not wilfully or consciously decide which events to remember and which to forget. The events that get enduringly remembered are the ones that make an impact, either positively or negatively, in terms of the achievement of objectives. Such impact will have generated emotion, and somehow it seems that emotion plays a major role in determining which experiences get remembered.

Why are certain memories remembered?

When the memory of an emotional event is laid down the emotion gets laid down with it. Strong, accompanying emotion increases the likelihood of an event being remembered and renders its recall easier and more intense. Sometimes I am surprised that I have remembered certain events. They are events that I (outer me) would not have considered to be worth remembering. The fact that I have remembered them indicates that they had struck the inner me as being important (in terms of the attainment of objectives). I am then inclined to reevaluate them. I am struck by the number of events from my early childhood that I have remembered, some of them with great vividness; particularly those of a sexual nature. Obviously the inner me considered them important.

The ineffectualness of the outer me in laying down memories

The outer me plays only a minimal role in the laying down of memories. It can consider that I ought to remember something, or I ought not to forget something, but that does not cause me to remember it, or stop me forgetting it. I may try to remember the contents of a book by reading it over and over in the hope that eventually the facts will stick, like something sticks to an adhesive surface. This is not an act of remembering. It is doing something that hopefully will cause remembering to happen. Ultimately, it is the inner me that determines whether an experience will be remembered or not. Repetition will help, but a more important factor is the degree of stimulation or interest that the experience evokes. It is extremely difficult to remember boring things, because the inner me has no incentive to remember them. Therefore, as every good teacher knows, the secret is to make the facts to be remembered stimulating or interesting. Another trick, as many a student has discovered, is making silly jokes about boring things. The emotion of the joke gets tagged on to the boring fact and renders it memorable. The hard work of cramming in facts during my student days contrasts with the ease with which I have remembered many events from the same period. Presumably this is because these events struck the inner me as important.

The retrograde reinforcement of memories

Events that precede an important event also seem to get remembered. This has survival value, for the precursor to an important event may serve as a warning that the event may be about to happen again. If I were walking along a particular stretch of road when an accident happened, the next time I walked along that stretch of road I would begin to feel anxious, presumably because I would recall the accident. Therefore I would take particular care. The recollection and feeling anxious are completely automatic (inner me) responses, though the taking care is more an outer me one.

When I was aged 10, I fell out of a tree and landed at my father's feet. I had severed an artery in my arm. In the middle of an empty field, for what seemed like an eternity, my father bent over me, trying to stem the flow of blood, while my mother ran for help. Of course I remember the experience vividly, but what is more important, I also remember the events that led up to it. I remember standing in the tree before I fell, telling my father that I could not get down, and the moment I slipped. Before that even, I remember how we had spent the afternoon picking blackberries, and had stopped to have a picnic. I even remember the day my parents bought the pale-blue shirt that I was wearing, which got soaked in blood. Had I not fallen out of the tree I would not have remembered these things.

The memory store

I must have an elaborate system for classifying memories that facilitates recall and also the linking of one memory to another. This classificatory system must be phenomenal, and is based upon a wide variety of different classes of attribute. A smell can trigger off the recall of an earlier time when that smell was experienced. Even a particular shade of colour can evoke the memory of a particularly important object that had this colour. Soon after the war ended, my father bought me what I considered to be a magnificent bicycle, which I rode everywhere, and which became almost a part of me. It was a pale, metallic green. Whenever I see that particular shade of green I feel emotional and remember the bicycle, and all that it meant to me.

The classification of memories is not restricted to links with simple sensory experiences like smell and colour. It works for complex inputs as well. One flower can trigger off the recall of a similar kind of flower. One building can trigger off the recall of a similar kind of building. One person's face can trigger off the recall of a person's face that is similar. One type of situation can trigger off the recall of a similar type of situation; for example, being rejected, or making a fool of myself, gets linked up with another occasion when I was rejected or I made a fool of myself.

Beyond this, the classificatory system can make bridges between ideas and concepts. It is only when I consciously decide to pay attention to this that I become aware of its frequency and extent. It is a much more complicated process than simply connecting words or shapes. The inner me has the capacity to link one idea or concept with another. Here are some examples: I turn up late for an appointment and I am reminded of a different occasion when I was late for an appointment. I think of a person from a foreign country having difficulty understanding English customs, and I am reminded of a different person from a foreign country having similar difficulties. I notice something being an exception to a rule and I remember something else that is an exception to a different rule. Perceiving the similarity between two or more events, phenomena, processes or ideas leads to establishing a relationship between them. Making connections is an important component of understanding and formulating theories. It is also a factor in aesthetics.

Memories that extend over space and time

Memories are stored not only in categories, but also across space and over time. I remember things in wholes, not in parts of wholes. When I imagine an elephant, I imagine the whole thing; I do not think of the separate parts and stick them together. A memory can spread outwards in many directions. I can remember a face, a whole person and all kinds of things about that person. I can remember a building, like Saint Paul's Cathedral or the Royal Festival Hall, an entire scene or landscape, the map of the world or any particular country; or I can remember the layout of an entire town.

Remembering sequences

Memories can also extend over periods of time. I may remember a story, the sequence of events of a book or a movie, a melody or even a long and complex piece of music, like a symphony. The capacity to remember sequences is not restricted to humans. Remembering routes has advantages for most forms of animal life, for it enables them to remember sources of food and breeding grounds, and how to get to them. When I am trying to remember how to get somewhere the first thing I remember is the starting place. From this point on, each point on the journey triggers the recall of the next point, and that triggers off the recall of the next point, and so on. Animals probably do the same thing.

Remembering music

The automatic remembering (laying down) of music is particularly striking. Often, I have the experience of walking through a shop, which is playing background music, and having left the shop I find I have a particular piece of music on my mind, and I do not know where it has come from. The memory must simply have picked it up as I was walking round the shop. Some days after having attended a concert, even of quite unfamiliar music, I find I have fragments of the music on my mind. In a much more complete way, some autistic savants can recall entire pieces of unfamiliar music after only one hearing.

FAMILIARITY AND PREDICTABILITY

It is difficult to put into words what the experience of familiarity is. In the previous chapter, the experiments of Zajonc (1980) were described, which demonstrated that which has been experienced before evokes, when it is recalled, an experience of pleasure. Perhaps this pleasure is what the feeling of familiarity is. When I experience something I have experienced before, there is a heightened intensity to the experience, due presumably to an earlier memory trace having been traversed. Sometimes people get this heightened intensity when they could not have had the experience before, a condition called *déjà vu*. Some people with temporal lobe epilepsy get this experience frequently. Presumably then there is a mental process that generates this feeling of familiarity, which sometimes is triggered off inappropriately. I sometimes have the experience of watching an old movie, and one or two aspects of the movie begin to feel familiar. As the movie continues, the feeling of familiarity increases until I am convinced that I have seen the movie before. I am then able to start predicting what happens next.

Predictability is important from a survival point of view. If, when I see something familiar, that which happened next when I first saw it comes to mind, it may warn me about an imminent danger, and give me time to take evasive action. Memories must be stored in time sequences, so that once one familiar event is recalled, the next event in the sequence comes to mind; like when listening to a long-playing record, when one track comes to an end I find the next track coming into my mind.

Explicit and implicit memory

The terms explicit and implicit are used to differentiate between the deliberate, conscious (outer me) cognitive system and the automatic, unconscious (inner me) one. Since all memorising is effected unconsciously, the distinction between explicit (declarative) and implicit (nondeclarative) memory seems rather odd. Spiegel and Li (1997) described implicit memory as being, by nature, relatively less "conscious" than explicit memory (their quotation marks). They state that ". . . explicit episodes clearly lead to the creation of implicit memory stores" (page 178). The difference between implicit and explicit relates to the ability of bringing memories into consciousness. Explicit memories can be recalled but implicit memories cannot, though their effects can be observed.

A much cited example of implicit memory (Claparède, 1911) involves a woman who, following an accident, could not commit anything new to memory. Even though she saw her doctor every day, she was never able to recognise him. One day, the doctor entered her room with a sharp pin secretly attached to his palm. On shaking the doctor's hand she received a mild pinprick and withdrew her hand abruptly. The next day when the doctor came into her room, even though, as usual, she did not recognise him, she refused to shake his outstretched hand.

Schachter (1987, 1992) and others have consistently found that amnesic individuals are seriously impaired on standard tests of explicit memory but perform at normal levels on a variety of implicit memory tasks, which depend upon the motor-perceptual or sensory aspects of experience. Cloitre (1997) observed that the dissociation in performance on these two types of memory task has led to the suggestion that explicit and implicit memory are distinct and relatively independent memory systems. In a number of circumstances, explicit memory for an event becomes impaired and implicit memory remains intact.

Share (1994) referred to a particular form of implicit memory, though he was not the first to describe it (Broadbent et al., 1986), which Reber (1993) considered to be based upon a relatively primitive memory system. Invariably it concerns early traumatic experiences. Its presence can be deduced only from various behavioural enactments, pictorial representations and the entering into consciousness of inexplicable ideas and fears. In many instances, there is no way of proving that what appears to be being "remembered" actually happened, but Mollon (1998) provided a case study in which the events were finally corroborated. The study is long and detailed and matches each implicit memory with an actual event or situation.

Most so-called implicit memories are sensory rather than verbal. Van der Kolk and Fisher (1995) observed that traumatic memories are more likely to be kinaesthetic, iconic, proprioceptive, sensory and affective, but lacking a coherent narrative, and therefore stored in the right cerebral hemisphere. DelMonte (2000) proposed that "Learning to put words on to these non-verbal fragments develops one's narrative competence, and may help to trans-fer the memory to the left hemisphere where it becomes more linguistically encoded" (page 6). Once in this verbal form, it can be discussed, examined and made sense of.

Implicit learning

Lewicki et al. (1992) demonstrated that people can learn rules without being aware that they have done so. Subjects were shown a set of photographs of people who varied widely in their facial appearance. The people in the photo-graphs were described as being kind or persistent across a range of facial features except that each adjective was consistently matched with a certain hair length. Later the subjects were shown another set of pictures and asked to decide which ones appeared kind or persistent. Though they did not realise it, their choices varied according to whether the people in the photographs had long or short hair.

The retrieval of memories

Automatic, nondeliberate (inner me) retrieval

Just as I do not consciously commit experiences to memory, I also do not consciously make connections with remembered material. Sometimes an appropriate quotation comes into my head. One evening I was expecting a visit from someone important, and the phrase "The king comes here tonight" (from Shakespeare's *Macbeth*) came to me. On another evening, I was driving my ex-boss to a party, and the phrase "I'm a main line train and I'm carrying the king, Weeeooee" (from a children's storybook) came to me. The words of songs that come to mind are sometimes astonishingly appropriate. One Christmas Eve, I was driving into a packed, supermarket car park, and I found myself singing, "Somewhere, there's a place for us" (from Leonard Bernstein's *West Side Story*). Walking home one evening, I noticed a sad-looking woman walking towards me. I found myself singing, "Are you lonely just like me?"

(from the Roy Orbison song "Pretty Woman"). Freud (1904) provided some astonishing examples of words, phrases or ideas coming into people's heads, which were appropriate to the situation. Sometimes the connection between the words and the experience was unclear until Freud helped the person to work it out.

The recall of emotion

Because emotion is locked in with memories, when memories are recalled, the emotion is recalled too. If a particular recalled event, location or person is associated with success, pleasure is aroused; if it is associated with danger, fear is aroused; if it is associated with failure, depression is aroused. Sometimes I had not realised that that which I had recalled had the particular emotion associated with it, and I was surprised to be feeling the emotion. That is, I (outer me) had not realised the emotional significance that the inner me had accorded to it. I might not have realised how much a person had meant to me until I experienced the emotion that had accompanied my remembering that person.

The emotion associated with past events is linked to the issue of repression, (considered in Chapters 4, 5 and 15). The in-between me seems able to block the recall of particular memories associated with unpleasant emotion. Orr (1999) noted that the question of traumatic amnesia across a range of experiences was noncontroversial until it became associated with sexual abuse.

Deliberate (outer me) retrieval

Even with deliberate memory retrieval, all that I (outer me) do is trigger it off. I play no part in the actual retrieval process. Ideally, I vaguely think of that which I am trying to remember, and almost instantaneously, that which I am trying to remember enters consciousness. Because this happens quickly and effortlessly, I would normally pay no attention to how it happens. Is it like going to a public library and asking the librarian (inner me) to find me a book? Does that which is the equivalent of the librarian first find the right "room," then the right "shelf," and then move along the shelf until it finds the right "book;" and then, hey presto, emerge with the "book"? In these days of computers, the idea of tapping into a memory store is not so difficult to conceptualise as it used to be; but is the brain's method of retrieving a memory the same as this?

If it is true that the inner me is unaware of the existence of the outer me, and this is one of my basic assumptions, it can hardly be said that the outer me and the inner me cooperate in the retrieval of the memory, so perhaps the librarian analogy is not a good one. It is more that I (outer me) have a way of "milking" the inner me. What essentially I do is hold within consciousness something approximating to what I want; and somehow then, the inner me, quite automatically, picks out that which I want from the memory store. But what is it that I hold? It cannot be the memory itself, so it must be some kind of forerunner to it. In Chapter 13, I write of Pinker's (1994) use of the term mentalese to refer to what he calls the language behind language, the thing that the language becomes an embodiment of. Perhaps then what I hold on to is something like this. I recognise it as that which I was looking for when it arrives, so I must have had something in mind that matches that which arrives.

Sometimes (and this happens increasingly as I get older) the memory does not come. Is the book no longer on the library shelf? I know what I am trying to remember (the name of the book); so I must still have that forerunner somewhere in my consciousness (at the back of my mind, wherever that is). Usually, I find that the memory is still there, because eventually I manage to retrieve it; but it may require some ingenuity to do so. I have the experience of the memory being on the tip of my tongue. Presumably the memory trace (whatever that is) has become weaker. I get glimpses of it, but not quite enough to grab hold of. I try one association after another. What is the first letter? Is it a long word or a short word? I often actually know these things. Eventually, perhaps due to the summation of all these associations, the memory comes. Sometimes trying to remember something blocks the retrieval (see Chapter 2 on trying) and when I stop trying, it happens.

Delayed retrieval

What is impressive is that once the request for a memory is put to the inner me, the inner me seems to be put on alert regarding that memory, sometimes for several days. It is like a detective keeping a case open. It remains sensitised to any additional cue that might help to make a connection. A few years ago, I read of the death of the American woman athlete Florence Joiner. I recalled (wrongly as it turned out) an incident when some people believed that she had caused another woman athlete to fall during the course of a race. (I have recently discovered it was not Florence Joiner who did this, but a different American athlete (Mary Decker-Tabb) – but that does not affect the story.) I could visualise the incident (having originally seen it on television) and I knew that the woman who fell was South African and ran in bare feet, but I could not remember her name. Some days later, I was watching a football match on television when the commentator mentioned the name of one of the players, Gianfranco Zola. Within a minute or two, but not immediately, the name Zola Budd came to mind, and that was the name of the athlete who fell. Once the name has been recalled, the pathway to it somehow becomes easier and the next day I find I can remember it with ease. The memory trace has been reinforced.

Memory recall and hypnosis

Under hypnosis, people can be asked to imagine they are a certain age or at a certain place and invited to describe the circumstances or what they can see.

In this state, they have access to memories that otherwise they would not have. While hypnosis is a way of establishing a more direct contact with the inner me, a complicating factor is that people are more suggestible than usual under hypnosis; so the recalled memories may not always be true ones. This will be considered further in Chapter 15.

Filling in the gaps

The principle of filling in the gaps applies not only to the interpreting of sensory input. It also applies to remembering. When a person has only fragments of a memory, the inner me embellishes them to make them resemble something more definite. Somehow the embellishments get added on to the memory, so I cannot remember the fragments without also remembering the embellishments. Consequently, I cannot distinguish between the actual memory and the embellished version of it. This happens with witnesses of a crime. They think they saw something or someone in more detail than they really did.

Filling in the gaps is also a feature of confabulation. When a demented person cannot remember something, s/he makes it up. If you ask her/him what s/he did one morning, s/he will say something s/he might have done that morning, like have breakfast or read a book. This could be a straight (outer me) lie, but it is more likely to be a piece of (inner me) gap-filling. If it is a lie, s/he will be aware that s/he has lied, but if it is confabulation, s/he will not. The confabulator has no idea that s/he has confabulated.

Inaccurate or false memories

It is an established fact that the recollection of past events can be grossly inaccurate, if not completely wrong. Greenwald (1980) has argued that we tend to create biases that support our self-esteem. He likened this to an Orwellian government's rewriting history to present itself in the most favourable light. Bahrick et al. (1996) showed that when students were asked to recall their high school grades, approximately 80 per cent inflated their remembered grades, but only 6 per cent reduced them. Ross and Conway (1986) proposed that we revise memories of how we were in the direction of consistency with how we are now. This is in keeping with a theme that runs through the book that I (in-between me) tend to protect myself against unpleasant emotion.

The issue of false memory was brought to prominence by the debate over the accuracy of people's recollection of sexual abuse by their parents, particularly during psychotherapy (Mollon, 1998). When adults have confronted their parents with this, their parents have been shocked, and accused the psychotherapists of planting ideas in their patients' minds. It is quite likely that their parents have repressed the memory. The complexity of the debate is admirably summarised by DelMonte (2000), who concluded that "The research suggests that there are false memories, true memories and everything in-between" (page 10).

Garry et al. (1994) have described four different kinds of study concerning the experimental distortion of memory. In three of them modifications to existing memories were successfully suggested, but in the fourth an entirely untrue memory was implanted into the mind of a 14-year-old boy by his older brother.

Memories of which I am not aware

I can never know how much there is in my memory that I do not have access to. Sometimes I accidentally hit upon an item of information, which brings back a memory that I did not know I had. I have come across an unfamiliar surname and recalled a man from my past who had that name. I saw a man in a movie wearing a particular type of shirt and I remembered a time, many years ago, when I had a shirt like that, but I would not have been aware of that without seeing the movie. It is a sobering thought that there must be vast numbers of memories within my memory store that I will never recall, simply because I do not have the appropriate cues to connect up with them.

People have remembered far more than they think they have. When shown a list of words, people are able to pick out these words from a subsequently shown larger list, even though they were unaware that they had remembered them, simply because the words feel familiar. Claxton (1998) referred to a number of experiments, which showed that people are reluctant to commit themselves about what they can remember for fear of being wrong. If instead, they are asked to guess, or to say which words or shapes they prefer, most of the guesses or preferences turn out to be the words or shapes that they were shown.

The neurophysiology of memory

At the end of each neuron (nerve fibre) there is a multiplicity of branches called dendrites. The endings of the dendrites that connect with other dendrites are called synapses. Electrical impulses pass from neuron to neuron by crossing the synapses. When impulses cross synapses they have the effect of strengthening the synapse, that is facilitating the passage of further impulses. Memory is thought to be something to do with this strengthening process.

There is no clear understanding of what exactly happens in the brain when a memory is formed. There are a number of hypotheses around the idea that learning brings about changes in the structure of certain brain neuroproteins (Hyden, 1977). The new neuroproteins formed during the learning process would be lost during the normal recycling process unless there were some mechanism for transcribing and translating them over and over again, but no such mechanism has been found.

It is thought that long-term memories are laid down through some permanent changes in the structure and function of neurons. Newly formed neuroproteins may alter both the structural and functional capacity of a neuron. Most theoretical models of memory assume some type of association or connection among neurons to form a network. Larger brains allow greater interaction among neurons through extensive dendritic and axonal arborisation. Brain size among species appears to be well correlated with learning capacity.

The intensity of a memory can be a useful guide to the recentness of the recalled event; the more recent the event the more intense is the memory. When I try to remember whether I have performed some routine act like locking a door, I try to imagine myself locking the door, and if this imagined experience feels intense, I know it was recently remembered, and therefore I am reassured that I did perform the act. Intensity is also associated with the importance of the event. Memories of important events have a greater intensity, even though these events occurred many years ago. This is why I say, "I remember it as though it were yesterday." This is like thinking that a sound is close because it is loud. When a memory is recalled, i.e. brought into consciousness, its intensity is increased (the synapses are strengthened), which makes it easier to recall the memory again.

Reinforcement through recollection

The memories of people or events I have not thought about for some time fade, so I have difficulty recalling them. If, after some effort, I do recall them, remembering them another time becomes easier. Recalling a memory increases its intensity, and repeatedly recalling it increases it still further. Since I recall important events more frequently anyway, their intensity is further enhanced by their repeated recollection.

Brain structures involved in memory

LeDoux (1998) observed that there are multiple memory systems in the brain, each devoted to different memory functions. The hippocampus is of central importance to declarative memory but not to procedural memory. With hippocampal lesions there is amnesia for the one but not for the other (Squire, 1983). When procedural memory is concerned with physical skills, like swimming or riding a bicycle, it involves the motor areas of the cerebral cortex, the cerebellum and the basal ganglia (Eccles, 1989). When it is concerned with cognitive processing skills, like the skills involved in analysing and making sense of information, different cortical areas are involved (Kihlstrom, 1987).

Patients who have received bilateral hippocampectomies for the treatment of severe, incapacitating hippocampal epilepsy remain incapable of remembering even just a few seconds earlier (anterograde amnesia) for the rest of their lives (Milner, 1966). Experimental bilateral hippocampectomy in monkeys has brought about a similar result. One hippocampectomy patient (H.M.), who has been the subject of intensive study, had retrograde amnesia for the three years prior to the operation, though his memories from before this period remained intact. It seems therefore that memories are ultimately stored in the neocortex, but it takes up to three years for them to become fully established there. During this time, the hippocampal input to the cortex has to be repeatedly replayed; that is, the memories have to be repeatedly recalled.

The hippocampus is not just a mechanism for laying down memories. It also brings together information from the various sensory cortices and integrates them into a coherent memory at the time of retrieval (Bremner et al., 1995). As LeDoux (1998) put it, ". . . the hippocampus encodes space" (page 199). According to O'Keefe and Nadel (1978) it forms sensory-independent spatial representations of the world, which provide a context within which to place memories. Animals that hide stores of food and find them again have a larger hippocampus than animals that do not.

LeDoux (1998) explained that information from the cortical areas for each of the various senses (see Chapter 9) are passed on to what is called the transition cortex. Here the information from the different senses are mixed together. This creates representations of the world that include all senses at once (Eichenbaum et al., 1994). By this means, we leave the purely perceptual and enter the conceptual domain of the brain. The transitional cortex then passes these conceptual representations on to the hippocampus, where even more complex representations are created. Rudy and Sutherland (1992) proposed that the hippocampus creates configurations that transcend the individual stimuli that contribute to them.

That which is called affective or implicit memory appears to function independently of the hippocampus. Its probable site is the amygdala, and this fits in with its association with strong emotion. Milner et al. (1968) showed that a patient with severe hippocampal damage could not remember a visit to his mother in hospital, but he did express the vague idea that something may have happened to her. Gloor (1986) observed that the electrical stimulation of the amygdala often evoked fear; but sometimes it evoked the memory of a traumatic event.

Part V

The active me

In contrast to Part IV, this part is concerned with action. It considers three kinds of action: motor action, communicative or linguistic action and mental action. The outer me plays a much greater role in all three of these areas than it did in any of the areas of Part IV. It seems then that the outer me evolved as a means of extending human striving, adaptability and enterprise. Human motor action is far more flexible than that of any other animal, but it is in communicative and linguistic action and in mental action that humans outstrip all other animals.

12 Motor action

The most fundamental difference between animals and plants is that animals move. Originally, animals needed to move in order to find and eat plants, and this is still the case for herbivores. Since plants do not contain much energy, animals need to eat lots of plants to get enough energy to enable them to move, to find more plants. Herbivores spend the greater part of their waking hours finding and eating plants. Since animals contain more energy than plants, carnivores are able to spend less of their time searching for and eating animals, and this frees them up to do other things.

Because movement is so complex, animals needed a nervous system to coordinate it, and because the nervous system is so complex, they needed a brain to coordinate that. Once the brain evolved, it continued to evolve further, becoming larger and more diverse in its range of functions; so the complex brain that we have today originated simply as a coordinator of movement, and this continues to be one of its more important functions.

Why do humans move?

In civilised societies, food is so plentiful that finding food accounts for only a fraction of human movement; yet humans spend a great deal of their time moving. Essentially, humans move in order to attain and maintain the inner me's objectives, so the impetus to move originates in the inner me. The outer me may think it decides, but the outer me exists solely for the purpose of serving the ends of the inner me, so it simply thinks up more effective ways of doing what the inner me requires to be done.

The inner me is not simply the source of the objectives, it is also an executor of various bodily functions, including movement; so the inner me provides the impetus, then the outer me thinks up the action, and then the inner me takes over the execution of the action. This is a perfect combination in that the outer me is a specialist whose job it is to convert intention into action, to think up how best to do things. It need not concern itself with how the action is executed.

Anatomical and physiological consequences of the need to move

To enable them to move, animals need muscles. These muscles need a constant supply of highly concentrated, energy-containing substances called sugars, a constant supply of oxygen to enable them to metabolise these sugars, and the constant removal of the end products of their metabolism. For this they need a digestive system to extract the energy-containing substances from the food, a respiratory system to extract oxygen from the air, an excretory system to dispose of the biproducts of metabolism, and a circulatory system to convey sugars and oxygen to the muscles and the biproducts of metabolism to the excretory system.

The skeleton

All but the simplest of animals, like slugs and worms, have muscles that contract against a rigid structure called a skeleton. Small animals, like beetles and crabs, manage with an external skeleton, but the larger animals, called vertebrates, need an internal skeleton of bones that articulate at joints. Muscles extend from the bone on one side of a joint to the bone on the other side. For movement to take place, one set of muscles has to contract while an opposite set relaxes.

The muscles

The muscles that contract against the skeleton are called skeletal or striatal muscle. They are structurally different from the smooth muscles that control the alimentary canal and the bladder. Smooth muscles, like the muscles of slugs and snails, do not contract against a skeleton. The heart is, in effect, one complete muscle, called the cardiac muscle. It has a unique structure because it has to perform the unique function of producing one pulsatile contraction, a little over once every second, throughout waking and sleeping. This it does from the time we are born to the time we die.

Together, the smooth muscles and the cardiac muscle are called the involuntary muscles, because they are not under voluntary (outer me) control. They are under the control of that part of the inner me that is called the autonomic nervous system. Although I can feel them moving, I have no power to control them. I am quite unaware of what they are doing, and yet, throughout life, they continue to function purposely and efficiently.

Although the skeletal muscles are called voluntary, they are largely not under voluntary (outer me) control. If I decide to kick a football or scratch my head, I (outer me) decide upon the action, but then the action takes place by way of a whole series of inner me-directed and monitored operations. My body needs to be maintained in a suitably supportive posture in order that I do not fall over during their execution, and when I move one part of my body all kinds of muscles in other parts of my body have to be brought into play to correct the balance, and all this has to happen quite automatically and instantaneously. Later I will describe how many actions involving the skeletal muscles, like jumping out of the path of a fast-approaching car, pulling my hand away from a hot plate, epileptic seizures, blinking, nervous tics, laughing and smiling, are not even initiated by the outer me.

Some actions can be initiated by either the outer me or the inner me. I can blink my eyes either wilfully and deliberately or as part of a reflex response. I can open my mouth either as a deliberate act or reflexly, as in an expression of surprise. I can withdraw my hand from something hot either deliberately or involuntarily.

The coordination of movement

The nervous systems of all animals are organised in such a way as to cause many muscles, or groups of muscles, to operate in a smooth and coordinated fashion. The organisation of a single action is complicated enough, but considering that many movements occur in long sequences, the neural connections and adjustments that are necessary to bring them about are extremely complex. Such operations enables millipedes to move their legs in purposeful progression, swallows to catch flies on the wing, gibbons to leap from branch to branch and humans to play piano sonatas.

A crucial component of the coordination of the movement of all muscles, whether they be voluntary or involuntary, is the continuous interplay between motor output and sensory input. This is called a servomechanism. The relevant regions of the brain need to be fed continuously with information about what is happening in those parts of the body where the movement is taking place. This information comes from receptors in the skin, joints and the muscles themselves. Within the neural circuits, there is a constant checking of action against intention. Any deviations from the intended action are corrected in response to the incoming information.

Unlearned (inner me) motor activity

Prenatal motor activity

Once organs reach a degree of maturity, they become functional even before birth. The heart needs to beat from an early stage to promote the circulation of the blood. The limbs move inside the uterus. They even move purposefully, as when they withdraw from a painful stimulus.

Postnatal, innate actions

In many species, the young are able to perform complex actions from birth. Flying insects can fly; fish can swim; turtles can crawl down the beach to the sea; and kangaroos can climb into their mother's pouch. Even for humans, some actions are possible from birth. Newborn infants can cry which, in terms of muscular coordination, is a complex action. They can clutch at objects and feel for and feed from the breast. They can open and close and move their eyes, and evacuate their bowel and bladder.

Movements that follow shortly after birth

Horses, cows and deer can stand and walk within hours of birth. Within days, birds can take flight from the nest. Compared with most animals, humans develop their motor skills slowly. Within days of birth, infants can track a moving object with their eyes, reach out and take objects that are offered to them, and smile at their parents, but it is weeks before they can crawl and months before they can walk. Some have proposed that humans are born prematurely in order that the head can pass through the birth canal before it grows too large.

Preprogrammed behaviour

All spiders can construct a web; all bees can construct a honeycomb; all birds can build a nest. All birds of a particular species sing the same song, and build the same kind of nest with the same materials. Some butterflies, fish and birds instinctively migrate at the same time and go to the same distant places. Much courtship, mating behaviour and parenting behaviour is pre-programmed. All ducklings follow the first encountered moving object, which usually is the parent.

Humans have some preprogrammed behaviour. Infants do not need to learn how to shiver, cough, sneeze, suck at the breast, swallow, vomit, yawn, laugh or blink. They do not even need to learn how to crawl, walk or run. These actions happen when the limbs and the appropriate components of the nervous system reach an adequate level of maturity. They do not even need to learn how to speak. Innately, they know how to make particular sounds, but they cannot do this until around three months when the larynx descends deep into the throat, opening up the cavity behind the tongue that allows the tongue to move forwards and backwards to make vowel sounds (Pinker, 1994).

The muscles of the head and face

The musculature of the head and face is more complex than that of any other part of the body. The eye muscles can move the eyeball so as to point the pupils in the direction of that which is being looked at. The small muscles of the iris can dilate or contract the aperture of the pupil so as to control the intensity of light that impinges upon the retina. The muscles of the larynx, tongue and mouth perform the actions involved in creating the multiplicity of sounds, variations of pitch, tone and loudness that are necessary for speaking, whistling and singing. Some of these movements, like those of the iris, are entirely involuntary; others, like moving the eyeball are voluntary, with the proviso of course that the outer me would not know what muscles to use to move the eye to where it needs it to be.

Facial gestures

Certain facial gestures occur in relation to certain emotional states. Laughing and smiling, weeping and the expression of despondency are perhaps the commonest, but there are wincing, grimacing, frowning, scowling, and there are the looks of puzzlement, horror, surprise and amazement. They probably evolved before we had language as a means of conveying to others what we are feeling. We do not learn how to make these gestures. They just happen at the appropriate moment as an accompaniment to the appropriate emotion. Furthermore, we cannot make them happen at will. The outer me can do its best to imitate them but the gestures it makes never looks exactly right, because outer me neural routes are different from inner me ones. I can try to imitate laughing, but unless I am truly amused, I cannot make a proper laugh. Actors try to imagine themselves into a situation in which a particular gesture happens spontaneously in the hope that it will. I have sometimes noticed that when I consider the possibility of some appalling accident, my face automatically winces. It is quite uncanny that I (outer me) find that I (inner me) have winced.

Facial gestures may also be a means of conveying interpersonal messages. We do not learn these; they just come naturally. Lowering the head, turning the head away, shaking the head, pulling in the chin, puckering the brow, half-closing the eyes and tightly closing the lips all seem to be ways of avoiding involvement. Lifting the head, looking straight at the other person, thrusting the chin out, raising the eyebrows, opening the eyes wide, opening the mouth (though not too wide) and smiling all seem to be ways of seeking involvement.

The interesting thing about facial gestures, as also about some bodily gestures, is that they seem to be a visual representation of what they are trying to convey. Closing the eyes, puckering the brow and closing the lips are an enactment of the message "You can't come in." Pulling the chin back tightly is an enactment of withdrawing into yourself. Shaking the head is a way of making it difficult for the person to get close to you. Opening the eyes, or the mouth (or the arms) are ways of saying "The way is open. Please come in." It could be argued that an exception to this is the expression of shock and horror, when the eyes and the mouth are opened wide. However, in the entry gestures, the face is relaxed, but in the horror gesture it is tense. Although the eyes and the mouth are open wide, they do not look like friendly places to go; and the eyes are not directed at the person.

Sexual invitation is also conveyed by the face, but it is more subtle and ambiguous, because it is not safe to make it too obvious. The head may be turned away or bowed down but the eyes are directed towards the recipient. The eyelids may flutter. The lips may be slightly opened and the tongue may be slightly exposed.

Bodily gestures

Certain bodily gestures also seem to be innate means of expression, again perhaps originating from a time before we had language. Shrugging the shoulders conveys "I do not know." Lifting the arms with the palms turned upwards conveys "I give up," "I don't mind," "Please yourself." Moving forward with the arms outstretched is perhaps a prelude to an embrace. Beckoning means come; and holding the arms out with the palms turned towards the other means keep away. Holding the finger to the lips conveys be quiet. Clasping the hands behind the head expresses frustration. Burying the head in the hands is an expression of failure. There must be many more. A person standing in the open air making hand gestures while speaking into a mobile phone is a common sight. Since the recipient cannot see these gestures, it reveals how automatic these gestures can be.

Lakoff (1997) expressed the view that bodily movements are a metaphor of what the person is feeling. For example, someone weighed down by responsibilities may carry her/himself as if s/he had a heavy load on her/his shoulders. Lowen (1967) described how people who are withdrawn and turned in on themselves walk with an arched back and their head bent down. In *Relating in Psychotherapy* (1999/2002) I described the typical postures and gestures of upper people and lower people.

Learned motor activity

The motor behaviour of early-evolved animals is the result of rigid, instinctive, sequences. In more later-evolved animals, increasingly more behaviour patterns are learned after birth, so their behaviour is more adapted to changing needs. Humans have the least amount of behaviour preprogrammed from birth. Humans must be the only animals that must learn how to swim.

If it is assumed that all innate behaviour is mediated through the inner me and noninnate behaviour has, initially at least, to be learned via the outer me, then it must be concluded that most animals have some kind of outer me, because most animals are capable of learning some new forms of behaviour. Or perhaps there are two kinds of learning, which could be called inner me (implicit) learning and outer me (explicit) learning; inner me learning being the fairly minimal modification of innate, instinctual behaviour, which happens automatically, and outside of consciousness, and outer me learning being that which is deliberately planned and carried through, involving the objective examination of the nature of a problem and the conscious development of a plan or strategy for resolving or overcoming it. Where humans are capable of both, most animals are capable only of inner me learning.

Inner me learning

Much animal learning involves remembering the location of food sources, and the routes to them, or the avoidance of hazards. Most animal learning experiments are constructed around either the need and the search for food, or the escape from danger, and involve pressing buttons or running mazes, which ultimately lead either to the reward of food or the avoidance of pain. In effect, this is little different from the animal's normal food-seeking or danger avoiding behaviour. When the animal encounters food it registers the equivalent of pleasure, and the route to and from the food becomes associated with this pleasure. When it encounters danger it registers the equivalent of fear, and the dangerous circumstances become associated with this fear. In animal training, the animal is either rewarded with food when it does what the trainer requires of it or punished with pain when it does not. (The carrot and the stick.)

In the wild, a particularly important form of animal learning is the assessment of its strength in comparison with that of another. Parker (1974) called the animal's overall capabilities, in terms of size, height, fitness and so on, its resource holding potential (RHP), and Lorenz (1981) called the testing of the relative strengths of two animals the ritual agonistic encounter. In this encounter, the animals confront each other and, by some means or other, assesses their respective resource holding potentials. The one that "concludes" that the other's RHP is the greater withdraws, and in all subsequent encounters it defers to the other. Where there is no obvious, perceived difference, the confrontation proceeds to an actual conflict. A stage is reached in the conflict at which one concedes to the other, and again, thereafter it always defers to the other.

Humans largely retain these inner me forms of learning. They become excited by the anticipation of food, and they associate learned routes to food with pleasure. They become anxious when approaching dangerous places. They probably also defer to people they have previously experienced as their superiors. They are however capable of modifying these reactions by way of the outer me's further knowledge about places and circumstances. The outer me may know that the restaurant that was always so good is now under new management and should now be avoided; that the place in the road where an accident occurred is no longer covered with ice and is no longer dangerous; and that the person who was always so good at chess has recently lost to a number of indifferent players; so is no longer a threat.

Outer me learning

The outer me is less reliant upon innate behaviour patterns and has far greater flexibility and adaptability to changing circumstances. Human infants are vulnerable because they have relatively few innate behaviour patterns; but humans learn quickly and they rapidly acquire a repertoire of behaviours that make them far more versatile than any other animal. They make up their own motor routines and they are also able to draw upon routines that others have developed.

Once routines are established, they get passed down to the inner me, and are indistinguishable from innate behaviour patterns. Children learn such skills as tying shoe laces, which would be beyond the capability of any other animal. I become unaware of the actions that I learn in this way, like doing up the buttons on a coat, reaching for the light switch when entering a dark room, and preparing to turn over as I get closer to the bottom of a page. I am also capable of unlearning and relearning when circumstances change, though there is usually an overlap period when I tend to slip back into the earlier routine, like reaching for the buttons in the wrong place when putting on a new coat and reaching for the light switch in the wrong place after it has been moved.

Humans are capable of astonishing feats of learning. Once they have learned a certain set of motor skills, like riding a bicycle or driving a motor car, they can apply them in a diverse range of circumstances. They can learn not only how to perform certain motor skills like tap-dancing or walking a tight-rope; they can also learn long sequences of motor actions like the choreography of a ballet or playing a piano concerto.

The inner me and the outer me in the acquisition of motor skills

Some actions are controlled entirely by the inner me, like the startle response, noise, blinking, laughing, tics, twitching, wincing, sneezing, teeth chattering, shivering, trembling, vomiting, involuntary spasms, the movements that are involved in reaching an orgasm and the labour contractions when giving birth. Some actions, like breathing and blinking, can be either inner me or outer me controlled.

A whole range of acts are performed without thinking, like raising an arm to shade the eyes from the sun, flicking away a fly, raising the arms as a protective gesture when being attacked, ducking to avoid a flying object, stepping aside to avoid colliding with someone, grabbing a sheet of paper as it starts to blow away, flattening the skirt as it is caught in the wind and taking action to avoid falling when slipping on ice. These are all inner me controlled, and some may even be innate. The inner me can orchestrate all the adjustments in posture and movement that are necessary, say, for a person to catch a ball. Catching a ball is an extremely complex act, which most children can master before the age of 10. It involves tracking the movement of the ball with the eyes, judging how fast it is travelling, and moving the arms and hands to where it is anticipated it will be at the end of its trajectory; then opening the hands at the exact moment the ball arrives and immediately clasping them shut.

The actions controlled by the outer me are deliberate ones, like peeling an orange, hammering in a nail, unscrewing a lid and touching the toes. The outer me comes into its own in new and unfamiliar situations, which have no established routine. In these, the outer me has to think up what to do. The more routine an action becomes, the more it becomes taken over by the inner me. When new motor tasks are learned, the outer me is in control, but once they are learned, they come under the control of the inner me. This frees up the outer me to concentrate on new problems.

Once humans have learned how to perform certain complex actions, like juggling, acrobatics, high-board diving, high-jumping, ice-skating routines and dance movements, these actions are performed best when there is no interference from the outer me. Hence, they are passed over to the inner me (cerebellum in this instance). Athletes are trained to allow the inner me to take complete control and not to think of what they are doing when performing these tasks. The less they are aware of what they are doing, the better they perform the tasks. After making a match-winning 173 not-out against the Australians, the English batsman, Mark Butcher said, "You have periods of batting where you can't do anything wrong and you're not thinking about your technique, you're just watching the ball and playing it and any batsman will tell you that when you get into that sort of mode, that's the most perfect way for batting" (Engel, 2001).

DRAWING UPON BASIC SKILLS

There are many situations in which an accumulated repertoire of basic skills can be drawn upon and brought into play in novel situations. This is particularly evident in various kinds of sporting activity. Professional footballers, tennis players, ice-hockey players, baseball players and basketball players learn a range of basic skills, but they do not learn specific situations in which they may be used. When participating in their particular sporting activity, the speed of play is so great that there is no time for players to decide which skill to call upon and exactly how to use it. Performing quite unselfconsciously, they find that they have done exactly the right thing.

Combining inner me and outer me functioning

Once they have been learned, routine activities, which have become predominantly inner me executed, can also be monitored and modified by the outer me. It will cut in when something unusual occurs or some new variation is required. Superimposed upon these basic, routine functions there can be outer me directed actions. The act of typewriting may be automatic but the outer me may be deciding what should be typed and how it should be typed: where paragraphs begin and end, what sequence the paragraphs should follow, when to use bold type or italics. Playing an instrument may be automatic but the outer me may be deciding what should be played and how it should be played. It may notice when something is wrong with the instrument or with the acoustics of the hall. Driving a car may be automatic but the outer me may be deciding where to drive and how fast to drive. It may be noticing that someone is wanting to overtake and wondering when it might be best to let her/him to do so. The footballer may be using all his footballing skills but the outer me might be thinking up ways of outwitting the opponent, looking to see where fellow members of the team are and to whom it would be best to pass the ball. Humans are functioning at their best when the inner and the outer me are interacting in this way.

When the inner me makes up its own mind

Since thinking so much about the outer me and the inner me, I have been surprised how often the inner me seems to make up its own mind about what to do. While screwing in a screw in an awkward situation, I notice that I have changed position to get a better grip on the screwdriver. Having picked up the milk bottles from my door step, I have no arms free to close the door, but I notice that my head has pushed the door to. Damasio (2000) provided the following recollection:

> I was coming up to my study with a book in my left hand and a cup of coffee in my right. Earlier, midway up the stairs, I had left two pens on a step. As I climbed the stairs, without noticing any thought on the matter whatsoever, smoothly and swiftly, I transferred the cup to my left hand, a skilled action that required a precise movement so as not to spill the coffee and that also entailed slipping the book under my left arm; I then proceeded to pick up the pens with the right hand. In retrospect, all of these actions, which are not routine in the setting and sequence, were occurring seamlessly and seemingly thoughtlessly. In fact, I only noticed that there was a "plan" behind these actions when I saw how my right hand had adopted the shape necessary for the prehension of the two pens given their spatial orientation (page 129).

Damasio observed that Jeannerod (1994) has shown that the process of executing motor activity masks the mental process that constitutes the preparation of the movements.

This is reminiscent of what I wrote in my book about psychotherapy (Birtchnell, 1999/2002). As I sit doing psychotherapy I notice that I have made remarks in response to what the client had said which, objectively, seem to have been highly appropriate, though I do not recall having consciously decided to make them. What is going on here? Has the inner me been "watching" me in action for so long that it has learned how to behave like an outer me? Has it noted what I have done and said in certain situations that now it simply knows what I am going to do and say in these situations and gets in before me?

THE ALIEN (OR ANARCHIC) HAND SYNDROME

This condition, also called the post-commissurectomy syndrome (Ferguson et al., 1985), is the result of damage to the corpus callosum, sometimes following a stroke and sometimes as the result of the deliberate, surgical splitting of the corpus callosum as a treatment for epilepsy. In it, one arm or hand appears to have a life of its own, making movements or performing actions that were not intended or voluntarily initiated by the person, and that frequently cause the person extreme distress. The hand may grab hold of a door handle and not let go, so that the person cannot proceed through the door. It may repeatedly snatch an article on display in a shop, even though the person has no intention of buying it. It may even try to strangle the person of whom it is a part. Sometimes it will repeatedly reverse an action performed by the unaffected hand, like opening a door that the unaffected hand has closed, or pulling off a garment that the unaffected hand has pulled on. The person is amazed, shocked and angered by what the alien hand has done, and the unaffected hand tries to combat or restrain the actions of the alien hand. What is so striking about this condition is that the actions of the alien hand appear to be of no benefit to the person. It is as though the alien hand is at war with the person and is intent on causing her/him the maximum inconvenience. Since the inner me is unaware of the outer me, this cannot be a conflict between them. Perhaps, since they have been artificially separated, it is a conflict between the motor cortex of the two cerebral hemispheres which, when they are not separated, work in a coordinated fashion.

SECOND ORDER NEURAL PATTERNS

Damasio (2000) made the important point that somewhere, somehow, there must be an overall coordination of the multiple complex motor activities going on at the same time. This is what he called the second order neural pattern. He gives the following example:

> Imagine yourself in a room when a friend enters and wishes to borrow a book. You get up and walk over, picking up the book as you do, and begin talking; your friend says something amusing; you begin laughing. You are producing movements with your whole body, as you rise and begin your trajectory, and as a certain posture is being adopted for that purpose; your legs are moving and so is your right arm; so are parts of your speech apparatus; so are the muscles in your face, rib cage, and diaphragm as you laugh. As in the analogy of behavior as orchestral performance, there are half a dozen separate motor generators, each doing its part, some under voluntary control (the ones that help you pick up the book), others not (the ones that control body posture or laughter). All of them, however, are beautifully coordinated in time and space so that your

movements are smoothly performed and appear generated by a single source and by a single will (page 179).

Damasio considered it unlikely that the second order neural pattern arises within a single brain region. His guess was that it arises transiently out of interactions among a select few regions. These might include what he called a slew of brainstem, cerebellar and basal ganglia circuits, interacting by cross-signalling.

Motor activity and the awareness of space

We tend not to realise how much our mobility contributes to our awareness of space. When I move my limbs, I am constantly aware of the position of my limbs in space. In Chapter 8, I proposed that our conception of how we relate to people is organised within a spatial framework. Because I can move around in my room or my house, I have an awareness of where everything is. I know where the bookshelves are, and in the bookshelves, I know where various books are, and within various books, I know where certain references are. I even know where on a particular page a certain reference is. I am sure that you are aware of this too, but you may not realise it. As I move about my house, I make all the right turnings to get me from one room to another. I move to the right drawer or the right cupboard to reach for what I am looking for. I could extend this to my street, my town, my country, even the world. If I did not move I would not care where things or places were, so motor activity and spacial awareness go hand in hand.

How outer me inventions have enhanced motor activity

In Chapter 9 I explained how, by various devices, like telescopes, humans have enhanced their perceptual capabilities. In the same way, they have enhanced their motor capabilities. I have referred to bicycles and motor cars, though not in this context. By their various, invented forms of transport, including submarines, ships, tanks, airliners and spacecraft, humans have vastly extended their ability to move about, and even travel beyond the planet. If aggression is also included within the definition of motor activity, then the appalling range of weaponry, including nuclear weaponry, that humans have invented, aimed ironically, entirely at their own kind, has resulted in their becoming by far the most destructive animal ever to have evolved.

13 Communication and language

While communication and language are closely interlinked, they are not the same thing. It is possible to communicate without language, as in nonverbal communication, and language is used for purposes other than communication, as when personal thoughts and fantasies are expressed in language.

Communication

Communication is the passing of messages across space and/or time, from one organism to another. For it to be possible organisms require emitters and receptors. It occurs almost entirely between animals, but it could be said that some plants communicate with animals by way of their flowers, their scent and the bright colour of their fruit. However, such communication is entirely one-way, since these plants emit communications but they do not receive them. While a degree of communication occurs between one animal species and another, the greater part occurs within a species, and as such, it has a powerful uniting function.

Communication is closely linked to relating (Chapter 8), though it is not the same as relating. Relating is far more than simply the passing of messages. It is a person's interpersonal involvement with another, in terms of closeness or distance and upperness or lowerness. Communication may be a means by which relating intents and needs are expressed and responded to, and relating behaviour is conducted and maintained.

Communication between nonhumans

The communication between nonhumans is almost entirely nonverbal. Animals in the wild do not use words and they certainly do not have language. They communicate by appearance, gesture and sound. The gestures and sounds they make are innately given and innately recognised, and entirely stereotyped. Different gestures and sounds communicate different messages. The communicating animal instinctively makes a gesture or sound under certain circumstances, and the recipient animal instinctively comprehends what that gesture or sound conveys. Eccles (1989) observed that animals are automata, lacking anything equivalent to human self-consciousness. They communicate by a limited vocabulary of signs, but lack speech. When bees communicate to each other the location of particular flowers, they do not *know* that they are communicating.

Like some plants, animals (and that includes, reptiles, fish, birds and insects) communicate simply by the way they look. By their appearance they are recognisable as members of a particular species. By this means they are attractive to members of their own species and repellent to those of another. In most species, the appearance of the two genders is different, and this serves to render the members of one gender attractive to the members of the other. Animals sometimes repel other animals by their colouring or marking. One kind of butterfly has markings on its wings that resemble snakes' heads. Animals that fear snakes are deterred by this.

Communication in animals by posture, gesture and movement

Animals also communicate by posture. They communicate hostility or friendly cooperation. They assume hostile postures that cause them to look big and powerful; they make aggressive movements and gestures; adopt ferocious facial expressions and make frightening noises. They do not think this out; it is purely instinctive. When two animals confront each other, they seem to have a way of assessing which one would have won had there been a fight, and the one that assesses it would have lost backs off.

Animals sometimes need to cooperate. Since hostile defensiveness is the predominant communication, they need to adopt a communication that negates this, particularly when they come together to mate. Males make appeasement gestures that indicate nonaggression, and females make submission gestures that indicate acceptance.

Animal noises

Animals have an innate understanding of what noises mean what. Some animals have a wide repertoire of noises, each conveying a specific message. There are probably some innate meanings to the noises of others, even for humans: some noises and some inflections mean the same in all languages; for instance the high notes that a parent makes when communicating with a baby. Animal noises serve specific functions, like warning off predators and laying claim to territory. They are linked with emotion and are controlled by those brain structures that are concerned with emotion. Pinker (1994) stressed that they are not the precursors to human language. The cortical areas that control human language are not present in the brains of other animals (Pinker, 1994).

Communication and the senses

One organism emits messages that are picked up by the sense organs of another. The most important senses for communication are vision and hearing, though smell and touch also play a part. People who are blind need to compensate by the greater use of hearing and touch. People who are deaf need to compensate by the greater use of vision. Smells are both pleasant and unpleasant. Pleasant smells invite proximity, particularly in mating. They also ensure the close proximity of parents and their young. Each learns to recognise the other's smell shortly after birth. Unpleasant smells drive others away. Some plants and some animals have a permanently unpleasant smell as a means of keeping others at bay. Animals stake out the boundaries of their territory by depositing urine or excrement, which other animals find repellent.

Touch is a powerful expression of the need for, and the indulgence in, closeness. Tentative touching is a communication of wanting to become close. Touch is permitted only if closeness is acceptable. Animals and humans maintain and reinforce closeness by frequent physical contact.

Human communication

Human communication may be nonverbal or verbal. Since all communication between animals is nonverbal, human nonverbal communication is likely to have evolved first.

Human nonverbal communication

It is possible that early human communication was entirely nonverbal. It can be either inner me-generated or outer me-generated. It is likely that early human nonverbal communication was entirely inner me-generated. It was probably much more extensive than it is today. Some forms of inner me-generated, nonverbal communication persist to the present day, and is significant because it *is* inner me-generated. Argyle (1988) argued that nonverbal communication expresses emotion more intensely than verbal communication, which ties in with its link with the inner me. Because of the greater efficiency of linguistic communication, outer me-generated nonverbal communication is not much used in humans. Inner me-generated nonverbal communication continues to be important. Because the inner me is incapable of deception, inner me-generated nonverbal communication is always genuine. It sometimes contradicts the more contrived, outer me-generated, linguistic communication.

Human language

Some apes are capable of learning to communicate within a limited range, but Pinker (1994) explained that, although humans are evolutionarily related to other primates, the human capacity for language did not evolve from the capacity of chimpanzees to learn artificial sign systems. Therefore, human language is analogous to but not homologous to (did not originate from a common ancestor) all other animal communicational abilities. Pinker also pointed out that human sign languages did not evolve from the nonverbal communication of other animals. Such languages are every bit as complex as vocal languages and depend upon the same brain areas. The human language capability is infinitely greater than that of any other animal. The only explanation for this is that a whole line of ancestors through which this capability evolved, over several hundred thousand generations, has become extinct.

Language is first and foremost representative, that is it represents things, thoughts, phenomena etc. Apart from this, it has three separate, though related, functions: It is an aid to rational thought; it is a means by which I may communicate with myself; and it is a means by which I may communicate with others. The first will be dealt with at length in the next chapter, but will be briefly touched upon here.

Language is a two-way process, and incorporates two sets of skills and two sets of information processing. These are the motor skill of communicating to others and the sensory skill of picking up and comprehending, through the sensory system, the communications of others. Language externalises inner thoughts into a neutral, outer space, where they may exist as vocal sounds, transmitted sounds, recorded sounds, signs or scripts. They can then be picked up by the recipient and reconverted into thoughts. People need to have the neural capacity to speak, make signs, or write, and to comprehend the speech, signs or writing of others. Brain defects may impair either the outgoing or the incoming language capabilities.

It is important to differentiate between spoken language and written language. Whereas spoken language is acquired effortlessly, written language has to be laboriously learned. Whereas almost all people can speak and understand the speech of others, until recently, the majority of people in the world could not write or read, and in many parts of the world this is still the case.

Once language is acquired, the child cannot stop using it. It thinks in language, it communicates with itself in language, it speaks in language, it may make signs in language, it communicates in language, and eventually it learns to read and write in language. There develops this incredible relationship between almost everything the person experiences and knows and the language that can represent it. What is so remarkable about language is that just about everything that is capable of being thought is capable of being expressed in language. Language becomes interchangeable with ideas, experience and knowledge. Language enables knowledge, experiences and ideas to be transmitted from person to person, to be recorded outside of the brian, so that when a person dies, her/his knowledge, experiences and ideas are not lost. Language enables one generation to pass information on to another.

Language as an instinct

Pinker (1994) observed that:

> Language is a complex, specialised skill, which develops in the child spontaneously, without conscious effort or formal instruction, is deployed without awareness of its underlying logic, is qualitatively the same in every individual, and is distinct from more general abilities to process information or behave intelligently (page 5).

Pinker preferred to refer to it as an instinct, and observed that people know how to talk in more or less the same sense that spiders know how to spin webs. Pinker explained that language is not just a single instinct: it is a whole set of instincts, and these are carefully and systematically described in his (1994) book.

One universal language

It was Chomsky (1957) who first proposed the idea that there are remarkable similarities in the structure of the world's languages. Subsequent investigators have discovered hundreds of universal patterns across languages. Possible explanations for this are that all languages evolved from one original language, or that languages reflect universals of thought; but the explanation that best fits the facts is that there is a single plan just beneath the surface of all languages; a common plan of syntactical, morphological and phonological rules and principles, amounting to a universal grammar, and that this plan is innate. Pinker (1994) compared such a plan to the archetypal body plan that is found across vast numbers of animals, like the anatomical structure of all vertebrates. Chomsky considered that when children learn a particular language, they do not have to learn a long list of rules, because they are born knowing them, and Pinker observed that, if this theory of language learning is correct, it would help solve the mystery of how children's grammar explodes into adult-like complexity in so short a time.

Language and memory

Language is perhaps the most remarkable manifestation of memory. That which is called semantic or categorical memory contains stores of learned words, verbal symbols and semantic relationships. When I speak or write, exactly the right words come into my head, simply because I am thinking of the ideas that I want to express. Although the outer me uses language in order to think and communicate, it relies upon the inner me to supply the words at the right time and in the right sequence for this to be possible. This is similar to the relative roles of the outer me and the inner me in voluntary muscular action, which were described in the last chapter. Somehow in the memory, thoughts and words must be paired off, so that I only need to think the thought and the word comes into consciousness. This has to happen so quickly that I am able to speak or write the thoughts the moment I think them. This enables me to continue speaking or writing without pause. Eccles (1989) pointed out that not only does language rely heavily upon memory, but also memory relies heavily upon language, since so much of the human cognitive memory is coded in language.

Learning a language

Eccles (1989) observed that, before they actually learn to speak, human infants repeatedly make noises with their mouths, which represents a kind of limbering-up for actual speaking. No other animal, not even apes, does this. Infants and young children have innate, language-specific processors that cause them to have a phenomenal capacity for learning languages. As they grow older this capacity becomes greatly reduced, so it is preferable that they learn languages at this optimal age. Children can pick up languages much faster than adults, which is why non-English speaking immigrants become so dependent upon their children. Whatever innate, language-learning abilities a child may have, it does not learn a language unless it has the experience of other humans talking. Children who are deaf from birth are also mute, and children who have grown up in the wild or shut away in attics or dark rooms are mute, and often remain so.

Different languages have different forms of pronunciation, which require specific motor skills to be acquired, in childhood, when the language is learned. People who, when they are adult, learn a new language, find it hard to adopt the forms of pronunciation that feature in the new language that did not feature in the original language. For example, Japanese does not contain the syllable "l," and Indian does not contain the syllable "w." When Japanese adults learn English, they substitute an "r" for an "l," and when Indian adults learn English they substitute a "v" for a "w." When children learn to speak a language, they hear the sounds and somehow know (at an inner me level) what muscle actions are required to make the sound. By the time they become adults this capacity to reproduce some of the sound they hear is much reduced, and the capacity to reproduce others is lost completely.

Almost instinctively, parents slip into what is called motherese or child directed speech. It occurs in many, but not all cultures. It is slower, more repetitive, grammatically less complex and has shorter utterances (Dockrell and Messer, 1999); but it is far from certain that this facilitates language acquisition (Messer, 2000). However, when given a choice, infants prefer to listen to motherese than to speech intended for adults (Pinker, 1994).

There are two components to language: There are the words and there are the rules that determine how the words should be combined in order to create meaning. The words belong to specific classes, like nouns, adjectives, verbs and adverbs, and it would seem that the child has an innate under-standing of what these classes are, though obviously it does not know the words by which they are described. The child is able to allocate each new word it learns to one of these classes. Since children know what a noun, adjective or verb is, all they have to learn are the words that are specific to their own particular language. This is not easy because sometimes the same word can be either a noun or a verb. In the sentence *John likes fish* the word fish is a noun, but in the sentence *John might fish* it is a verb. It is necessary for the child to learn that the word likes always precedes a noun and the word might always precedes a verb.

Pinker (1994) convincingly demonstrated the astonishing fact that many of the rules of the use of words and the rules of grammar are innate, which is why children get irregular verbs wrong (i.e. they apply the rules even when they do not apply). Eventually, of course, when they hear irregular verbs used in context, they are able to assimilate them into their repertoire. Pinker wrote, "The three year old, then, is a grammatical genius – master of most constructions, obeying rules far more often than flouting them, respecting language universals, erring in sensible, adultlike ways and avoiding many kinds of error altogether" (page 299).

There are two ways of learning a language. They might be called inner me and outer me learning. Inner me learning is the automatic picking up of words and their meaning, simply by hearing the language spoken. Outer me learning is consciously and deliberately listening to the instruction of a teacher, and doing translations and set exercises. Ideally, children should learn the greater part of their language by the inner me approach, and only top up their understanding of it by a more didactic, outer me approach. The outer me approach makes conscious and deliberate that which happens unconsciously and automatically; and this can sometimes make a difference. I remember the day clearly when, at secondary school, I learned about clauses (adverbial, adjectival etc); it improved the way I write, though not the way I speak; presumably because I do not speak in clauses.

How many words do we know?

This is a much more difficult question than would at first appear. For one thing, what do we mean by a word and what do we mean by know? Do we count singular words and plural words separately? Do we count all the word endings? Do we count the words we could deduce the meaning of even though we had never heard them before? Pinker (1994) pointed out that people can recognise vastly more words than they have occasion to use. In the whole of Shakespeare's collected works there are only 15,000 words; yet it has been estimated that an average six year old commands around 13,000 words and the average American high school graduate knows around 60,000. To attain this total, the student would have had to learn 10 new words a day from age 1 to age 18. As Pinker pointed out, learning a word is no simple matter: It is necessary to learn what kind of a word it is, what it means and in what context it can appropriately be used.

Speaking more than one language

It is not uncommon for a person to be able to speak several languages. In fact, children sometimes learn more than one language at the same time. People who communicate in more than one language constitute a majority in the world (Zulueta et al., 2001). Somehow, the inner me is able to set itself into the particular mode of the language that is being listened to, read or spoken, so that all the connections are being made within that language. At conferences I have always been impressed by the way the translators are able to switch from one language to another at such astonishing speed, listening to what is being said in one language, then repeating it in another. Zulueta et al. (2001) demonstrated that, in some polyglot patients, psychotic symptoms, in the form of thought disorder, delusions or hallucinations, can be apparent, or can be more marked, when the patient speaks in one language than in another.

Why so many languages?

If so much of language is innate, why is not the whole thing innate, and why does not everyone speak the same language, like all birds sing the same tune? Pinker (1994) explained that an entire language could never be innate because it would take up more space than any genome could accommodate; secondly, since evolution has made the basic computational units of a language innate, there is no need to replace every bit of learned information with innate wiring; and thirdly, there is a need for flexibility: new objects, new experiences, new phenomena and new ideas all require new words. Here again we have the same general principle that the inner me dictates the basic framework and the outer me provides the details to fit specific circumstances.

Language in relation to the inner me and the outer me

The relationship of language to the inner me and the outer me is complex. The instinctive nature of language, and the enormous dependence of language upon memory, places it fairly and squarely in the domain of the inner me, yet, as I explained in Chapter 2, and will discuss further in the next chapter, the outer me draws heavily upon language, and there is a special relationship between language and outer me functioning. One further twist is that language, like any other acquired skill, gets taken over by the inner me. As I speak or as I write, the words that I (outer me) need simply get expressed vocally (or in sign language, if I have that ability), in handwriting or typewriting, and at the same time, the ideas I am expressing get experienced in consciousness.

Language and the outer me

The outer me and the development of language go hand in hand, in terms of both evolution and the individual. As the outer me evolved, so also did language. As the individual acquires an outer me, s/he also acquires language. The outer me functions in a linguistic way. The kind of self-conscious, step-by-step way of describing things, analysing situations and working things out is almost entirely set within and based upon language. The outer me could not function the way it does without language. For the outer me to evolve, language also had to evolve. Paradoxically, although the outer me depends so heavily upon language, the larger part of the management and execution of language, just like the larger part of any learned skill, is managed by the inner me.

In language, the outer me and the inner me work hand in hand. The outer me has the thoughts and the inner me (the memory store) supplies the words to express them. The outer me does not even realise that it is calling upon the inner me in this way. Sometimes, however, the outer me calls upon the inner me in a more self-conscious way, as when the thought arises but the appropriate words do not come. The person then has to piece together a sentence that has a contrived quality, rather like a forced smile. Other times, particularly with the recall of a name, the inner me does not have enough associations for the name to be retrieved. The outer me then has to consciously think up and feed additional information into the inner me for the link with the word to be made.

Language and rational thought

The issue of language and rational thought will be considered in detail in the next chapter. Using words, which name things, events, actions and so forth makes it easier to progress logically, step-by-step, and to record each step as you go. Barlow (1987) suggested that conscious thoughts are often like imagined verbal communications to others. Eccles (1989) wrote:

> though the monkey and the ape have good development of all the neural machinery for cognitive and motor learning, they are greatly handicapped in a novel situation by being unable to think of the problem linguistically. So in hominid evolution we again have presented to us the tremendous role of language in evolutionary success (page 166).

Without language I could not record each step of a sequence of thoughts, and if I did not think, a great deal of language would become redundant. Eccles (1989) observed, and Pinker would agree, that even apes have nothing equivalent to human thinking, and apes cannot ask questions. Eccles considered that, because apes have nothing to say, language would be of little benefit to them.

Mentalese

Pinker (1994) proposed that behind all expressed language there has got to be an internal language upon which the expressed language draws. He called this language mentalese. No one ever hears this language, so its presence can only ever be inferred. He explained that when we say we have got the gist of what someone is saying, there has got to be a gist that is different from, and more fundamental than, what is actually being said. Presumably mentalese is not made up of words: It is more the ideas, meanings and concepts that lie behind the words, to which the words give expression. Without mentalese I could not think up a word, because I would have nothing for the word to represent. Similarly, I could not make a translation from one language to another. Mentalese is the vehicle by which the idea can be transferred. It is that which is common to, and underlies all languages. It is because children already have mentalese that they are able, in learning a language, to infer what their parents mean. Might it be that mentalese belongs to the province of the inner me, or is it the means by which, or through which, the inner me is able to conceptualise and reach its conclusions? Might it also be that the mentalese of the inner me needs to be converted into the specific language of the outer me? On the other hand, when I am trying to remember a word (even over a long period of time) am I holding the gist of that word, in the form of mentalese, in consciousness, or preconsciousness, so that I can be aware of the word that I am trying to remember?

Contrasting inner me speech with outer me speech

Although language facilitates outer me functioning, the inner me also uses language, though it may not use it in the way the outer me does. Since the inner me does not think, the term saying something without thinking is an appropriate description of an inner me utterance. Inner me speech is fast, emotive, free-flowing, spontaneous, uncensored, more natural, frank, messy, ill-disciplined and to the point. Outer me speech is slower, more deliberate, more carefully prepared, formal, impersonal, cautious, evasive, laboured, verbose and circumspect. A person will blurt out something, quickly adding that s/he did not mean it. The inner me certainly did mean it, but it had slipped through the in-between me's censor. Had the outer me realised what was about to be said, it might have decided it was unwise to say it. People are reluctant to allow the inner me free rein, fearing that they will let slip something they did not want to reveal.

Language and emotion

Language, particularly spoken language, is an important vehicle for the expression of emotion. Depressed people speak less, though the few words they do speak are laden with emotion. Anxious people speak fast, constantly repeating those things that are worrying them. Manic people also speak fast and sometimes continuously. They have what is called a pressure of speech: words and sentences come out jumbled up (word salad). There are frequent changes of direction, with wild associations, some due simply to sound similarities (clang associations). They can be quite incoherent. Angry people shout, often using swear words and obscenities. It is because swear words are disapproved of that using them provides such relief. They permit us to take emotional expression up a gear. It is because they provide such relief that they can become so addictive.

Disorders of communication

At the simplest level, Andreasen (1979) distinguished between quantity and content of speech. In terms of quantity, some people are frustratingly laconic, not saying enough to convey their meaning, while others are tediously verbose, speaking at great length and yet still conveying very little. It seems likely that inner me speech is of optimum length, and that laconic speech or verbosity are forms of outer me speech; that is, the person is intentionally being noncommunicative. In laconic speech the person is reluctant to give anything away and in verbose speech s/he is avoiding coming to the point.

In terms of content, linguists draw a distinction between texts and randomly organised sentences. For a text to be coherent, the sentences have to be linked. People are aware, though not normally consciously, of ways of establishing links. Deese (1978) considered that, for a text to be comprehensible, there has to be a hierarchical organisation of ideas, so that one idea is meaningfully connected to the previous one. Hierarchical organisation requires the speaker to have a goal to which her/his sentences are directed. Andreasen (1979) wrote of what she called derailment in which the speaker drifts either into an obliquely related idea or one that is completely unrelated. She also wrote of distractible speech in which the person switches, sometimes even in mid-sentence, from topic to topic. The topics are not obviously related but, on close examination, they do reveal a loose connection.

Thomas (1995) made the point that what psychiatrists call thought disorder is more appropriately called communication disorder, for disordered speech is not necessarily a reflection of disordered thinking. Psychiatrists are much preoccupied with the phenomenon of thought disorder, and Edwards (1972) found that over 80 per cent of American psychiatrists considered it to be the single most important symptom in diagnosing schizophrenia; though Harrow et al. (1983) observed that so-called schizophrenic thought disorder occurs in other psychiatric diagnoses, notably mania and depression. It is also apparent in the speech of normal people. Thomas and Fraser (1994) considered there to be a specific disorder of language processing in acute schizophrenia, and Frith (1992) concluded that the failure of communication in schizophrenics is related to their inability to take account of the listener's needs in following their speech. However, Andreasen (1979) observed that only 16 per cent of schizophrenics exhibited clearly disorganised speech and Frith (1995) considered that language disorder is not the whole picture.

Communication with myself

It would be difficult to communicate with myself without the use of language. When I communicate with myself, it is not the outer me communicating with the inner me; it is one part of the outer me communicating with another part. People do not confess to talking to themselves, or perhaps they do not let themselves talk to themselves, because they equate talking to oneself with being mad. Psychotic people do not so much talk to themselves as talk to a hallucination, which they experience as another person. This is more like the outer me talking to whatever it is (inner me, in-between me or a combination of the two) that has created the hallucination. I communicate with myself because I find it useful to have someone to relate to. I like the company. I do it to encourage or console myself. When I am in a predicament, I discuss with myself how I might get out of it.

Conversation

By way of language, people can convey to each other what it is like to be them, and what is going on inside their head. No other animal can do this. Because of this, language greatly enhances the capacity of humans to form close relationships. The bonds between parents and children and children and other children are strengthened when they start talking. The most important function of conversation is maintaining contact between people: the content is less important. The value of chatlines and telephone helplines is that they maintain contact between people. When people are trying to become close they talk a lot. Once they have become close they talk less; in fact they can tolerate long periods of silence.

In the next chapter, I will describe how, for most of the time, within the consciousness of most people, there is a continuous flow of ideas (CFI). A conversation becomes an intermingling of the CFIs of two people. The CFI of each person continues while the conversation is taking place and, from time to time, each person chooses to give expression to selected portions of her/his CFI, leaving long stretches of it unexpressed. When engaged in a conversation, I (outer me) am thinking about what I am thinking, and what the other person is saying, and wondering what I might usefully say next, and when to say it and how to say it, and how what I say might affect the other. This is similar to the way I conduct psychotherapy (Birtchnell, 1999/2002).

On a more constructive plane, two or more people can work together, trying to understand or solve a problem, bouncing ideas off each other, and carrying the process forward with each exchange. On a longer-term basis, human understanding progresses by one person recording her/his ideas, and these ideas being read and extended by another person who records her/his ideas.

Language function and the brain

The location of language function varies to some extent among individuals. In almost all right-handed people, and the majority of left-handed people, it is located in the left cerebral hemisphere, but in some, it is located in the right, and in a few, particularly left-handers, it is located in both. There is a greater right hemisphere contribution in bilinguals than in monolinguals, and there is a more complicated distribution of language functions in polyglots than in bilinguals (Albert and Obler, 1978). Critchley (1991) considered the right hemisphere to be involved to a greater extent in reading than in speech. Even though the right hemisphere is more concerned with visuospatial abilities, Bellugi et al. (1992) found that even sign language is controlled by the left hemisphere, indicating that it is language, and not simply the processes supporting it, which is controlled. Within the hemisphere, it is located in a number of brain structures that are distributed around the Sylvian fissure. This is the fissure that separates the temporal lobe and the frontal lobe. The region is called the perisylvian region. The two main locations for language function within this region are called Broca's area, which is on the frontal side of the fissure, and Wernicke's area, which is on the temporal side, and there are neural connections between the two. Damage to the two areas, and to the connections between them, produces different language disorders. Damage to Broca's area commonly causes impairment of grammar, and damage to Wernicke's area results in speech, which is more or less correct grammatically, but makes little sense and includes words, which only approximate to real words. Wernicke's area damage also results in the patient showing few signs of comprehending the speech of others. Sometimes, damage to the basal ganglia, two neural centres buried within the frontal lobes, also results in a language disorder similar to that caused by Broca's area damage. Gomez-Tortosa et al. (1995) reported selective impairments in one or more languages following surgery in the left perisylvanian region. Sometimes a patient with a lesion in the vicinity of Wernicke's area can have a Broca-like aphasia, and a patient with a lesion in Broca's area can have a Wernicke-like aphasia; so despite the wealth of clinical information about people with damage to different regions, the specific functions of the locations within the perisylvian region is still not clearly established (Pinker, 1994). Vocalisations other than language, such as laughing, sobbing, moaning and shouting with pain, are controlled by those subcortical areas that are associated with emotion, and not by the cortex.

14 Mental activity

Chance (1988), an ethologist, distinguished between what he called "two antithetical types of social system with markedly different functional thrusts" (page 1). He called them the agonic mode and the hedonic mode. In the first, the primary concern is with survival and security. The organism is constantly on the alert. Information processing systems are designed to recognise, attend and respond to potential threat. In the second, there is more trust and the emphasis is upon mutual support. Because the organisms are released from a self-protective preoccupation, group members are able to give a free rein to intelligence and creativity and to developing systems of order in their thoughts and social relations. Chance considered both modes to be found in both animals and humans, but that the hedonic mode is commoner and more fully developed in humans. This explains why humans can be more contemplative.

Cerebration can be divided into an active and a passive form. In the active form (outer me), there is a definite decision to generate thoughts and organise them in a directive and purposeful fashion; in the passive form (inner me), thoughts and ideas, even purposeful ones, happen automatically. Active cerebration endeavours to exclude emotion, but passive cerebration is much more linked to emotion.

Active (outer me) cerebration

Cloitre (1997) observed that one of the basic principles of the information processing perspective is that humans select out and attend only to a subset of the rich and varied amount of information available in the environment. She believed that the basic purpose of this selecting process is to organise information, make experience comprehensible and facilitate goal-directed behaviour. Damasio (2000) considered that what he called extended consciousness (see Chapter 2) included a means of preparing the way for mental activity. He wrote, "Extended consciousness has to do with exhibiting knowledge and with displaying it clearly and efficiently so that intelligent processing can take place" (page 199). This has much to do with the cognitive concept of the working memory (Baddeley, 1986) that was discussed in Chapter 5.

Intelligence

Intelligence is the human capacity to manipulate knowledge: to see the point of, conceive the application of, make sense of, perceive connections within, draw conclusions from, generate new ideas from and make predictions from, a set of information. Intelligence testing is based upon the assumption that there is one specific and precisely definable capability that contributes to all these mental tasks. Weir et al. (2002) argued that toolmaking and tool use are important indicators of intelligence, but were able to show that a crow could bend a piece of wire to make a hook to retrieve a piece of meat out of a tube; performing the task within two minutes in nine out of ten attempts. This demonstrates that (1) humans are not the only intelligent beings and (2) intelligence does not require an outer me. However, humans are easily the most intelligent animals, and the outer me contributes greatly to human intelligence.

Curiosity

Thirty years after his paper on the synthetic function of the ego, Nunberg (1961) wrote a book called *Curiosity*. In this, he considered that curiosity comes close to being an instinct. Certainly, in children, it is immense. Adults vary in the extent to which they retain their childhood curiosity. Professional researchers retain it to a greater extent than others. Nunberg described a patient whose insatiable curiosity appeared to be the result of unsatisfied early sexual curiosity, and speculated that all adult curiosity is really sublimated sexual curiosity. Curiosity is a major precursor to mental activity. It is an extension of the more fundamental drive of exploration. It is more than just wanting to get somewhere; it is concerned with discovering how and why things happen.

Thinking and objectives

Humans only think because they have objectives, and with objectives come emotions. The big difference between humans and computers is that they are motivated: they badly need to find the answer, to solve the problem. When I think, I catch glimpses of the answer, and that excites me; it also prompts me to change direction and move towards where it seems the answer is more likely to be. Computers are to thinking what telescopes and microscopes are to sensory perception. They are devices that humans have invented to increase their mental capacity in certain directions. Their advantage over humans is that they are fast, they never tire and they never complain. Logical rules are programmed into them and they are programmed to apply these rules to specific situations. Because they are not motivated and because they have no emotion, they cannot, like humans, see when they are getting close, and change direction or take short cuts; but because they are so fast this does not matter.

Rational thought

The enormous advances humans have made in both understanding and manipulating the environment is a consequence of the process that is called rational thought, which is primarily an outer me activity. Rational thought has led to the discovery and recording of natural laws. It proceeds by way of algorithms; these are logical sequences in which each step is the logical derivative of its predecessor. Logic has its own rules that apply across all areas of study. One such rule is the rule of inclusiveness, that is, if all B's are included within the category A, then all B's must also be A's, though all A's are not necessarily B's.

Claxton (1998) used the term deliberate conscious thinking to describe the kind of rational, logical, step-by-step reasoning that is one of the strengths of the outer me. He said that such thinking works well when the problem being unravelled is well defined and easily conceptualised. He used the abbreviated term d-mode (the d standing for deliberate) to define the state of mind the person is in when functioning in this way. He said that someone who is described as bright, clever or smart is good at operating within this mode. There is an undertone here that bright, clever or smart people are not necessarily the best thinkers. He referred (page 7) to the busy conscious mind that does not relax enough to allow new ideas to enter into it.

Thinking and language

While I know that thinking can occur without language, for occasionally I catch myself doing it, language certainly makes thinking easier. It enables ideas to be represented and problems to be formulated in words and sentences. This gives them an objectivity, an external reality. McGuigan (1978) has observed small movements of the speech muscles, called subvocalisation during thinking. I can listen to an idea if it is spoken, even if only in my head, and I can look at it if it is written down, and see it as something separate from me. It may originate as my thought, but once I have thought it, it exists in its own right. Language enables the stages in a sequence of thoughts to be recorded, so that I can build edifices out of thoughts, which are similar to building a building. Once I have built up to and recorded one layer, I can start building beyond that layer and then record that; so if I go away and come back I can resume where I left off; and I do not have to start again from scratch. If something has gone wrong in my thinking, I can go back over the steps and find and correct the error, and then start again from there. Not only can I do this with my thoughts, but everyone can do it both with their own thoughts and with other people's thoughts. This creates a common fund of knowledge that everyone can contribute to and take from. If there were a nuclear holocaust, and all the knowledge stores were destroyed, the whole scientific world would have to start again from scratch.

Mathematics

Mathematics is a totally nonverbal system within which reality is represented numerically. It is closely allied to logic. Mathematics is an abstraction of reality. Because of this, the same set of symbols and rules can be applied to a diversity of problems. At the end of a calculation, or series of calculations, mathematical representations have to be translated back into reality. Mathematics can only handle data that can be expressed numerically, that is that can be expressed in terms of how many or how much. Humans are not born with mathematical skills. We have to learn them, though perhaps as with language, we have innate dispositions that makes mathematics easier for us. Some young people are able to acquire mathematical skills easily, and people who gain early entry to university, and get degrees at an early age, have usually specialised in mathematics. The youngest professors are mathematicians, and people do their best mathematical work when they are young.

Where is the outer me taking us?

Having worked out how things work, the outer me has taken the next two steps of (1) changing the way they work and (2) creating things that work that never existed before. Examples of the first are genetically modified crops, cloning and extending the length of life. Examples of the second are the manufacture of vaccines and antibiotics, creating weapons and tapping the earth's energy sources. The outer me will continue to enable us to make such changes and innovations, but although these are directed towards furthering our individual objectives, they will not necessarily be for the ultimate good of the species.

Passive (inner me) mental activity

The continuous flow of ideas (CFI)

Consciousness is a kind of space where mental activity takes place. During waking hours, and possibly also through long stretches of sleep, this space is rarely empty. Because it is there, it has to be filled, so ideas just drift into it. No idea stays there long, because as each association is made, the incoming idea pushes out the existing one; but there is rarely a time when an idea is not there (when the mind is a complete blank). It is an ever changing scene. Although the flow of ideas goes on all the time, people seem unaware of it. It happens quite automatically, and the outer me has no control over the ideas that come and the connections that are made. William James called it the stream of consciousness. Others have called it the interior monologue. James Joyce used it to great effect in his novel *Ulysses*. It is possible that it plays a part in determining the content of dreams. It is a ticking-over of the brain, perhaps keeping the brain geared up for those moments when it needs to move into action.

I have to step outside myself to watch it. The continuous linking of one idea with another is quite astonishing. Each idea lasts less than a second, so within a few seconds, I have shifted attention from one idea to one that is quite distant from it, and apparently quite unrelated to it. I (outer me) sometimes try tracking back to follow the sequence of the associations and how they were made. By doing this, I can see the sense of them, even though I played no part in making them.

On a walk I can make a remark to my wife, which seems to have come out of the blue, but it is the end of a sequence of associations that I have not spoken out loud. I might see a pheasant in a field, and remember the day a local farmer came to the door with a brace of pheasants, and our son Tom said, "Poor things." Then I jump to one Christmas morning when Tom came running through the house shouting, "Mummy, Daddy, Father Christmas has come." Then I jump to the time when he said, "I don't believe in Father Christmas, but I do believe in God." Then I remember the time when our other son, Bill, was so excited by Richard Dawkins' Christmas Lecture, because he had made such a strong case for the nonexistence of God. Then I remember Jung's statement that "I know that there is a God." Then I begin to wonder whether a belief in God might be innate. At this point, I might say to my wife, "Do you think a belief in God is innate?" The CFI can even impose itself upon other mental activity. This is when it is said that the mind is wandering. I can be watching a movie in the cinema, watching a play in the theatre, or listening to a piece of music in a concert hall; all of which I believe I am totally absorbed in, and yet I am aware that the CFI is continuing.

There must be some means by which the rate of CFI is regulated, for in the condition of mania it gets out of hand. The manic person gives utterance to a flow of ideas, which enables the listener to perceive the connections that are being made. Many of the connections are personal, and the listener does not know enough about the person's life to understand where they are coming from. Ideas flow so fast in mania that they run into each other, and talk becomes incoherent. The person simply cannot stop speaking. I used to tell myself that if I noticed that my head was spinning and I was getting a headache, I was in the presence of a manic patient.

Some people seem not to like allowing their minds to drift in this way, and they adopt various methods of stopping it, which include actively doing something, distraction and meditation. Many are inclined to believe that doing anything is preferable to doing nothing. Distraction involves paying attention to something, like listening to the radio, watching television, listening to music, or reading a book, magazine or newspaper. Meditation is a particular form of distraction, which involves sitting still in a silent place and repeating a meaningless noise or mantra over and over.

The usefulness of the CFI

The CFI is useful because it connects one idea to another and establishes a relationship between the two. The connections are not random: they are based upon a similarity. Beyond this, the connections most likely to be made are to an idea or an image that is emotionally charged. Hence, within just a few connections they arrive at something significant. The direction that the CFI takes may be linked to what Bargh (1990) has called priming. If I am pre-occupied by a particular problem, sooner or later I will end up thinking about it. In this sense, all roads lead to Rome. It would not be too surprising that I would have got to the topic of the belief in God so quickly, since it is something that is presently on my mind. There is an obvious continuity between CFI and thinking. The CFI has to be slowed down or stopped, before the more orderly sequence of rational thought can begin; but perhaps it is common to move from passages of one to passages of the other.

Non-linguistic thinking

Eccles (1989) has stressed the value of language in thinking, and it is difficult to dissociate thinking from language, but the idea of the primacy of language in thinking is at variance with the view expressed by Pinker (1994) that people do not think in their own native language, but in mentalese (see previous chapter). He considered that it must be simpler than spoken language and yet be richer because it incorporates more concepts than there are words for. When I think without words, it seems that I think more quickly. If language and the outer me are inseparable, when I am thinking without words, it must be the inner me, and not the outer me, which is doing the thinking. It may seem odd that the inner me can think, but considering that the inner me can take over any task, like gymnastics, working a machine or playing an instrument, which began its existence at the outer brain level, there is no reason why it should not take over the task of thinking.

Creative intelligence

There are people who are good at solving specific problems, which are set within clearly defined limits, and there are others who are more flexible, inventive and ingenious, who can turn a problem on its head, tackle it from a different angle, redefine it, see it in different terms, or see it as not the real problem. Such people are less disciplined and more playful, and are capable of considering ideas that more conventional thinkers might consider to be absurd. Lateral thinking is one aspect of creative intelligence.

Emotional intelligence

There are those who consider stark rationality to be cold, callous, ruthless and inhumane. Computers, robots and Mr Spock (of the *Starship Enterprise*) are good at solving problems, but they lack emotion. Intelligent, but unemotional people are dangerous, because they do not consider the human implications of their decisions. That which is called emotional intelligence

(Goleman, 1995, 1998) is the capacity to be comfortable with emotional and relational issues. It was introduced to stress the fact that there is a limit to how far standard intelligence can take us. Relationship problems are every bit as complex and important as technical problems, but they require a different type of person to solve them.

Synthetic thought

The psychoanalyst, Nunberg (1931), described what he called the synthetic function of the ego. By this he meant the human capacity to organise facts in such a way that they appear to make sense. This is related to the inner me's tendency to make guesses and to fill in gaps. He considered that the ego's tendency to unite, to bind and to create goes hand in hand with a tendency to simplify and to generalise. This may cause us to jump to conclusions. Such conclusions may be wrong but there is a chance that they may be right, and if they are, that could be an advantage. If I meet three people who have red hair, and they are all bad tempered, I may conclude that all red-haired people are bad tempered. If on all three occasions that I go to Blackpool it rains I may conclude that it always rains in Blackpool. This is the basis of formulating hypotheses, and without it, science would not get off the ground. The next step is to try to find red-heads who are not bad-tempered or bad-tempered people who do not have red hair.

Nunberg introduced the term rationalisation to mean a way of making meaningful connections, or producing explanations, which fall short of a rigorous scientific analysis. The human need to explain and to make sense of is so great that we will create quite unsubstantiated explanations rather than have no explanations at all. He considered rationalisation to be particularly prevalent in children and primitive people, who have a limited capacity for rational thought. He also considered it to be present in psychotic people. Thalbourne (1991) observed that in states of elation, manic patients develop insights into the connectedness of previously unrelated events. Such people differ from children and primitive people in that they have been logical, and may well become logical again, but they have temporarily lapsed into an irrational way of thinking.

Recognising connections and similarities

An important feature of working things out is recognising when something (a shape, a texture, an idea, a feeling, a sequence of words) is like something else. This seems to be largely a function of the inner me. It is something to do with the way that memories are stored. When something enters consciousness that resembles, in any way at all, something else, either in the present or the past, that something else also enters consciousness. If the similarity does not strike me as useful, I will discard it; but at least the connection has been made.

This process of recognising similarities leads to the idea of classification. The inner me seems to have a natural tendency to classify. Any object, idea or whatever can belong to any number of different classes. A rabbit, for example, can be classified as an animal, as something to eat, as something furry, as something with four legs, as something with big ears, as something that lives in holes in the ground, as something that eats dandelion leaves, as something that breeds rapidly, as something we find squashed on roads and so on. The inner me seems to feel, "Ah yes, I know something else like that, or that does that", and then that something else pops into consciousness. The simple process of recognising similarities leads on to more elaborate groupings like concepts, analogies and metaphors.

Solving a problem without trying

A number of writers, Claxton (1998) in particular, have pointed to a particular method of solving a problem, which involves not actively trying to solve it. Trying to do something is an outer me action; it deliberately sets the mind in a specific direction; and sometimes, because we do not know exactly where to find the answer, we need a less committed approach. Claxton introduced the term the intelligent unconscious to describe that part of the nervous system that takes in information and works out the answers to problems; as he put it, "below the horizon of conscious awareness" (page 103). In contrast to the step-by-step progression of rational thought, it involves what he called playing around with the problem. He emphasised that sometimes this method of working things out can be a very slow process. It is similar to the process described in Chapter 11, of waiting for a forgotten name to come. It is another example of the inner me sometimes being very slow rather than very fast. Claxton provided a number of examples of people just waiting for the answer to pop into consciousness. He suggested that much of that which is normally called intuition can be explained by this process. He considered that it has been overshadowed by an undue emphasis upon rational thinking and recommends that more attention be paid to it. This resonates with Ehrenzweig's (1953) surface mind and depth mind and Milner's (1987) undirective thinking (Chapter 4).

Intuitive problem-solving

Claxton distinguished between what he called explicit, articulate thinking or figuring something out and the implicit approach or intuition. Spinney (1998), a science journalist, reviewed research into intuitive problem-solving. She referred to:

> mechanisms that enable the brain to soak up and ruminate on informa-
> tion, looking for subtle patterns and connections, behind your back –

without the aid of words, and in many cases without your even being conscious of what's going on (page 44).

She cited Schooler as maintaining that the nonverbal condition can sometimes be essential. His advice was that, if you want to get the most from your intuitive brain, don't strive to put into words pieces of knowledge that are essentially nonverbal. Schooler concluded that the brain handles verbal and nonverbal knowledge in different ways and is not happy to mix the two. Claxton also cited a number of works by Schooler and his associates (e.g., Schooler and Engstler-Schooler, 1990).

Where rational (outer me) thinking proceeds step by step, making sure that one step is secure before proceeding to the next one, irrational or intuitive (inner me) thinking proceeds by what are sometimes called intuitive leaps, or leaps in the dark, or leaps of faith. It is perhaps because the inner me has no sense of time that it does not, cannot, proceed in stages. Where it might take the outer me years of painstaking progress to reach a particular conclusion, the inner me might get there in a single leap. It probably does this because it ignores conventions, jumps over boundary lines and plays fast and loose with ideas. It does undoable things and thinks unthinkable thoughts, which sometimes, somehow turn out to be brilliant. Where the outer me makes sensible connections, the inner me makes crazy connections, which do, when you think about them, have their own kind of crazy logic.

Filling in the gaps

The inner me's capacity to fill in the gaps, which has been referred to in relation to memory, is also useful in working things out. A thing needs only to have a slight resemblance to something to cause the inner me to think of that something. There are any number of games that are based upon the principle of gradually adding more information (clues) until the answer becomes clear. With small amounts of information, there is a large range of possibilities, which gradually become whittled down as more information is added. This does not happen only in games. When I am trying to solve a problem, I make jumps to what the solution might be by filling in the parts of the picture that I do not yet know. As I get nearer to the solution the gaps get smaller and easier to fill.

Unconscious reasoning

Since thinking is a skill that has to be learned, it seems likely that many thought routines, just like many learned motor skills, start as conscious, deliberate, outer me procedures, but get taken over by the inner me, so they become automatic. Such automatic thoughts would have to be called unconscious thinking.

Damasio (2000) described an experiment that revealed how the unconscious (inner me) can sometimes reach conclusions before the conscious (outer me) can. Participants were invited to play a game of cards in which some packs had been loaded positively (with more cards that led to financial rewards) or negatively (with more cards that led to penalties). A stage was reached when players were consistently choosing from the good packs and avoiding the bad ones. At this stage they were producing systematic skin-conductance responses (indicating anxiety) immediately prior to selecting a card from a bad pack, though not when doing so from a good one. Damasio asked himself how does the brain get to know without consciousness?

Claxton (1998) made the important point that it is possible to try too hard to solve a problem, that the solution may come if we relax. The implication of this is that the inner me, or what Claxton called the undermind, goes on trying to solve a problem while I am not thinking about it. This is what he called the incubation period. This is an important point because it means that consciousness is not necessary for problem-solving, and that the inner me is capable of grasping the nature of a problem and working on it. One implication of this is that animals, which largely only have an inner me, may also be able to solve problems.

Thinking in mental images

Pinker (1994) observed that many experiments have shown that there is such a thing as visual thinking, which uses not language but a ". . . mental graphics system, with operations that rotate, scan, zoom, pan, displace, and fill in patterns of contours" (page 68). He argued that many creative people insist that, in their most inspired moments, they think not in words but in mental images. He wrote that physical scientists are even more adamant that their thinking is geometrical, not verbal. Some solutions are visuospatial solutions, such as, for instance, Kekulé's visualization of the benzene ring and Crick and Watson's visualisation of the double helix. The idea that we solve problems within a visuospatial framework is not so strange when we consider that our experience of the world, and probably also our internal representation of it, is visuospatial. Also, in Chapter 8, I described how we tend to conceptualise the way we relate to people and the way that people relate to us in spatial terms.

Inspirational thinking

At this point I am driven to the conclusion that thinking without words is not strictly thinking at all. There is a whole cluster of ideas and phrases that run into each other that point to a different way of coming to conclusions. Take the phrase I did not have time to think. What does it mean? It means that I arrived at a decision without thinking. So how did I arrive at the decision? I have to conclude that a different system was involved. This is reminiscent of Gilbert's (1998) fast-track and slow-track distinction. What I am talking about here is what he would call fast-track. Fast-track does not involve words, does not involve proceeding step by step. Whatever happens, happens in a flash. We speak of a flash of inspiration. So the decision did not involve breaking down the problem into its component parts. The problem was treated as a whole. In other words it was experienced as a shape or a pattern. This takes us from a dominant hemisphere process to a minor hemisphere one.

We speak of someone making an inspired guess. Claxton (1998) has argued that the process of guessing is more reliable than we realise. In psychological experiments, when people are invited to guess the answer, they get it right more times than they would have done by chance. Guessing is, by its nature, not a thought process. We say in a derisory way, "You just guessed." So what do I do when I guess? I cast aside rational thought and say the first thing that comes into my head. Where does it come from? It comes from a quick assessment of the situation. When people guess, they do not say absurd things. When asked to guess the weight of a baby, they guess within the range of weights the baby is likely to fit into; so their answer is not likely to be that far out. People do not realise that, somewhere inside them, they know roughly how much babies of different sizes weigh. My mathematics teacher at school had an expression called intelligent guesswork. This is a method he encouraged us to use to work out roughly what the answer to a mathematical problem should be before we started to solve it properly. Guessing is a quick and dirty way of coming to conclusions. In evolutionary time it probably preceded the slow and clean process of rational thought, but sometimes it is better to make a quick guess than to pass through the slow process of thinking it out logically; and sometimes the quick guess is better than the carefully thought out conclusion.

Just knowing

Guessing is linked to the idea of just knowing. Someone might say, "I just knew that the plan was not going to work." What does just knowing amount to? Here it is not necessary to implicate what some have called a sixth sense. This belongs to that category of knowing that is called knowing without realising that I know. These judgements are based upon an accumulation of knowledge that I have that has a bearing upon the decisions that I make. I may not be able to put a finger on exactly what it is that contributes to these decisions, but it is there. The inner me matches up (in some kind of nonverbal and automatic way) how things are with how they ought to be. If they match up, it feels right, and if they do not match up, it feels wrong.

Autistic savants

Certain very rare people called autistic savants are capable of solving problems very quickly without knowing how they do it. Autistic savants are a subcategory of people with autism, is a condition in which the individual has a limited capacity to become socially involved with others, combined with a limited capacity to infer what other people are thinking, an ability sometimes referred to as mindreading or the theory of mind. Most autistic people have general learning difficulties and low intelligence. Autism affects one in a thousand members of the population, but only one in ten autistic people are considered to be savants. Different savants have different capabilities. Many involve pattern recognition, like doing jigsaw puzzles, even picture-side down, drawing complicated scenes from memory and playing a tune after hearing it only once; others are mathematical, such as working out the square root of any number, dividing one very large number by another, or working out the day of the week of any given date in history.

Autistic savants do not know how they get their answers. They just come to them. You ask them what is the square root of 74, and they tell you. I cannot believe that they have learned the square roots of all numbers and just draw upon their memory store. They do it on the spot. They take in the problem as a whole and tackle it as a whole. They visualise it, and they visualise the answer. This ties in with eidetic imagery. Some autistic savants can remember an entire scene or an entire piece of music. They perceive problems in their entirety. All this fits in with the idea that the outer me appears to be less well developed in autistic people.

My younger son, who is not autistic, used to infuriate his mathematics teacher by coming up with the answer to a problem without knowing exactly what steps he had taken to get there. When he got to university he ran into difficulties because there is only so far you can get with this approach; but perhaps some autistic savants can carry this process a lot further.

Frith (1989) proposed that both the assets and deficits in autism might have one and the same origin. This she called weak central coherence; that is, autistic people are not good at pulling information together for higher level meaning. Frith argued that people with autism show detail-focused processing, that is, features are noticed and retained at the expense of global configuration and contextual meaning. One autistic child identified a baby's pillow as a piece of ravioli, thus ignoring the size of the pillow and where it was placed. Kanner (1943), who named the disorder, observed that people with autism are unable to experience wholes without full attention to the constituent parts. This seems to run counter to much else that is written about autism. It even argues against autistic ability being an inner me process, because concept formation is that which the inner me is good at. Autistic children are thought to process faces in terms of their individual features, rather than the overall configuration. Savant artists tend to draw from one contiguous detail to the next rather than sketching an outline first. They see shapes for what they are rather than for what they represent. They do not interpret them. This enables them to be quick at identifying embedded figures (Happé, 1999).

Piven et al. (1995) have shown that some people with autism have larger or heavier brains, with increased cell density in certain areas. Cohen (1994) and Happé (1999) have argued that this probably results in an increase in the number of neurons, and that this makes it less necessary for the autistic individual to extract the essence of a set of data, and thus permits her/him to process information piecemeal, with the entire data set, rather than globally, with generalisations derived from it. Thus the autistic brain may work more like a computer; but can it work as fast as a computer? It would need to, to solve some of the problems autistic savants are able to solve.

The appeal of the irrational

Often, when cognitive psychologists use the term irrational they do not mean that which is not sensible, or that which flies in the face of reason; they mean that which does make sense, even though it is not entirely clear why it makes sense. In other words, it makes sense to the inner me and I (outer me) simply have to take it on trust that the inner me knows what it is doing. On the other hand, there are those who find the irrational appealing because they consider that it transcends the rational. They prefer to believe that not everything is explicable, and that there are phenomena that are beyond our comprehension. They find the idea of the supernatural appealing. They even like to align themselves with it. Personally, I see this as a way of trying to upstage the rest of us.

Part VI

The complex me

The phenomena described in this part of the book are the most difficult to explain. They involve interactions, if not actual conflicts, between the inner me and the outer me; and the role of the in-between me in resolving these must be crucial. The issue of deceiving others, covered in the first part of Chapter 15, is the most straightforward, since it is outer me determined. From this point on things become more complicated. The most likely factor in explaining the phenomena considered is the extent to which the in-between me controls the emergence of disturbing ideas into consciousness.

15 Deception and self-deception

Some plants are capable of deception. The leaves of certain insectivorous plants have evolved in order to deceive insects, and cause them to respond to them as though they were flowers. Insects that settle upon them, or enter them become trapped. Later they are digested by the plant's secretions. Challoner (2000) observed that many evolutionary biologists consider deceit to play an important part in the animal world, and to be important for survival. Some animals have evolved with deceptive characteristics that are advantageous to them, the commonest being camouflage. They have shapes and colouring that cause them to merge into the background of their usual environments. Some animals change their colouring with the seasons, and some even change when they move from one environment to another. Stick insects and leaf insects have evolved in order to deceive insectivorous predators that they are sticks or leaves. The forms of deception of plants and animals differ from human forms of deception in that they are simply the evolved characteristics of these animals and plants. The plants and animals are not aware that they are being deceptive and, of course, they do not decide to deceive.

Humans do not have an evolved deceptive appearance, but they do have an evolved disposition to deceive; but where the evolved deception of plants and animals is directed mainly at other species, the evolved disposition of humans to deceive is directed mainly at other humans. The inner me is naive, and quite incapable of deception, so deception has to be 100 per cent outer me. An awareness of time is a necessary prerequisite for deception. The deceiver needs to be able to envisage what might be the consequences of a particular form of behaviour, and also to imagine what it is like to be the person who is being deceived. Autistic children (see Chapters 8 and 14) are not capable of deceiving people (Happé, 1999) because they cannot imagine themselves into the mind of another person. They cannot comprehend that, if they tell a lie, the other person will believe it, and act as though it were true. This suggests that they have a less influential outer me.

Deceiving others

The capability to deceive has reached new heights in humans. Camouflage was probably one of the earliest forms of human deception, used as a protection from predators and as a form of concealment in hunting. Humans developed the skill of deceiving other animals in order to catch them. They dug holes in the ground and covered them with branches and leaves so that animals would fall into them. They used other animals, or objects that resembled other animals as bait to lure their prey into traps.

The outer me weighs up the pros and cons, and considers the possible consequences of what the inner me appears to be intending to do or say. If it concludes that, in the long run, this would not be advantageous, it will step in to prevent it. From this, it is but a small step in giving the impression of acting in a particular way, in order to induce another to respond in a way that would be advantageous to the deceiver. An essential component of such deception is concealing from the other that s/he is being deceived.

Evolutionary explanations of cheating

Some evolutionists argue that people cheat because they are essentially selfish, and maintain that a person will only grant a favour to another if there is a reasonable chance that the favour will be reciprocated. The most obvious way to cheat is to convey the intention of repaying the favour and then not doing so. Trivers (1971) argued that the more subtle way is to partially repay the favour, and thus put the recipient in the quandary of either accepting the partial repayment or insisting upon equity and risking the cheater pulling out altogether. Trivers (1981) discussed a number of variants of this, like pretending to be angry that the other has not returned the favour in order to induce the other to offer a further favour, or pretending to be guilty for not returning a favour as a means of suggesting that the person has reformed, and then again not returning the favour. Feigning concern may induce another to feel better disposed towards the feigner; feigning indignation may induce another to make redress; and feigning distress may induce another to be helpful.

The combination of deception and self-deception

Trivers (1976) further argued that false emotions are more convincing when the deceiver is able to deceive himself of his sincerity. This, he claimed, may be the basis of the evolution of self-deception. The ability to deceive myself that I am not deceiving someone is an advantage. Lying while at the same time denying to myself that I am lying is a kind of double lying, and is a particularly effective strategy. I may maintain that something is, or is not the case, and really believe this to be so, even when the evidence suggests otherwise. It is possible that there is a degree of self-deception in almost all acts of deception in order to make deceiving possible, or easier to do.

Pretending

This is the simplest form of deception. There are advantages of pretending to be older (for children) or pretending to be younger (for older women), or pretending to be ill or disabled (to gain sympathy or avoid having to do something) or pretending to be richer or have more qualifications (to impress a potential mate or to get a better job).

Lying

This is the verbal equivalent of pretending. I may claim to be someone that I am not, or deny being someone that I am. I may claim to have done something I did not want to do, or claim not to have done something that would have got me into trouble. I may give false information that would put me in a favourable light or withhold information that may put me in an unfavourable light. Children are excited when they discover that they can lie, not only because it gives them the power to deceive but because it enables them to conceal from others what they are really thinking. It provides for them a protection for a secret interior that others cannot reach. It contributes to a sense of privacy and a sense of self. A patient once boasted to me that her children never lied to her. It concerned me that she did not appreciate that, by expecting them always to tell her the truth, she was denying them this control over what they revealed of themselves to her.

Lying does not come easily to most people for they (outer me) are having to behave in a way that is unnatural to them. They feel uneasy when they lie, and often give themselves away, largely by way of an inner me act, for the inner me cannot lie. Even hardened criminals are anxious when they lie, which is why lying can be detected by measuring the galvanic skin response, a physiological correlate of anxiety. People are also less inclined to lie under the influence of sodium amytal (the truth drug), which diminishes the controlling influence of the outer me. Practiced liars learn to present a blank facial expression, sometimes called a poker face.

For pathological liars, lying is a compulsive habit. They probably started to lie out of a fear of others getting to know them too well. They come to lie automatically and without thinking. They tell one lie to cover up another, and another to cover up that, and reach a point where they cannot remember what is true and what is not. Some create an entirely false life story by which they live. Strangely, it seems possible that when lying becomes second nature it gets taken over by the inner me.

Gaining upperness by deception

Cheating

Some people make a living out of cheating. Conmen need to acquire the capacity to lie convincingly. They play upon the sympathy of others by telling hard luck stories and asking for money; or play upon the gullibility of others by persuading them to pay out sums of money on the expectation of profitable returns. By this means they may deprive people of their entire life's savings. To be able to do this they must be able to deaden themselves to any awareness of the distress that others experience in response to being cheated. Because cheating only works if the cheater is not found out, concealment is an essential part of cheating, and every cheater needs to be able to deny convincingly that s/he is cheating. Cheaters acquire the art of feigning innocence. Because the advantages of cheating are so great, cheating is universal and extremely common. It occurs on both a small scale and a grand scale; individuals cheat, but so also do major financial institutions.

Devising methods of cheating is a major occupation. Because cheating is universal, cheat detection is also universal. Cheaters try to circumvent cheat detectors, so cheat detectors have to become ever more sophisticated. This results in cheaters developing ever more subtle methods of cheating. An extra twist to cheating is when two cheats agreeing not to cheat on each other, and then one or both of them breaks the agreement. The only rule in the cheating game is you cannot trust anyone, which is the basis of the much cited prisoner's dilemma.

The response to cheating

Because everyone denies that they cheat, people respond to being cheated with righteous indignation, the implication being that they themselves would never cheat which, of course, is not true. People hate cheats and hate being cheated. Those who are cheated are angry and seek revenge and retribution. People who are caught cheating are shamed, ostracised and punished. Because of this, the motivation not to be found out is great. Societies try to control cheating by proclaiming it to be dishonest or immoral, and instil into people the fear that a ubiquitous deity can see when they cheat. This makes them feel bad about cheating, but it does not stop them cheating.

Recognising cheats

Cosmides (1989) discovered that people are particularly sensitive to being cheated and are able to perform logical deductions much more efficiently when they involve detecting cheaters. When given a fairly meaningless task, like testing the rule that if a card has a D on one side of it, it must have a 3 on the other side, few people are able to select the right procedure, but when given the task of testing which people in a bar are underage drinkers, people are more likely to select the right procedure. Their motive to catch the cheater is much greater, so they try harder.

Crime

Children who are not good at school work may compensate for this by cheating, like copying other children's work or looking up answers in a book and pretending to have worked them out for themselves. This does not benefit them in the long run, but it provides them with temporary approval. Similarly, adults who are not conventionally successful may seek illegal routes to success, which sometimes become a permanent lifestyle. People follow a life of crime as an alternative means of achieving upperness (Birtchnell, 1993/96). A professional criminal may consider his lifestyle to be the equivalent of that of a legitimate professional, and will work hard to become good at it. Criminals gain at the expense of others' loss so, like the cheat, they have to live with the knowledge that their gains have caused others to suffer. They may justify this by maintaining that others can afford the loss, or that they deserve to gain because they have suffered losses themselves. A necessary part of the life of the professional criminal is the need to evade detection, so the endeavours of the successful criminal are split between the crimes and the evasion of detection. Such evasion may extend over months or years, and as the crimes accumulate, the evasion becomes more complicated.

Gaining lowerness by deception

Feigned helplessness

Realising that certain others derive satisfaction from helping them, some people feign or exaggerate their helplessness or incompetence. Helplessness evokes a feeling of wanting to help, and beggars rely upon this response. Considering helplessness to be a feature of the dependent personality, Millon (1981) wrote, "By acting weak, expressing self doubt, communicating a need for assurance, and displaying a willingness to comply and submit, dependents are likely to elicit the nurture and protection they seek" (page 114).

Malingering

Malingering is a conscious decision to feign illness or disability in order to get out of doing an unpleasant task. It is a calculated act. The person (outer me) consciously tries to impersonate someone who is ill or disabled.

Self-inflicted injury

People sometimes inflict injuries upon themselves and maintain that they have had an accident or that others have done it to them. This they do either to gain sympathy or to cause others to get blamed. It is not the same as inflicting injuries upon themselves as an expression of frustration, like slashing the arms or other parts of the body; or inflicting injury or pain as a form of self-punishment; or cutting the wrists or throat in a suicide attempt; though probably all these motives overlap, and the person is not aware which it is.

Hospital addiction

Some people pretend to have a serious medical condition by claiming to be in pain, or creating the false signs of illness by, for example, putting blood in their urine. This they do to gain sympathy, to have the experience of being looked after, to be admitted to hospital and to be operated upon. Such behaviour becomes addictive. They do it repeatedly over a number of years, sometimes travelling from town to town and from hospital to hospital.

Compensation neurosis

In compensation neurosis, the person stands to gain financially by not being capable of acting in a particular way. People who suffer industrial injuries for which they may gain substantial financial compensation are tempted to feign or exaggerate disability. Soldiers who are injured in battle, who know that they may be taken from the field of action are similarly tempted. In many instances, these people know quite well that they are trying to deceive, but because the gains are so great, they (in-between me) may succeed in convincing even themselves that they have the disability. Because the person is so reluctant to perform well, it is often difficult to determine the severity of injuries under these circumstances; but when there is a financial settlement or when the soldier is taken from the front, there is a dramatic improvement in the disability, sometimes even to the surprise of the complainant.

Self-deception

Central to the whole issue of deception and self-deception is the point that the inner me cannot and does not deceive, because deceiving is not within its comprehension; so all forms of deception must be outer me led. This is easy enough to understand when one person is deceiving another, but what about when one part of the person is deceiving another part? If the outer me is what is doing the deceiving then who is it deceiving? The answer has to be that one part of the outer me is deceiving another part. That part that does the deceiving is the in-between me. Perhaps deceiving is not the right word; it is simply keeping the awareness of something out of consciousness.

The psychoanalytic view of self-deception

One of the great strengths of psychoanalysis is that it has always taken for granted that what people say they are doing or feeling may not be what they really are doing or feeling. Quite reasonably, psychoanalysts watch what people do or say and draw their own conclusions. Although it has become something of a joke that psychoanalysts can have it both ways by claiming that when a woman says "Yes" she means yes, but when she says "No" she really means yes. The truth is that people sometimes really do mean yes when they say "No," and vice versa – and they (outer me) simply do not know that this is so. What can be so frustrating for the psychoanalyst is that s/he may never get outright confirmation of this from the client. S/he may tell the client (by way of an interpretation) that s/he is doing or feeling something, and the client may just laugh or deny it, a phenomenon psychoanalysts call resistance. A person (inner me) may actually hate someone s/he (outer me) thinks s/he loves, or actually love (inner me) someone s/he (outer me) thinks s/he hates, or even more confusingly, both love and hate a person at the same time. The psychoanalyst may get further confirmation of her/his hunch from the way that things eventually turn out, and Freud (1904) correctly observed that people can sometimes give the game away by an unthinking act or a slip of the tongue.

Why do people deceive themselves?

The expression never let your left hand know what your right hand is doing indicates that we know that we are capable of deceiving ourselves; but how and why do we do it? In a nutshell, we deceive ourselves in order to avoid experiencing unpleasant emotion. We (the in-between me) block out memories that are linked with unpleasant emotion or we block out thoughts that give rise to unpleasant emotion. In Chapter 10 I said that we should not make happiness our aim, rather we should aim to attain our objectives and, with their attainment, the happiness will come. In fact, we can only guess at what our objectives are, so all that we can realistically aim for is that happiness that comes with the attainment of an objective. In other words, we are emotion driven: We seek pleasant emotion and strive to avoid unpleasant emotion. This then is the key to self-deception: Sometimes our awareness of unpleasant emotion is simply blocked out, even though somewhere it must still exist.

Depressive realism

It is now well established that we have a more optimistic outlook than our circumstances would justify. We judge things to be better than they really are and we have higher expectations of success than realistically we should have. We have a more accurate judgement of our circumstances, abilities and prospects when we are depressed; a phenomenon known as depressive realism (Albright and Henderson, 1995). This implies that, most of the time, we deny to ourselves the true nature of reality in order not to become too unhappy. It is the in-between me that causes us to see things through rose-tinted spectacles.

Self-deception is the norm

We divert our attention away from those things which, if we thought about them, would cause us distress. This kind of self-deception comes easily to us. Those of us who live in the affluent West are able to turn a blind eye to those in Africa who are starving or dying of AIDS. There are enormous disparities across the world, or even within the same city, between those who have and those who have not, yet we turn a blind eye to them, and we are not motivated to do much about them. We continue to fly in supersonic aircraft that pollute the atmosphere and increase global warming. We do not restrict the sale of motor cars that can travel over 100 miles an hour, even though the speed limit, even on motorways, is only 70 miles an hour; and we pay little attention to the thousands of people who are killed on our roads every year. We deny to ourselves that we are capable of appalling acts, and then are shocked when some people do.

WE DECEIVE OURSELVES TO AVOID FEELING BAD ABOUT OURSELVES

The more civilised part of ourselves (outer me) know the way we ought to behave and how we ought to feel. We know that we should give to the poor, feel sympathy for those who are ill and suffering, feel bad about those that we cheat. If we avoid thinking about the misfortune of others we do not need to feel bad about them. It is the in-between me that keeps these thoughts at bay. Therefore, another function of the in-between me is to enable us to live with ourselves, and to suppress our feeling of guilt. Westen (1998) pointed to how people who pride themselves on being nonracist reveal their racist tendencies by avoiding sitting next to a black person or checking their wallet after a black person has walked past. It is widely accepted among psychoanalysts that people who protest most strongly against certain attitudes are probably defending against such attitudes in themselves. Adams et al. (1996) showed that people identified by questionnaire as being homophobic, in contrast to nonhomophobics, had increased penile circumference when exposed to a videotape showing male, homosexual activity.

HYSTERIA

Hysteria is the most complete form of self-deception. Laing (1959) wrote, "The hysteric characteristically dissociates himself from much that he does" (page 95). This means that one part of the person is apparently unaware of what the other part is doing. In the condition called conversion hysteria, the in-between me enables the person to believe that s/he is incapacitated in some way, like being paralysed or blind, in order to avoid having to do something s/he does not want to do. An example would be a daughter feigning a paralysis in order to avoid staying at home to care for her disabled father. Szasz (1962) explained that, in this condition, the person knows what she should be doing, but she cannot bring her/himself to do it. It would be shameful for her to admit that she did not want to do it, since this would cause her to appear heartless and selfish. The solution is to deceive others while, at the same time, denying to herself that she is deceiving others. Her outer me is unaware of what her in-between me is doing, so she genuinely believes that she is paralysed.

HYPNOSIS

Oakley (2000) has argued that hypnosis shares many of the characteristics of hysteria. The hypnotist is able to function like an in-between me and suggest to the outer me of the hypnotised subject that a limb is paralysed. The hypnotised subject is as puzzled as is the hysteric that she cannot move the limb. The subject's outer me has obeyed the hypnotist's instruction to behave as if the limb were paralysed, just as it would obey the restriction of the in-between me; or perhaps the hypnotist gains access to the in-between me, for something has to keep the instruction from the outer me.

Hypnosis is sometimes used as a treatment for hysteria, but presumably not simply by overriding the imposition of the in-between me (Erdelyi, 1985). Perhaps, in the hypnotic state, the hypnotist can make contact with the in-between me and even conduct a conversation with it. In this way, in the example given above, the daughter may be able to explain to the hypnotist why she was electing not to move the limb, but this would not be enough to cause her to unparalyse it in the waking state, unless she could find an alternative strategy for coping with the intolerable situation.

Keeping information out of consciousness

Lord Platt (1967), who was neither a psychiatrist nor a psychologist, wrote, "Man has from earliest times built up an elaborate series of defences lest his carefully sublimated emotions and motivations come disturbingly into consciousness" (page 442); and Erdelyi (1985) cited Dostoyevsky (1864) as saying that there are some things that a man is afraid to tell even to himself. Keeping information out of consciousness is one of the most important forms of self-deception. This issue comes under the general heading of repression, which has also been considered in Chapters 4 and 11. Psychoanalysts distinguish between two forms of keeping things out of consciousness, which they call suppression and repression. Rycroft (1995) defined suppression as the conscious, voluntary inhibition of activity by "an act of will," and contrasted it with repression, which he considered to be unconscious and automatic and "instigated by anxiety." I find this distinction unconvincing.

I have difficulty with the idea that there are two places: one called the conscious and one called the unconscious, and that disturbing material is expelled out of the conscious and into the unconscious. The way I see it is that the memories that are retained in the memory store can move freely into consciousness unless they are held back by some mechanism, which I call the in-between me. When I remember emotional experiences I remember the emotion along with the experience. The memories that the in-between me holds back are those that have unpleasant emotions remembered with them. I am not aware of the in-between me holding back memories. I only know that there are some memories that I cannot recall, and I propose that there is this unconscious component of the outer me that has the ability to block them, that is to stop them entering consciousness. The inner me is not a place, as the unconscious is a place; it is simply a set of mental mechanisms, so memories cannot be banished to it. What the psychoanalysts call the unconscious is simply, in my parlance, the memory.

Psychoanalysts use the word repression to describe the automatic exclusion of painful thoughts from consciousness (Chapter 4). Freud (1915) wrote, "The essence of repression lies simply in turning something away, and keeping it at a distance from the conscious" (page 147). Erdelyi (1996) considered that, in such a situation, attention is simply directed away from something that is disturbing. He called this intentionally not thinking about something. Others have used the terms cognitive avoidance and selective inattention (Chapter 5). I would wish to distinguish between intentionally not thinking about something (outer me) and automatically, unconsciously and defensively not doing so (in-between me).

Repression is common in people who have experienced sexual abuse by a parent in childhood. The in-between me of the abused person keeps out of consciousness the knowledge that the abuse ever took place. When the abused person has a child of her/his own, s/he may find her/himself avoiding a situation whereby the child is left alone with another adult even though s/he does not know why. Here, the inner me has access to the memory of the abuse and is alerted by the prospect of it happening in a similar situation while, at the same time, the in-between me is keeping the memory out of consciousness.

One of the more astonishing features of hypnosis is that which is called hypnotic age regression. The hypnotist asks the subject to return to an earlier age. The subject then appears to behave in a way that is appropriate to that age. I saw this happen once in Cheltenham. In the present the person spoke with a refined accent, but at the earlier age she spoke with a Gloucestershire accent. Claxton (1998) observed that, while at this prescribed age, the subject may gain access to apparently long-forgotten childhood memories. By linking up with the specified age (going to a specific "library shelf") the blocking mechanism of the in-between me gets circumvented. In a recent report, Addley (2001) described how a stage hypnotist told a woman to act as though she were eight. This released memories of her being abused by her great uncle, and over the ensuing months, she became depressed and attempted suicide. Evidence such as this confirms that disturbing episodes are present in the memory store, but they are being forcibly kept out of consciousness.

People are sometimes able to gain access to repressed, painful material when in the relative security of a psychotherapy session. Typically, the memories come back in fragments and initially, the patient appears unable to make any sense of them. The final fragment is usually the one that is associated with the pain. Spinelli (1994) described such an uncovering, which was accompanied by a period of relative calm. Some weeks afterwards the patient asked to see him again. She said:

> I hadn't really forgotten the event. I'd thought of it in a kind of detached way lots of times. But I just hadn't connected to it. It was kind of there and not there in my thoughts. It was like a thought that didn't bother me (page 144).

The experience profoundly affected Spinelli, who gradually came to acknowledge that whenever he had remembered a seemingly forgotten event, he had felt, often immediately, that he had known it all along. He wrote, "In some way the 'I' who knew the material and the 'I' who defined my sense of who I was had become, seemingly, disassociated" (page 145). These two I's would correspond to the in-between me and outer me. After this Spinelli referred to disowned thoughts and memories rather than repression.

The ego defence mechanisms

In psychoanalytic theory, repression is but one of a range of mechanisms by which it is assumed the ego defends itself against the intrusion of the id. I acknowledge the existence of these mechanisms, but I would consider them to be the in-between me protecting the outer me against experiencing excessive mental pain. It was Anna Freud (1936), Sigmund Freud's daughter, who introduced and defined them. All were believed to operate unconsciously, by way of the unconscious ego, and all, with the exception of sublimation, were considered to be manifestations of neurosis. Some psychoanalysts maintain that repression is the basic defence mechanism, and that all the others either reinforce it or are brought into play after it has failed. I list them here because I consider them to be forms of self-deception.

Dissociation

Mollon (1998) drew a distinction between repression and dissociation. Where repression is the separation of the unconscious material from consciousness, dissociation is the splitting of consciousness into separate compartments. Mollon cited van der Kolk et al. (1996) who proposed three stages in the dissociative process: the fragmenting of a traumatic memory, imagining leaving the body and observing it from a distance, and the splitting of consciousness into a number of separate ego states or mental states, such that what is known or experienced in one state may or may not be known in another. This seems to be what happens in hysteria, and perhaps also in multiple personality.

Denial and projection

Related to dissociation is the (psychoanalytic) defence mechanism of denial. In this, the person (in-between me) denies to her/himself (consciousness) unacceptable truths about her/himself. Klein [1934] (1968) proposed the further step of projection, by which the person projects these unacceptable parts of her/himself on to another person, and attributes to this other person that which s/he is denying in her/himself. From what I have already said, it is clear that denial is widespread and present in everyone, not just neurotics.

Splitting

This process tends to be linked with denial and projection. It involves conceptually splitting either the self or another person into two, the one part being seen as all good and the other as all bad. Usually only the all good part is acknowledged, the all bad part being relegated to the unconscious (or in my terminology, being kept out of consciousness). Hence only the good part is owned and the bad part is denied. This is comparable with the Jungian concept of the shadow (Chapter 4).

Isolation

This is a process by which a traumatic experience becomes separated off, so that it is not in continuity with other memories. It is deprived of its emotion and all associative connections.

Undoing

This is a kind of magical device, more commonly adopted by children, by which a form of acceptable activity is introduced in order to conceal (keep out of consciousness) the existence of a less acceptable one. The intention is to "blow away" the unacceptable activity and make it as though it did not happen.

Reaction formation

This is a process by which unacceptable negative feelings are replaced by equally strong positive ones. Thus a person is exceptionally nice towards someone s/he really hates. The energy of the unacceptable negative feelings has been channelled into positive ones.

Sublimation

This is a process by which less acceptable, particularly sexual, pursuits are replaced by more acceptable cultural ones. Thus sexual curiosity is replaced by scientific curiosity and playing with faeces is replaced by modelling in clay, and painting in oils. The implication is that the scientific curiosity and artistic behaviour are simply displacements of disapproved sexual behaviour and the energy that drives them is rechanelled sexual energy. In fact, science and art are worthy pursuits in their own right, though I would not deny that sublimation sometimes happens.

Regression

This is a process by which an adult, in order to avoid the stresses of adult sexual behaviour, regresses to an earlier stage of sexual development. Rycroft (1995) observed that a sublimating person may regress to the sexual behaviour against which the sublimation is a defence.

Reversal

This is a process by which a feeling becomes transformed into its opposite. Thus voyeurism is transformed into exhibitionism and sadism is transformed into masochism. This may be linked to projection in that the voyeur is projecting her/his voyeurism on to the person s/he is exposing her/himself to, and the sadist is projecting her/his sadistic feelings on to the person s/he is inviting to hurt her/him.

Turning against the self

This is a process by which an act of aggression directed towards another is, out of shame, redirected against the self. Some people believe that suicidal behaviour is murderous behaviour directed back on to the self.

The false self

Winnicott (1956) wrote of the creation of a false self, which is a kind of pretend self through which the person lives, in order to not truly be part of what is happening. This is not one of the defence mechanisms, but it functions like one. It is believed to protect the real self, which hides behind it. There may be certain similarities between the false self and the Jungian persona (Chapter 4).

Multiple personality

Multiple personality is an extreme example of the brain's capacity for compartmentalisation. It might be considered an extension of dissociation, and it possibly has a similar origin. Recently it was renamed dissociative identity disorder (Kluft, 1996). People with multiple personality frequently have a history of childhood sexual abuse, but Mair (1999) considered that the theory that multiple personality results from severe childhood trauma rests upon extremely shaky foundations, and can neither be proved nor disproved. A woman with multiple personality once explained to me that, following each episode of abuse, she would create a new personality into which to escape. By the time I saw her she had a large number of personalities that she called the tribe. Each had a name and distinct characteristics that she could describe. A case reported by Walker (1998) said, "They are all me – they're different parts of me." Ludwig et al. (1972) observed that when one personality was asked to learn information already learned by another, that personality learned much more easily than the first, suggesting a degree of integration.

16 Delusions and hallucinations

Loosely, delusions are firmly held, irrational beliefs, which are considered not to be true by most other people, and hallucinations are sensory experiences that seem real to the person experiencing them, but which have no counterpart in reality. Do delusions and hallucinations originate in the outer me or the inner me? The answer must surely be neither. The inner me is concerned with the attainment of objectives. It is not, cannot be, devious. The outer me is devious in so far as it pretends, lies and cheats, but these are all conscious contrived behaviours. Delusions are not consciously contrived, and hallucinations are not consciously created. This only leaves the in-between me, functioning as it does on the border between the inner me and the outer me.

The interconnection of delusions and hallucinations

Delusions and hallucinations are frequently interconnected in that a delusional belief is frequently a way of explaining a hallucinatory experience and a hallucinatory experience frequently gives expression to a delusional belief. A person may believe that her/his neighbours can communicate with her/him through the central heating system as a way of explaining where the voices s/he is hearing are coming from. A person who believes her/himself to be worthless may hear voices telling her/him that s/he is.

Delusions, hallucinations and mental illness

It is commonly assumed, particularly by psychiatrists, that people who have delusions and experience hallucinations have a mental illness, notably schizophrenia. Making such an assumption does not contribute greatly to our understanding of these phenomena. The illnesses in which delusions and hallucinations are considered to occur are called psychotic, which simply means that the person is out of touch with reality. Only psychiatrists have the legal right to determine whether people are mentally ill, to compulsorily admit them to, and detain them in, a mental hospital, and to treat them with psychotropic drugs. Some psychiatrists, notably Szasz (1962), and rather more clinical psychologists, dispute the concept of mental illness, and the right of psychiatrists to admit people to, and detain them in, a mental hospital.

Because psychiatrists are inclined to view delusions and hallucinations as symptoms, which have to be elicited in order to establish a diagnosis, they are less interested in their nature and content, since they believe that, once the illness is treated, the symptoms will go. The main thrust of much psychiatric research is to seek the genetic or organic origins of psychotic illness and to develop drugs to control it. Clinical psychologists are more inclined to view delusions and hallucinations as psychological phenomena that are worthy of study in their own right. Since psychologists cannot prescribe drugs, they aim to develop techniques for eliminating, modifying or coping with them.

Is there a connection between psychosis and dreams?

The view has sometimes been expressed, even by psychiatrists, that psychosis is like dreaming when awake. While there are similarities between psychosis and dreams, there are also important differences. Where a psychosis extends over months or years, a dream lasts for only part of one night. When I awake, I invariably recognise the experience as a dream and quickly forget about it. In a dream, I may have strange experiences, but I do not normally hold irrational beliefs. In a dream, I have sensory perceptions that do not correspond with external reality, but they always form part of the entire dream experience. They are not, as in psychosis, isolated voices or visions occurring within a setting of normality. Perhaps the most disturbing feature of psychosis is the way it contrasts with the normality in which it is set. Rarely, if ever, do people act in response to what they have experienced in a dream, but acting in response to psychotic experiences is much more common.

Greenfield (2000) wrote, "Schizophrenia has often been compared to dreams, in that both states are characterised by strong emotion yet a paucity of logic and reasoning ability" (page 75). She linked this description with the fact that the prefrontal cortex (the area of the brain that is associated with logical reasoning, and therefore a possible locus of the outer me) has been shown to be underactive in both dreams and schizophrenia. A characteristic that is shared by dreams and psychosis is a disconnectedness from normal surroundings. The dreamer is asleep and the psychotic is distanced from people. Millon (1981) observed that the more estranged an individual is from her/his social environment, the more out of touch s/he becomes with the conventions of reality and with the checks against irrational thought and behaviour that are provided by reciprocal relationships. Such distancing is a feature of schizotypal personality disorder. Millon believed that the withdrawn and isolated existence of the schizotypal causes her/him to develop oddities of thought such as suspiciousness, magical thinking, ideas of reference and illusions, all of which occur also in schizophrenia. The fact that dreams and psychosis occur more when the input from the exterior is diminished strengthens the idea that they are derived from material stored in the memory. This issue is further considered in the section on hallucinations.

Is psychosis a struggle to contain blocked out material?

Some support for the hypothesis that delusions and hallucinations are the equivalent of waking dreams is the idea put forward by Hingley (1992), that people who are prone to delusions may have a genetically determined failure to limit the content of consciousness, that is they have a restricted capacity for repression, or an ineffectual in-between me. As a result, threatening contents of the unconscious break through into consciousness. To compensate, the defences of denial, distortion and projection are brought into play, through which negative affect or intent is perceived within the other rather than within the self. Frith (1979) expressed the view that psychotic people have difficulty limiting the contents of consciousness. A similar theory, originating in Jungian theory and later revised by Royston (1989), is that psychosis involves either an unusually strong unconscious forcing its way into consciousness or a weak consciousness that cannot keep back unconscious material. Thalbourne (2000) introduced the term transliminality to mean the ease with which psychological material, such as imagery, ideation, affect and perception, can cross into or out of consciousness. He predicted that high transliminality and psychoticism would have something in common.

If psychosis is a consequence of the struggle of the in-between me to contain emerging, disturbing ideas, then a delusion would represent the breaking into consciousness of ideas that the person would normally succeed in keeping out of consciousness; and a hallucination would be the projecting into a created voice, of ideas that the person would normally wish to deny. Respectable people sometimes report that their hallucinatory voices speak obscenities to them, just as people sometimes experience in dreams what they would not permit themselves to experience when awake. The recovery from psychosis would be a returning of this unacceptable material back into a shut-off part of the memory.

Delusions

That so many criteria are required to define a delusion indicates the elusiveness of the concept. Garety and Freeman (1999) observed that research has promoted a number of changes to the definition. Harper (1992) systematically worked through the criteria, revealing how each is capable of being challenged, and ultimately questioned the validity of the concept of delusions. A delusion is a false belief, but to the deluded person it is not false. Sims (1991) argued that a delusion is more an assumption or a notion than a belief. Some people who have given up delusions maintain that they never really believed them; that they always knew that they were not true. A delusional belief is one that is not ordinarily accepted by other members of the person's culture or subculture, but a scientist, who has just made a new discovery of which the members of her/his culture are unaware, is clearly not being deluded. On the other hand, religious beliefs that are shared by most members of a culture are not factually true and, might, therefore, be considered delusions. It is maintained that a delusional belief is held with absolute conviction, but Garety and Freeman (1999) observed that levels of conviction are not always absolute, and may fluctuate. It is further maintained that the belief is not amenable to reason, but there is now evidence that some people with delusions are able to reason about them and can be responsive to contradictory ideas or experiences (Garety and Hemsley, 1997). The belief is considered to be unshakeable, but delusions now can be shaken by recently developed forms of cognitive therapy (Kuipers et al., 1997). Chadwick and Lowe (1990) have shown that delusions may be given up in the face of evidence, providing this is presented to them in a nonconfrontational manner.

Are delusions the extreme of normal attitudes and beliefs?

It could be argued that delusions are nothing more than extreme versions of normal attitudes and beliefs. A paranoid delusion that a person is being followed or spied upon, that gangs are out to get her/him, may be incorrect in this particular incident, but sometimes it would be correct. It is not always easy to tell whether a person's paranoid beliefs are justifiable, particularly in these days of closed circuit television. There have been instances of people being committed to mental hospital for maintaining that they were in danger, and later being shown to be right (Harper, 1992). A grandiose delusion, such as claiming to have immense wealth or supernatural power, may not be strictly true in one particular instance, but where does one draw the line? A delusion of badness, evil or worthlessness, of being the cause of all the ills in the world, may simply be the extreme of normal feelings of incompetence or of being in people's way. It is pertinent to ask what it might be that causes a normal attitude or belief to be converted into an exaggerated one, namely a delusion? The answer might be the intensity of felt emotion. Perhaps then, extreme ideas, which are normally held in check by the rational outer me, push through the normal restraints when the accompanying emotion builds up to an irresistible level; and perhaps tranquillisers dispel delusions by subduing the associated emotion. Argyle (2000) made the important point that irrational beliefs are sustained by emotion. They cannot be dispelled by reason alone: the underlying emotion has to be tackled.

Delusions as a rational explanation of abnormal experiences

Maher (1974) has explained at least some delusions as an attempt to make sense of perceptual anomalies, fundamentally biological in nature, which involve vivid and intense sensory experiences, some of which, but not all, are actual hallucinations. The delusion is entirely rational given the abnormal experience, and is arrived at by an entirely normal process of reasoning. Maher (1974) observed that the delusion is reinforced by the reduction in anxiety that follows the development of an explanation. Given the intensity of the hallucinatory experience, what else can a person do but try to find an explanation, however absurd it may seem, for where it is coming from? Hallucinated people sometimes think it is God who is speaking to them; others believe that there is some kind of radio transmitter; others believe it is telepathy. The idea that s/he is generating the experience her/himself might be considered an even more absurd explanation. Similarly, it never occurs to a dreamer that s/he is putting the words into the mouths of the people in her/his dreams.

Does the attitude of others affect psychotic people?

The psychiatrist, R.D. Laing (1959), wrote a great deal that is relevant to our understanding of delusions. He considered that orthodox psychiatrists were simply creating distance between themselves and their psychotic patients by classifying their delusions and hallucinations as the signs and symptoms of an illness. Gagg (1999) referred to the stand-off approach of orthodox psychiatrists to deluded patients. Laing (1959) provided an account by the psychiatrist Kraepelin (1905) of the behaviour and utterances of a schizophrenic patient. Laing maintained that Kraepelin considered that the patient was talking nonsense, but Laing made a convincing case for interpreting the patient's remarks as parodied responses to the way that Kraepelin was treating him.

Kotowicz (1997) observed that Laing had no trouble meeting psychotic patients on their own territory, and that he had an effortless facility to engage in "the barmiest of conversations" with them. In his obituary of Laing, Schatzman (1989) described how Laing always tried to see people's strange behaviour as a consequence of how other people had treated them, and were continuing to treat them. Laing and Esterson (1964) introduced the term mystification to describe what they considered to be the way the parents of some schizophrenics behaved. One form of this would be denying something that is obviously true, like opening the patient's letters; then when the patient insisted that they did this, maintaining that the patient was deluded.

Schatzman (1989) said that Laing believed that, in the presence of someone who listened carefully to a psychotic person's communications and responded with understanding, the psychotic's distress and peculiar behaviour diminished and even disappeared. I have observed how, even in the course of a single session, a patient can fluctuate between expressing frank paranoid delusions and simply being paranoid, according to how secure s/he felt. Bannister (1987) referred to the enormous distrust of certain schizophrenics and observed that, during psychotherapy, trust continues to be tested time and time again. Hayward and Taylor (1956) quoted a schizophrenic as saying,

"The problem with schizophrenics is that they can't trust anyone. The doctor will usually have to fight to get in, no matter how much the patient objects" (page 218).

It seems likely that, by distancing themselves from their patients, and pressing them to give more details of their delusions, psychiatrists may be pushing their patients deeper into their psychosis. If for instance they ask, "And how do you think this transmitting machine might work?" the patient may be forced to think up some additional explanation. The opposite approach, which Rowe and MacIsaac (1989) called empathic attunement, involves the psychiatrist behaving encouragingly and giving the patient the time and space to be her/himself. This is derived from Kohut's (1984) distinction between the experience-distant, probing approach, and the experience-near, supportive approach.

Tarrier (1992) proposed that the evidence suggests that people are constitutionally disposed to develop schizophrenic symptoms (delusions and hallucinations), and that schizophrenic episodes occur when the level of environmental stress reaches the threshold for any particular individual's level of vulnerability. Such stress creates overstimulation that overloads the person's limited capacity for information processing. As far back as the late 1950s, Brown et al. (1958) observed that schizophrenics who returned to live with their families were more likely to relapse than those who returned to live alone in lodgings. The stress that family members generate came to be called expressed emotion (Brown, 1985). Families were classified according to their level of expressed emotion (EE), and relapse was shown to be greater in schizophrenics who lived in high EE families. When families were trained to reduce their level of EE, relapse was reduced.

Some characteristics of deluded people

Garety and Freeman (1999) reviewed a large number of experimental studies carried out on deluded patients. These showed that they are more inclined than nondeluded patients to jump to conclusions, that is to reach conclusions on a minimum of evidence. McCormick and Broekma (1978) demonstrated that paranoid patients have an abnormally strong tendency to organise ambiguous information in a meaningful way (filling in the gaps). Huq et al. (1988) showed that deluded people, more so than nondeluded people, make overconfident decisions when presented with limited evidence, and make less effort than nondeluded people to seek out further evidence. Even so, in the tasks they had to perform, they made fewer errors than nondeluded patients. It was concluded that this may cause them to be more likely to accept incorrect hypotheses. Another set of studies showed that patients with persecutory delusions are more inclined to blame others, though not situations, when things go wrong. Further studies suggested that deluded patients may be poor at representing the mental state of others. In this respect they resemble autistic individuals. They have a less influential outer me.

Delusions as metaphors

A number of writers (Laing, 1967; Bannister, 1987) have suggested that delusions can be better understood if they are considered metaphorically rather than taken literally. When a patient was in a highly emotional state, he would speak about the mafia, and would refer to people he knew who were members of the mafia. When he was less emotional, he would say that there isn't really a mafia, and that he simply meant that these people behaved as though they were part of a mafia. Turning a factual statement into a metaphor gives it greater emphasis. When emotion is high the literal statement is not enough, and the more exaggerated metaphor is needed to give it full expression. The person states the metaphor as if it were reality. When the emotion drops it is accepted as the metaphor that it really is.

Hallucinations

A hallucination is a sensory experience that is not part of reality. Many people who experience hallucinations are aware that they are not the same as reality. Fenwick (2001) observed that it is very common for bereaved people to hallucinate a dead partner. This is most common during the first 10 years after death but it can last for many years. It is usually experienced as helpful. Hallucinations occur in all sense modalities. They must be the result of activity arising in those parts of the brain that receive and interpret incoming sensory information, but are generated without the incoming sensory information. Neuroimaging has shown that the same structures are active when a patient imagines a voice as when s/he is hallucinating (Frith, 1995). Weiss and Heckers (1999) observed that the neural systems involved in the perception of hallucinations appear to involve the same modality specific cerebral structures as are involved in normal perception.

Johnson and Raye (1981) considered the ability to discriminate between the real and the imaginary to be an inferential skill. They argued that a person does not automatically know whether a perceived event is generated by the self or by the external world, and that s/he has to guess between these two possibilities on the basis of the available evidence. Bentall (1990) observed that, in normal reality discrimination, people determine the source by unconsciously applying a set of criteria. Factors that they take into account are properties of the stimulus, contextual cues and expectations. When these criteria fail, the person concludes that the experience is coming from outside her/himself.

All that we see and hear in our dreams are hallucinations. This is evidence that everyone is capable of hallucinating. It is significant that hallucinations are predominantly of other people. They must reflect the problems that we have in our relating with other people. We relate to, and are related to by, hallucinations; that is, we enter into a relationship with them. Dreams emerge when, in sleep, we block out external reality. The withdrawal of external stimulation also predisposes people to hallucinations. In other words, if there is no sensory input from outside, the person is more aware of his/her internal sensory experiences. People immersed in flotation tanks have experienced hallucinations (Lilly, 1956) as have solitary sailors (Slocum, 1948) and prisoners subjected to long periods of solitary confinement (Grassian, 1983). Progressive sensory loss renders elderly people in particular vulnerable to hallucinations (Hammeke et al., 1983). Deaf people are particularly prone to them. Hallucinations are also likely to occur during periods of unpatterned stimulation, such as white noise or traffic noise (Bentall, 1990). Even though schizophrenics are more tolerant of sensory deprivation than most (Harris, 1959), they are more inclined to spend long periods of time on their own, and schizophrenic hallucinations are less likely to occur when the person is attending to meaningful stimuli, such as speech (Margo et al., 1981).

Are hallucinations exaggerations of normal experiences?

It is not difficult to evoke within one's head the sound or the image of another person. Perhaps hallucinations are similar to this, only louder and more vivid. Some theorists consider hallucinatory voices to be a genus of inner speech. If I am by myself, and I am not speaking, I can hear words and sentences inside my head that I recognise as my thoughts. I can hear myself thinking. I cannot describe these as hallucinations since I know that they are me and not someone else. I (outer me) can decide to bring images into my head. I can decide to hear the voice of my mother or my father, even though they have been dead for many years. I can decide to visualise the face of someone I know well. I can even decide to experience the smell of petrol or the taste of an orange. I can visualise things that I have never seen, like a fish riding a bicycle. I can hear someone saying things that I know I have never heard that person say. All these are the necessary ingredients of both dreams and hallucinations; but the missing element is that in the dream or the hallucination, I (outer me) do not determine what the person in the dream or the hallucination gets to say. So what does? It can only be the in-between me. What seems to happen in both dreams and hallucination is that certain highly emotional themes become released from the memory store, and words and phrases are generated that give expression to them. Finally, another person's voice is created to give utterance to these words.

Visual hallucinations

A visual hallucination, just like an auditory hallucination, is an internally generated sensory perception experienced as though it were outside the person. Visual hallucinations are predominantly pleasant experiences, which suggest that we create them because we want them. It is not unusual for visual hallucinations to speak, so they are both visual and auditory. The commonest form of visual hallucination is seeing someone who has died. We want the person back so much that we create the image of her/him. Ghosts are probably an extension of this phenomenon. Ghosts invariably are of someone thought to have once lived in a particular place. We imagine the ghost in the costume of the time we thought s/he lived. It is commonly believed that ghosts return to complete some form of unfinished business. Ghosts are part of our denial that when we die we cease to exist (see Chapter 20). Beyond ghosts, there are visions. These are very much a part of religious belief. They are kindly people who say comforting things. People tend to worship them as though they were a form of deity. The places where they were seen are considered to be holy, and people build shrines there. Often they are believed to have healing powers. Other kinds of vision are angels and faeries. In more recent times, people have started to have hallucinations of aliens from outer space who, interestingly, are able to speak the language of the person who sees them. Beyond aliens, there are spacecraft or flying saucers, seen either in the sky or having landed; and sometimes aliens are seen emerging from them. Interestingly, visual hallucinations tend not to be considered pathological, though I recall a morbidly jealous woman who claimed to have seen a woman entering and leaving her husband's bedroom.

Auditory hallucinations

Auditory hallucinations are more common and more disturbing than visual ones. A little under 5 per cent of the population hear voices regularly (Leudar and Thomas, 2000). Antipsychotic medication sometimes dramatically dispels them, but sometimes it has no effect at all, and they may persist for many years. Hallucinatory voices can claim the person's attention to the exclusion of all else. Sometimes a voice provides a kind of running commentary on everything the person is doing and the person (outer me) cannot understand how this other person can know so much about her/him. Sometimes a voice booms abuse at the person and threatens her/him. Sometimes a voice tells the person to do things, even extreme things like kill somebody or kill her/himself, and sometimes the person obeys; but is this not someone projecting into the voice something that s/he really wanted to do? Sometimes the person hears two or more voices talking together about her/him. However, many voice hearers do not mistake hallucinatory voices for other people speaking (Leudar and Thomas, 2000), and voices are not always unpleasant. Sometimes a person experiences the voice as a friend or an adviser. Joan of Arc considered that she heard the voices of saints. Socrates allowed his life to be directed by his demon. Some voice hearers do not want to lose their voices.

Where do the voices come from?

An important consideration with auditory hallucinations is where the hearer experiences the voices as coming from. In effect, this means whether s/he believes that s/he has generated them or whether s/he believes them to have arisen from an external source. Of course, all hallucinatory voices are self-generated. In Chapter 14, it was noted that small movements of the speech muscles, called subvocalisations, can be measured during normal verbal thought. Similar movements can be measured when a person is hearing hallucinatory voices (McGuigan, 1966). Thus, although the hearer is generating the sound of the voices, and is determining what the voices are saying, s/he is disowning them and projecting them on to this imaginary other person. This mechanism is similar to the child's creation of an imaginary companion (which is not normally considered to be a form of psychopathology) and making the companion say what s/he is thinking. The process would appear to be one in which the in-between me creates an imaginary external other who gives voice to certain fears or needs. Sometimes the hallucinator (outer me) enters into conversations with the hallucinatory (in-between me generated) other.

Holloway (2000) provided a graphic account of what voice hearing is like. At first, she wrote, the voice was barely audible, but as time passed, the whispers became louder. Initially, she could not hear what the voice was saying, but gradually she became tormented by its continuous criticism. It told her that she was no good at her job and that she should drown herself. In fact, she did make two suicide attempts. She was admitted to hospital and the voice was silenced by medication. As the pressures in her life increased, the voice returned, and was joined by a second one and the two voices spoke to each other about her, referring to her laziness, selfishness and worthlessness. Further hospital admission brought temporary respite. During times of stress the voices became louder and more insistent. The voices have persisted and she has learned to live with them. They may well represent what others have said about her.

A most useful and insightful account of voice hearing was provided by Exell (2001) who initially was not sure what his voices were. One day when listening to, and replying to, a voice that he believed was from a friend, he realised that he was creating the voice, just as he was creating the reply. This led him to conclude that he created all the voices he heard. He wrote, "It seems that my voices are simply my idea of what others would say to me, or my idea of what others are thinking of me" (page 15). He noted that his voices matched his mood: If he was feeling bad he got bad voices, if he was feeling good he got good ones, and if he was feeling guilty he got accusing ones. He wrote, "The voices only accentuated what I was already feeling" (page 15). He considered voices to be caused by things not dealt with, and suggested that hearing a voice telling you to kill someone might represent unexpressed anger that might be better dealt with in other ways.

Romme et al. (1992) examined a sample of 173 voice hearers who responded to a television appeal. Two-thirds of the sample considered themselves unable to cope with their voices. Romme and Escher (1993) concluded that open discussion with others about the voices makes it easier to come to terms with the experience. In the UK there are now over 80 self-help groups that provide an opportunity for mutual communication between voice hearers. They form part of the Hearing Voices Network. There are similar groups in other European countries. Romme and Escher (2000) considered engaging with the voices to be an essential part of the process of gaining control over them. Beyond this, the hearer is able to do deals with the voices by giving them free rein for limited periods. Assuming that voices are a means of projecting parts of the self into an imaginary other person, or other people, entering into an agreement with them can be a way of uniting with, rather than resisting, these split-off parts of the self.

A convincing account of (the outer me) entering into an agreement with voices was provided by Thomas (1994/95). After many years of suffering hallucinations, and hospital admissions, he was told by a fellow patient that he had two halves to his brain, and that he occupied one half and his voices were coming from the other half. The patient told him to think of his brain as a car with two drivers, the one being himself, the other being the voices. Instead of wanting to drive all the time, he should let the other driver take the steering wheel sometimes. He reported this to his therapist who agreed with it. She said, "Tell your other half that you are prepared to time-share with it, that you will let it in and give it control" (page 14). He did this and the voices gradually went away.

Delusions, hallucinations and relating

Delusions and the content of hallucinations are not just random ideas. They make clear reference to the person's interpersonal circumstances and represent how s/he views her/himself in relation to others. They will be summarised here under the four main headings described in Chapter 8.

Closeness–distance

Closeness

Taking first the horizontal axis, a lonely or isolated person may develop the delusional belief that a particular other person is in love with her/him. The other person may be someone s/he has never had involvement with and may be someone of some prominence. A woman may believe that a particular man visits her in the night and has intercourse with her. She may even believe that she has been made pregnant by him. Such a condition is called erotomania (Seeman, 1978). Sometimes hallucinations are regarded as pleasant companions (Romme et al., 1992).

An insecurely close person may harbour the delusional belief that her/his partner has sexual involvement with someone else. S/he may have visual or auditory hallucinatory experiences of the other person coming into the house or into the shared bed, or believe that stains on clothes, furniture or bed linen, are the semen resulting from her/his partner's infidelity. Such a condition is called morbid jealousy (Cobb, 1979).

Distance

A person may feel unable to keep others out. S/he may believe that others can put thoughts into her/his head or can read her/his thoughts. S/he may hear a hallucinatory voice commenting on everything s/he does. S/he may believe her/his thoughts are being broadcast over the radio or that articles in news-papers are making reference to her/him. S/he may believe that others are out to get her or to harm her/him and s/he may hear threatening hallucinatory voices.

A person may go into a state of withdrawal from others and become totally preoccupied with her/his inner self. S/he may mutter to her/himself, perhaps in response to auditory hallucinations. Sometimes the person feels quite unable to emerge from this condition. A patient of Fromm-Reichmann's (1959) said, "Hell is if you are frozen in isolation into a block of ice" (page 9).

Upperness–lowerness

Upperness

Taking now the vertical axis, delusions of upperness may be viewed as an overcompensation for feelings of inferiority. What may be called the manic defence was originally proposed by Klein (1934). It was further elaborated by Segal (1964) as having three components: a denial of dependence, a feeling of triumph and omnipotence, and a contempt for others. People in a state of mania sometimes have upper delusions; so does the state of well-being that the mania gives rise to cause the person to imagine her/himself as having the kind of relationship to others that might justify this feeling of well-being? Wing et al. (1974) described four categories of upper delusions: (1) delusions of assistance in which an organisation, force or power is direct-ing the person's life in some advantageous way, like enabling her/him to perform miracles; (2) delusions of grandiose identity in which the person believes her/himself to be famous, rich or titled, or related to a prominent person. S/he may believe her/himself to be someone of great importance, such as Napoleon, the Prime Minister or the ruling monarch. S/he may assume the manner of such a person and demand that others behave towards her/him with respect and deference; (3) delusions of grandiose ability in which s/he may believe her/himself to have outstanding abilities; to have extraordinary powers such as the power to perform miracles, to heal or to see into the future; or to have been chosen for a special mission or purpose; and (4) religious delusions in which s/he considers her/himself to be God, Jesus Christ, a saint or an angel.

Lowerness

Just as upper delusions are sometimes linked with euphoria, lower delusions are sometimes linked with depression. Beck's (1983) description of defeat depression corresponds with the condition of negative lowerness. In such a condition, a person may have delusions of uselessness, worthlessness, help-lessness and hopelessness. S/he may consider herself to be in the way, the cause of other people's problems and better off dead. People with lower delusions often have obsessive suicidal feelings, or hear hallucinatory voices telling them to kill themselves.

17 Dreams

Unlike hallucinations, dreams are experienced by everyone. In an average night's sleep of seven to eight hours, an adult is thought to dream for one and a half to two hours. Children are thought to dream more than adults. The amount of dream time per night is thought to fall off with increasing age. When I am dreaming I am not aware that I am. It is just like being awake. However absurd the dream may be, it never occurs to me that I am dreaming. This is like a psychotic person not being aware that s/he is psychotic. The moment I awake from a dream, and enter wakefulness, I realise that I have been dreaming and now I am awake; but the moment that I start to dream I do not have the experience that I have just stopped being awake. The moment I awake from a dream I remember it in some detail and I recognise it as having a bearing upon some current preoccupation.

What commonly happens to me is that I wake in the night, having had a dream, and note, sometimes with some surprise, the dream's content. Normally, I can see what the dream was getting at, and can appreciate why this might have been a concern for me; but it has been useful to have learned this extra bit about myself. Sometimes, I stay awake a while, thinking about the dream and its implications.

It is said that people are more inclined to dream shortly after they have fallen asleep and shortly before they wake up. If I happen to drop off to sleep for a few minutes during the day, I notice that I invariably dream. When I dream, I seem not to be aware of what is happening around me. I do not hear what people around me are saying, and if the radio or television is on, I am unaware of what is being transmitted; yet some part of me does appear to be monitoring what is happening, for I am not woken by familiar sounds, but I am woken by unfamiliar ones.

What makes dreams so difficult to investigate is that they are so easily forgotten. People forget them so quickly that either they think that they hardly dream at all, or they consider their dreams to be irrelevant. It may not be so much that we forget our dreams as that we have no way of connecting up with them, for if something happens during the day, or even some days later, that reminds me of a dream, I am able to recall it. Also, there are certain dreams that recur throughout life, and each time I have one, I recognise it as one that I have had before. It may be that people are able to train themselves to remember their dreams, for patients in psychoanalytic psychotherapy, in which dream analysis often plays an important part, seem able to remember them in great detail.

Greenfield (2000) considered dreams to resemble more the experiences of early childhood, " . . . in which one has a kind of passive experience without engaging in complex thought . . ." (page 76). She concluded that they are a consequence of the way an immature brain functions; but since adults of all ages dream, how can this be? When I dream, I almost always dream as an adult; my dreams are of adult situations, and the thoughts I have are often quite complex. She wrote, "In my own view, dreaming represents the lowest end of a continuum of consciousness, low on logic and high on feeling, resulting from small assemblies of brain cells driven by residual brain activity" (page 180).

The distinction between the dream world and the real world

Dream life, unlike waking life, has no continuity. When I dream, I do not resume where I left off in a previous dream. If I awake and then fall asleep again, the next dream I have does not normally carry on from the one I had in the previous period of sleep. My impression is that most dreams are of short duration, probably lasting no more than a few minutes. There is no continuity between the so-called unreal world of the dream and the real world of wakefulness. The moment I wake up I am flooded with sensory cues that bring me back, in both space and time, to where I was when I fell asleep. In fact, the dream world is every bit as real as the waking world. Of course, the experiences I have in dreams are real experiences, that is, I really do have them; and sometimes they have a powerful effect upon me.

In wakefulness, the input is almost entirely from the sense organs, and in dreaming it is almost entirely from the memory store. When I dream I have minimal input from the sense organs, so that, although I am conscious in the dream, I am unconscious of what is going on around me; though I mention below how sometimes some sensory input becomes incorporated into the dream.

Confusing dreaming and waking

Day-dreaming is quite different from dreaming. When I am day-dreaming I am awake, and I know I am awake. A day-dream is never fantastic, or difficult to make sense of, in the way that a dream is. Sometimes I wake up during the night and start to think about a disturbing aspect of my life. It is probable that this disturbing aspect of my life has woken me up. Perhaps, had I stayed asleep, I would have dreamed about it instead.

Damasio (2000) distinguished between being awake and being conscious, and described how either state could be present without the other. A number of states are described that appear to fall mid-way between sleeping and being awake. They are called parasomnias. In these states, which are also called altered states of consciousness, the person is conscious but is not awake. Sleep-walking is one example. Sometimes in these states, acts of extreme violence, even murder, can take place. In law, the person is deemed to be not responsible for such acts, even though presumably the motivation to commit them arose in the inner me.

The Dutch psychiatrist, van Eeden (1913), maintained that he sometimes became conscious while dreaming. This is a strange statement since I consider that we are conscious in dreams. Perhaps he meant that he was aware that he was dreaming. He called this state lucid dreaming. He considered that, in it, he (outer me) could direct the course of a dream or exercise some control over its content. Campbell (1996) described a woman who had narcolepsy, a condition in which the person suddenly falls asleep during periods of wakefulness. Mollon (1998) described this as a dream-like hallucinatory state invading waking life without the person realising that s/he has entered a state of altered consciousness. Campbell described how the woman's constant falling asleep caused her to blur the boundary between sleeping and waking, so that she could not tell her dreams from reality. She said, "The memories I have of lucid dreams are only distinguished from my memories of reality if I make a really massive effort to label them, file them away. So when I wake up, I quickly go through what was in the dream and recognise it as a dream." She went on, "When I go to sleep, my body goes to sleep but my mind stays awake. I'm totally conscious through my sleep. And I dream as well" (page 44). I am not sure that Damasio would agree with these terms. She described how she could have the experience of someone coming into her room and sitting on her bed and talking to her, and not knowing, when she woke up, whether it happened in reality or in the dream. Hays (1992) reported several instances of narcolepsy patients making false but sincere accusations of sexual assault upon themselves. In other words, the rape occurred in the dream and not in reality.

LaBerge (1985) used the term lucid dreaming to mean having dreams that make perfect sense. This is a quite different definition. He cited the example of a man who dreamed that he had inoperable lung cancer. He saw a huge shadow on a radiograph of his chest. He experienced being physically examined and being told that he had extensive lymph node involvement. He suffered the anguish of knowing that he would never see his children grow up. He had the thought that none of this would have happened if he had given up smoking. When he awoke he experienced immense relief and actually did give up smoking.

The possible functions of dreaming and sleeping

It may be difficult to separate the functions of dreaming from those of sleeping. Most, but not all, animals sleep, so it seems likely that sleeping performs a function. Vital organs, like the heart and the lungs, slow down, but do not stop, during sleep. Other organs, like the digestive system and the excretory system, appear to function as usual. Since I change position from time to time, my muscles must be functional. Metabolism within the muscles continues, since when I wake up, muscles that I overused the previous day have started to ache. In sleep, wounds heal and the body continues to combat infection. Something beneficial must happen during sleep, for when I wake up, I do not feel tired like I did when I went to sleep. During wakefulness, repeated neurotransmitter release in the brain depletes the glycogen stores in the glial cells. This cause the release of adenosine, which induces non-REM sleep, during which the glycogen stores are replenished (Bennington and Heller, 1995).

After several hours of wakefulness I begin to feel tired. This is comparable to feeling hungry after several hours of not eating. The longer I go without sleep, the more compelling the tiredness becomes, just as the longer I go without food, the more hungry I get. When I am tired, I find it increasingly difficult to concentrate and solve problems, I am less able to cope with the unexpected, and I make more errors than usual. Eventually, the need to sleep becomes irresistible. This is a problem for long-distance drivers, who sometimes have fatal accidents when they fall asleep at the wheel. It seems that during tiredness, the outer me functions fail before the inner me ones so, for a time, the driver can rely upon those (inner me) functions that have become second nature to him. It is possible that the outer me needs more sleep than the inner me does, and that perhaps what happens during dreaming is that the outer me gives up some of its normal control over the inner me.

DREAMING AND REM SLEEP

Once it was believed that when a person dreams the eyes move rapidly from side to side. This is called rapid eye movement (REM). The sleep when this is happening is called REM sleep. However, Solms (1997) observed that REM sleep occurs regularly approximately every 90 minutes throughout the sleep cycle, and that it is switched on and off by a simple oscillatory mechanism located in the brainstem. Damage to this area does not cause the cessation of dreaming. It has been shown that a 26-week-old human foetus spends all its time in REM sleep, which could hardly mean that it spends all its time dreaming. Foulkes and Vogel (1965) demonstrated that far more dreams occur outside of REM sleep than earlier studies have suggested, and that as many as 50 per cent of awakenings from non-REM sleep elicit dream reports; so does this mean that we dream for at least half the time we are asleep?

Since the presence of REM is not a reliable indicator of dreaming, there can be no way of telling whether animals dream. Sometimes, when a dog is asleep, it makes muffled barking noises and makes slight, excited movements of its limbs, indicating that something equivalent to human dreaming is happening. Reptiles show no REMs, so perhaps REM came relatively recently in evolutionary time. Greenfield (2000), apparently still believing there to be a connection between REM sleep and dreaming, wrote, "Although we may toss and turn in dreamless sleep, in REM sleep our muscles become paralysed to stop us acting out our dreams. Only our eyes dart about, perhaps looking at the images moving about in the dream world" (page 179). If this is so, and the foetus is in continuous REM sleep, why is it not permanently paralysed? Jouvet (1975), apparently believing that animals dream, observed that both animals and humans get up and act out their dreams when the brain centres responsible for this paralysis are deactivated.

If people have been deprived of REM sleep, or if they have been deprived of sleep at all, when they finally go to sleep, they spend longer than usual in REM sleep. This suggests that any loss of REM sleep, whether or not this is the same as dreaming, has to be made up, and that something happens during this part of sleep that is essential to well-being. Considering people do not remember most of what they dream, this is remarkable; though we have encountered other instances of beneficial things happening outside of conscious awareness.

DREAMING AND ACETYLCHOLINE

The neurotransmitter acetylcholine plays a key role in sleep, wakefulness and arousal. Drugs that boost the level of acetylcholine trigger the rapid brain-waves that are characteristic of wakefulness and dreaming. Drugs that stop the production of acetylcholine (e.g., hemicholinium) cause a sharp reduction in the amount of dreaming sleep.

DREAMING AND THE ELECTROENCEPHALOGRAM

During dreaming, the electroencephalographic (EEG) slow wave sleep pattern reverts to the waking pattern of faster, irregular brainwaves. Does this mean that I am nearer to wakefulness when I dream than when I am not? Was it this that led Greenfield (2000) to consider that "dreaming is a form of consciousness" (page 75)?

The content of dreams

Dreams do not come from nowhere. The raw material for dreams must be past or recent experiences that have been stored in the memory, though these experiences can become modified in various ways within the dream. In a dream, I can be anywhere and at any time in my life, or a mixture of different places or different times. People can feature from different periods in my life. They can be people who have died, and (e.g., my children) they can be much younger than they are now. Sometimes I do not recognise either the place or the people. It is important to register that none of this strikes me as strange.

Current events can also influence dreams. Sometimes, when I was a child, my mother would wake me to tell me that it was time to get up and get ready to go to school. I would fall asleep and dream that I was getting up. Sometimes external noises, like someone using a vacuum cleaner, get incorporated into a dream and become the sound of something else. This illustrates the inner me's capacity to make the most of the information that it has. It may be that a similar process takes place with images entering into the dream space from within. The inner me integrates them into the dream.

Bodily sensations, like sexual desire, hunger or the pressure of a full bladder, get incorporated into dreams and I find myself enacting my satisfaction of them. When I am hungry, I dream that I am eating. Adolescent boys ejaculate in their sleep, presumably as part of being sexually aroused. At times when I have had a full bladder, I have dreamt that I was peeing. When I was a child, I would wake to find that I had wet the bed, but in adult life, the peeing has remained restricted to the dream. Recently, in a dream, a woman I did not know very well, sat on the toilet and peed. I remember admiring her for being able to do this. I awoke to find that I needed to pee.

Because people often experience themselves as the passive recipients in dreams, they are inclined to believe that dreams are things that just happen to them, that they have no part in their construction. They view dreams in much the same way as psychotics view delusions and hallucinations, that they come from somewhere outside of themselves. This is very much an outer me viewpoint. There is a joke about dreams that succinctly corrects this view. A woman has a dream that a big, hairy cave-dweller picks her up and carries her to his cave. As he holds her above a pile of animal skins, she looks up at him and asks, "What are you going to do to me?" The cave dweller replies, "Please yourself, it's your dream." The implication of this joke is that some part of us really does determine what we dream about.

Forms and theories of dreams

The association of ideas in dreams

In Chapter 11, I referred to the phenomenon of automatic recollections; and in Chapter 14 I referred to the continuous flow of ideas (CFI). It seems likely that these two related phenomena continue into our dreams, but I need to stress that neither of these is random. One idea triggers off another because it is meaningfully related to it, and the associations that are made are made because of their emotional significance; so ultimately by this sequence important themes are reached. Llinas (as cited by Greenfield, 2000) proposed that the brain, even during waking, is in a constant state of dreaming. By this he meant that I am continually generating images inside my head that represent the reality outside my head. To support his contention, he demonstrated that in both dreaming and wakefulness, but not in nondreaming sleep, neurons in the thalamus and the cortex are synchronised, with both areas generating rhythmic waves of electrical signals in step with each other.

Making sense of random information

Hobson and McCarley (1977) proposed that what they called a dream state generator bombards the forebrain with randomly synthesised misinformation, which the cerebral cortex tries to make sense of. I would not discount the idea that a lot of random material finds its way into dreams and that the inner me does its best to fashion this material into something meaningful; but this does not explain why we dream about certain people and certain problems.

The disposal of unwanted material

Greenfield (2000) wrote, "A common idea is that dreaming helps us to sort out the experiences of the day" (page 180). This does not get us very far. Besides, since the inner me has no conception of time, dreams can concern any part of a lifetime, and frequently do. Winson (1990) considered the primary function of dreams to be sifting through information gathered during the day and selecting out that which should be kept (remembered) from that which should not. It is hard to think of an experiment that would confirm or disconfirm this. Some writers have proposed that dreams are a kind of mental excretion. Crick and Mitchison (1983) considered that dreaming was a way of disposing useless information, and that, in the process of dreaming it, we are unlearning it. This kind of theory completely overlooks the obvious meaningfulness of most dreams. It is reminiscent of psychiatrists who discount the content of delusions and hallucinations.

The reliving of traumatic experiences

People who have had extremely disturbing experiences, such as fighting in a war, killing people, or seeing their comrades being killed, being in a concentration camp, being in a serious accident, or being raped, often repeatedly relive these experiences in their dreams and re-experience the associated emotions. Van der Kolk and Fisher (1995) have argued that, whereas normal memory is largely a left-brain function, traumatic memory mainly remains stored in the right parietal lobes. This means that traumatic memories are predominantly visual and only minimally verbal, so they are more readily transformed into dreams.

Revisiting unresolved earlier problems

Sometimes problems of earlier times resurface in dreams, probably because a link has been made with a present difficulty. The dreamer is back in the earlier predicament and experiencing the accompanying emotion. Recently I dreamed of someone I had been at school with, but whom I had not met for over 40 years. In the dream he was older than when I knew him but not as old as he would have been now. At school, he had been more successful than me and more favoured by the staff, and I had felt inferior to him. In the dream I was trying to get even with him, and even rise above him.

Reworking long-standing anxieties

For any person, there are common and recurrent themes in dreams. These comprise lingering anxieties that get reworked and incorporated into new settings. Such themes might be concerned about not being popular, being incompetent in one's work, the fear of being found out, the fear of rejection, the unfaithfulness of a partner and the inability to have a child.

Enacting current anxieties

This is probably the commonest content of dreams. Worrying current circumstances get woven into a drama that permits the expression of strong emotions. Since the in-between me is less effective during sleep, disturbing ideas that are blocked out during the day emerge in dreams and get enacted in dramatic form. This is not to say that any resolution of them takes place. One of the most important functions of dreams may be the opportunity they provide for the expression of emotions that have been set aside during the course of the day. Sometimes the emotions are so strong that they wake the dreamer. Then the dreamer continues to worry about the unearthed material.

Dreams as a representation of frustrations and predicaments

In a dream, I (outer me) frequently find myself in a predicament. I ask myself questions like, "What is going on here?" and "How can I get out of this mess?" I appreciate that I am in a problematic situation and I try to think of ways out of it. This is all outer me activity. A common feature of my dreams is that the problematic situation I am in is quite insoluble. Commonly this is because something that would normally be there is not there, or something that was there a moment ago has now gone. I reach for it and it is not there. I think to myself "How can this be?" I never think that this must be another of those crazy dreams. I wake, with some relief, but also feeling that I have been conned again. This effect may be a consequence of the fragmentary nature of dreams and the lack of continuity.

Some frustrating dreams are recurrent: One is that I cannot remember where I have parked my car. This has never happened to me in reality. During the dream, I move from location to location, but I am sure I know where the car is going to be. When it is not there I conclude with horror that it has been stolen. In the dream I recall that this has happened to me several times before, and I have the feeling of "Oh not again." I report the loss of the car, but it is never found. A variant of this dream, which I do not recall so clearly, is that the car has been found to be seriously defective or is seriously damaged. Again, I have this "Oh not again" feeling and this is followed by the thought that I am hopeless.

False insights in dreams

Sometimes in a dream, I am explaining a theory to someone, or a group of people. I see things with greater clarity than ever before. An expression comes to me that seems to sum up everything. When I awake, I remember the expression, but it is quite banal and does not explain anything.

Dreams and anticipation

If a major event is due to happen the following day, whether it be pleasant or unpleasant, I will sometimes dream of it happening. As a student, I used to dream I was taking the examination I was due to take the next day. Once I had two dreams; in the first I had failed and in the second I had passed.

Improvements on present reality

It is a common belief that people dream of things that they would like but they do not have. This is in line with Freud's (1902) conception of dreams as wish fulfilments. This may be one form of dream, but there are many others. In unpleasant circumstances, people dream of better times in the past or good times in the future. Frankl (1967) wrote of how prisoners in Nazi concentration camps escaped from the unpleasantness of their surroundings by dreaming. Old people dream of times when they were younger and healthier. Dreams sometimes bring compensation for present deficiencies. We dream of things that are not, or no longer, available to us.

A psychodynamic view of dreams

Freud (1902), quite correctly, referred to dreams as the royal road to the unconscious. Therefore, they are a valuable means of discovering those things with which the unconscious mind is preoccupied. Freud (1902) considered there to be a constant struggle in dreams between emerging material that could overwhelm the ego and the repressing forces of the superego. He introduced the term the censor to represent these restraining forces. Rycroft (1995) called the censor the theoretical ancestor of the superego. Freud proposed the censor as a kind of gatekeeper that bars the entrance to the conscious of disturbing ideas. For Freud, the unconscious was a place where material that is unacceptable to the censor is kept. Presumably, if the censor had its way, it would destroy it. In dreams, we have access to it, but Freud (1902) believed that in its efforts to keep it from the conscious mind, the censor distorts it. Freud called the distorted version of the dream material the dream's manifest content and the undistorted version, the latent content. Commonly in dreams, the person appears to be expressing several ideas at once, something that happens commonly in poetry and art. In other words, all the associations get heaped up together within the same scene, image or phrase. Freud (1902) called this condensation. Sometimes a disturbing idea becomes incorporated into an innocuous image, where it is more acceptable. Freud (1902) called this displacement. Finally, all of the disparate images get combined into a harmonious whole, a process which Freud called secondary elaboration.

The outer me, the inner me and the in-between me in dreams

Outer me

I (outer me) have no influence upon the content of my dreams. Dreaming is like walking into a cinema. I do not determine what I am going to see. Yet, apart from this, I, the I of the outer me, am very much present in the dream. I am both the watcher and the watched. I am the central character in the dream, and it is always about me. Dreams mostly involve my being in places, with other people. I do things, I say things, things get done and said to me, and I respond emotionally to what is happening. I have thoughts, I use words and sometimes I try to reason things out and argue with people. Sometimes I turn into one of the other characters in the dream.

In another sense, the outer me plays a minimal part in dreams, for dreams are not very verbal or very rational. The outer me is not as controlling of the inner me in dreams as it is in waking life. Maquet (cited by Greenfield, 2000), using positron emission tomography (PET), observed that the parts of the brain involved in arousal and emotion light up in just the same way during dreaming as when we are awake, but that large expanses of the cortex, particularly the prefrontal cortex, are far less active. Could it be, asked Greenfield (page 75), that the prefrontal cortex is the key area for differentiating the inner world of our imagination and dreams from the outer world of reality? Later, she asked, "Is what takes place in a dream, the brain freewheeling without restraint from the prefrontal cortex?" (page 76). Since certain areas of the cortex, and particularly the prefrontal cortex, are the areas most likely to be linked with the outer me (see Chapter 2), Maquet's observation and Greenfield's comments support the idea that the influence of the outer me is diminished during dreams.

Inner me

Because of the diminished influence of the outer me, the inner me comes into its own in dreams, which are highly visual and emotional. Situations are created in dreams that have no equivalent in reality, and yet the dreamer is entirely accepting of them. Although outside noises can get incorporated into dreams, the dream content arises largely from the memory store.

Since emotions emanate from the inner me, it is not surprising that emotions feature prominently in dreams. It seems likely that emotions play a prominent role in determining the content of dreams. Emotionally charged memories press for expression in dreams, and I am more emotional in dreams than in my waking life. Sometimes the intensity of the emotion wakes me up.

Since the inner me has little awareness of time, there is often a timeless quality to dreams. Events from different time periods get meshed together, presumably because they have some conceptual similarity. Greenfield (2000) correctly observed that, in dreams, it is hard to ascribe a precise location or time to an experience. She wrote of this, "Unable to reflect on the past or speculate on the future, we become trapped in the present moment, the passive recipients of tastes, colours, smells and sounds stripped of personalized memories and significance" (page 180). In fact, tastes, colours and smells rarely feature in dreams, and when they do I would not agree that they are stripped of personalised memories and significance. In dreams, I experience the images but I am usually not aware of their colour. The one exception is when the colour has some significance. I once had a dream in which it seemed important to distinguish between a green and a blue tampon packet, the colour of the packet indicating the degree of absorbency. The packet in my dream was green, and it was exactly the shade of green that the packet of this particular brand usually was. I remember noting when I woke up that I had had the experience of dreaming in colour.

The inner me is very much concerned with concepts. People and events are often united in a dream because they share or represent the same concept. As far as the inner me is concerned, a memory is an image, irrespective of the time period it comes from. Memories are stored according to their conceptual similarity, rather than from the time period they come from. Beyond concepts, the inner me appears to be capable of generating metaphors. A metaphor is the representation of an abstract thought in terms of something that is more concrete. Lakoff (1997) presented reasons for believing that metaphors feature prominently in dreams; so one reason why dreams are so difficult to understand is that we are inclined to interpret them too literally. In the last chapter I described how metaphors also feature in psychosis. The vivid, visual images in dreams, like for example my car, make more sense when they are viewed as metaphors.

In-between me

I have no problem with much of what Freud wrote about dreams, though I would wish to rephrase it in terms of my own terminology. There are obvious similarities between the Freudian censor and the in-between me. There is much to support the idea that the controlling influence of the in-between me is relaxed in dreams; yet despite its diminished influence, it seems not to relinquish control altogether. There appear to be moments in dreams when it is still trying to keep disturbing thoughts at bay; and there may well be, as Freud said, strange compromise positions in which they become half-expressed or expressed in a camouflaged or distorted form.

Disturbing, early memories emerge in dreams accompanied by strong and upsetting emotion. People entertain in dreams thoughts that they may not be prepared to entertain in wakefulness. A young woman, who was shy and religious, told me that she sometimes had what she called X-rated dreams. I sometimes have sexual dreams about women patients and women patients sometimes have sexual dreams about me. Such fantasies would not be acceptable in wakefulness. In dreams, the in-between me creates scenes that represent early or current preoccupations, by way of which emotions get expressed. In this respect, dreams resemble art.

There is also a reason to believe that the in-between me, which after all is a component of the outer me, is less influential in dreams. Painful and disturbing memories are more likely to emerge, which are accompanied by the release of strong emotion. The dreamer may escape from these nightmares by waking up, and the in-between me regains control. Claridge et al. (1997) have shown that a susceptibility to nightmares correlates with psychoticism. This supports the idea expressed in the last chapter of a link between the inability to limit the escape of emotion and psychosis. It is possible that the reasonably controlled release of emotion in dreams helps to prevent people becoming psychotic. This could be why people who are prevented from dreaming quickly become disturbed.

Interpreting dreams

People have always tried to interpret dreams, though often without any sound understanding of how dreams come about. Some psychodynamic therapists, both Freudian and Jungian, rely heavily upon dream interpretation, but it is all too easy for the therapist either to fit the dream into a pre-existing theoretical framework, or to link it to her/his own personal preoccupations. Webster (1996) accused Freud of both these failings; but it is likely that Jungians are equally open to such criticism. Freud believed that the task of the psychoanalyst is to decode the manifest content and reveal the latent content, that is, to outsmart the censor. Not everyone agreed with Freud's view. Jung was never able to agree with Freud that the dream is a "façade" behind which meaning lies hidden. Instead, he described it as a part of nature that harbours no intent to deceive. It is simply the mind trying to express itself as best it can.

Since the dream may be heavily camouflaged, the therapist cannot know, simply from the description, what the dream is about. It is always safer to assist the client to discover this for her/himself rather than have it imposed upon her/him. Either way, there is always the danger that the client's censor (in-between me) will not allow her/him to know the dream's meaning or even to accept the therapist's interpretation of it. An effective strategy is to invite the client to free associate about the dream. This often brings forward new material that makes the dream clearer. As with doing therapy with a psychotic patient, the principle should be to establish trust and keep down the level of anxiety.

The creativity of dreams

One of the strangest things about dreams is that I am sure that new images and scenes, which are not part of the memory store, get created in them in order to represent ideas that need to be expressed. People are amazingly creative in dreams; though, of course, such creativity is entirely automatic and not wilfully executed. When I awake from a dream, and the experience is still fresh in my mind, I am sometimes struck by its inventiveness, originality and sheer aesthetic quality, which seems to suggest that everyone is capable of creative synthesis. Perhaps it is our awareness of our creativity in dreams that inspires us to be creative in our waking life, or perhaps dreaming and waking aesthetic creativity are variations of the same process. Unpacking even an apparently simple dream can be a long and complicated process, and is similar to unpacking a work of art or even a joke. Freud (1905b) linked dreams with jokes.

Part VII

The social me

In this final part I want to spread the net wider in order to apply the same two-me approach to three vital areas of social functioning. There is a clear continuity from the issues dealt with in Part VI to those dealt with in this part, but whereas self-deception, delusions, hallucinations and dreams are created internally (inner me, in-between me), without any conscious deliberation, the arts, humour and to a large extent religion, are deliberately and consciously created, though unconsciously (inner me, in-between me) motivated. The arts, humour and religion have quite different, though overlapping functions.

18 The arts

The earliest art work, found in a cave north of Verona, Italy, dates from 35,000 years ago (Willan, 2000). In evolutionary time, this is recent. It is a sobering thought that art did not exist before that time. Presumably, the early humans who did this work realised that certain marks and shapes that, by chance, resembled real things, excited them; so they started to create such marks and shapes intentionally. The realisation and decision to make marks and shapes would have been the outer me; so the outer me thought up the idea of art; though, as we shall see, the role of the inner me in both the execution of, and the response to, art is crucial.

The arts are a means of creating replicas of reality, such that, when I experience them, I respond to them as though they were the real thing. The replication may be only slight and suggestive or extremely detailed and elaborate. A likely explanation for this effect is that the inner me cannot discriminate between reality and replicas of reality. There are enough cues in the replica to trigger off the response. Part of the fascination of the arts is the awareness that what is being experienced feels like the real thing, and affects me as the real thing would, even though it is not the real thing. Through the arts I am able to feel as though I am experiencing reality in the absence of true reality. Even in the partial replication of reality I am able to have the subjective experience of attaining my objectives, which is sufficient to satisfy the inner me.

Reality can be replicated through the entire range of the senses. Touch, taste and smell play a minimal role because they have such a simple input. Vision and sound predominate because their input is so much more complex. Although the representation of reality is central to art, the straightforward representation of something is not necessarily art. Reality is sometimes represented simply to show to others what something looks like. Since the straightforward representation is not necessarily art, what is the extra component that makes it so? Taking something out of context, placing a frame around it and hanging it on a gallery wall can in itself sometimes be aesthetically effective. Putting something in a gallery that is not normally in a gallery can have an aesthetic effect, similar to the mere exposure effect (Zajonc, 1980); but at the end of the day, what makes the representation aesthetic is its power to evoke emotion.

Beauty

Once it was thought that the aim of the arts is the creation of beauty. Beauty is a harmonious arrangement of shapes, words sounds or whatever that generates a sense of well-being in the person who witnesses it. It is linked to perfection. There is natural beauty, as in a face, a body, a flower or a landscape, and before the invention of photography, the aim of most artists was either to capture this natural beauty, or to create the representation of an artificial assemblage of people, things and so forth that supposedly contained it. To do this, artists needed extreme skills, which had to be learned. It was therefore much more outer me dependent. Beauty is associated more with women, and perhaps also young children, than with men. The association of beauty with women is a consequence of evolution: Men are genetically programmed to be attracted to women who are healthy and likely to produce healthy offspring, which is largely what beauty amounts to (see Chapter 7). While beauty continues to have its appeal, it is no longer the primary objective of most contemporary artists.

Distortion in art

When a conventional artist paints a still life or a landscape, s/he remains in a fixed position in relation to what s/he is painting. When painting a portrait or a nude, the sitter or the model is required to remain in a fixed position in relation to her/him. Creating pictures this way is totally unnatural, which is why we find it so difficult to do, why it requires so much training and why the resulting picture looks so contrived. Normally, no one ever does stand still in front of what s/he is looking at, and no person or animal ever stands still in front of us, so what we normally see, if we allow ourselves to acknowledge it, is a mixture of perspectives. Representation continues to be an important component of art, but since the invention of the camera, attention has increasingly been paid to what would normally be called nonrepresentational, or abstract art.

Photography did a great service to the visual arts for, with the advent of photography, there was no longer any point in accurately representing anything, since the camera could do this so much better. Picasso, in particular, developed ways of representing things which, though grossly distorted, somehow looked more strikingly like the real thing than a photographic reproduction did. When I first encountered his art I could not understand what he was trying to do. Now, it is hard to believe that it took me so long to come to terms with it. Increasingly, more people are finding his work, and that of other abstract artists appealing, but there remain many who find it incomprehensible, even offensive. Such people cannot stop seeing a work of art from an outer me perspective, that is seeing it as they think it logically ought to be.

So, what then was Picasso doing, and why did his pictures look so much more real than a photograph did? One thing he was doing was allowing his hand to do whatever it wished; that is allowing what he did to be almost entirely dictated by the inner me, which essentially did the work for him. Another thing he did (though probably quite unselfconsciously) was mix together, in the same picture, a number of different perspectives of the same object or person. His mixture of the frontal and profile view of a face has now become almost a cliché.

Nonrepresentational art

Many abstract artists aim to create art that does not look like anything. This is an impossible aim because almost anything intentionally drawn or painted looks like something. It is perhaps the slight resemblance to something that provokes the reaction in the viewer. Artists have tried painting a uniformly black canvas. Yet even this evokes a reaction because the viewer is reacting to what s/he perceives the artist is trying to do, i.e. not to represent anything. I suspect that the appeal of abstract art is its just perceptible resemblance to real things or real experiences. These things and experiences have been stripped of almost all their recognisable features, but certain basic shapes and shades of colour have been retained. Much abstract art appears to resemble nothing at all, but it is probable that certain small cues have been retained that are sufficient to strike the viewer as familiar, and it is this familiarity that give the creations their appeal. It provides an opportunity for the inner me to fill in the gaps.

The arts and dreaming

There are obvious similarities between the arts and dreaming, and it may be that the arts and dreaming perform similar functions. Perhaps the arts are important to us for some of the reasons that dreams are; though where dreams are fleeting experiences that are quickly forgotten, the arts create a permanent record. Some surrealist artists tried to paint pictures of their dreams (Birtchnell, 2002). One thing that both the arts and dreams do is permit the expression of the socially unacceptable. In art, as in dreams, things can be represented ambiguously. An object can be depicted that looks partly like something that is acceptable and partly like something that is unacceptable. The experiencer can maintain that what s/he is experiencing is the thing that is acceptable. This is the basis of the double entendre, which is also the ingredient of some forms of humour. Beyond ambiguity is the subtler process of metaphor. In metaphor, one idea is hidden within another. The metaphorical representation of something bears no resemblance to that something, but the inner me can connect with it by perceiving a conceptual similarity.

Although representations of reality remain a prominent feature of the arts, the arts must, from an early stage, have been used as a means of representing that which is not real. As do dreams, they afford the means of creating representations of unreal fantasies (like angels, giants and mythical creatures) or unattainable or unrealisable wishes. Within the context of art, anything is possible. Things that are not possible can be represented and, through perceiving these representations, people can, indirectly, experience them. Through such experience, even though it is only a representation, people can derive satisfaction and feel the appropriate emotion.

The role of emotion in the arts

The arts appeal to us because they generate emotion. Although, in Chapter 3, I stated that the inner me is able to perceive whether something is aesthetically effective, I do not believe that there is a specific emotion that is associated with aesthetic experience. Until recently, it was assumed that the emotion in the arts had to be a pleasurable one; but now it seems it can include any emotion, even disgust. When people create art they are trying to create something that makes them feel emotion each time they experience it. It is the generation of emotion that guides them in the creation of their work. They preserve the parts that generate emotion and discard or modify those that do not. Thus, initially, the work is created for the creator, but because people are basically similar, it is likely to have a similar effect upon others who experience it. The advantage of experiencing strong emotion in a work of art is that, at the outer me level, the person knows that the work of art is not the real thing, and this makes the experience of the emotion acceptable.

Although the aim in producing a work of art is to create something that generates emotion, the experiencer sometimes does not know what it is about the work that provokes the emotion. LeDoux (1998) wrote, "We can be drawn toward the aesthetic beauty of a painting without consciously understanding what it is we like about it" (page 22). Sometimes the link is obvious. Quite often what happens is that, in the process of playing around with the work, the creator hits upon something that makes her/him feel emotional. S/he then tries adding to it and subtracting from it until s/he gets the maximum emotional response. S/he may be able to make a guess about what it is about the work that generates the emotion, but s/he will never know for sure. What I am describing here is most pertinent in the more abstract art forms, like abstract art, music and modern poetry, but it applies, in varying degrees, to all the arts.

Some art works, like drawings, paintings, photographs and sculpture are experienced in an instant: I look at the work and I respond immediately. Others, like poems, stories, novels, plays, movies, music, opera and ballet, extend over periods of time. They take a long time to read, watch or listen to. This provides for the creator the opportunity to change the emotional content over different segments of the work, and gradually to build up an overall, emotional effect. The experiencer passes through these different emotions at different stages of the work and comes to the ultimate climax. Extended works seem to work best when the emotional content varies. A sad passage is more disturbing if it follows a happy one, and a happy passage is more exciting if it follows a sad one. People like having their emotional responses manipulated in this way. The standard procedure used to be to introduce frightening and depressing passages during the early and middle stages of the work, and then to bring it to a happy ending, but more recently, the formula has been less predictable.

People vary in the intensity and nature of the emotion they like to experience in a work of art. Some prefer it to be of low intensity and mainly happy or humorous, and others prefer to be taken on an emotional roller coaster, so that, by the end, they are emotionally drained. Some like to be terrified; some like to experience violence and aggression; some like to be depressed; and some like to be sexually aroused. People tend to choose (though not necessarily consciously) a work, which either resonates with their present circumstances or emotional state, or that facilitates the release of pent-up emotion.

Sometimes people are surprised that a certain incident or passage in a book, play or movie, arouses strong emotion in them (perhaps makes them cry). It seems likely that this incident or passage has connected up with some emotional experience in their memory store. A patient will sometimes tell me about such an experience and this may enable us to identify and explore an unresolved area of difficulty.

In Chapter 6, the issue of risk-taking was considered. The excitement of risk-taking was attributed to the safe experience of fear. Part of the experience of fear is arousal, and arousal, just as in sexual arousal, can generate euphoria. During the Falklands war, in the heat of battle, an officer is reported to have raised both arms in the air and shouted, "Isn't this fun." Seconds later he was shot and seriously wounded. Works of art provide a way of experiencing fear within a safe setting, and this is part of their appeal. Funfairs and sporting events are not normally included within the definition of art, but they serve a similar function. They are representations of real life, which are sufficiently like the real thing to generate, and facilitate the release of strong emotion.

The difference between pornography and art

The aims of pornography and art are similar though different. Pornography is quite simply to stimulate sexually. It is direct and purely functional. Art has more diverse functions. In pornography, people are represented in sexually arousing poses or performing sexual acts. Art evokes a range of emotions, usually of a more complex and subtle nature. Of course there is a degree of artistry in pornography and sexual arousal is not necessarily absent from works of art, but the principal difference between the two is that pornography is blatantly and uncompromisingly arousing and art is more broadly representational and is only incidentally arousing. While nudity features prominently in art, it is not normally considered to be pornographic. Whether it is depends upon what the nude is doing.

There are many sound reasons why nudity is acceptable in art. A drawing, painting, statue, photograph or even a movie, however clearly it depicts the naked person, is not the actual person; it is just paper, canvas, stone or celluloid. In this sense it is like artificial flowers. The inner me responds to the image though the outer me knows that it is not the real thing. In earlier times, though less so today, the nude was depicted as someone other than the model her/himself, usually a character from mythology, or religion. This created yet a further degree of distancing from the original model.

Regulation or restraint play a part in distinguishing art from pornography. A life-class is not pornographic because it is so well regulated. The model is separated from the artists; s/he does not move; they do not touch her/him. The art teacher is present to ensure that the rules are kept. Similar principles apply in the theatre. When an actor is naked on the stage, the understanding is that it is really only the person who is being depicted by the actor who is naked but, of course, it is also the actor. When the story is compelling enough, the audience find it easy to experience the nude as the person in the story and not as the actor her/himself. As long as the actor keeps to her/his lines, the audience does not get to know her/him as who s/he really is; though this is not the case with a well-known actor.

In a pornographic video or movie the characters are not actors playing a part in a story. They are people being themselves. Actors in a play or in a film never actually perform a sexual act. They simulate it, albeit sometimes convincingly. In pornography, there is no simulation; it is the real thing. In the play or in the art film the audience feel more comfortable knowing that the actors are not actually having sex.

Creating a work of art

It is quite likely that everyone is born with artistic ability. This is borne out by the power of child art, primitive art and outsider art, but what we are born with is the ability to depict things as they really are, not as we think they ought to be. Depicting things the way we think they ought to be is unnatural, and requires much professional training. Picasso had been thoroughly trained and was capable of creating conventional art, but when he changed his style he had to untrain himself. He was influenced by certain forms of primitive art, so primitive artists had got there before him. His work came to resemble child art, and people objected that a child could do what he did; but an adult behaving like a child has a different effect from a child being a child.

Many art forms require an extensive knowledge of the underlying theory, and the acquisition of considerable skill of execution. This all starts at an outer me level, but over time, this knowledge and these skills become second nature, and get taken over by the inner me. This frees up the artist to work unselfconsciously. The outer me may, quite consciously, think up the general structure of the work, but the inner me has to provide that which the outer me cannot provide, namely that which generates the emotion and the representation of it. The outer me may try out ideas that it thinks might be aesthetically effective, but it then has to try these out against the inner me to see whether they are; that is whether they generate emotion. The outer me needs to assume that the inner me knows what it is doing and where it is going, and to give it free rein; but at times it needs to make practical interventions like selecting different equipment or different materials.

Of the art of painting D.H. Lawrence (1952) wrote, "The knowing eye watches sharp as a needle; but the picture comes clean out of instinct and sheer physical action. Once the instinct and intuition gets into the brush-tip the picture happens, if it is to be a picture at all." The knowing eye here is obviously the outer me. The instinct and intuition are the inner me. The outer me has to stop itself interfering in the inner me's creativity. The creator of the art work is its first audience. If the creator is excited by it, s/he lets it loose on other people. John Constable, the English landscape artist observed that painting is a science of which pictures are but the experiments. Evans (2001) suggested that the (outer me) skill of the artist lies in distinguishing between the experiments that work and those that do not.

Getting it right

There is such a thing in aesthetic creation as getting it right. In all art forms, the creator believes s/he knows when s/he has got it right, and the experiencer can tell when it has been got right. Neither the creator nor the experiencer can say for certain why s/he considers it to be "right" when it is "right." Aesthetic creation works best when the creator trusts her/his intuition and tries not to allow the rational outer me to interfere. Sometimes the outer me (of either the creator or the experiencer) decides that it ought to be right because the creator appears to have done all the right things, and yet it does not feel right. Something is not right and the inner me knows when it is not right and rejects it.

The whole process of getting it right is an inner me one, but I, the outer me, have to try to understand what it amounts to. I think it amounts to getting the representation of reality as close as possible to how reality impinges upon the inner me. Art (in any of its forms) cannot be put together by the contrivances of the outer me. What the artist is groping towards in any artistic creation is something that is recognised by the inner me as real and exciting. This is why, as far as possible, the outer me has to keep referring back to the inner me and letting it decide what lines to make, what shades to use, what notes to play, what words to write and so on.

It is as important to "get it right" in nonrepresentational art as it is in representational art. Mondrian was an artist who produced pictures comprising rectangular shapes of various colours. In a television programme on art and neuroscience, an experiment was described in which pairs of pictures were presented to a class of art students. One picture was of a genuine Mondrian and the other was a fake. To a very significant degree, the students were able to identify the genuine Mondrian, to pick out the pictures in which the artist had got it right. Mondrian's pictures are so simple in structure and design that it would seem easy to fake them, yet the students were able to pick out the fakes. What was it that they were recognising? I would guess that what Mondrian was doing when he made up his compositions was unconsciously representing the bare essentials of the shapes and colours of familiar scenes. These were readily recognisable to the inner me's of the students. Evans (2001) observed that when asked to choose between a selection of abstract paintings, most people prefer the same one, and it is usually one that was painted by a famous artist. He considered that such a painting embodies features that the human visual system is programmed to find most appealing and that the good artist has some intuitive appreciation of what these are.

Responding to a work of art

All of the arts have their effect through the generation of emotion, and all art appreciation takes place by way of the inner me. The outer me takes me to the work of art, but I have to wait to see whether the inner me responds to it, that is generates emotion. It matters not whether the outer me believes that I (inner me) should respond to it. If it doesn't it doesn't, and that's an end to it.

People try to rely upon the outer me to judge a work of art. They look at it and ask, "What is it supposed to be?" Of course, there are art works that are supposed to be something, and with these, the outer me can make a judgement about whether they really look like that something. It can, for example, judge whether the artist has got the proportions or the perspective or the shading right; but art can sometimes work (as indicated by the inner me's response) even though the proportions or the perspective or the shading are not right.

Filling in the gaps plays a major part in responding to a work of art. As was explained in Chapter 6, filling in the gaps is an important survival mechanism: we cannot afford to wait until we have the whole picture before we try to escape from danger. Because we fill in the gaps so effectively, we do not need the whole picture. In fact, it has become tedious to have to look at an entire picture. This is probably because a rigidly created picture leaves no scope for gap filling.

The appreciation of the art work

Once the art work is presented or performed it enters a kind of no-man's-land, out of which it is perceived by the experiencer. The experiencer experiences it in the way he might experience anything else, that is, irrespective of the fact that it has been created or performed by another person or other people. What s/he may make of it may or may not correspond to what the creator or the performers had intended. Thus any aesthetic experience is a mixture of what is given out by the creator and what is taken in by the experiencer.

People frequently do not know why they like or dislike a work of art (because the inner me is not able to tell them). Liking depends upon the release of emotion, not necessarily pleasurable emotion. If they experience no emotion they say it does nothing for them.

Poetry

Poetry, like most other art forms, has undergone major transformations over recent years. It has become much more loosely structured. It is no longer necessary for it to scan or to rhyme, and it is no longer written in stanzas. In modern poetry, words are frequently used in strange combinations that are not always easy to understand. You simply allow the words to wash over you and leave it to the inner me to make of it what it will. The writing of poetry has become far less contrived. Poets almost allow the poems to write themselves. Claxton (1998) cites the American poet Amy Lowell's description of how she writes. She said that she just drops the subject into her unconscious, "much as one drops a letter into the mailbox" (page 60), and six months later the words of the poem begin to come into her head. In reply to the question, "How are poems made?" she said, "I don't know. It makes not the slightest difference that the question as asked refers solely to my own poems, for I know as little of how they are made as I do of anyone else's. What I do know about them is only a millionth part of what there must be to know. I meet them where they touch consciousness, and that is already a considerable distance along the road of evolution" (page 67).

The performing arts

Certain forms of art (music, ballet, opera, drama and the cinema) are created in the form of a notation or script that has to be interpreted by a performer or performers. The art work has to be interpreted by the performer and different performers produce different interpretations. There may also be an intermediary between creator and performer (conductor or director) who guides the performers. In ballet, there is a composer and a choreographer and in opera there is a composer and a librettist. Beyond this, the final performance depends upon the capabilities of the performers. Each person in this sequence has an input to the final effect, so the art work is not a simple and direct communication between the creator and the person who experiences it.

Music

Music is by far the least representational of the arts. At a rational (outer me) level it is difficult to understand what I might like about music. It can only be liked at an irrational, intuitive and therefore inner me level. Even if I (outer me) do not understand music, it seems to say something to me if I accept it unquestioningly. It is difficult to understand what advantages music might have for the individual, or to identify the evolutionary precursors to it. Pinker (1997) wrote, "As far as biological cause and effect are concerned, music is useless" (page 528). He maintained that, ". . . music could vanish from our species and the rest of our lifestyle would be virtually unchanged" (page 528). He doubted Darwin's suggestion that music grew out of our ancestors' mating calls, though he conceded that if we include all other emotional noises like weeping, moaning, snarling and yelping, there might be some link. My own view is that music works like all other art forms work, because it generates emotion, and we just like experiencing emotion.

There is a vast range of types of music. The music of different cultures is sometimes quite different in structure, and uses different instruments. It is sometimes difficult for members of one culture to appreciate the music of another. Even within the same culture, there are contrasting musical styles, and devotees of one style may find another style incomprehensible or distasteful. On the other hand, music is not as culture-specific as language. While English is the only language in which I am fluent, I can be affected by the music of many parts of the world.

Although a few pieces of music have been composed in order to represent certain specific experiences, like waves breaking, horses galloping or birds singing, most forms of music are not strictly representational. How then do they create their effects? It is unlikely that there is a single explanation. A central feature of much music is its rhythm. It is particularly prominent in primitive music, which suggests that it was one of its earliest features. The linking of rhythm with the heart beat may be significant. Normally, I am not aware of my heart beating, but when I am, it is when I am feeling emotional. When I hear a musical rhythm, the similarity to the heartbeat may be sufficient to evoke in me the subjective experience of being emotional. This suggests that the physical component of emotion is the precursor to the subjective experience.

Besides rhythm, there are a number of other variables in music, like loudness, speed, key, scales, pitch, tone, overtones, chords and the characteristic sound of different instruments. Each of these, in its separate way, contributes to the overall effect. So many combinations of variables are possible that new compositions are continuously being composed. When I listen to music, I am not aware of which component is having which effect.

Music creates abstract sounds, like swirling, soaring, drifting, swooping, thudding, scraping, grunting, juddering, jangling, ranting, rasping, pounding and pattering. Such sounds occur in nature and they must remind me of these natural experiences, but it is the nonspecific nature of music that frees me from making connections to particular experiences.

The composer can only go so far in representing her/his creation in the form of a notation, and from this, the performer has to try to understand the composer's intention; that is to interpret it. Just as the composer in her/his composing has to "get it right" so the performer, in her/his performance of it, has to "get it right." Ideally, the performer's inner me is in tune with the composer's inner me and both inner me's work as one. It is possible that the performer can improve upon the composer's intention, by seeing what the composer was trying to do and carrying the process further.

Music and emotion

It is because it is so abstract that music is so readily linked with emotion. Music is played on occasions when it is necessary to generate emotion. In Nazi Germany, military music was played with great effect at Hitler's, highly orchestrated, political rallies. It is often played when soldiers march to war or march into battle. It is commonly played at religious services and at weddings and funerals. It is played in the theatre or the cinema to enhance the emotion of the action. It is sometimes played in psychological experiments to generate certain mood states.

It is generally accepted that music has its effect through analogy. Notes rising up a scale create the effect of progress and success, and generate good feelings, and notes falling down a scale create the effect of regress and failure, and generate bad feelings. Just as we like stories that tell of unhappy events that progress to happy ones, we also like music that takes us down a scale and then takes us up again. When I listen to music I am being taken on an abstract journey. The fast bits and the slow bits make me feel I am moving quickly or slowly, and the ups and downs are lifting my emotions up and dropping them down.

Songs

Songs are a category of music in which words are arranged so as to fit the structure of the music. In this way the words and the music reinforce each other. This makes it possible for the music to make reference to specific areas of reality. It is noteworthy that where the words of songs are processed in the dominant (verbal) hemisphere, the music is processed in the minor (spaces and shapes) hemisphere. Because of the structure of the music, songs can only include simple statements. In the chapter on memory I noted how the inner me projects into consciousness a few simple words of a song that capture the essence of the situation I am in. This adds to their impact. The music as well makes its contribution. Opera is a particularly potent art form in which music, singing and drama are combined.

Dance

Music, particularly when it has a regular beat, induces us to tap our hands or feet, and even to want to dance to it. In primitive cultures, music and dance are almost inseparable. In dancing, music and muscular activity are intertwined. There is a compulsion to move the body in time to the music. The dancer gives her/himself up to the music and becomes absorbed into it. Sometimes particular kinds of dance music require specific dance movements and even specific costumes. Ballet is an art form in which there is a precise and often complex choreography for a specific piece of music. In ballet the choreographer is the creator and the dancers are simply the interpreters of her/ his creation. The choreographer has contributed as much to the art form as has the composer of the music.

The arts and the cerebral hemispheres

The dominant (usually the left) cerebral hemisphere is more concerned with logic, mathematical calculation and language than the minor (usually the right) hemisphere. The minor hemisphere is more concerned with recognising shapes and faces and appreciating art and music. Challoner (2000) reporting upon studies by Perry on people who had had their cerebral hemispheres surgically separated (in an attempt to cure severe epilepsy) observed that they could copy drawings better with their left hand (usually controlled by the right hemisphere) than with their right, even if they were right-handed.

An area located in the temporal lobe of the minor hemisphere is concerned with musical ability and musical appreciation (Eccles, 1989). People who have had a right temporal lobectomy have difficulty identifying a musical memory and continue to hum the rest of a tune after it has been started and stopped (Shankweiler, 1966). It is significant that music is located in the hemisphere that is specialised for spatial and imagistic abilities, for though words can be added to music, music itself is a totally nonverbal experience.

19 Humour

I will consider first the outward expression of humour.

Smiling

Smiling is not only an expression of amusement. It is a form of communication to others. It is a powerful communication that only humans have. As with all facial expressions, it originates in the inner me, and only an inner me-generated smile looks genuine. The outer me does not have access to the neural mechanisms that give rise to the smile. However, an outer me-generated smile can resemble the genuine article sufficiently to fool the inner me of a recipient. Consequently, forced smiles are commonly adopted to put others at their ease, particularly by television announcers, air hostesses and politicians. Smiling is an expression of peace. It conveys the message, "I mean you no harm." With the eyes wide open, it can be a means of seduction. Smiling is also a bonding gesture. Parents smile at their children and children and friends smile at each other. People smile at the camera when they are being photographed. Finally, forced (outer me) smiling is an act of defiance. People put on a smile, or wear a smile, as a way of pretending that they are happy when they are not. People are urged to smile when they are oppressed and soldiers are urged to smile in times of war.

So how does smiling come to be associated with humour? In the absence of other people, smiling is an expression of contentment. I smile to myself when things are going well for me. Beyond this, I may smile when watching someone doing something that is obviously going to fail. I will say, "I had to smile," meaning I could not hold back that feeling of smugness; so I am smiling at someone else's misfortune; and this is the basis of a lot of humour.

Laughing

Some people laugh more easily than others, and there is evidence that this may have a genetic basis. A pair of identical twins, who met for the first time in adult life, discovered that they laughed much more than most people. There is evidence that people who laugh a lot are healthier. They attract other people around them. Laughing is infectious. If I break into laughter, this can only be an inner me eruption. The outer me cannot decide that I should laugh. I can decide to pretend to laugh, but a pretend laugh, just like a pretend smile, is not inner me driven, and does not sound or look like the real thing.

Certain monkeys, e.g. chimpanzees, laugh, but they are probably the only animals that do. Their laughter appears to be an expression of triumph, which is certainly a common ingredient of humour; so it is possible that human laughter, and possibly also human humour, has evolved out of this. Eibl-Eibesfeldt (1989) observed that monkeys make a laughing like sound when they gang up against a common enemy. I laugh when I have won a game, particularly if I did not expect to.

Laughing as a response to being tickled

Chimpanzees tickle each other and they laugh when they are tickled. Being tickled is a strange experience. I cannot tickle myself, even though I do exactly what someone else would do to tickle me. The brain (inner me) is aware that the part that is being touched is not being touched by me. There-fore, as with sexual arousal, I am responding to someone else touching me. Certain parts of the body, the soles of the feet for example, are more respon-sive to being tickled than others. When I laugh when I am being tickled, I experience the same kind of pleasure that I experience when I am amused, but I also want the person to stop, because I find the degree of stimulation intolerable. Babies appear to like being tickled, and laugh with obvious pleasure. Children also like being tickled, and like tickling each other. Laughing would appear then, like smiling, to intensify social bonding.

Nervous laughter

Laughing can be an expression of a particular kind of nervousness. When I was in my late teens and early twenties, I often laughed when I was nervous, and people sometimes misunderstood this. It had nothing to do with being amused, and it was difficult to control. It arose only in social situations. In the sixth form at school, we had an attractive, young biology mistress. Some-times, in her classes I, and my (male) neighbour, would break into uncontrol-lable giggling. I imagine that this was our attempt to suppress our sexual feelings towards her; so laughing appears to be a way of covering up, or denying, an emotion. There is a common association between laughter and embarrassment.

Laughing and crying

Laughing varies in intensity, according to the degree of emotion released. At its most intense, the whole body rocks and shakes, just as it does in intense weeping. In fact, sometimes tears are shed in laughter, and sometimes it is difficult to tell whether someone is laughing or crying. Sometimes the one turns into the other, and sometimes both occur together. People sometimes say, "If I didn't laugh I would cry." This kind of laughing is a defence against crying, a kind of manic defence (Klein, 1934). When people alternate between laughing and crying, they are trying to conceal their unhappiness with humour, but the unhappiness keeps breaking through. Children sometimes convert their crying into laughing, indicating their recovery from being upset, but it can be a frail recovery.

Laughing together

Pinker (1997) observed that laughter is noisy so that others may hear it; which means that laughter is a form of communication. This is like the bonding quality of smiling. Provine (1991) found that people laugh 30 times more often when they are in the company of others than when they are alone. There is a difference between laughing at someone and laughing with someone. When people laugh together it serves as a reinforcement of togetherness. Perhaps it is an expression of shared upperness (Chapter 8). People speak of having a good laugh, when they are all laughing together at the same thing. However, more often than not, what they share is laughing at someone else's misfortune. Sometimes when people are having a good laugh together (as with defiant smiling) they are trying to drown their sorrows. One person laughing can trigger off another. This is why television comedy programmes are accompanied by recorded laughter. Once people have started to laugh, small cues can keep the laughter going. This is why comedians start their act with their funniest joke.

Laughing and sex

Once, in a survey of young, married couples, I asked each partner what it was s/he had found attractive about the other. Often, the woman would say, "He could make me laugh." Men often feel, perhaps quite rightly, that if they can make the woman laugh, sexual excitement will follow. Couples sometimes generate laughter by doing silly things, and once they have started laughing, they soon become sexually excited.

Laughing at somebody

Laughing can take on an offensive quality. It can be cruel, mocking, humiliating and ridiculing. Ridicule shares the same origin as the Latin word *ridere*, meaning to laugh. Laughing falls short of outright aggression. It is like the monkeys who laugh as they gang up on a common enemy. Perhaps the aggression is not necessary, for the laughing acknowledges that the enemy are already defeated.

Laughing at the misfortunes of others

A common trigger for amusement is the sudden and unexpected misfortune of another. This is an expression of the German concept of *Schadenfreude*, taking pleasure in another's misfortune. In effect, it is the pleasure of gaining upperness (Chapter 8). Clowns perform the function of pretending to experience misfortune in order to cause people to laugh at them. The pretend component is an important one, for if the clown were to seriously harm himself during a performance it would stop being funny. As with the arts, the inner me cannot distinguish between reality and pretence, and so it is responding to the pretend action as though it were real. Pinker (1997) observed that both children and members of primitive tribes are able to laugh even when people are seriously harmed. People with an antisocial personality can laugh when they inflict pain on, or cause serious injury to, others. Tantam (1988) observed that certain disconnected individuals, called schizotypals, can laugh when they hear of people being burned to death. Here, the inner me is able to escape the restraint of the outer me.

What is humour?

It is impossible to identify a single, essential ingredient of humour, but certain features stand out. It is always a positive and pleasurable experience, and presumably is accompanied by the release of endorphins. It is a response to a sudden and unexpected event. It is catching myself feeling an emotion that I realise I ought not to be feeling. The laughter is the outcome of the ensuing struggle; though laughter does not have to contain this element of conflict. Take, for example, the triumphant laughing of monkeys.

Humour offers me a way of giving expression to socially unacceptable feelings, largely by denying that I am really feeling them. It arises out of the conflict between the selfish urges of the inner me and the decent or moral impositions of the outer me. It is more easily experienced in a crowd setting in which the in-between me seems to have less influence, and people seem able to give expression to their more selfish and less moral tendencies; or under the influence of alcohol, which appears to reduce the restraints of the in-between me.

Amusement

Amusement is what Damasio (2000) would have called a secondary or social emotion; that is a basic emotion that is experienced under particular circumstances. The basic emotion is pleasure, but it is pleasure from a position of upperness, and pleasure that is not freely felt. It usually also needs to incorporate a degree of guilt.

Amusement, like an aesthetic effect, may be natural or created. If it is natural, something funny simply happens, like a bird's dropping lands on a lady's clean hat. If it is created, someone has to think up an action, saying, story or situation that others might consider to be funny. Just like the artist, the comedian needs first to try out the creation on her/himself to see how her/his inner me responds to it.

The sequence of events that leads to the experiencing of amusement

Humour depends upon the release of emotion, but the association between humour and the release of emotion is complex. Amusement commonly happens in three stages, but the stages usually follow so quickly that people are not normally aware of them. First, I respond to an event or a statement with an appropriate emotion, but the emotion is not amusement; often it is something like triumph or sexual arousal. Next, I become aware of my response, and realise it is not a nice or acceptable response to have made, and I feel bad about having made it. Finally, I try to dissociate myself from this unacceptable emotion, by concealing it or apologising for it, and somehow this distorted or disguised emotion emerges as amusement. What the amusement is saying is, "I'm sorry, I didn't really mean to make that response. It was wrong of me. Forgive me." The important point is that the emotion still gets released, and the denial, disowning or apology is sufficient to allow it to be released. The essential feature of the emotion of amusement then is an attempt to hold back, or become dissociated from, or apologise for, an emotion I know I should not be feeling; so there is always the feeling of something pressing for expression coupled with a determination to dam it back. It is the feeling bad bit that generates the humour. Laughing then is an expression of a half-way state in which I both mean and do not mean what I am feeling.

Let us take the example of the bird's dropping landing on the lady's hat. My immediate response is one of triumph. The lady's hat has been ruined. She is down and I am up. I suddenly realise what a terrible thing it is to be feeling, so I try desperately to conceal or deny it. Despite my efforts, the emotion comes out, but it is acceptably disguised or diminished by the expression of laughter. Essentially then humour is a way of converting unacceptable emotion into a kind of apologetic or diluted version of it that is acceptable. I like humour because it allows me at least the partial expression of feelings that I otherwise would not have been able to allow myself to express.

A SPLIT-BRAIN EXPERIMENT IN HUMOUR

Schiffer (2000) reported upon an experiment carried out by Sperry. Ostensibly it was to test whether the right hemisphere of a split-brain patient (who had had her cerebral hemisphere's surgically separated) could register the meaning of words. The words were momentarily flashed by tachistoscope to her left visual field. This was registered only by the right hemisphere; for in split-brain patients, the image cannot be transferred to the other side. Suddenly she began to laugh. When asked why she was laughing, she replied, "Doctor, you have a funny machine." Since the right hemisphere has no speech function, this verbal response must have been made by the left hemisphere, which could not have known what had been flashed. In fact, a nude woman in a provocative pose had been flashed. The right hemisphere had reacted with embarrassment to the nude photograph, which had caused the patient to laugh; but it had not been able to convey to the left hemisphere what was funny. One hemisphere had been amused, but the other hemisphere did not know why, so it had to make up a reason. Since laughter is inner me-generated, it is likely that even non-split-brain people sometimes do not know why they are laughing – like me with my biology mistress.

HUMOUR AND SURPRISE

Surprise is a common component of humour because the emotion is felt before the in-between me has a chance to kick in and prevent or modify its expression. Comedians are aware of this: They lead their audience along a neutral path, then abruptly change direction. They describe an innocent scene, then unexpectedly introduce a new and disturbing feature of it. They lull the audience into a state of calm, then suddenly shock them. Audiences are aware of this, and sit in apprehension, waiting for the shock to come. Consequently, they are all the more emotional when the punch-line lands.

PUSHING HUMOUR TO ITS LIMITS

Humour only works if it contains the element of a forbidden truth. Using psychoanalytic terminology, in much humour, there is the innocent, manifest content and the not so innocent latent content. The innocent, manifest content serves as a cover for the not so innocent latent content. I resort to humour as a means of giving expression to feelings that I have but that I do not dare to express openly. A joke is not a joke unless it contains a hidden, forbidden message. I will only laugh if I recognise the truth of the hidden message. The closer the joke gets to the forbidden message without actually saying it, the greater the anxiety it arouses, and the greater amusement it generates. It has to be a balance between the shockingness of the message and the adequacy of the cover.

Telling jokes is a form of risk-taking. The term *risqué* joke is derived from the French word *risquer*, which means to take risks. A *risqué* joke is one that borders upon impropriety. The professional comedian knows that the more shocking the hidden message is, the more the audience will laugh when they pick it up; yet if it is too shocking, the consciences of the audience will step in and stop them laughing. A joke is like a party dress: it has to reveal enough to be provocative, but not so revealing as to be indecent. Comedians have to live dangerously, knowing that they need to get as close as they dare to the unspeakable, without slipping into impropriety. Consequently, a number have been banned because they have overstepped the limits.

Varieties of humour

Humour and escapism

Some people have difficulty taking life seriously, and joke about everything. This is particularly so of people who are trying to avoid unpleasant circumstances or unpleasant memories. The private lives of many professional comedians are unhappy, and their comedy is a way of keeping their unhappiness at bay. It is difficult to pin them down and persuade them to give serious answers to personal questions. They are popular because they are able to help other people to be escapist. In contrast, people who are forever serious are unpopular, and are accused of having no sense of humour. They are rejected because they are a reminder of the unpleasantness of reality. In one respect, humour performs a similar function to religion. Like religion, by playing down certain unacceptable aspects of reality, it makes life more acceptable. What is so striking about religion is that there is no humour in it, though of course people do make jokes about it.

Humour and the forbidden

Humour is something that happens unexpectedly, that catches me off guard, that makes reference to a forbidden hope or desire, in either a pretend or an oblique way, that allows me to release the emotion that would be appropriate to an event of this kind had it happened in reality. Clearly there is an element of guilt involved in that I am acknowledging that I have been caught out feeling something that I know I should not have been feeling. The veneer of civilisation has been allowed to slip. Ambiguity is a useful tool in humour. A remark (the double entendre) is made which has both a neutral meaning and a more emotionally charged one. The more emotionally charged meaning is able to slip through, under cover of the more neutral one. The laughing person is trying, at the outer me level, to hold on to the more neutral meaning, while the more emotionally charged meaning is getting picked up by the inner me.

Humour and hostility

Humour is often directed at people we have misgivings about, like those who are our enemies, members of a political party we do not support, or members of another country or race. The humorous remark is not normally an overtly offensive one; the offensiveness is oblique or implied, and this allows us to find it amusing. We are able to say offensive things to people if we are laughing while we are doing it. The message we are conveying by our laughter is "Do not take this seriously. I am only joking." What does only joking mean exactly? Why does laughing at the same time make being offensive permissible? The reverse of this particular coin is "Many a true word is spoken in jest." In fact, everything spoken in jest is true. If it were not true it would not be funny. Adding laughter provides the speaker with a kind of immunity. If someone does take offence at a remark made under cover of humour, we say, "What's the matter, can't you take a joke?" An offensive remark made within the setting of humour is understood to be proffered as an offensive gesture rather than a true assault. Expressing an offensive remark within the setting of a joke is supposed to be saying "I do not really mean it."

Humour echoing my own feelings

If I am feeling irritated by or intolerant of another person, and someone makes an unkind remark about that person, I laugh, because the remark resonates with my own irritation or intolerance, which I have been trying to conceal not only from others but also from myself. Similarly, if I am feeling sexually desirous of someone, and someone makes a remark, which alludes to her attractiveness, I will laugh because I have been caught out harbouring desirous feelings that I am trying to conceal.

Humour and cruelty

Humour enables people to describe extremely cruel acts, and laugh because they are not really true. An example of a cruel joke is: After an operation the surgeon said to the patient, "I have some bad news and some good news. The bad news is I have cut off both your legs. The good news is the man in the next bed has made an offer for your slippers."

Racist humour

A lot of humour has a basis in fear. We laugh when something that we fear is alluded to in a joke. We would not laugh if the object of our fear were referred to openly. Most people fear foreigners, so xenophobia is a common source of humour. Different nations choose different foreigners to make fun of. In Western cultures Jews, West Indians, Indians and Pakistanis have been fruitful sources of humour. There have also been members of these racial and national groups who have become comedians and made jokes against themselves. In recent years, many countries have made serious attempts to integrate different racial and national groups into multi-racial and multi-national societies. These attempts have been thwarted by outbreaks of open hostility towards minority groups. The upshot of this is that racial humour has become increasingly frowned upon.

Sexual humour

Allusions to sexuality or sexual behaviour or feelings are common ingredients of humour. Frequently, we are not prepared to acknowledge openly that we have certain sexual intentions or feelings, but when oblique reference is made to them we find ourselves laughing. The reference has been sufficient to evoke a sexual response. Here again, if there is a pretend element that it is not exactly the real thing, it makes it easier to laugh. Humour and pornography are closely linked. Through humour, we are able to approach closer to disapproved of or forbidden sexual ideas and sexual practices. Jokes that allude to sex are called dirty jokes. Their popularity, particularly among the young, indicates the extent of anxiety we have about sex and sexually transmitted diseases. The walls of public toilets are daubed with sexual poems and sexual drawings, which often have humorous overtones. People who have an open attitude towards sex and sexual perversions do not find dirty jokes funny.

Humour and relief

Some jokes are funny because they create anxiety and then provide immediate relief from it. A boy says to a girl, "Do you know what lips are for?" (The listener feels anxious at the thought of the boy making a sexual advance to the girl.) The girl replies, "To stop our mouths fraying at the edges?" (The listener laughs with relief that the girl has deflected the man's advance.) Here is a similar kind of joke: A woman says to a man, "Rub my tummy and tell me that you love me." The man does as she asks. The woman says, "Lower." (The listener feels anxious at the woman's suggestion.) The man repeats "I love you," but in a deeper voice. (The listener laughs with relief that the man had not understood the woman's instruction.)

Slips of the tongue and slips of the pen

In the slip of the tongue or the slip of the pen, the person is showing that part of her/himself that s/he is trying to keep hidden, that which Jung called the shadow (Chapter 4). I laugh because I have been caught thinking that which I know I should not be thinking, that which is socially unacceptable or undesirable. One of the funniest moments for me was when I was sharing a psychotherapy supervision session with some fellow trainees. One of us, a rather correct young man, was describing a psychotherapy session he had had with an attractive, young, woman patient. He said that she told him that she was feeling hot and that she took off her sweater. I, and my fellow trainees, fell about laughing, somehow knowing that what she had taken off was not her sweater, but her coat. There were a number of reasons why I laughed: One was that, by saying that she was hot, the young woman was suggesting that she was feeling emotional; another was that she had given utterance to what we all would like to have happened, and had released our shared sexual fantasies about her; another was that he and I were rivals on the same psycho-therapy course, so I enjoyed seeing him slip up in front of the supervisor; another was that he had expressed strong disapproval of my sexual interest in a woman member of the course, which had made me feel both guilty and intolerant of him; but probably the main one was that, by his slip of the tongue, he had revealed that, behind his correct manner, he also had sexual fantasies about the patient, which he had obviously been trying to conceal. When our laughter subsided, he said quietly to the supervisor, "She did not take off her sweater."

The joke

A joke is a form of contrived humour. A good joke, like a good dream or a good work of art, condenses a number of ideas into one brief event, statement or representation. Freud (1905b) drew parallels between jokes and dreams and considered they performed a similar function. The joke happens in the split second when all its components get registered at the same time. It is often the overtones of the composition that contribute to the humour, but since it is the combined inner me and in-between me (both unconscious) that cause me to be amused, I do not always know what it is about the joke that I have found amusing. In fact, I can only ever guess at what it was, and I might be wrong in my guess.

A good joke, like a good work of art, depends upon a multiplicity of circumstances coming together at the same time. The setting and the timing have to be right. The choice of words has to be right. The way the joke is told has to be right. The professional comedian is acutely aware of all this. Quite rightly the comedian, Frank Carson, used to boast, "It's the way that I tell 'em." A good comedian can tell a joke and get a laugh where a poor comedian can tell the same joke and not get a laugh. The good joke has to catch the listener unawares. For this reason, the good comedian tries to keep a straight face when telling the joke. If the listener can see the joke coming it loses its impact. Good comedians never laugh at their own jokes, though many people do, perhaps because they hope that their laughter will be infectious.

Freud (1905a) made the point that one cannot keep a joke to oneself. One has to tell it to someone, like showing a work of art to someone. In telling a joke I have to make the other laugh. If I do not, I experience a horrible sense of failure. Often, when the recipient laughs I also laugh, and Freud argued that the teller uses the recipient to release her/his own emotion.

Freud also made the point that the joke only works the first time of telling, because the ending has to be unexpected. If the listener guesses the ending s/he does not laugh; so we have to keep producing new jokes.

There is a process in responding to a joke called getting it. Sometimes a person tells a joke and the impact is immediate: All the components strike home together, and they are immediately assimilated and interpreted. Some-times there is a delay, lasting up to several seconds, before the person hearing the joke gets it, that is experiences the rush of emotion that indicates that the joke has been recognised. What exactly is going on during this delay? Perhaps the person has got stuck at the manifest content and has not been able to make contact with the hidden message. Sometimes, by way of the outer me, the person works through the joke bit by bit, and eventually sees the point; but a joke that has to be worked through in this way does not have the same impact. It is possible that the person does not get it because its message is too disturbing and the in-between me has not allowed her/him to register it.

The complicated joke

Some jokes are ingenious, or subtle, and need to be thought about, by way of the outer me, before the point is got. Sometimes the listener has to be clever or needs to have access to special knowledge in order to get the point, as with the in-joke. The ingeniousness, when it finally penetrates, contributes to the impact of the joke, and sometimes an audience will actually applaud an ingenious joke as well as laugh at it. This places it closer to a work of art. Although, in the end, it is the combined inner me and in-between me that decide whether the joke should be registered as funny, the outer me is needed here to pass judgement upon the skill of the teller.

Creating humour at one's own expense

People who are the butt of humour, like people in social, racial, sexual or religious minorities, sometimes make jokes about themselves. People often admire them for doing this and consider them to be brave, or to have a good sense of humour. In fact, what they are doing is anticipating the criticism or the insult of the majority and getting the criticism or insult in before the majority do. It is those who are in the majority who find such jokes funny. A variation of this practice is people who are the butt of humour actually laughing at the joke that is directed at them. They actually laugh with the joker and almost align themselves with the joker. This again is considered to be brave; but people who do this are accepting the humiliation that the joker is imposing upon them. A black person who makes jokes about black people, or who laughs at the racist humour of white people, is denying her/his racial status in an attempt to join the ranks of, or win the favour of, the white people who find the joke funny. This is a betrayal of the dignity of her/his own racial group. The person who is the butt of the joke places her/himself in the one-down position and elects to stay there, hoping that this way s/he will gain the favour of the teller of the joke.

Humour and swearing

Swear words are a particular category of word that is scorned upon, if not frankly forbidden, in a polite society (see Chapter 13). The whole point of swear words is that they are forbidden, so those who use them are being defiant. They have their impact because they are forbidden, and people use them because they are forbidden. The listener laughs at the swear words because the teller of the joke is daring to use them. Another way of viewing swear words is that they are words that are reserved for the expression of strong emotion. Not surprisingly, swear words feature commonly in humour, particularly in dirty jokes. Stand-up comics frequently use them. The Scottish comedian, Billy Connolly, uses the word fuck liberally in his performances. He has confessed that people stopped laughing at him when he stopped using it.

The length of a joke

Usually, humour works best when the message is compressed, so that the emotion is held within a small sensory input, whether this be verbal or pictorial. A pun is a highly concentrated form of joke that usually rests upon a single word having two meanings. Some double meanings are funny and some are not. Presumably the funny ones are the ones in which the second meaning has certain emotional overtones. Recently, I heard the joke: What do you call a fly with no wings? Answer: A walk. I confess that I did not see the joke immediately. It took me several seconds to realise that the word fly had two meanings: the one a noun that describes a kind of insect, the other a verb that describes what the fly does. I suspect that the power of the joke rests upon the idea that it is cruel to pull off the wings of a fly to make it walk, and, by this rather indirect play on words, one is permitted to enjoy that sense of cruelty, without feeling too bad about it. The joke makes no mention of pulling off the wings. The emotion only hits when you visualise this poor fly walking around with no wings.

There is also the long, drawn out joke, sometimes called a shaggy dog story. The effectiveness of such a joke depends upon the comedian holding the audience in suspense. He leads and the audience follows, almost like being hypnotised. The audience becomes tense, knowing that eventually something funny is going to be said. That something funny is called the punchline which, when it comes, has to be concise; but it has to be related to the story that leads up to it, so that it binds the story together. This creates a release of tension which precipitates the laughter. Freud (1905b) observed that the discharge of an inhibitory cathexis is increased by the height of the damming up.

Deconstructing a joke

It might require several paragraphs to unpack and reveal the interlocking of the many components that resulted in the humorous effect (just like unpacking a dream or a work of art). It is often said that if a joke has to be explained it ceases to be funny. The explaining process lifts it out of the automatic sequence described at the beginning of the chapter and places it into a piece of rational thought. The joke only makes me laugh if it catches me unawares and I have not had time to assimilate it into a logical explanation. However, it is sometimes instructive to take a joke apart to try to understand where the humour has come from. In the process, of course, the joke completely loses its humour, but that is not the point. I will take the example of an old, but compact joke. One man says to another, "Who was that lady I saw you with last night?" The other replies, "That was no lady, that was my wife." The whole force of the joke rests upon the various meanings of the word lady. At its simplest, it means a female person, as opposed to a male person. It may also mean a respectable female person, as opposed to a woman, who is not necessarily respectable. When the first man asked, "Who was that lady I saw you with last night?" he may, at the most innocent of levels, have meant, "Who was that female person I saw you with?" The fact that he added "last night" suggests that he was using the word lady to mean lady friend, that is a casual woman he has picked up for the evening. In his reply, the man was trying to explain that he was not philandering, because he was out with his wife; so when he replied, "That was no lady" he was trying to deny that the woman he was with was a lady friend, but inadvertently, he was insinuating that his wife was not a lady, that is, not a respectable person. The reason why people laugh at this joke is that they suspect that the man really did think of his wife as not being respectable, and that he was allowing his true feelings to show.

20　Religion

The fact that every known culture has religious beliefs should mean that humans have an innate disposition to be religious; but this seems unlikely. During the course of its history, each culture lays down its own religious beliefs, which are specific for that culture, but which share common themes with the religious beliefs of other cultures. Probably the earliest forms of religion concerned good spirits and bad spirits that inhabit rocks, ponds and so forth. During the course of social evolution, the nature of religious beliefs and rituals has tended to change from a belief in multiple gods, like the sun god, the moon god and the rain god, to a belief in one single god, the creator, controller and supervisor of the universe.

People used to believe that the gods had the power to determine the nature of events: like the sun god brought the sun and the rain god brought the rain. People thought that the gods caused certain things to happen in response to the way they behaved. Consequently, they were careful not to offend the gods. If bad things did happen, people would try to appease the gods. Certain members of communities served as intermediaries between the community and the gods. They conveyed messages to and from the gods and decided what or whom should be sacrificed. People built shrines, which served as access points to the gods, where they felt close to them, where they prayed to them and where sacrifices were made.

Religion and the supernatural

Religious belief is a category of the more general belief in the supernatural; that is belief in spirits, demons, ghosts, angels, faeries, witches, superstition, magic, voodoo, witch-doctors, prophets, fortune tellers, spiritualism, astrology, telepathy, psychokinesis, aliens and corn circles. Despite the universal acceptance of scientific explanations, Pinker (1997) reported that recent polls have shown that 69 per cent of Americans believe in angels, half believe in ghosts and a quarter believe in witches.

Nunberg's (1931) term rationalisation, introduced in Chapter 14, refers to the human (inner me) capacity to make irrational causal connections. It is particularly evident among children and primitive people, who are pre-rational, that is, although they have the potential for rational thought (outer me), they have not yet been schooled in it. Children and primitive people accept uncritically what they are told about the world. When I was a small child and it thundered, my mother told me that it was the old man mending his shoes, and I believed her.

The variability of religious conviction

For some people, the conviction that their god exists is intense and unshakeable. It is held with the same conviction as a delusion. In fact, it has all the characteristics of a delusion. It is irrational and it is not amenable to reason. You cannot destroy a religious belief with logic, because religious people argue that it transcends logic. They often radiate euphoria because they know that they are right. Jung (1938) described religious experience as an absolute, which cannot be disputed. Jung considered religious belief to be an archetype of the collective unconscious (Chapter 4). When asked if he believed in God, Jung (1959) replied, "I know, I don't need to believe, I know." Perhaps in this sense, everybody "knows" there is a god.

For some people, religious belief is weak or totally absent. As far back as I can remember I have not believed in God. However hard I might have tried I could not do so, though I do not remember trying very hard. I understand the concept of God. I think I know what it would be like to believe in God. Perhaps I (inner me) really do, but I (outer me) am not allowing myself to admit it. Perhaps people who say they believe in God do not really, and they are not allowing themselves to admit it.

Is religion a delusion?

I have considered how children and primitive people are capable of believing that which is not true, but how is it that civilised adults are? They are and they do when they become psychotic. Being civilised does not protect people against becoming psychotic, neither does having a scientific education. Even eminent scientists become psychotic. Religion is one of the most remarkable of human characteristics. It is so obviously not true that it must be a delusion; but how can all humans share the same delusion; and how is it that when people take antipsychotic drugs, they stop being deluded but they do not stop being religious?

A recent book (Clarke, 2001) explores the overlap between religion and psychosis. In it Lenz (1983) is quoted as saying that a major difference between a religious belief and a delusion is the course of development on which the belief takes the person. Fulford (1989) observed that where spiritual experiences have adaptive and life-enhancing consequences, similar phenomena experienced by psychotics often lead to social and behavioural impoverishment. This is an extremely important distinction. It points to the fact that there can be both beneficial and harmful delusions. In so far as religion serves as a protection against the harsh realities of existence, it is more like a massive denial, i.e. a form of self-deception, than a delusion.

It is probable that the in-between me plays a major role in the development and sustainment of religious belief. People do not normally make a conscious decision to believe: It is something they do naturally and unconsciously. Argyle (2000) produced a substantial body of evidence that religious belief is accompanied by a sense of well-being, which is in accord with the assumption that the in-between me protects us against unpleasant emotion.

The modification of religious belief by the outer me

In primitive cultures, the inner me predominates, and the outer me has a relatively feeble influence. Consequently, all members of the culture hold the religious beliefs of the culture. People can only disbelieve if, at an outer me level, they are able to think about their beliefs and wonder how they could be possible. In modern societies, people apply the rational thought of the outer me to the irrationality of religious belief. Consequently, in modern societies, increasingly higher proportions of the population are either agnostic or atheist. A recent British poll (Opinion Research Business (ORB) for the British Broadcasting Corporation, 2000) revealed that 62 per cent of a British representative sample of 1,000 believe in God (compared with 76 per cent in 1980). Pinker (1997) observed that polls have shown that 96 per cent of Americans still believe in God or a universal spirit. However Larson and Witham (1998) observed that only 40 per cent of American scientists were religious believers. This figure dropped to 7 per cent when the sample was restricted to those elected to the National Academy of Sciences; so Freud's (1927) prediction that religion would disappear as we moved into the rational age of science may have been borne out. The American Religious Identification Survey of 2001 (cited by Dawkins, 2002) showed that the number of Americans classified as nonreligious or secular (nearly 30 million) has more than doubled since 1990. It is extremely difficult to know to what extent people are able, by way of the outer me, to argue themselves out of a religious belief. People who claim not to have a religious belief pray to their particular god for help when facing disaster. I have caught myself doing it.

The rational (outer me) arguments against religion

Pinker (1997) pointed out that religious beliefs do not conform to the laws of physics and biology; therefore, they cannot be true. He continued, "How does religion fit into a mind that one might have thought was designed to reject the palpably not true?" (page 554). Dawkins (2002) wrote, "We are all atheists about most of the gods humanity has ever believed in – some of us just go one god further" (page 12). A *Guardian* reader wrote to ask how he could avoid his non-religious feelings being hurt by religious people. Another reader replied, "You do not entertain 'non-religious feelings.' You experience the universe as it is. There is nothing 'non' about where you stand. It is they who are in denial, they who cannot accept reality" (Gilbert, 2002). Religious explanations are pseudo explanations that cover up areas with which we would rather not concern ourselves.

Religions set humans apart from all other life forms. It is as though all other life forms were provided by the deity for the benefit of humans. The evidence that humans evolved from earlier life forms is overwhelming. If all life forms were created by the deity, is it not ironic that only humans are able to be aware of this? Dennett (1995) maintained that Darwinian theory has rendered a belief in God an impossibility. He asserted that there is no future in a sacred myth, and that there can be no returning to pre-Darwinian inno-cence. God, he claimed, is a myth of childhood, like Santa Claus; it is not anything that any sane, undeluded adult could literally believe in. This clearly is not the case. The majority of humans still do believe in a god and the teaching of Darwinian theory is prohibited in at least one American state.

THE SOCIAL BENEFITS OF RELIGION

Even within the modern, materialist world, religion remains massively important. Because Marx considered religion and communism to be incompatible, religion was banned from the communist empire; but when it collapsed, people flooded back to religion. Religious leaders are held in high esteem. Religion has provided the inspiration for outstanding music, art and architecture. Suttie (1935) considered rational science to represent a flight from tenderness, and he saw the Christian religion as a counterbalance to this. The best forms of religion stress the importance of compassion; though the worst forms engender intolerance and hatred. People turn to religion at times of tragedy and suffering. The church, mosque or synagogue provide a meet-ing place, and mass worship serves a powerfully uniting and supportive function. There are important religious rituals surrounding birth, marriage and death.

The function of religious beliefs

The appeal of religion is that it can be anything that people want it to be. It protects them against intolerable truths. Gods exist because people need them to; and because their need is so great, they find a way of allowing themselves to believe in them. The religious beliefs of all cultures concern the same issues. These will now be considered.

The creation of the universe

Pinker (1997) reported that half of Americans believe in the creation as it is described in the book of Genesis. Dawkins (1988) wrote, "Nearly all people have developed their own creation myth, and the Genesis story is just the one that happened to have been adopted by one particular tribe of middle eastern herders" (page 316). The Genesis story is that the entire universe was created, by a single being, over a six-day period.

The current scientific view of the creation of the universe is as hard to believe as the Old Testament one. It claims that the universe came into existence in a fraction of a second rather than in six days; that to start with it was infinitely small, but that gradually it has expanded to the enormous size it is today, containing many millions of astral bodies. Even harder to believe is that the present universe is of finite size and has a boundary. What is outside that boundary? There cannot be a boundary with nothing outside it. De Jong and Faulkner (1972) observed that, among American faculty members, physicists were the most religious; and Argyle (2000) suggested that this may account for some of the quasi-religious notions of modern physics.

Within the universe, things always come from somewhere; that is, one thing gets transformed into another, but how can anyone ask, "Where did everything come from?" You cannot get everything from nothing. Surely the answer is that it did not come from anywhere. If it came from somewhere, then where did that somewhere come from?

The general scientific consensus is that the vast majority of astral bodies have no life on them and that, for the greater part of its existence, the earth had no life on it. Life, it is claimed, came into existence around 3.6 billion years ago in the form of simple molecules. Eccles (1989) reported that there then followed ". . . the unimaginably slow biological processes of the creation of the nucleotides and proteins with the biochemical developments of the genetic codes with mutations and natural selection" (page 240). From this point on, Darwinian theory takes over, explaining how simple organisms proceeded to more complex ones, and how, over many millions of years, with progressive modifications, the vast array of plant and animal species of today came into being. For the greater part of this time period, humans did not exist. They only gradually came to exist, around 90,000 years ago, by the modification of human-like creatures.

Dawkins (1988) distinguished between those theologians who believe in instantaneous creation and those who believe in guided evolution. The latter are prepared to concede that humans evolved, but maintain that such evolution was supervised by God. Postulating either that the universe was created by a god or that evolution was supervised by a god begs the question, where did that god come from? As Dawkins (1988) observed, such a god must be a creature of prodigious intelligence and complexity, who too must have evolved somehow, sometime.

Where do we go when we die?

This is similar to the where did everything come from question. Instead it is asking "Where does everyone go to?" The answer is, they do not go anywhere.

Where could they go? Many people do not want to believe that when they die they cease to exist. Instead, they believe that an essential, though weightless part of them, called the soul, does not die. It goes to a special place called Heaven, where the soul of everyone else who has ever died continues to exist for ever. Such a belief is a source of great comfort for many people. In a survey of 36 studies, Spilka et al. (1985) found a reduced fear of death for religious people in 24 of them. Walsh et al. (2002) in a prospective study, demonstrated that people with a strong religious belief recover more rapidly and more completely from the death of a close other than people with no religious belief.

Many, including even Eccles (1989), the authority on brain evolution, believe there is an essential part of us, the soul, that survives the death of the body. Some believe in an underworld, or a heaven, where they become reunited with their loved ones who have died. Others believe that the soul transmigrates into a new body, and that they come back to earth as a different person, or even as an animal. Some claim to remember themselves as they were in a previous existence. Some claim to be able to communicate with those who have died.

No one has ever been to Heaven and returned, though many now have been resuscitated after cardiac arrest, and some of these people claim to have had strange experiences during their period of unconsciousness. In the ORB 2,000 poll, 69 per cent of a British population sample said that they believed that they have a soul and just over half believe in an afterlife. No one has ever experienced a soul, though many would say that ghosts are souls, and Pinker (1997) reported that half of Americans believe in ghosts, and many people claim to have seen a ghost. There are many unanswered questions about the soul and Heaven like, Where is Heaven? How does Heaven cope with its continually expanding population? Why is there only a Heaven for humans? Do people stay the age they are when they die; if so, what happens to newborn babies? How do people pass their time in Heaven, since survival is assured and reproduction is not necessary?

Are we alone in the universe?

The answer to this is, yes, we probably are. Eccles (1989) wrote, "There is such an inherent improbability that life can exist elsewhere in the cosmos and that it could evolve into intelligent beings that biologists tend to assume that human life on Planet Earth is inscrutably unique" (page 242). The consequence of this is that we are surrounded by inert space. There is nobody else out there. The cosmos is indifferent to us. But why should this matter? There are six billion of us on the planet. Is that not enough? How many of those will we meet up with in a lifetime? Suppose there were a thousand other planets inhabited by people like ourselves: How would that help us?

The human need for closeness

Closeness is a basic human need (see Chapter 8). As we go through life, we accumulate what I have called an internalised close other (Birtchnell, 1993/96), an amalgam of all the close others we have encountered. This may contribute to the subjective experience of God, and account for the expression God is love. The small child fears that when the mother goes away she will not return, until it can create an internalised representation of the mother that can be held on to in her absence, which is called object constancy. Erikson (1965) called it basic trust. Winnicott (1958) stressed the internalisation of a good internal object in the acquisition of what he called the capacity to be alone. Not everyone has the good fortune to experience in childhood a constant and loving parent, and some people never acquire basic trust or the capacity to be alone.

People who have had inconsistent or unreliable experiences of love are hesitant to allow themselves to get close to people. Committing themselves to a close other person will render them vulnerable to being hurt should the other person break away. People vary in the extent to which they allow themselves to become close to others. Opening yourself to love means allowing yourself to be receptive to close involvement with another. This requires a considerable degree of trust.

The Christian God is comparable to the imaginary companions of children and the phantom lovers of certain adults (Chapter 16). The advantage of a make-believe love object is that it can be anything you want and it will do anything you want. God knows everything about everyone, takes a personal interest in everyone and is constantly available to everyone. The way that God is conceptualised is that everyone has their own direct access to Him. They can speak to Him whenever they want to and pretend that He speaks back to them. There is the expression opening yourself to God. You can let God into your heart in the way that you can let a lover into your heart, but unlike a lover, He will never reject you. Tamminen (1994) observed that 95 per cent of a large sample of young, Finnish children had felt at times that God was close to them; and Pollner (1989) found that reported closeness to God correlated with happiness, independently of church attendance.

The human need for protection

Freud (1927) proposed that religion is the result of the human inability to tolerate the loss of the familiar world of childhood, symbolised by the protective father. Despite this view, many psychoanalysts are religious. Lowerness is another basic human need (see Chapter 8). One way of viewing God is as someone to watch over me, which is one important aspect of lowerness. Humans need to know that there is someone above them who will take responsibility for them and take care of them, someone they can turn to in times of need, who will comfort, console, encourage and reassure them. These are the qualities that humans have endowed God with. He is conceived of as having the interests of everyone at heart. He will let no harm come to anyone.

The human need to idolise

Gods are conceived of as supremely powerful. Consequently, people wish to align themselves with them in order that they may share their power. Watts (1996) argued that emotions like awe and reverence are central to religion. People do their best to please their gods, by building elaborate edifices to them in which they worship them, and make sacrifices to them. In return, they hope that they will cause good things to happen to them and be on their side. What, in effect, the worshipper is saying is, "You are great, magnificent and powerful and I am small, insignificant and weak. If I place myself help-lessly at your feet and continue to tell you how wonderful you are will you view me with favour?" The aim of the worshipper is to humble her/himself in the extreme in order to present her/himself as the feeble and wretched one. Worshipping may be an extension of the hierarchical system that is evident in many animal species, including our immediate ancestors, the primates. In order to survive in the herd, the less powerful animals must behave in a deferential manner towards the more powerful ones, and this may be the origin of the human tendency to idolise. There are hierarchical systems in all human communities and those lower in the hierarchy act deferentially and respectfully towards those higher in the hierarchy.

The human need to be told what to do

Religious people have argued that, without religion, life has no meaning. If this is so, then does the existence of all those life forms other than humans, who have no religion, have no meaning? Does the life of people who have no religious beliefs have no meaning? Humans, like all other life forms, have objectives (see Part II) and the attainment of these objectives is a source of satisfaction. What then do religious people mean by meaning? Common to all religions is a set of rules concerning what people should and should not do. These rules are set down by the deity, but how can they be made known to humans? In the Christian religion, there were two ways: In the first, Moses met with God on a mountain top. In the second, God sent His son to earth.

Jesus Christ

The Christian religion is greatly strengthened by the story that, 2,000 years ago, God was able to impregnate a virgin, a married woman called Mary, and cause her to give birth to His son, who was called Jesus. Jesus somehow knew that he was the son of God. He was able to demonstrate his godly powers by performing miracles, by turning water into wine, by feeding 5,000 people with five loaves and two fishes, by walking on water, by healing the sick by touching them, and by raising at least one person from the dead. When he was killed he rose from the dead. He gathered around him 12 male followers, who went everywhere with him, but he revealed no sexual interest in men or women.

Drawing upon an additional power

In the act of prayer people can draw upon a power that is greater than themselves to help them through difficulties. People pray for good weather, for rain, for a good harvest, to have a child, to have a healthy child, for recovery from illness, for the recovery of a friend or relative from illness. People pray for success in sport, in a business venture, in competition and in battle. When different people (say opponents in a battle) pray for opposite outcomes, how does their god decide whose prayer should be granted? When people suffer misfortune, they sometimes lose faith in their god.

Religion and metaphor

As with delusions, some people are able to shift from accepting religious beliefs in a strictly literal sense to considering them simply as metaphors. As with delusions, they are able to do this when they feel safe. Such a shift is a possible step towards disbelieving, and people are able to position themselves at, or move between, various positions between the literal and the metaphorical. Many aspects of religion, such as the resurrection of Christ, may be safely discounted without abandoning fundamental religious principles.

Good and evil, right and wrong

Good and evil

The Christian religion, like most other religions, is based upon two contrasting forms of behaviour called good and evil. Good is difficult to do and evil is easy to do and pleasurable. We are told that God approves of good and disapproves of evil. Therefore, people should strive to take the difficult path and be good and resist the temptation to take the easy path and be evil. People pray to God to give them the strength to resist the easy path and take the difficult one. The word evil is also used as an adjective. As such, it is offered as an explanation for bad behaviour. A person does something bad because s/he is evil; s/he has the quality of evilness. It is a quality that witches have; as do leaders like Adolf Hitler, Pol Pot, Idi Amin, Slobodan Milosevic, Saddam Hussein and now Osama bin Laden. It is not a concept that psychologists study; but it is something that could be explicable in terms of life history and personality.

Sin

Evil acts are called sin. Sargant (1957) wrote insightfully of the methods of evangelists, particularly the eighteenth-century British preacher, John Wesley, to evoke a sense of shame in members of a religious congregation by warning them that they would go to Hell. He offered them redemption from sin if they were prepared to believe in God. The confession of sin and the forgiveness by a human representative of God (particularly a Roman Catholic priest) continues to be a powerful device for reinforcing religious belief.

The Devil

The presence is proposed of another being, who has various names like Satan, the Devil, Old Nick and Beelzebub. He is a kind of god, though he is never referred to as such. In Pinker's reported poll, half of Americans believe in the Devil. Where God resides in Heaven, the Devil resides in Hell. Conceptually, Heaven is somewhere up above and Hell is somewhere down below. Heaven is a wonderful place and Hell is a terrible place. When people die, those who have consistently done good things go to Heaven, and those who have consistently done evil things go to Hell. In Hell, they stay forever in a fire, but somehow they do not burn up. They just endure the pain of being burned forever. The Devil aims to tempt people to commit sin, and in one Bible story, he tried to tempt Jesus Christ. Those who are tempted by the Devil are called lost souls, and it is said that the Devil has gained possession of their souls.

Right and wrong

The concepts of right and wrong have links with religion but they can be quite separate from it. Right and wrong are quite independent of religious rules (though they may coincide with them). They are something that I (outer me) feel. They are to do with my personal standards of correctness and decency. They are to do with how I behave towards another person. They are a consequence of the capacity of the outer me to imagine what it must be like to be the other person, to identify and empathise with the other person. Right is being fair, straight and honest with someone, and wrong is the opposite. I know when I have done wrong, that I have cheated or deceived someone. It makes me feel bad inside. I feel ashamed and want to say I am sorry. This is a consequence of identifying with, feeling for, or empathising with the other person. Cold, self-centred, detached, antisocial people are less inclined to concern themselves with issues of right and wrong.

All religions externalise these natural feelings in the form of rules concerning what is and is not acceptable. Such rules provide guidelines for the efficient running of a community, but they are presented to the community as the commands of the deity. In the Bible there are many such rules, but there is also a special set of rules called the Ten Commandments which were conveyed to Moses by God on the mountain top. Thus instead of using their own internal (outer me) judgements concerning what feels right or wrong, people obey their deity. There are rewards (eternal life) for doing right and punishments (eternal damnation) for doing wrong.

Free will

People are given the option (outer me) to pursue either the good path or the evil path. This option is called free will (see also Chapter 2). That which urges people towards being good is the conscience, which causes people to feel guilty if they are tempted towards being bad. Christians believe it is the internal presence of God, but even nonbelievers feel guilty when they act in a way that, while benefiting themselves, brings harm to others. Psychoanalysts consider the conscience to be a manifestation of the superego (Chapter 4) (Freud, 1923), the result of an internalised judgemental and punitive parental figure, which comes close to the Christian view of God. Rasmussen and Charman (1995) reported a strong correlation between superego strength and religiosity. In terms of brain function, the conscience appears to be located in the frontal cortex, and people with damage to this region are inclined to lack the capacity for moral judgement. An emotion that is particularly associated with religion is shame. It is difficult to differentiate between shame and guilt (Gilbert and Andrews, 1998) but the experience of Eve in the Garden of Eden could not be anything other than shame. Thus part of shame is having evoked the disapproval of God and having been cast out.

Why does everyone not choose to be good?

It is never explained what determines whether people choose the good path or the evil path. It is easy to be good when I have been treated well and when everything is going my way. When I have been unjustly treated, and when I see others gaining undeserved advantages, it is difficult, if not impossible, for me to avoid becoming bitter, and determined, by whatever means I can, to get what I believe I deserve. If I were starving, the temptation to steal would be irresistible. If I were sufficiently provoked, I probably could not resist committing murder. Religious people would argue that, if your faith is strong, you can resist the most powerful temptation; but how do you get such a strong faith, and why does not everyone have it?

Good and evil in terms of the outer me and the inner me

From the point of view of the outer me and the inner me, there are two contrasting approaches to the issue of right and wrong. The religious struggle between the difficult path to good and the easy path to evil feels very much like the outer me's struggle to resist the inner me's inclination to act for the moment. Because it can think in terms of future, possible consequences, the outer me can see the point of deferring immediate gratification. Where the inner me may be inclined to hit someone or shout out something offensive, the outer me can perceive that tact and diplomacy may be the better course of action. Where the inner me impels me to give up, the outer me can see the point of struggling on.

The opposite approach is to do with the inner me's naivety versus the outer me's deviousness (Chapter 15). The inner me is incapable of lying, deceiving or cheating, so its capacity for committing harmful acts is limited. In the long run, the outer me is capable of plotting and planning and committing far worse offences; so the outer me can be the source of both good and evil.

Religion and the suppression of sexuality

Where did the idea originate that sex is sinful? Did eating the apple in the Garden of Eden allude to sex? Why did it cause Adam and Eve to feel shame, and believe it to be wrong to be naked? In some cultures nudity is not considered to be wrong and genitals appear prominently on sculpture. The suppression of sexuality did not come from Christ's teaching, but it became incorporated into historical accounts of Christ. The virgin birth could be a way of dissociating Christ from sexuality, though it could also be that this was the only way that Christ's supernatural powers could be imparted to a human. Christ did not refer to sex in his teaching and showed no sexual interest in men or women. In the Roman Catholic version of Christianity, sexual suppression was considered to be a means of increasing the power of the Pope. Forbidding contraception was a means of preventing having sex simply for pleasure; and having large families became a byproduct of this. The Christian ideal was celibacy. The next best was a sexless marriage. The next best after that was to have sex only for the purpose of reproduction, though it was never made clear why having sex for pleasure should be regarded as sinful. There is a tradition that sexual urges should be punished. Self-flagellation is one such form of punishment, yet self-flagellation may cause sexual arousal. In masochism, pain and pleasure become intertwined. The pain gets turned into ecstasy.

Punishment

A passage in the Bible goes "Vengeance is mine; I will repay, saith the Lord." Christians are urged to turn the other cheek. Despite such admirable sentiments, most religious people believe that those who do wrong should be punished. When someone is punished for a wrong s/he has committed, it makes the person who was wronged feel better, but it also assuages the wrong doer's guilt. Punishment is linked with revenge. In terms of relating (Chapter 8) it compensates for the loss of upperness resulting from the offence, by depriving the offender of upperness.

Religion and the brain

The universality of religious belief strongly suggest that it is a manifestation of inner me functioning. If it is, then perhaps there is a brain structure that predisposes people to hold religious beliefs. Updike (2000) wrote, "We know that human brains are hardwired with a religious instinct" (page 1). Some people refer to the god spot, a location in the brain that is concerned with religious belief. If there were such a location, there should, by now, have been someone who, as a result of damage to it, had lost her/his religious belief.

Temporal lobe epilepsy and religious feelings

One experience that has been reported by some patients with temporal lobe epilepsy is a religious one. Ramachandran, cited by Challoner (2000), described a man who, following a series of temporal lobe seizures, became intensely religious and who perceived religious or cosmic significance in everything, sometimes even believing himself to be God. Persinger (1987), using a device called a transcranial magnetic stimulator, which could stimulate any part of the cerebral cortex, was able to induce in himself the same kind of religious experiences by stimulating his temporal lobes. However, Sensky and Fenwick (1982) discovered that people with temporal lobe epilepsy were no more inclined towards religion than those with generalised epilepsy, and that epileptics under-reported mystical and psychic states compared to the general population.

The importance of the amygdala to the experiencing of emotion has already been described (Chapter 10). Ramachandran, cited by Challoner (2000), considered that the close proximity of the amygdalae to the temporal lobes explains why epileptic seizures arising in the temporal lobes are associated with the welling up of a range of emotions. It may explain why van Gough, who suffered from temporal lobe epilepsy, responded so emotionally to visual imagery and why his paintings were so vivid. Ramachandran, cited by Challoner (2000), explained that repeated seizures can produce permanent changes to the emotional pathways, an effect known as kindling. He considered that kindling the neural pathways between the amygdalae and the temporal lobes might bring about the sensation of "glory" so that almost anything can be imbued with emotional significance.

Bibliography

Adams, H.E., Wright, L.W. and Lohr, B.A. (1996) "Is homophobia associated with homosexual arousal?" *Journal of Abnormal Psychology*, 105, 440–445.

Addley, E. (2001) "Payout for stage hypnosis trauma". *The Guardian*, 26 May, page 13.

Adler, A. (1954) *Understanding Human Nature*. New York: Fawcett.

Albert, M. and Obler, L. (1978) *The Bilingual Brain: Neuropsychological and Neurolinguistic Aspects of Bilingualism*. New York: Academic Press.

Albright, J.S. and Henderson, M.C. (1995) "How real is depressive realism? A question of scales and standards". *Cognitive Therapy and Research*, 19, 589–609.

Anderson, J.R. (1983) *The Architecture of Cognition*. Cambridge, MA: Harvard University Press.

Andreasen, N.C. (1979) "Thought, language and communication disorders. 1. Clinical asessment, definition of terms and evaluation of their reliability". *Archives of General Psychiatry*, 36, 1315–1321.

Anthony, S. (1940) *The Child's Discovery of Death: A Study in Child Psychology*. London: Kegan Paul, Trench & Trubner.

Argyle, M. (1988) *Bodily Communication*, 2nd edn. London: Methuen Academic.

Argyle, M. (2000) *Psychology and Religion: An Introduction*. London: Routledge.

Baars, B.J. (1997) *In the Theatre of Consciousness: The Workspace of the Mind*. New York: Oxford University Press.

Badcock, C.R. (1986) *The Problem of Altruism: Freudian–Darwinian Solutions*. Oxford: Blackwell.

Baddeley, A.D. (1986) *Working Memory*. Oxford: Oxford University Press.

Bandura, A., Underwood, B. and Fromson, M.E. (1975) "Disinhibition of aggression through diffusion of responsibility and dehumanisation of victims". *Journal of Research in Personality*, 9, 253–269.

Bannister, D. (1987) "The psychotic disguise". In Dryden, W. (ed.) *Therapists' Dilemmas*. London: Harper & Row.

Bahrick, H., Hall, L.K. and Berger, S.A. (1996) "Accuracy and distortion in memory for high school grades". *Psychological Science*, 7, 265–271.

Bargh, J.A. (1990) "Auto-motives: Preconscious determinants of social interaction". In Higgins, T. and Sorrentino, R.M. (eds) *Handbook of Motivation and Cognition*. New York: Guilford Press.

Barlow, H. (1987) "The biological role of consciousness". In Blakemore, C. and Greenfield, S. (eds) *Mindwaves*. Oxford: Blackwell.

Bateson, G. (1973) *Steps to an Ecology of Mind*. St. Albans, Herts: Paladin.

Beck, A.T. (1983) "Cognitive therapy of depression: New perspectives". In Clayton, P.J. and Barret, J.E. (eds) *Treatment of Depression. Old Controversies and New Approaches*. New York: Raven Press.

Beevor, A. (2002) *Berlin: The Downfall, 1945*. London: Viking Penguin.

Bellugi, U., Bihrle, A., Neville, H., Doherty, S. and Jernigan, T. (1992) "Language cognition and brain organization in a neurodevelopmental disorder". In Gunnar, M. and Nelson, C. (eds) *Developmental Behavioral Neuroscience: The Minnesota Symposia on Child Psychology*. Hillsdale, NJ: Lawrence Erlbaum Associates Inc.

Bennington, J.H. and Heller, H.C. (1995) "Restoration of brain energy metabolism as the function of sleep". *Progress in Neurobiology*, 45, 347–360.

Bentall, R.P. (1990) "The syndromes and symptoms of psychosis". In Bentall, R.P. (ed.) *Reconstructing Schizophrenia*. London: Routledge.

Bibring, E. (1941) "The development and problems of the theory of the instincts". *International Journal of Psychoanalysis*, 22, 102–131.

Birtchnell, J. (1981) "In search of correspondences between age at psychiatric break-down and parental age at death ('anniversary reactions')". *British Journal of Medical Psychology*, 54, 111–120.

Birtchnell, J. (1987) "Attachment–detachment, directiveness–receptiveness: A system for classifying interpersonal attitudes and behaviour". *British Journal of Medical Psychology*, 60, 17–27.

Birtchnell, J. (1990) "Interpersonal theory: Criticism, modification and elaboration". *Human Relations*, 43, 1183–1201.

Birtchnell, J. (1993/96) *How Humans Relate: A New Interpersonal Theory*. Westport, CT: Praeger (hardback, 1993); Hove, Sussex, UK: Psychology Press (paperback, 1996).

Birtchnell, J. (1994) "The interpersonal octagon: An alternative to the interpersonal circle". *Human Relations*, 47, 511–529.

Birtchnell, J. (1997) "Attachment in an interpersonal context". *British Journal of Medical Psychology*, 70, 265–279.

Birtchnell, J. (1999/2002) *Relating in Psychotherapy: The Application of a New Theory*. Westport, CT: Praeger (hardback, 1999); Hove, Sussex, UK: Brunner-Routledge (paperback, 2002).

Birtchnell, J. (2002) "Surrealism: Desire unbound (Tate Modern, London, 20 September 2001–1 January 2002)". *British Journal of Psychotherapy*, 18, 556–562.

Birtchnell, J. and Shine, J. (2000) "Personality disorders and the interpersonal octagon". *British Journal of Medical Psychology*, 73, 433–448.

Bisiach, E. and Luzzatti, C. (1978) "Unilateral neglect of representational space". *Cortex*, 14, 129–133.

Blackmore, S. (2001) "State of the art: Consciousness". *The Psychologist*, 14, 522–525.

Borkovec, T.D. and Lyonfields, J.D. (1993) "Worry: Thought suppression of emotional processing". In Krohne, H.W. (ed.) *Attention and Avoidance*. Toronto: Hogrefe & Huber.

Bornstein, R.F. (1992) "Subliminal mere exposure effects". In Bornstein, R.F. and Pittman, T.S. (eds) *Perception without Awareness: Cognitive, Clinical and Social Perspectives*. New York: Guilford Press.

Bower, G. (1981) "Mood and memory". *American Psychologist*, 36, 129–148.

Bowlby, J. (1969) *Attachment and Loss, Vol. 1: Attachment*. London: Hogarth Press/ Institute of Psychoanalysis.

Bowlby, J. (1980) *Attachment and Loss, Vol. 3: Loss, Sadness and Depression*. London: Hogarth Press/Institute of Psychoanalysis.

Bowlby, J. (1988) *A Secure Base*. New York: Basic Books.

Bremner, J.D., Randall, P., Scott, T.M., Bronen, R.A., Seibyl, J.P., Southwick, S.M., Delaney, R.C., McCarthy, G., Charney, D.S. and Innis, R.B. (1995) "MRI based measurement of hippocampal volume in combat-related post traumatic stress disorder". *American Journal of Psychiatry*, 152, 973–981.

Brenner, C. (1957) *An Elementary Textbook of Psychoanalysis*. New York: Doubleday Anchor.

Brewin, C.R. (1989) "Cognitive change processes in psychotherapy". *Psychological Review*, 96, 379–394.

Brewin, C.R. and Andrews, B. (1997) "Reasoning about repression: Inferences from clinical and experimental data". In Conway, M. (ed.) *Recovered Memories and False Memories*. Oxford: Oxford University Press.

Brewin, C.R. and Andrews, B. (2000) "Psychological defence mechanisms: The example of repression". *The Psychologist*, 13, 615–617.

Broadbent, D.E., FitzGerald, P. and Broadbent, M H P. (1986) "Implicit and explicit knowledge in the control of complex systems". *British Journal of Psychology*, 77, 33–50.

Brown, G., Carstairs, G. and Topping, G. (1958) "Post hospital adjustment of chronic mental patients". *Lancet*, ii, 685–689.

Brown, G.W. (1985) "The discovery of expressed emotion". In Leff, J. and Vaughan, C. (eds) *Expressed Emotion in Families*. New York: Guilford Press.

Buss, D.M. (1994) *The Evolution of Desire: Strategies of Human Mating*. New York: Basic Books.

Calder, A.J., Young, A.W., Rowland, D., Perrett, D.I., Hodges, J.R. and Etcoff, N.L. (1996) "Facial emotion recognition after bilateral amygdala damage: Differentially severe impairment of fear". *Cognitive Neuropsychology*, 13, 699–745.

Campbell, K. (1996) *Brainspotting*. London: Channel Four Books.

Capgras, J. and Carrette, P. (1924) "L'illusion des sosies et complex d'oedipe". *Annales Societé Medical-Psychologique*, 82, 48–68.

Chadwick, P. and Lowe, C.F. (1990) "The measurement and modification of delusional beliefs". *Journal of Consulting and Clinical Psychology*, 58, 225–232.

Challoner, J. (2000) *Equinox: The Brain*. London: Channel Four Books.

Chance, M.R.A. (1988) "Introduction". In Chance, M.R.A. (ed.) *Social Fabrics of the Mind*. Hove, UK: Lawrence Erlbaum Associates Ltd.

Chomsky, N. (1957) *Syntactic Structures*. The Hague: Mouton.

Christie, A. (1936) *The ABC Murders*. New York: Bantam Books, 1967.

Claparède, E. (1911) "Recognition and 'me-ness' ". In Rapaport, D. (ed.) *Organization and Pathology of Thought*. New York: Columbia University Press, 1951.

Claridge, G., Clark, K. and Davis, C. (1997) "Nightmares, dreams and schizotypy". *British Journal of Clinical Psychology*, 36, 377–386.

Clarke, I. (ed.) (2001) *Psychosis and Spirituality: Exploring the New Frontier*. London: Whurr.

Claxton, G. (1998) *Hare Brain, Tortoise Mind: Why Intelligence Increases When You Think Less*. London: Fourth Estate.

Cloitre, M. (1997) "Conscious and unconscious memory: A model of functional amnesia". In Stein, D.J. (ed.) *Cognitive Science and the Unconscious*. Washington, DC: American Psychiatric Press.

Cobb, J. (1979) "Morbid jealousy". *British Journal of Hospital Medicine*, 21, 511–518.

Cohen, I.L. (1994) "An artificial neural network analogue of learning in autism". *Biological Psychiatry*, 36, 5–20.

Concar, D. (1998) "Out of sight into mind". *New Scientist*, No. 2150 (5 September), 38–41.

Cork, R.C. (1996) "Implicit memory during anaesthesia". In Hammeroff, S.R., Kaszniak, A. and Scott, A.C. (eds) *Toward a Science of Consciousness: The First Tucson Discussions and Debates*. Cambridge, MA: The MIT Press.

Cosmides, L. (1989) "The logic of social exchange: Has natural selection shaped how humans reason? Studies with the Wason selection task". *Cognition*, 31, 187–276.

Crick, F. and Koch, C. (1995) "Are we aware of neural activity in primary visual cortex?" *Nature*, 375, 121–123.

Crick, F.H.C. and Mitchison, G. (1983) "The function of dream sleep". *Nature*, 304, 111–114.

Critchley, E.M.R. (1991) "Speech and the right hemisphere". *Behavioural Neurology*, 4, 143–151.

Damasio, A. (1994) *Descartes' Error: Emotion, Reason and the Human Brain*. New York: Putnam.

Damasio, A. (2000) *The Feeling of What Happens: Body, Emotion and the Making of Consciousness*. London: Vintage.

Damasio, A. (2002) "A neurobiology for emotion and feeling". Paper read to the conference on Emotion, Evolution and Rationality, King's College, London, 27–28 April.

Darwin, C. (1872) *The Expression of the Emotions in Man and Animals*. Chicago: University of Chicago Press, 1965.

Dawkins, R. (1976) *The Selfish Gene*. Oxford: Oxford University Press.

Dawkins, R. (1988) *The Blind Watchmaker*. London: Penguin.

Dawkins, R. (2000) Open letter to Prince Charles. *The Observer*, 21 May, page 21.

Dawkins, R. (2002) Preaching atheism is no sin. The Editor, *The Guardian*, 3 August, page 12.

Deese, J. (1978) "Thought into speech". *American Scientist*, 66, 314–321.

De Jong, G.F. and Faulkner, J.F. (1972) "Religion and intellectuals: Findings from a sample of university faculty". *Review of Religious Research*, 14, 15–24.

DelMonte, M.M. (2000) "Retrieved memories of childhood sexual abuse". *British Journal of Medical Psychology*, 73, 1–13.

Dennett, D. (1995) *Darwin's Dangerous Idea: Evolution and the Meanings of Life*. New York: Simon & Schuster.

D'Esposito, M., Detre, J., Alsop, D., Shin, R., Atlas, S. and Grossman, M. (1995) "The neural basis of the central executive system of working memory". *Nature*, 378, 279–281.

Dobzhansky, T. (1967) *The Biology of Ultimate Concern*. New York: The New American Library.

Dockrell, J. and Messer, D.J. (1999) *Children's Language and Communication Difficulties: Understanding, Identification and Intervention*. London: Cassell.

Dolan, R. (2002) "William James and emotion revisited". Paper read to the conference on Emotion, Evolution and Rationality, King's College, London, 27–28 April.

Eagle, M.N. (1987) "The psychoanalytic and the cognitive unconscious". In Stern, R. (ed.) *Theories of the Unconscious and Theories of the Self*. Hillsdale, NJ: Lawrence Erlbaum Associates Inc.

Eccles, J.C. (1989) *Evolution of the Brain: Creation of the Self*. London: Routledge.

Edwards, G. (1972) "Diagnosis of schizophrenia: An Anglo-American comparison". *British Journal of Psychiatry*, 120, 385–390.

Ehrenzweig, A. (1953) *The Psycho-analysis of Artistic Vision and Hearing*. London: Routledge & Kegan Paul.

Ehrenzweig, A. (1957) "The creative surrender". *The American Imago*, 14, 3.

Eibl-Eibesfeldt, I. (1989) *Human Ethology*. New York: Aldine de Gruyer.

Eichenbaum, H., Otto, T. and Cohen, N.J. (1994) "Two functional components of the hippocampal memory system". *Behavioral and Brain Sciences*, 17, 449–518.

Ellenberger, H. (1970) *The Discovery of the Unconscious: The History and Evolution of Dynamic Psychiatry*. New York: Basic Books.

Engel, M. (2001) "England rejoice . . . for now". *The Guardian*, 21 August, page 1.

Epstein, S. (1991) "Cognitive-experiential self-theory: An integrative theory of personality". In Curtis, R. (ed.) *The Relational Self: Convergences in Psychoanalysis and Social Psychology*. New York: Guilford Press.

Epstein, S. (1994) "Integration of the cognitive and the psychodynamic unconscious". *American Psychologist*, 49, 709–724.

Erdelyi, S. (1985) *Psychoanalysis: Freud's Cognitive Psychology*. San Francisco: Freeman.

Erdelyi, M.H. (1996) *The Recovery of Unconscious Memories, Hypermnesia and Reminiscence*. Chicago, IL: University of Chicago Press.

Erikson, E. (1965) *Childhood and Society*. London: Penguin.

Evans, D. (2001) *Emotion: The Science of Sentiment*. New York: Oxford University Press.

Evans, D. and Zarate, O. (1999) *Introducing Evolutionary Psychology*. Cambridge, UK: Icon Books.

Exell, J. (2001) "Voices from within and without". *Open Mind*, 111, 15.

Fehr, F.S. and Russell, J.A. (1984) "Concept of emotion viewed from a prototype perspective". *Journal of Experimental Psychology, General*, 113, 464–486.

Fenwick, P. (2001) "The neurophysiology of religious experience". In Clarke, I. (ed.) *Psychosis and Spirituality: Exploring the New Frontier*. London: Whurr.

Ferguson, S.M., Rayport, M. and Corrie, W.S. (1985) "Neuropsychiatric observations on behavioral consequences of corpus collosum section for seizure control". In Reeves, A.G. (ed.) *Epilepsy and the Corpus Callosum*. New York: Plenum Press.

Fonagy, P. and Cooper, A.M. (1999) "Joseph Sandler's intellectual contributions to theoretical and clinical psychoanalysis". In Fonagy, P., Cooper, A.M. and Wallerstein, R.S. (eds) *Psychoanalysis on the Move: The Work of Joseph Sandler*. London: Routledge.

Fordham, F. (1968) *An Introduction to Jung's Psychology*. Harmondsworth, Middlesex: Penguin.

Foulkes, D. and Vogel, G. (1965) "Mental activity at sleep onset". *Journal of Abnormal Psychology*, 70, 231–243.

Frankl, V.E. (1967) *Psychotherapy and Existentialism: Selected Papers on Logotherapy*. London: Souvenir.

Freud, A. (1936) *The Ego and the Mechanisms of Defense* (translated by C.M. Bains). New York: International Universities Press, 1946.

Freud, S. (1900) "The interpretation of dreams". *Standard Edition*, Vol. 4. London: Hogarth Press, 1953.

Freud, S. (1902) "On dreams". *Standard Edition*, Vol. 5. London: Hogarth Press, 1953.

Freud, S. (1904) "The psychopathology of everyday life" (translated by A.A. Brill). In *The Basic Writings of Sigmund Freud*. New York: Modern Library, 1938.

Freud, S. (1905a) "Three essays on the theory of sexuality" (translated by J. Strachey). *Standard Edition*, Vol. 7. London: Hogarth Press, 1953.

Freud, S. (1905b) "Jokes and their relation to the unconscious" (translated by J. Strachey). *Standard Edition*, Vol. 8. London: Hogarth Press, 1960.

Freud, S. (1911) "Formulations regarding the two principles in mental functioning" (translated by M.N. Searl). *Collected Papers*, Vol. 4, pp 13–21. London: Hogarth Press, 1925.

Freud, S. (1913) "The unconscious" (translated by C.M. Bains). *Collected Papers*, Vol. 4, 98–136. London: Hogarth Press, 1925.

Freud, S. (1915) "Repression". *Standard Edition*, Vol. 14. London: Hogarth Press.

Freud, S. (1920) "Beyond the pleasure principle" (translated by J. Strachey). New York: Liveright Publishing, 1950.

Freud, S. (1923) "The ego and the id". *Standard Edition*, Vol. 19. London: Hogarth Press, 1961.

Freud, S. (1927) *The Future of an Illusion*. New York: Liveright Publishing, 1949.

Frith, C.D. (1979) "Consciousness, information processing and schizophrenia". *British Journal of Psychiatry*, 134, 225–235.

Frith, C.D. (1992) *The Cognitive Neuropsychology of Schizophrenia*. Hove, UK: Lawrence Erlbaum Associates Ltd.

Frith, C.D. (1995) "Functional imaging and cognitive abnormalities". *Lancet*, 346, 615–620.

Frith, U. (1989) *Autism: Explaining the Enigma*. Oxford: Blackwell.

Fromm-Reichmann, F. (1959) "Loneliness". *Psychiatry*, 22, 1–25.

Frosh, S. (1997) *For and Against Psychoanalysis*. London: Routledge.

Fulford, K.W.M. (1989) *Moral Theory and Medical Practice*. Cambridge, UK: Cambridge University Press.

Furnham, A., Lavancy, M. and McClelland, A. (2001) "Waist-to-hip ratio and facial attractiveness: A pilot study". *Personality and Individual Differences*, 30, 491–502.

Fuster, J.M. (1989) *The Prefrontal Cortex*. New York: Raven Press.

Gagg, S. (1999) "Re-cognising voices". *Context: Magazine for Family Therapy and Systemic Practice*, 46, December, 19–21.

Gardner, R. (1991) Personal communication.

Garety, P.A. and Freeman, D. (1999) "Cognitive approaches to delusions: A critical review of theories and evidence". *British Journal of Clinical Psychology*, 38, 113–154.

Garety, P.A. and Hemsley, D.R. (1997) *Delusions: Investigation into the Psychology of Delusional Reasoning* (Maudsley Monograph No. 36). London: Psychology Press.

Garry, M., Loftus, E.F. and Brown, S.W. (1994) "Memory: A river flows through it". *Consciousness and Cognition*, 3, 438–451.

Gazzaniga, M.S. (1985) *The Social Brain: Discovering the Networks of the Mind*. New York: Basic Books.

Gilbert, P. (1992) *Depression: The Evolution of Powerlessness*. Hillsdate, NJ: Lawrence Erlbaum Associates Inc.

Gilbert, P. (1998) "The evolved basis and adaptive functions of cognitive distortions". *British Journal of Medical Psychology*, 71, 447–463.

Gilbert, P. and Andrews, B. (eds) (1998) *Shame: Interpersonal Behavior, Psychopathology and Culture*. New York: Oxford University Press.

Gilbert, S. (2002) Notes & Queries. G2, *The Guardian*, Thursday, 15 August, page 12.

Gloor, P. (1986). "Role of the human limbic system in perception, memory and affect: Lessons from temporal lobe epilepsy". In Doane, B.K. and Livingston, R.E. (eds) *The Limbic System: Functional Organization and Clinical Disorders*. New York: Raven Press.

Goldman-Rakic, P.S. (1993) "Working memory and the mind". In Freeman, W.H. (ed.) *Mind and Brain: Readings from Scientific American Magazine*. New York: Freeman.

Goleman, D. (1995) *Emotional Intelligence: Why it Can Matter More Than IQ*. London: Bloomsbury.

Goleman, D. (1998) *Working with Emotional Intelligence*. London: Bloomsbury.

Gomez-Tortosa, E., Martin, E., Gaviria, M., Charbel, F. et al. (1995) "Selective deficits of one language in a bilingual patient following surgery in the left perisylvanian area". *Brain Language*, 48, 320–325.

Grassian, S. (1983) "Psychopathological effects of solitary confinement". *American Journal of Psychiatry*, 140, 1450–1454.

Graybiel, A.M. (1998) "The basal ganglia and the chunking of action repertoires". *Neurobiology of Learning and Memory*, 70, 119–136.

Greenfield, S.A. (1995) *Journey to the Centres of the Mind: Towards a Science of Consciousness*. New York: Freeman.

Greenfield, S.A. (2000) *Brain Story: Unlocking our Inner World of Emotions, Memories, Ideas and Desires*. London: BBC Worldwide Ltd.

Greenwald, A. (1980) "The totalitarian ego: Fabrication and revision of personal history". *American Psychologist*, 35, 603–608.

Groddeck, G.W. (1923) *The Book of the It*. New York: Mentor Books, 1961.

Grunbaum, A. (1993) *Validation in the Clinical Theory of Psychoanalysis: A Study in the Philosophy of Psychoanalysis*. Madison, CT: International Universities Press.

Hammeke, T.A., McQuillen, M.P. and Cohen, B.A. (1983) "Musical hallucinations associated with acquired deafness". *Journal of Neurology, Neurosurgery and Psychiatry*, 46, 570–572.

Haritos-Fatouros, M. (1988) "The official torturer: A learning model for obedience to authority of violence". *Journal of Applied Social Psychology*, 18, 1107–1120.

Happé, F. (1999) "Understanding assets and deficits in autism: Why success is more interesting than failure". *The Psychologist*, 12, 540–546.

Harper, D.J. (1992) "Defining delusion and the serving of professional interests: The case of paranoia". *British Journal of Medical Psychology*, 65, 357–369.

Harris, A. (1959) "Sensory deprivation and schizophrenia". *Journal of Mental Science*, 105, 235–237.

Harrow, M., Silverstein, M. and Marengo, J. (1983) "Disordered thinking: Does it identify nuclear schizophrenia?" *Archives of General Psychiatry*, 40, 765–771.

Hays, P. (1992) "False but sincere accusations of sexual assault made by narcotic patients". *Medico-Legal Journal*, 60, 265–271.

Hayward, M.L. and Taylor, J.E. (1956) "A schizophrenic patient describes the action of intensive psychotherapy". *Psychiatric Quarterly*, 30, 211–248.

Hillman, J. (1975) *Revisioning Psychology*. New York: Harper & Row.

Hingley, S.M. (1992) "Psychological theories of delusional thinking: In search of integration". *British Journal of Medical Psychology*, 65, 347–356.

Hobson, J.A. and McCarley, R.W. (1977) "The brain as a dream-state generator: An activation-synthesis hypothesis of the dream process". *American Journal of Psychiatry*, 134, 1335–1368.

Holloway, J. (2000) "Learning from voices". *Open Mind*, 103, 16.

Holmes, B. (1998) "The zombie within". *New Scientist*, No. 2150 (5 September), 31–37.

Horney, K. (1945) *Our Inner Conflicts*. New York: Norton.

Humphrey, N.K. (1983) *Consciousness Regained*. Oxford: Oxford University Press.

Huq, S.F., Garety, P. and Hemsley, D.R. (1988) "Probabilistic judgements in deluded and non-deluded subjects". *Quarterly Journal of Experimental Psychology*, 40A, 801–812.

Hyden, H. (1977) "The differentiation of brain cell proteins, learning and memory". *Biosystems*, 8, 213–218.

Imperato-McGinley, J., Peterson, R., Gautier, T. and Sturla, E. (1979) "Androgens and the evolution of male gender-identity among male pseudohermaphrodites with a 5a-reductase deficiency". *The New England Journal of Medicine*, 300, 1233–1237.

Ingvar, D.H. (1985) "Memory of the future: An essay on the temporal organization of conscious awareness". *Human Neurobiology*, 2, 177–189.

Jacobi, J. (1959) *Complex/Archetype/Symbol in the Psychology of C.J. Jung*. Princeton: Princeton University Press.

Jacobsen, C.F. and Nissen, H.W. (1937) "Studies of cerebral function in primates: IV. The effects of frontal lobe lesions on the delayed alternation habit in monkeys". *Journal of Comparative and Physiological Psychology*, 23, 101–112.

Jacoby, L.L., Lindsay, D.S. and Toth, J.P. (1992) "Unconscious influences revealed: Attention, awareness and control". *American Psychologist*, 47, 802–809.

James, O. (2000) "Basking in the son". *The Guardian*, G2, 22 May.

Jeannerod, M. (1994) "The representing brains: Neural correlates of motor intention and imagery". *Behavioral Brain Sciences*, 17, 187–202.

Johnson, M.K. and Raye, C.L. (1981) "Reality monitoring". *Psychological Review*, 88, 67–85.

Johnson-Laird, P.N. (1988) *The Computer and the Mind: An Introduction to Cognitive Science*. Cambridge: Harvard University Press.

Jouvet, M. (1975) "The function of dreaming: A neurophysiologist's point of view". In Gazzaniga, M.S. and Blakemore, C. (eds) *Handbook of Psychobiology*. New York: Academic Press.

Jung, C.J. (1938) *Psychology and Religion*. New Haven, Conn: Yale University Press.

Jung, C.J. (1939) "Conscious, unconscious and individuation". In Adler, G., Fordham, M. and Read, H. (eds) *The Archetypes and the Collective Unconscious. The Collected Works of C.J. Jung*, Vol. 8. London: Routledge & Kegan Paul, 1959.

Jung, C.J. (1953) *Two Essays on Analytical Psychology*. New York: Meridian.

Jung, C.J. (1959) Interview with John Freeman. *Face to Face*. BBC Television.

Kanner, L. (1943) "Autistic disturbances of affective contact". *Nervous Child*, 2, 217–250. Reprinted in Kanner, L. (1973) *Childhood Psychosis: Initial Studies and New Insights*. Washington, DC: Wiley.

Kelly, G.A. (1955) *The Psychology of Personal Constructs*. New York: Norton.

Kendrick, D.T. and Keefe, R.C. (1992) "Age preferences in mates reflect sex differences in reproductive strategies". *Behavioral and Brain Sciences*, 15, 75–133.

Kiesler, D.J. (1983) "The 1982 interpersonal circle: A taxonomy for complementarity in human transactions". *Psychological Review*, 90, 185–214.

Kihlstrom, J.F. (1987) "The cognitive unconscious". *Science*, 237, 1445–1452.

Klein, M. (1934) *Contributions to Psychoanalysis, 1921–1945*. London: Hogarth Press, 1968.

Kluft, R.P. (1996) "Treating the traumatic memories of patients with dissociative identity disorder". *American Journal of Psychiatry*, 153, 103–110.

Knussman, R., Christiansen, K. and Couwenbergs, C. (1986) "Relations between sex hormone levels and sexual behaviour in men". *Archives of Sexual Behavior*, 15, 429–445.

Kohut, H. (1984) *How Does Analysis Cure?* Chicago: University of Chicago Press.

Kotowicz, Z. (1997) *R.D. Laing and the Paths of Anti-Psychiatry*. London: Routledge.

Kraepelin, E. (1905) *Lectures on Clinical Psychiatry*, 2nd rev. edn. London: Ballière, Tindall & Cox.

Kuipers, E., Garety, P., Fowler, D., Dunn, G., Bebbington, P.E., Freeman, D. and Hadley, C. (1997) "The London–East Anglia randomised control trial of cognitive-behavioural therapy for psychosis I: Effects of the treatment phase". *British Journal of Psychiatry*, 171, 319–327.

LaBerge, S. (1985) *Lucid Dreaming*. New York: Ballantine Books.

Labouvie-Vief, G. (1989) "Modes of knowledge and the organisation of development". In Commons, M.L., Sinnot, J.D., Richards, F.A. and Armon, C. (eds) *Adult Development*. Vol. 2. New York: Praeger.

Laing, R.D. (1959) *The Divided Self: An Existential Study of Sanity and Madness*. Harmondsworth: Penguin, 1965.

Laing, R.D. (1967) *The Politics of Experience*. Harmondsworth, Middlesex: Penguin.

Laing, R.D. and Esterson, A. (1964) *Sanity, Madness and the Family*. Harmondsworth, Middlesex: Penguin.

Lakoff, G. (1997) "How unconscious metaphorical thought shapes dreams". In Stein, D.J. (ed.) *Cognitive Science and the Unconscious*. Washington, DC: American Psychiatric Press.

Larson, E.J. and Witham, L. (1998) "Leading scientists still reject God". *Nature*, 394, 313.

Lawrence, D.H. (1952) "Making pictures". In Ghiselin, B. (ed.) *The Creative Process*. Berkeley, CA: University of California Press.

Leary, T. (1957) *Interpersonal Diagnosis of Personality*. New York: Ronald Press.

Le Bon, G. (1895) *The Crowd: A Study of the Popular Mind*. London, Ernest Benn, 1952.

Lecky, P. (1961) *Self Consistency: A Theory of Personality*. Hamden, CT: Shoe String Press.

LeDoux, J. (1989) "Cognitive-emotional interactions in the brain". *Cognition and Emotion*, 3, 267–289.

LeDoux, J. (1995) "Emotion: Clues from the brain". *Annual Review of Psychology*, 46, 209–235.

LeDoux, J. (1998) *The Emotional Brain: The Mysterious Underpinnings of Emotional Life*. London: Weidenfeld & Nicolson.

Lenz, H. (1983) "Belief and delusion: Their common origin but different course of development". *Zygon*, 18 (2 June), 117–137.

Leudar, I. and Thomas, P. (2000) *Voices of Reason, Voices of Insanity: Studies of Verbal Hallucinations*. London: Brunner-Routledge.

Levy, J. (1974) "Psychological implications of bilateral asymmetry". In Diamond, S.J. and Beaumont, J.G. (eds) *Hemisphere Function in the Human Brain*. New York: John Wiley & Sons.

Lewicki, P., Hill, T. and Czyzewska, M. (1992) "Nonconscious acquisition of information". *American Psychologist*, 47, 796–801.

Libet, B. (1981) "The experimental evidence of subjective referral of a sensory experience backwards in time". *Philosophy of Science*, 48, 182–197.

Libet, B. (1993) "The neural time factor in conscious and unconscious events". In Block, G.R. and Marsh, J. (eds) *Experimental and Theoretical Approaches to Consciousness* (CIBA Foundation Symposium 174). New York: Wiley.

Libet, B., Freeman, A. and Sutherland, K. (1999) *The Volitional Brain: Towards a Neuroscience of Free Will*. Thorverton, Devon: Imprint Academic.

Lilly, J.C. (1956) "Mental effects of reduction of ordinary levels of physical stimuli on intact, healthy persons". *Psychiatric Research Reports*, No. 5, 1–9. Washington, DC: American Psychiatric Association.

Lindisfarne, N. (1998) "Gender, shame and culture: An anthropological perspective". In Gilbert, P. and Andrews, B. (eds) *Shame: Interpersonal Behavior, Psychopathology and Culture*. Oxford University Press: New York.

Logie, R.H. (1999) "Working memory: State of the art guides to major topics in psychology". *The Psychologist*, 14, June, 174–178.

Lorenz, K.Z. (1981) *The Foundations of Ethology*. New York: Springer-Verlag.

Lowen, A. (1967) *The Betrayal of the Body*. London: Collier Macmillan.

Ludwig, A.M., Brandsma, J.M., Wilbur, C.B., Bendfelt, F. and Jameson, D.H. (1972) "The objective study of multiple personality: Or are four heads better than one?" *Archives of General Psychiatry*, 26, 298–310.

MacLean, P.D. (1949) "Psychosomatic disease and the 'visceral brain': Recent developments bearing on the Papez theory of emotion". *Psychosomatic Medicine*, 11, 338–353.

MacLean, P.D. (1990) *The Triune Brain in Evolution*. New York: Plenum Press.

Maher, B.A. (1974) "Delusional thinking and perceptual disorder". *Journal of Individual Psychology*, 30, 98–113.

Mair, K. (1999) "Development of a dogma: Multiple personality". *The Psychologist*, 12, 76–80.

Margo, A., Hemsley, D.R. and Slade, P.D. (1981) "The effects of varying auditory input on schizophrenic hallucinations". *British Journal of Psychiatry*, 139, 122–127.

Marlowe, F. and Westman, A. (2001) "Preferred waist-to-hip ratio and ecology". *Personality and Individual Differences*, 30, 481–489.

McCormick, D. and Broekma, V. (1978) "Size estimation, perceptual recognition and cardiac rate response in acute paranoid and non-paranoid schizophrenia". *Journal of Abnormal Psychology*, 87, 385–398.

McCrone, J. (1999) "States of Mind". *New Scientist*, No. 2178 (20 March) 30–33.

McGuigan, F.J. (1966) "Covert oral behaviour and auditory hallucinations". *Psychophysiology*, 3, 73–80.

McGuigan, F.J. (1978) *Cognitive Psychophysiology: Principles of Covert Behaviour*. Englewood Cliffs, NJ: Prentice Hall.

Meek, J. (2000) "Scientists create greedy mouse that stays thin". *The Guardian*, 27 July.

Messer, D. (2000) "State of the art: Language acquisition". *The Psychologist*, 13, 138–143.

Millon, T. (1981) *Disorders of Personality, DSM III, Axis II*. New York: John Wiley & Sons.

Milner, B. (1966) "Amnesia following operation on the temporal lobes". In Whitty, C.W.M. and Zangwill, O.L. (eds) *Amnesia*. London: Butterworths.

Milner, B., Corkin, S. and Teuber, H.L. (1968) "Further analysis of the hippocampal amnesia syndrome: Fourteen year follow-up study of H.M". *Neuropsychologia*, 6, 215–234.

Milner, M. (1987) *The Suppressed Madness of Sane Men: Forty Four Years of Exploring Psychoanalysis*. London: Routledge.

Moir, A. and Jessel, D. (1991) *Brainsex: The Real Difference Between Men and Women*. London: Mandarin.

Mollon, P. (1998) *Remembering Trauma: A Psychotherapist's Guide to Memory and Illusion*. Chichester, Sussex: John Wiley & Sons.

Morris, D. (1985) *Bodywatching: A Field Guide to the Human Species*. London: Jonathan Cape.

Morris, J.S., Ohman, A. and Dolan, R.J. (1998) "Conscious and unconscious emotional learning in the human amygdala". *Nature*, 393/6684, 467–470.

Morris, J.S., DeGelder, B., Weiskrantz, L. and Dolan, R.J. (2001) "Differential extrageniculostriate and amygdala responses to presentation of emotional faces in a cortically blind field". *Brain*, 124, 1241–1252.

Myers, L.B. (1998) "Repressive coping, trait anxiety and reported avoidance of negative thoughts". *Personality and Individual Differences*, 24, 299–303.

Myers, L.B. and Brewin, C.R. (1994) "Recall of early experience and the repressive coping style". *Journal of Abnormal Psychology*, 103, 288–292.

Neumann, F. and Kalmus, J. (1991) *Hormonal Treatment of Sexual Deviations*. Berlin: Diebach.

Nisbett, R.E. and Wilson, T.D. (1977) "Telling more than we can know: Verbal reports on mental processes". *Psychological Review*, 84, 231–259.

Nunberg, H. (1931) "The synthetic function of the ego". *International Journal of Psycho-Analysis*, 12, 123–140.

Nunberg, H. (1961) *Curiosity*. New York: International Universities Press.

Oakley, D. (2000) "An extraordinary phenomenon". Report (by K. Cavanagh) of a symposium on hypnosis at the University of Luton. *The Psychologist*, March, 129–130.

Oatley, K. (1998) "Emotion: State of the art guides to major topics in psychology". *The Psychologist*, June, 285–288.

O'Keefe, J. and Nadel, L. (1978) *The Hippocampus as a Cognitive Map*. Oxford: Clarendon Press.

Olds, J. and Milner, P. (1954) "Positive reinforcement produced by electrical stimulation of septal area and other regions of rat brain". *Journal of Comparative and Physiological Psychology*, 47, 419–427.

Orr, M. (1999) "Believing patients". In Feltham, C. (ed.) *Controversies in Psychotherapy*. London: Sage.

Panksepp, J. (1999) *Affective Neuroscience*. Oxford: Oxford University Press.

Parfit, D. (1987) "Divided minds and the nature of persons". In Blakemore, C. and Greenfield, S. (eds) *Mindwaves*. Oxford: Blackwell.

Parker, G.A. (1974) "Assessment strategy and the evolution of fighting behaviour". *Journal of Theoretical Biology*, 47, 223–243.

Parkyn, A. (2000) Letter to *The Guardian*, 21 August.

Persinger, M.A. (1987) *The Neuropsychological Base of God Beliefs*. Westport, CT: Praeger.

Pinker, S. (1994) *The Language Instinct*. London: Penguin.

Pinker, S. (1997) *How The Mind Works*. London: Allen Lane/Penguin.

Pittman, T. (1992) "Perception without awareness in the stream of behavior: Processes that produce and limit nonconscious biasing effects". In Bornstein, R.F. and Pittman, T. (eds) *Perception Without Awareness: Cognitive, Clinical and Social Perspectives*. New York: Guilford Press.

Piven, J., Arndt, S., Bailey, J., Havercamp, S., Andreasen, N.C. and Palmer, P. (1995). "An MRI study of brain size in autism". *American Journal of Psychiatry*, 152, 1145–1149.

Platt, Lord Robert (1967) "Medical science: Master or servant?" *British Medical Journal*, 4, 439–444.

Pollner, M. (1989) "Divine relations, social relations and well being". *Journal of Health and Social Behavior*, 30, 92–104.

Popper, K.R. (1977) Part I of K.R. Popper and J.C. Eccles *The Self and Its Brain*. Berlin: Springer-Verlag.

Power, M. and Brewin, C.R. (1991) "From Freud to cognitive science: A contemporary account of the unconscious". *British Journal of Clinical Psychology*, 30, 289–310.

Provine, R. (1991) "Laughter: A stereotyped human vocalization". *Ethology*, 89, 115–124.

Rachman, S.J. (1978) *Fear and Courage*. San Francisco: Freeman.

Raichle, M.E. (1998) "The neural correlates of consciousness: An analysis of cognitive skill learning". In Gazzaniga, M. (ed.) *The New Cognitive Neurosciences*, 2nd edn. Cambridge, MA: The MIT Press.

Ramachandran, V. and Blakeslee, S. (1998) *Phantoms in the Brain*. London: Fourth Estate.

Rasmussen, L. and Charman, T. (1995) "Personality and religious beliefs: A test of Flugel's superego projection theory". *International Journal for the Psychology of Religion*, 5, 109–123.

Reber, A.S. (1992) "The cognitive unconscious: An evolutionary perspective". *Consciousness and Cognition*, 1, 93–133.

Reber, A.S. (1993) *Implicit Learning and Tacit Knowledge: An Essay on the Cognitive Unconscious*. New York: Oxford University Press.

Reynolds, M. and Brewin, C. (1999) "Intrusive memories in depression and post-stress disorder". *Behaviour Research and Therapy*, 37, 201–215.

Róheim, G. (1950) *Psychoanalysis and Anthropology*. New York: International Universities Press.

Rokeach, M. (1950) "The effect of the perception time upon the rigidity and concreteness of thinking". *Journal of Experimental Psychology*, 40, 206–216.

Rolls, E.T. (1997) "Brain mechanisms of vision, memory and consciousness". In Ito, M., Miyashita, Y. and Rolls, E.T. (eds) *Cognition, Computation and Consciousness*. Oxford: Oxford University Press.

Romme, M. and Escher, S. (1993) *Accepting Voices: A New Approach to Voice-hearing Outside the Illness Model*. London: Mind Publications.

Romme, M. and Escher, S. (2000) *Making Sense of Voices: A Guide for Professionals who Work with Voice-hearers*. London: Mind Publications.

Romme, M.A.J., Honig, E.O., Noorthoorn, E.O. and Escher, A.D.M.A.C. (1992) "Coping with hearing voices: An emancipatory approach". *British Journal of Psychiatry*, 161, 99–103.

Rosner, E. and Semel, S.R. (1998) *Williams' Syndrome*. Oxford: Blackwell.

Ross, C.A. (1989) *Multiple Personality Disorder: Diagnosis, Clinical Features and Treatment*. New York: John Wiley & Sons.

Ross, M. and Conway, M. (1986) "Remembering one's own past: The construction of personal histories". In Sorrentino, R.M. and Higgins, E.T. (eds) *Handbook of Motivation and Cognition*. New York: Guilford Press.

Rowe, C.E. and MacIsaac, D.S. (1989) *Empathic Attunement: The Technique of Psychoanalytic Self Psychology*. Northvale, NJ: Aronson.

Royston, R. (1989) "Schizophrenia, genetics and analytical psychology". *British Journal of Psychotherapy*, 6, 50–61.

Rozin, P. (1996) "Towards a psychology of food and eating: From motivation to module to model to marker, morality, meaning and metaphor". *Current Directions in Psychological Science*, 5, 18–24.

Rudy, J.W. and Sutherland, R.J. (1992) "Configural and elemental associations and the memory coherence problem". *Journal of Cognitive Neuroscience*, 4, 208–216.

Rumelhart, D.E., McClelland, J.L. and the PDP Research Group (1986) *Parallel Distributed Processing: Explorations in the Microstructures of Cognition*. Cambridge, MA: The MIT Press.

Rycroft, C. (1995) *A Critical Dictionary of Psychoanalysis*. 2nd edn. London: Penguin.

Samuels, A. (1997) *Jung and the Post-Jungians*. London: Routledge.

Samuels, A., Shorter, B. and Plaut, F. (1986) *A Critical Dictionary of Jungian Analysis*. London: Routledge & Kegan Paul.

Sandler, J. and Sandler, A.M. (1984) "The past unconscious, the present unconscious, and interpretation of the transference". *Psychoanalytic Inquiry*, 4, 367–399.

Sargant, W. (1957) *Battle for the Mind: A Physiology of Conversion and Brain Washing*. London: Heinemann.

Schachter, D.L. (1987) "Implicit memory: History and current status". *Journal of Experimental Psychology, Learning, Memory and Cognition*, 13, 501–518.

Schachter, D. (1992) "Understanding implicit memory: A cognitive neuroscience approach". *American Psychologist*, 47, 559–569.

Schatzman, M. (1989) R.D. Laing, Obituary. *The Independent*, 25 August, p. 14.

Schiffer, F. (2000) *Of Two Minds: A New Approach for Better Understanding and Improving Your Mental Life*. London: Pocket Books.

Schneider, W. and Shiffrin, R.M. (1977) "Controlled and automatic information processing: I. Detection search and attention". *Psychological Review*, 84, 1–66.

Schooler, J. and Engstler-Schooler, T. (1990) "Verbal overshadowing of visual memories: Some things are better left unsaid". *Cognitive Psychology*, 22, 36–71.

Scoville, W.B. and Milner, B. (1957) Loss of recent memory after bilateral hippocampal lesions. *Journal of Neurology and Psychiatry*, 20, 11–21.

Seeman, M.V. (1978) "Delusional loving". *Archives of General Psychiatry*, 35, 1265–1267.

Segal, H. (1964) *Introduction to the Works of Melanie Klein*. London: Heinemann.

Segal, H. (1999) "What is an object? The role of perception". In Fonagy, P., Cooper, A.M. and Wallerstein, R.S. (eds) *Psychoanalysis on the Move: The Work of Joseph Sandler*. London: Routledge.

Sensky, T. and Fenwick, P. (1982) "Religiosity, mystical experience and epilepsy". In Rose, C. (ed.) *Progress in Epilepsy*. London: Pitman.

Shankweiler, D.P. (1966) "Effects of temporal lobe damage on perception of dichotically presented melodies". *Journal of Comparative and Physiological Psychology*, 62, 115–119.

Share, L. (1994) *If Someone Speaks it Gets Louder: Dreams and the Reconstruction of Infant Trauma*. Hillsdale, NJ: Analytic Press.

Sherry, D.F. and Schachter, D.L. (1987) "The evolution of multiple memory systems". *Psychological Review*, 94, 439–454.

Sims, A. (1991) "Delusional syndrome in ICD-10". *British Journal of Psychiatry*, 159 (Supplement 14), 46–51.

Singh, D. (1994) "Ideal female body shape: Role of body weight and waist-to-hip ratio". *International Journal of Eating Disorders*, 16, 283–288.

Slocum, J. (1948) *Sailing Alone Around the World*. London: Rupert Hart-Davis.

Solms, M. (1997) *The Neuropsychology of Dreams*. Mahwah, NJ: Lawrence Erlbaum Associates Inc.

Speece, M.W. and Brent, S.B. (1984) "Children's understanding of death: A review of three components of a death concept". *Child Development*, 55, 1671–1686.

Sperry, R.W., Gazzaniga, M.S. and Bogen, J.E. (1969) "Interhemispheric relationships; the neocortical commissures; syndromes of hemisphere disconnection". In Vinken, P.J. and Bruyn, G.W. (eds) *Handbook of Clinical Neurology*. New York: John Wiley & Sons.

Spiegel, D. and Li, D. (1997) "Dissociated cognition and disintegrated experience". In Stein, D.J. (ed.) *Cognitive Science and the Unconscious*. Washington: American Psychiatric Association Press.

Spilka, B., Hood, R.W. and Gorsuch, R.L. (1985) *The Psychology of Religion: An Empirical Approach*. Englewood Cliffs, NJ: Prentice Hall.

Spinelli, E. (1994) *Demystifying Therapy*. London: Constable.

Spinney, L. (1998) "I had a hunch . . ." *New Scientist*, No. 2150 (5 September), 42–47.

Squire, L.R. (1983) "The hippocampus and the neuropsychology of memory". In Seifert, W. (ed.) *Molecular, Cellular and Behavioral Neurobiology of the Hippocampus*. New York: Academic Press.

Stebbins, G.L. (1982) *Darwin to DNA, Molecules to Humanity*. New York: Freeman.

Sutcliffe, J.P. (1961) "'Credulous' and 'skeptical' views of hypnotic phenomena: Experiments in esthesia, hallucination and delusion". *Journal of Abnormal and Social Psychology*, 62, 189–200.

Suttie, I.D. (1935) *The Origins of Love and Hate*. London: Kegan Paul.

Symons, D. (1979) *The Evolution of Human Sexuality*. New York: Oxford University Press.

Szasz, T.S. (1962) *The Myth of Mental Illness: Foundations of a Theory of Personal Conduct*. London: Paladin, 1972.

Talwar, S.K., Xu, S., Hawley, E.S., Weiss, S.A., Moxon, K.A. and Chapin, J.K. (2002) "Behavioural neuroscience: Rat navigation guided by remote control". *Nature*, 417, 37–38.

Tamminen, K. (1994) "Religious experiences in childhood and adolescence: A viewpoint of religious development between the ages of 7 and 20". *International Journal for the Psychology of Religion*, 4, 61–85.

Tantam, D. (1988) "Lifelong eccentricity and social isolation I: Psychiatric, social and forensic aspects". *British Journal of Psychiatry*, 153, 777–782.

Tarrier, N. (1992) "The family management of schizophrenia". In Bentall, R.P. (ed.) *Reconstructing Schizophrenia*. London: Routledge.

Teasdale, J.D. and Barnard, P.J. (1993) *Affect, Cognition and Change: Remodelling Depressive Thought*. Hove, UK: Lawrence Erlbaum Associates Ltd.

Thalbourne, M.A. (1991) "The psychology of mystical experience". *Exceptional Human Experience*, 9, 168–186.

Thalbourne, M.A. (2000) "Transliminality: A review". *International Journal of Parapsychology*, 11, 1–34.

Thomas, D. (1951) *Collected Poems, 1934–1952*. London: J.M. Dent & Sons.

Thomas, J. (1994/95) "An open letter to a worried friend". *Open Mind*, 72, 14.

Thomas, P. (1995) "Thought disorder or communication disorder: Linguistic science provides a new approach". *British Journal of Psychiatry*, 166, 287–290.

Thomas, P. and Fraser, W. (1994) "Linguistics, human communication and psychiatry". *British Journal of Psychiatry*, 165, 585–592.

Thornhill, R. and Palmer, C. (2000) *A Natural History of Rape: Biological Basis of Sexual Coercion*. Cambridge, MA: The MIT Press.

Trivers, R. (1971) "The evolution of reciprocal altruism". *Quarterly Review of Biology*, 46, 35–57.

Trivers, R. (1976) Foreword to Dawkins, R. *The Selfish Gene*. Oxford: Oxford University Press.

Trivers, R. (1981) "Sociobiology and politics". In White, E. (ed.) *Sociobiology and Human Politics*. Lexington, MA: D.C. Heath

Trivers, R. (1985) *Social Evolution*. Reading, MA: Benjamin/Cummings.

Turing, A.M. (1950) "Computing, machinery and intelligence". *Mind*, 59, 433–460.

Tversky, A. and Kahneman, D. (1983) "Extensional versus intuitive reasoning: The conjunction fallacy in probability judgement". *Psychological Review*, 90, 293–315.

Updike, J. (2000) "Confusions of a churchgoer". *The Guardian*, Saturday Review, 8 January.

van der Kolk, B.A. and Fisher, R. (1995) "Dissociation and the fragmentary nature of traumatic memories: Overview and exploratory study". *Journal of Traumatic Stress*, 8, 505–525.

van der Kolk, B.A., van der Hart, O. and Marmar, C. (1996) "Dissociation and information processing in post traumatic stress disorder". In van der Kolk, B., McFarlane, A. and Weisaeth, I. (eds) *Traumatic Stress*. New York: Guilford Press.

van Eeden, F.W. (1913) Meeting of the Society for Psychical Research, London.

Viesti, C. (1971) "Effects of monetary rewards on an insight learning task". *Psychonomic Science*, 23, 181–183.

Vuilleumier, P., Armony, J.L., Clarke, K., Husain, M., Driver, J. and Dolan, R.J. (2002) "Neural response to emotional faces with and without awareness: Event-related fMRI in a parietal patient with visual extinction and spatial neglect." *Neuropsychologia*, 40, 2156–2166.

Walker, M. (1998) Personal communication.

Walsh, K., King, M., Jones, L., Tookman, A. and Blizard, R. (2002) "Spiritual beliefs may affect outcome of bereavement: Prospective study". *British Medical Journal*, 324, 1551–1554.

Watson, M.W. and Getz, K. (1990) "The relationship between Oedipal behaviors and children's family role concepts". *Merrill-Palmer Quarterly*, 36, 487–505.

Watts, F.N. (1996) "Psychological and religious perspectives on emotion". *International Journal for the Psychology of Religion*, 6, 71–87.

Webster, R. (1996) *Why Freud was Wrong: Sin, Science and Psychoanalysis*. London: HarperCollins.

Wegner, D.M. and Wheatley, T.P. (1999) "Apparent mental causation: Sources of the experience of will". *American Psychologist*, 54, 480–492.

Weir, A.A.S., Chappell, J. and Kacelnik, A. (2002) "Shaping of hooks in New Caledonian crows". *Science*, 297, 981.

Weiskrantz, L. (1997) *Consciousness Lost and Found*. Oxford: Oxford University Press.

Weiss, A.P. and Heckers, S. (1999) "Neuroimaging of hallucinations: A review of the literature". *Psychiatric Research, Neuroimaging*, 89, 61–75.

Westen, D. (1998) "The scientific legacy of Sigmund Freud: Toward a psycho-dynamically informed psychological science". *Psychological Bulletin*, 124, 333–371.

Willan, P. (2000) "Oldest cave paintings ever found light up human history". *The Guardian*, 19 October.

Wilson, E.O. (1975) *Sociobiology: The New Synthesis*. The Belknap Press, Cambridge, MA: Harvard University Press.

Wing, J.K., Cooper, J.E. and Sartorius, N. (1974) *The Measurement and Classification of Psychiatric Symptoms*. London: Cambridge University Press.

Winnicott, D.W. (1956) "On transference". *International Journal of Psycho-Analysis*, 37, 382–395.

Winnicott, D.W. (1958) "The capacity to be alone". *International Journal of Psycho-Analysis*, 9, 420–438.

Winograd, T. (1975) "Frame representations and the declarative-procedural controversy". In Bobrow, D.G. and Collins, A.M. (eds) *Representation and Understanding: Studies in Cognitive Science*. New York: Academic Press.

Winson, J. (1990) "The meaning of dreams". *Scientific American*, November, 42–48.

Young, R.M. (1994) "The psychoanalysis of sectarianism". *Newsletter of the Psychotherapy Section of the British Psychological Society*, 15, 2–15.

Young-Eisendrath, P. and Dawson, T. (1997) *The Cambridge Companion to Jung*. Cambridge: Cambridge University Press.

Zajonc, R. (1980) "Feeling and thinking: Preferences need no inferences". *American Psychologist*, 35, 151–175.

Zulueta, F. De, Gene-Cos, N. and Grachev, S. (2001) "Differential psychotic symptomatology in polyglot patients: Case reports and their implications". *British Journal of Medical Psychology*, 74, 277–292.

Author index

Subject index